SOMEONE
IS OUT TO
GET US

SOMEONE IS OUT TO GET US

A Not So Brief History of Cold War Paranoia and Madness

BRIAN T. BROWN

TWELVE

NEW YORK   BOSTON

Twelve
Hachette Book Group
1290 Avenue of the Americas, New York, NY 10104

twelvebooks.com

twitter.com/twelvebooks

First Edition: November 2019

Twelve is an imprint of Grand Central Publishing. The Twelve name and logo are trademarks of Hachette Book Group, Inc.

The publisher is not responsible for websites (or their content) that are not owned by the publisher.

The Hachette Speakers Bureau provides a wide range of authors for speaking events. To find out more, go to www.hachettespeakersbureau.com or call (866) 376-6591.

Library of Congress Cataloging-in-Publication Data has been applied for.

ISBNs: 978-1-5387-2803-1 (hardcover), 978-1-5387-0023-5 (ebook)

Printed in the United States of America

LSC-C

10 9 8 7 6 5 4 3 2 1

With respect and love . . .
Stan Arkow
Maryellen Duffy Brown

CONTENTS

When people react out of fear, horrible things can happen.

—Mieke Eoyang, Third Way think tank, commenting on a 2018 text alert sent to Hawaiian residents warning, wrongly, of an inbound missile attack. A state employee had pushed the wrong button during a safety drill.

Paranoia: A mental disorder characterized by systematized delusions ascribing hostile intentions to other persons; often linked with a sense of mission.

It is dark. You are alone on a silent street in a dangerous neighborhood. Your senses have been instantly and sharply awakened. You suspect you are being followed. You turn around. No one is there.

If You're Not Paranoid You're Crazy

—headline in a 2015 *Atlantic* story that references the National Security Agency's new data center in Utah

Our life is what our thoughts make it.

—Marcus Aurelius

There is no fear in love; but perfect love casteth out fear: because fear hath torment. He that feareth is not made perfect in love.

—1 John 4:18 (KJV)

INTRODUCTION

In tone and temperature, the current cultural moment clearly bears a resemblance to the Cold War's undertow of suspicion, deceit, and peril. A killer is back in the Kremlin. There's a new round of chilling Russian subversion, and FBI counterintelligence experts are back digging to assess the depth of the damage. A cloud of disinformation won't clear. Once again, the Doomsday Clock is heading back toward midnight.

During the Cold War, Soviet defector Yuri Bezmenov confirmed that the KGB—the "Committee for State Security"—was trying to make us question the very nature of truth: "Most of the work, 85 percent of it, is a slow process which we call ideological subversion, active measures, or psychological warfare. What it basically means is: to change the perception of reality of every American to such an extent that despite the abundance of information no one is able to come to sensible conclusions in the interest of defending themselves, their families, their community, and their country."

During the 2016 U.S. presidential campaign, Russia's spy turned autocrat, Vladimir Putin, unleashed the kitchen sink of *aktivni meropriyatiya*—active measures—to damage Hillary Clinton, a perceived foe. Soviet military intelligence hacked into sites associated with the Clinton campaign and used a willing front organization, Wikileaks, to launder the stolen goods. The ubiquity and vulnerability of social media, Facebook in particular, was exploited by Russian-directed forgeries. In the *Washington Post*, a Russian troll explained how it worked: "You were in some kind of factory that turned lying, telling untruths, into an industrial assembly line.... There were huge numbers of people, 300 to 400, and they were all writing absolute untruths."

In 1964, Lyndon Johnson's most famous campaign commercial showed a young girl picking daisies before cutting to a blooming mushroom cloud. The scene, juxtaposing innocence with annihilation, was a coy warning of the dire threat presented by Johnson's alleged trigger-happy opponent, Barry Goldwater.

In 2016, the Clinton campaign consistently warned voters that candidate Trump couldn't be trusted with the nuclear codes. "There's always been a paranoid fringe in our politics," said Clinton. "But it's never had the nominee of a major party stoking it, encouraging it, and giving it a national megaphone."

Mr. Trump opened his bid for the presidency by demonizing immigrants, encouraging Islamophobia, and suggesting it was our turn to build a wall. He also expressed nostalgia for the days of Richard Nixon's Law and Order. Like Nixon, Trump has protested he is not a crook in spite of almost daily press bulletins indicating otherwise. In these times, we have become more mindful than ever that the tactics of Trump were taught to him by Roy Cohn, who powered Joe McCarthy's shameless witch hunts.

Lies have become alternative facts, problematic journalism is now called fake news, conspiracies inform policies, the president has his own state TV, and, going back to the future of *1984*, reality has to be seen through the eyes of the Party. "Just remember," Trump told a gathering of veterans, "what you are seeing and what you are reading is not what's happening."

As many of us continue to obsess over the danger posed by suicidal jihadists, recent annual statistics show death by lightning, shark, or white supremacist as far more likely. The effects of climate change are indeed leading us toward extinction, but many insist that gay marriage, Planned Parenthood, and gun control are greater threats to our national welfare.

Flying saucers, first "officially" sighted over America during the early days of the Cold War, are also back in the news. The Pentagon recently admitted it was still in the business of evaluating alien visitations. According to the *New York Times*, the Advanced Aerospace Threat Identification Program was charged with investigating an increasing number of UFO reports from service members. The program spent $22 million of "black money" secretly authorized by Congress and was "run out of an office on the fifth floor of the [Pentagon's] C Ring, deep within the building's maze."

A new documentary, *Bob Lazar: Area 51 and Flying Saucers*, profiles the man who told the world that captured alien technology was being reverse engineered "at a classified base known as S-4 out in the Nevada desert near Area 51." Lazar insists that the U.S. government is concealing the truth about extraterrestrial visitations and suppressing knowledge that has the power to shift "the entire world economy."

———

Your author, born in 1958, experienced three-quarters of the Cold War—as a child left largely unattended on the streets of Queens; as a teenager engaged by the daily news he was dispensing on a paper route in a freshly built suburban development in New Jersey; as a college student at Columbia, where the antiwar ferment of the sixties still had a romantic appeal; and, finally, as a budding journalist working for the *New York Times* (publisher of the Pentagon Papers) and the *San Diego Union* (a publication headed by former members of the Nixon administration).

My parents, as devout Irish Catholics, were virtually under papal obligation to vote for John Kennedy. Their fealty to the Democratic Party did not last much longer. Mom and Dad viewed communism as the presence of evil in the world and thought McCarthy had the right idea. My father often mentioned Bill Buckley's book *God and Man at Yale*. It made me wonder if Ivy League schools were almost as godless and sinful as the Soviet Union. I remember J. Edgar Hoover's *Masters of Deceit* being one of the titles in the family bookcase. I assumed that it was a spy thriller. I never had an urge to read it. I don't think my parents did, either.

One of my first memories is watching three-year-old John Kennedy Jr. saluting during his father's funeral. When Neil Armstrong walked on the moon, I was heading into sixth grade. The fuzzy live pictures from the moon had a dreamy, magical quality. I also understood, proudly, that by getting to the moon first, America had completely smoked the Russians. I saved copies of the "moon landing" editions of the *New York Times* and the *Daily News*. I had never seen bigger headlines.

One of my favorite board games was a Cold War creation. In 1957, Oscar-winning French filmmaker Albert Lamorisse introduced *La Conquête du Monde* (The Conquest of the World). When Parker Brothers bought the idea and brought it to America, it was renamed Risk. The game is played on a political map of the world. Participants take turns rolling dice and shuffling armies seeking to claim global dominion, continent by continent. Lamorisse's deeper ironic intention was to lampoon the imperialist behavior of the superpowers. I did not get the joke.

My freshman Columbia dorm had coed showers. Having attended an all-male Catholic high school, I was suddenly thrust into an alternative universe, although I'd only crossed the George Washington Bridge. The dean advised that he would be largely hands-off unless we committed a horribly violent crime. Every recreational drug known to man was available on campus. We used them with impunity.

Columbia didn't make me a liberal. I had already been radicalized by the Salesians of Don Bosco. I was the editor of the high school paper and the principal, Father Thomas Glackin, reviewed all the articles before publication. Stories he didn't like—such as a review of an R-rated film—were crumpled up and tossed into a wastebasket. When I first objected to this violation of my First Amendment rights, the normally humorless Fr. Glackin stunned me with a bellowing laugh.

One of my papers at Columbia was about FBI spying on Dr.

Martin Luther King Jr. My central source was the Church Committee report. I was floored by the litany of Hoover's despicable—and outrageously unconstitutional—behavior, in particular the apparent attempt to push Dr. King to suicide by threatening to release recordings of his extramarital sex. I read recently that James Comey, while he was FBI director, kept a copy of the King wiretap request on his desk as a reminder of the bureau's antidemocratic dark ages.

I was working on the foreign desk of the *Times* when Lech Wałęsa and his Solidarity labor movement rose to power. In response, Poland declared martial law. Communication was cut off into and out of the country. The *Times* correspondent in Warsaw, John Darnton, was among the Western press silenced. But Darnton figured out various work-arounds. One method was to photograph his stories and print the developed pages on easy-to-smuggle slides. He also found willing co-conspirators fleeing the country.

One of the couriers was a young American teacher who called the *Times* when I was answering the phones. After flying out of Poland, she had just arrived at Kennedy Airport and was waiting to make a domestic connection. She told me she had an envelope stuffed with Darnton's reports. I immediately jumped into a taxi to retrieve them, doing my small part for a reporter chronicling important history. Darnton won a Pulitzer.

In 1985, traveling behind the Iron Curtain, I had a chilling confrontation with the East German police. I was on vacation, driving a rented compact car. I'd picked up two East German hitchhikers, a young couple, at the Czechoslovakian border. After my human cargo was discovered while we were getting gas (the police were waiting to pounce, their car parked in a shadowy corner of the station), there was yelling, cursing, negotiating, and bribery—all of it complicated by a language barrier. Apparently, and not surprisingly, the East Germans were not supposed to be fraternizing with me.

Early in the encounter, I confidently waved a U.S. passport at eye level of one of the cops. In response, he wagged a finger menacingly and instructed, "Not U.S.A." Then, with the same finger, he pointed at the ground and added, slowly, "DDR." I offered him all my East German money, which I was happy to surrender since it was going to be impossible to exchange the bills when I returned to the Western world. It might as well have been money from Mars. The officer didn't want his country's cash, either. What he demanded was West German deutschmarks—so-called *hard* currency—and I enriched him by about $100.

One of the German words the couple had taught me was *arschloch*—asshole. As I left them behind, the two were using the word quite a lot. A few hours later, when I reached the bright lights of a buzzing West Berlin, the instant change had the feel of the famous movie moment when Dorothy transitions from the stormy black and white of Kansas into the Technicolor wonderland of Oz.

Had I been privy to top-secret CIA reports, I would have read that the agency was somehow claiming that the East Germans were recording greater per capita production than the West Germans. This assessment was about as valid as the flimflam produced by Dorothy's overhyped wizard. Like many who traveled in Eastern Europe during the Cold War, I had seen more than enough evidence that communism was a big, fat, stupid joke and, it appeared, about to croak.

———

The Cold War reengaged the purported rivalry between capitalism and communism that had been put in motion by the Bolshevik Revolution of 1917, which claimed to have ignited the rise of the proletariat and begun the demise of the bourgeoisie, as envisioned by Karl Marx. The bourgeoisie in New York, London, and Paris thought the message out of Russia was: You're next. It would not be the last time that the capitalist elite overreacted to the prospect of labor eating into profits.

The Western powers, plus the Japanese, responded to Bolshevism by sending troops to strangle the alarming ideology in its infancy.

What this did was make a large mess larger. After the Bolsheviks beat back enemies both domestic and foreign, they logically deduced that many people everywhere hated them and they put in place perhaps the most paranoid and secretive ruling establishment in the history of man, which they may have done anyway, since most of the revolution's top players were damaged and abused people who'd spent half their lives exiled to Siberia as enemies of the czar. The United States responded to the new Union of Soviet Socialist Republics by immediately ending diplomatic relations. The relationship got off to a horrible start.

Stalin, born in 1878, was among the essential figures in the founding story of the Soviet state. At the time of the 1917 revolution, he was in Petrograd, the center of Bolshevik power, and one of the chief aides to the leader of the gang, Vladimir Lenin, from whom he inhaled the prime directive of "no mercy." (Martin Amis described Stalin as "Lenin's industrious, underbred mascot, his shaggy dog.")

Stalin never had any interest in exporting warm, fuzzy, unadulterated Marxism. Once in charge, his primary goal was eliminating anyone who could challenge his authority. To that end, he dispatched assassins near and far. In the Cold War, Americans were told they were in a fight against communism. This was not the case. The new order in Moscow was an organized crime family with a horrible sense of fashion.

In the seventy-four-year history of the Soviet Union, no one created as much bloodshed as Joseph Stalin—estimates range from twenty to sixty million dead—and no one was as afraid of the truth. As the Cold War dawned, and for as long as it continued, what the Soviet Union feared the most was not American weaponry, nor the economic strength of the West. What it feared the most was any amplification of the fundamental facts of its very nature, which is this: It was all one big lie. "The dictatorship of the proletariat was a lie," Amis wrote of the USSR. "Union was a lie, and Soviet was a lie, and Socialist was a lie. The enemy of the people was the regime."

Inside this perpetual fraud, the subjects of the Russian empire in the first half of the twentieth century lived through incessant turmoil and suffering on a scale no other society may have ever experienced. If what occurred in the USSR had instead happened in the United States, this is what you would have to imagine...

Imagine...if the United States had lost a war with Japan in 1904. Imagine if America had a revolution in 1905, instead of 1776. Imagine if after fighting—and losing—in World War I, the United States endured another Civil War, in 1917. Imagine if the Depression had been even more horrific and resulted in the starvation of millions. Imagine if Franklin Roosevelt, at the start of his second term, in 1936, decided to eliminate his political opposition by ordering the FBI to arrest, torture, and kill every Republican senator and congressman. Imagine if Roosevelt also had the FBI shoot every top officer in the Army, Navy, and Air Force.

Imagine if after all those terrors—Civil War, starvation, the murder of the political and military elite—the United States next invaded Canada and Mexico.

Imagine if World War II had been fought on American soil with the same sweep and ferocity as occurred across Europe, North Africa, and Asia between 1939 and 1945. Imagine if New York had been bombed almost every night for months. Imagine if an enemy had marched to within twenty miles of the White House. Imagine every major factory in Detroit turned into scrap. Imagine Chicago surrounded by attackers for almost three years, with people dying at the rate of fifty thousand per month.

Imagine if millions of farm animals were slaughtered across Iowa, Kansas, and Nebraska. Imagine if millions and millions of acres of cropland had been poisoned.

Imagine Los Angeles stormed by amphibious invasion, or the Golden Gate Bridge blown apart.

Imagine airports, train stations, and bus depots clogged with thousands and thousands of homeless families, mothers and their children sleeping on floors, begging for help, too sick to move, on the verge of death.

Imagine towns and cities without electricity, without hospitals, without fuel, without a speck of food.

The people of the Soviet Union didn't have to imagine such things.

Stalin accepted full credit for winning the Great Patriotic War. That notion, however, is a howling profanity. Victory was attained, at a shocking price, by a multitude of unknown and ill-equipped Red Army soldiers, along with the sheer grit of ordinary people on the home front who withstood Hitler's Blitzkrieg. The D-Day invasion was not the decisive blow; the bulk of Hitler's army had already been dismantled by heroic Soviet sacrifice on the Eastern Front.

The Red Army suffered more combat deaths *at Stalingrad alone* than the U.S. armed forces accumulated in the *entire war*. During a single operation in 1944, Marshal Rokossovsky destroyed a collection of Wehrmacht divisions equivalent to the entire German deployment faced by the British and the Americans on the Western Front. And, as scholars now tell us, the war with Japan didn't conclude *only* because of two U.S.-made atomic bombs. Although the USSR entered the fray at the eleventh hour—as Japanese forces decimated in a string of punishing battles were offering ever feebler resistance—it seems the Soviets can still take credit for delivering the coup de grace. In deciding how soon to surrender, Hirohito and his war cabinet appear to have been more frightened of the approaching Red Army—a notoriously rapacious whirlwind—than of Curtis LeMay's attempt to bomb the country back to the Stone Age.

Of the fifteen Soviet republics, nine had been occupied by the Germans during World War II. Seventeen hundred cities and towns were either totally or partially destroyed, as were seventy thousand villages and approximately thirty-one thousand factories. In all, six million buildings were damaged in some fashion. Millions of acres of crops were gone. The slaughter of cattle, hogs, sheep, goats, and horses reached into the tens of millions. Of the approximately sixty million people killed in the war, twenty-five to thirty million were Soviets. An additional twenty-five million Soviet citizens were rendered homeless. By comparison, U.S. combat deaths in World War II totaled 407,000.

American schoolchildren, like me, were fed a one-sided view of that war, capped by the conclusion that our superlative industry and unsurpassed genius were the deciding factors in defeating Nazi Germany and Imperial Japan. What would the Cold War have been like if, during history class, American kids learned that the world forever owed a debt of gratitude to Soviet forces and Soviet citizens? Their remarkable resilience and triumphs saved democracy as much as did George Patton, Iwo Jima, and the atom bomb.

However, young American minds were presented with an all-consuming fairy tale that became America's version of *The Iliad* and that played on a loop of almost numbing heraldry. The victory over Fascism was almost instantly converted into a mythological struggle of Homeric glory, which therefore, in its telling, emphasized the good parts and generally left out the nasty bits. A pernicious culture of secrecy emerged from what the federal government didn't want to tell us about World War II, and by failing to learn the true costs of that experience, the United States continued to seek remedies through the practiced route of state violence and devoted far less attention to keeping the peace.

Mostly, Americans adopted the *Reader's Digest* version of the USSR—literally. When World II ended, the magazine told its sixteen million subscribers (in seventeen languages) that the Soviet state was the primary danger to America. "*The Digest* presented the U.S. and USSR as polar opposites," wrote Joanne Sharp. "As well as running clearly political articles that explained international relations and threats to peace, the magazine's ostensibly apolitical stories reinforced this image of two incompatible societies. Descriptions of everyday life in America and the Soviet Union detailed how different

Americans were from Russians, how different Russians' music was, their food, their sense of humor—even Russian sex lives were different. At the extreme, in 1981 a story about an American in Siberia seemed to suggest biological differences when it reported that the American's body rejected a Russian blood transfusion."

U.S. citizens knew more about craters on the moon than about any physical feature of the USSR, and we apparently met far more aliens than communists during the Cold War. A poll released in 1991 indicated that several million Americans believed they were regularly affected by alien abductions. For comparison, it was estimated that by 1956, membership in the U.S. Communist Party had dropped to five thousand, of which about fifteen hundred were FBI informants.

———

During the Cold War, the inflated menace of communism was intermingled in the public consciousness with the latent terror of Nazism, and, viewing the ideologies as two sides of the same coin, America's leading hawks saw defeating the Russians as unfinished business from World War II. At the same time, the Pentagon's propaganda machine ignored the general peace, warned about another Pearl Harbor, and lobbied for overpreparation. We were made to think more work was necessary in order to cleanse the world. The final warning from *The Thing from Another World* (1951) encapsulated our paranoia as a mantra: *Keep watching the skies!*

Facts were no match for a waterfall of fabricated frights. At the close of World War II, the United States of America had all but silenced its external threats and was about to embark on a stunning era of prosperity. It wasn't hyperbole to say that Americans were in position to rule the world. Nonetheless, from 1946 to 1989, from the conclusion of World War II to the fall of the Berlin Wall, we feared fear itself, even though this condition was counterfactual. Our forty-plus-year Cold War with the Soviet Union, a second-rate foe, was quickly entrenched and often defied logic, saddling what was the world's richest and most secure nation with a costly fortress mentality. Millions chased shadows. Millions lived scared to death. With the gift of hindsight, we can now say that the Cold War appears to have been a mind-boggling waste of money and lives to wage an inherently lopsided contest with a preordained outcome.

The Soviet Union and the United States were the chief combatants in what was never a fair fight. As America entered a period of unchallenged economic dominance, unleashing the biggest boom in personal consumption the world had ever seen, a stagnant Soviet society was unable even to feed its own people. Moreover, the Soviets tried playing catch-up in an arms race they couldn't afford while simultaneously attempting to tame a vast, restive conglomeration of republics and satellites that regularly required invasion—if not occupation—to subdue.

Yet in spite of living in a country that had a clear superiority by every metric, American citizens remained at high alert for an imminent invasion no Kremlin figure ever seriously contemplated. If anything, Soviet citizens had more to fear from dangerously insubordinate American generals who didn't see the point of having nuclear weapons if you couldn't use them. As we fought an enemy of our own making, we failed to understand that the real enemy was looking at us in the mirror.

"As a post-Soviet flood of archives has revealed," wrote national security expert Roger Morris, "Moscow's foreign policy was waged more often in caution than aggressiveness, more out of weakness than strength, and with an abiding parochial fear and ignorance of the U.S., a hostility that Washington's acts in kind only reinforced, justified, and prolonged. So much of the great 'superpower' rivalry was what John le Carré would aptly call a grotesque 'looking-glass war.'"

Consequently, some degree of distortion affected every important story told about the Cold War during the Cold War. It wasn't just the Soviets who were sitting on a mountain of secrets. The U.S. government was just as capable of classifying minutiae and criminalizing transparency. Both sides vomited disinformation as they flayed speech. Deviousness, dishonesty, and collateral damage were rationalized as acts of patriotism. As a result, the authors who have been writing the second draft of this history have learned—as did I—that there's a seemingly bottomless pit of buried truths.

Therefore, a tour of Cold War paranoia is a cautionary tale pointing to a misguided and troubling legacy of humiliation and hubris— Vladimir Putin hasn't gotten over losing it and the United States took too much credit for winning it. The period was a compendium of misconceptions, fallacies, frauds, comedies, tragedies, lies, and deceits. Some of our delusions linger even now, others securely tucked away as we try to forget how historically embarrassed we should be. We were more ready than ever to join a cult and call it a social movement, to conflate innuendo with truth, to assume the presence of unseen machines of oppression. We invented lethal invaders—terrestrial and extraterrestrial—and attacked spectral contagions. The era produced a nihilistic and potentially suicidal national defense posture called mutually assured destruction and gave us primal scream therapy, which posited that anger and frustration could be relieved by unrestrained yelling and hysteria. Or, put another way, an assertion that the most logical remedy for an age of self-induced anxiety was, paradoxically, self-induced *madness*.

CHAPTER 1

SCORCH, BOIL, AND BAKE

The plane is a dud. A very, very expensive dud. And your boss wants you to save the day. You are General Curtis LeMay and your boss is Hap Arnold, and Hap Arnold's ass is on the line because the B-29 is the most expensive weapon of the war and it's a dud and General Arnold wants you to rescue him from complete and total humiliation. So he has sent you to the war in the Pacific and you are stationed on a tiny volcanic island where every day is the same day, baking sunshine mixed with brief thunderstorms. Thank goodness the Quonset hut has air conditioning, because you've got a solid week of work ahead of you. You're going to ask for a pot of coffee and work the problem, a habit happily indulged, going back to your days as an engineering student at Ohio State.

Your predecessor, General Haywood Hansell, had been flummoxed by two formidable issues: the vagaries of Mother Nature and the debugging of a revolutionary aircraft. The B-29 is still a work in progress. Its engines, meant to push the plane high above the clouds, are incredibly powerful, but they often overheat. You also find out that even if the pilots manage to reach thirty thousand feet without the engines bursting into flames, there's another problem: fierce hundred-mile-per-hour jet stream winds in this part of the Pacific, which compromise accurate targeting. There's more. Even if the B-29s can be held steady rocketing through a wind-blasted sky, soupy clouds over Japan regularly make it impossible to even see targets at all. General Hansell had hoped the Soviets might supply more accurate forecasts, since the weather in Japan arrives from Siberia, but no cooperation has been forthcoming from Marshal Stalin. What a fucker.

You stay up into the early morning hours reading intelligence reports, studying reconnaissance photos. Every past attack tells you a story. You figure out that the Japanese have almost no air defenses left, and you come to the conclusion that the bombing campaign has to start over. You want the B-29s flying at night, at low altitude. This should help with putting bombs on targets. Just because the B-29s can fly above the clouds doesn't mean that's the only way to use them. You're also going to strip guns from planes. Since the Japanese have no fighters left, what's the point? That will decrease the size of the crews, which will allow the bomb capacity to be increased by five or six tons. At the next flight meeting, you're going to be telling everyone that they'll now be flying low…light…at night…with more bang.

You're also very aware that thousands of Japanese homes are made of paper and wood. And you know all about the recent devastation in Europe. Firebombing works. It might work even better in Japan. You are of the opinion that the best way to save lives is to end the war as soon as possible. You also know that the worst way for this war to end would be to make foot soldiers fight their way to Tokyo inch by bloody inch, with millions of suicidal kids rushing at them with bombs strapped to their bellies. That would be the biggest fucking nightmare in the history of war. Your B-29s are going to keep that from happening. They are going to scorch, boil, and bake the Japanese until they've had enough. When the B-29s next attack Tokyo, they'll be doing just what the British have been doing in Germany. The planes going to Tokyo will be packed with hundred-pound oil-gel bombs and six-pound gelled-gasoline bombs. You're going to turn the capital of Japan into one giant bonfire.

When the crews start bitching that the young hotshot general has a brand-new way of getting them killed, you'll explain that they are going to deliver the biggest firecracker the Japanese have ever seen. You'll also remind the airmen about the horrific fighting and towering sacrifice required by the U.S. Marines to claim Tinian, and Saipan, and Guam, which put their bombers a few thousand miles closer to the Japanese mainland. You'll remind them of the Imperial Army beheading their fellow airmen. You'll mention the kamikaze attacks sinking warships. You'll mention all the Boeing workers in Kansas who'd spent night and day and day and night building the B-29, the world's first intercontinental bomber, capable of a four-thousand-mile round trip, the largest and heaviest plane ever mass produced, with a 141-foot wingspan carrying 2,000-horsepower engines, with propellers sixteen and a half feet in diameter. But you also say this: You say this new plan is *your deal*. If this fails, you—General Curtis Emerson LeMay of the Twenty-First Bomber Command—will be *solely* responsible. Heck, you haven't even told Hap what you're doing. "In a war," you'll tell a reporter, "you've got to keep one punch ahead of the other guy all the time. A war is a very tough kind of proposition. If you don't get the enemy, he gets you. I think we've figured out a punch he's not expecting this time."

———

As the Air Force was becoming the sexiest branch of the service, the demanding and uncompromising Curtis LeMay became its guiding and often divisive figure. His leadership skills were undoubtedly precocious, and he rose rapidly. Stocky, stern, blunt, immensely self-confident, LeMay would be to the Air Force what George Patton was to the Army. Both were prototypical, unapologetic members of the warrior class.

LeMay spoke sparingly. Being on the verge of a growl was his steady state. His ferocious bearing was enhanced by the cigars he was constantly chewing, which would dangle from one side of his mouth. In truth, the cigars were a kind of prop, used as an act of concealment. It disguised the fact that one side of LeMay's face drooped from Bell's palsy, contracted during a flight in the inhumanely frigid conditions of high altitude, before the era of pressurized cabins.

The United States began World War II pursuing daytime, precision bombing of Nazi military and industrial targets, which was in theory more humane and accurate, but which also involved a much higher degree of difficulty and produced a higher rate of mortality for the airmen. The early results were paltry. In practice, pilots being assaulted by darting Nazi Focke-Wulf interceptors and blistering antiaircraft fire from 88-millimeter guns weren't maintaining position over their targets for the necessary amount of time. LeMay established a new rule: no more evasive action. "Having paid the price of admission to get over the target," LeMay told his airmen, "we've got to get the benefits."

Such an order required a giant measure of courage, and it was also, just as clearly, suicidal. But LeMay won the loyalty of those under his command because he backed up his words with tactical brains and personal courage. On November 23, 1942, in an attack on a fortified U-boat pen in Saint-Nazaire, France, LeMay piloted the lead plane. It was damaged by flak, but he and his crew nailed the target, as did the majority of the 101 B-17s on the mission. A month later, LeMay introduced the "combat box," which required bombers to break up into small box-shaped groups. By doing so, the planes were able to mass firepower from their defensive guns and, during raids, concentrate the release of bombs on a given target.

In recognition of his guts and, more significantly, his genius for improving the effectiveness of killing machines, LeMay would become the youngest four-star general in the Army, at age thirty-seven. As the Nazi threat diminished, he was dispatched to fix an ineffective bombing campaign in the Pacific theater, part of which involved nursing the temperamental, multibillion-dollar B-29 bomber, as costly to develop as the atom bomb. The plane's Wright Cyclone engines had come to be nicknamed the "Wrong" engines and ultimately required more than eighteen hundred modifications to fix leaking, overheating, fried cylinders, faulty exhaust stacks, and the tendency to conk out or catch fire. Hap Arnold, the commanding general of the Army Air Force, had to that point written a very big check for a plane that was all promise and no punch.

By 1945, when the concept of strategic bombing had morphed

into the barbarity of area bombing, LeMay had no qualms about this evolution. It could even be said the reverse was true: He readily became its most productive adherent when he determined that the ideal bombing strategy for mainland Japan was to turn the entire country into a heap of smoking rubble. "I'll tell you what war is about," he'd say. "You've got to kill people, and when you've killed enough, they stop fighting."

However, as strategy, area bombing—or, less euphemistically, the indiscriminate killing of noncombatants—proved to be mostly pointless and even counterproductive. The British had theorized that their air raids would cause German citizens to rebel against the Nazis, but, as Robert Pape noted, the opposite occurred: The attacks actually increased reliance on Hitler's government for basic necessities. "Air power has never driven the masses into the streets to demand anything," Pape wrote. Moreover, raids on cities had a negligible impact on German war production because many factories were outside city centers. The U.S. Strategic Bombing Survey estimated that the effect of all Allied city bombing probably depleted the German economy by no more than 2.7 percent. German production in 1944 was three times greater than it was at the start of the war. The most effective missions targeted such resources as oil facilities. By 1945, the Nazis were running out of gas.

Raids in Italy had long-term negative political consequences. During the American offensive, U.S. bombers targeted railroads, bridges, and factories. The rampant destruction dimmed Italian enthusiasm for the American liberators, especially among industrial workers. As a result, many Italians had a more favorable opinion of the Red Army, and during the Cold War, the country's working class backed the most vigorous Communist Party in Western Europe.

The Air Force didn't win the war in the Pacific, either. All the decisive battles were fought by the Navy. In June 1944, Admiral Chester Nimitz put 127,000 troops on 535 ships and began ejecting the Japanese from multiple island strongholds with a series of amphibious landings. The bloodshed was horrific. The first target,

Saipan, was attacked on June 15, 1944. On the beaches, exposed Marines were sliced and shredded by mines, mortars, and machine guns. Bodies were typically dismembered and even atomized into red bits. The Japanese fought to the point of futility, choosing hopeless banzai charges instead of permitting capture, making final stands in pillboxes and caves, many of which became coffins as American soldiers resorted to the use of flamethrowers.

To subdue Saipan, 13,000 U.S. troops were killed or wounded. Of the 30,000 Japanese soldiers defending the island, only 921 were taken prisoner. Even Japanese civilians joined this death cult. After being told the Americans would commit rape, castration, and torture, as many as 1,000 men, women, and children proceeded to the northern tip of the island and tossed themselves off a six-hundred-foot seaside cliff. Back in Japan, a newspaper praised the event as "the finest act of the Showa period."

———

Tinian, Saipan's sister island in the Marianas archipelago, was the next target. After being cleared of Japanese forces, this dot in the middle of the Pacific, some six thousand miles west of San Francisco, was transformed into the largest and busiest airport in the world. The Navy's can-do construction battalion, the Seabees, cut and paved six huge runways, each almost two miles long and as wide as a ten-lane highway. These jumbo dimensions were required to accommodate the B-29 Superfortress, half a football field in size.

Soon, each day on the island would conclude with the thrum of giant piston engines building to a deafening symphony of a single sustained note. Every fifteen seconds, another bomber choked with fuel and explosives would fitfully lift into the fading daylight, headed north into the night for an early morning attack on a Japanese target.

On March 9–10, 1945, the aerial bombardment of cities reached a new and even more sickening level when LeMay ordered 334 B-29s to attack Tokyo. The bombers each carried two kilotons of incendiary devices. What occurred, according to the Strategic Bombing Survey, was worse than a firestorm. It was termed "a conflagration." Thousands of bombs scattered what was described as a "flaming dew" above Tokyo's flammable wood-and-paper residences. Volatile gases merged and rose, becoming an invisible wall of boiling heat. Wind speeds climbed as the air became violent. B-29s were turned upside down. The fire spread madly, erasing everything until there was nothing left for the flames to consume.

"Fire winds with burning particles ran up and down the streets," said factory worker Tsuchikura Hidezo. "I watched people, adults and children, running for their lives, dashing madly about like rats. Flames ran after them like living things, striking them down. They died by the hundreds in front of me.... The whole spectacle with its blinding lights and thundering noise reminded me of the paintings of purgatory—a real inferno out of the depths of hell."

The United States later calculated that in the six-hour bombardment of Tokyo more people lost their lives than in any equivalent period "in the history of man." More than one hundred thousand men, women, and children were killed; a million more were made homeless. "I suppose if I had lost the war, I would have been tried as a war criminal," LeMay later conceded.

———

During the Cold War, LeMay's public image would eventually track downward, but it began with a long spell at rare heights. The bombing campaign by his B-29s ultimately established him as an unequivocal military superstar, with journalists of the day ignoring the unconscionable body count from attacks that ultimately reduced seventy Japanese cities to dust. His portrait on the cover of *Time* carried this blunt caption: *Can Japan stand twice the bombing that Germany got?* The esteem lasted into the 1950s as LeMay took over Strategic Air Command, a Cold War–era creation. SAC crews were put on a perpetual hair-trigger standby, and the division's nearly three thousand bombers packed enough megatonnage to instantly turn the Soviet Union—or any foe—into a radioactive ruin.

The emotional underpinning of SAC was a misplaced overpreparedness that could be attributed to a Pearl Harbor syndrome. Curtis LeMay was among the generation of officers who felt the sting of humiliation when the U.S. military was caught sleeping, literally, in the early hours of a Sunday morning in 1941 when Japanese fighters and bombers swarmed Hawaii. He was also intimately aware that the American forces at the time were incapable of swiftly mounting a counterpunch. With 200,000 troops, the 1941 version of the U.S. military was about the same size as Bulgaria's, and the Air Force had only a few hundred first-line combat aircraft.

By 1944, however, American air power was unchallenged. LeMay and other commanders were supervising 2.4 million personnel, up from 20,000, with a total of 80,000 planes. After being engorged with weaponry, LeMay fiercely fought to maintain a surplus of destruction for the rest of his military career.

He also cultivated an incestuous relationship with Hollywood, which spent the first half of the Cold War mythologizing the magnificence of American air power. *Command Decision* (1948) starred Clark Gable as a crusading Air Force general who stops the Nazis from deploying their frightening new jet fighters. *Twelve O'Clock High* (1949) portrayed a fictional underperforming U.S. bomber group motivated into greatness by General Frank Savage, a disciplinarian presented in a positive light by Gregory Peck. In 1952, MGM released *Above and Beyond*, based on the experiences of Paul Tibbets in training the B-29 squadron that dropped the atomic bombs. Those who bought a ticket watched a fraught relationship between Lucy Tibbets, a weary, worried, lonely wife, and a driven, distracted, distant, self-centered, and short-tempered husband. In one scene, Paul returns home late—yet again. As he carries one of his sleeping sons into the bedroom, Lucy joins him. While they are bonding over their children sedately snoozing, Paul volcanically erupts in a defense of using atomic weapons.

LUCY: They are wonderful, but you know every time I look at them sleep I get sad. Terribly sad.

PAUL: Why?

LUCY: Oh, I keep thinking of this war and how somewhere at this very moment bombs are being dropped and children like that are being killed.

PAUL: Lucy, don't ever say that again! Not to me...Look. Look. Let's clear up one little piece of morality right now.... War is what's wrong, not just its weapons. Sure...innocent people are dying and that's horrible. But to lose this war to the gang we're fighting would be the most immoral thing we could do to those kids in there. And don't you ever forget it!

In the real world, LeMay would become yet another general stuck fighting old battles and anxious for the next one to start. In the Korean conflict, U.S. bombers resumed the scorched-earth tactics of World War II, decimating cities and villages, and in the process killing two million North Korean civilians, or, as LeMay proudly calculated, "20 percent of the population." But, as in World War II, this savagery was not determinative. The entry of Mao's ground troops into the Korean conflict, in massive numbers and commanded to fight without reason, ultimately produced a stalemate.

Army general Matt Ridgeway was unalterably opposed to LeMay's supposition that modern nuclear wars could be fought quickly, easily, and antiseptically. He had witnessed the worst fighting in World War II and Korea, and in Korea, particularly, he saw what the Air Force had *promised* to do with strategic bombing and how *limited* it was in fact as an instrument of policy and power. When the United States bombed, Ridgeway argued, it inevitably ended up using ground troops. He compared air power to an aspirin; it gave some immediate relief, but it did not cure the underlying problem. Ridgeway also deemed the "strategic bombing" of residential areas fundamentally immoral.

In 1954, when LeMay was asked what he would do if hostilities resumed in Korea, he said he would drop a few atomic bombs on China, Manchuria, and southeastern Russia in the hope it might escalate into World War III and allow the United States to finish off the Soviets before they were an equal match in nuclear firepower. By that point, it's important to note, the Soviets had ended the U.S. atomic monopoly, had two hundred atomic bombs of their own, and were on the verge of testing a hydrogen device, one of which, if dropped on New York City, could have caused millions of deaths, with the destruction reaching Boston and Washington, D.C. LeMay simply refused to grasp that the atomic destruction of Hiroshima and Nagasaki *wasn't* the beginning of a new age of warfare. It was just the opposite: a warning that such a war could never, ever be fought.

Hollywood—with LeMay as an unofficial executive producer—nonetheless found a way to even glamorize thermonuclear destruction. *Strategic Air Command* (1955)—the first in a so-called SAC trilogy that also included *Bombers B-52* (1957) and *A Gathering of Eagles* (1963)—advertised that it had been filmed in "the sky-filling grandeur of Vista Vision." A barking narrator told moviegoers: "Now for the first time the Air Force throws opens its guarded gates to reveal the amazing story of America's top-secret striking force, its earth-quaking power ready for defense at a moment in history when the world trembles in the shadow of an H-bomb."

The star of *Strategic Air Command* was Jimmy Stewart, who had flown twenty bombing missions in World War II. He played Dutch Holland, an ex–bomber pilot and baseball legend who is called back to duty by the Air Force to fulfill a need for senior leadership. The man doing the recruiting is a character named General Ennis C. Hawkes, modeled on General Curtis LeMay, who tells Dutch that SAC is only interested in deterrence. "We're here," he says, "to stop a war from starting."

However, it began to leak out that Curtis LeMay had long been hoping to start a war with the Soviet Union, more or less by himself.

By the time of the 1962 Cuban Missile Crisis, LeMay had become a member of the Joint Chiefs of Staff as head of the Air Force, and he viewed the high-stakes showdown as an opportunity to subvert John F. Kennedy's blockade. He covertly told SAC airborne-alert nuclear bombers to soar past their customary turnaround points, and he failed to halt a ridiculously ill-timed West Coast test launch of a nuclear missile. On October 19, 1962, as Kennedy was about to announce a blockade, LeMay denigrated the idea and said it would encourage the Soviets to attack Allied forces in West Berlin. Here's a portion of the secretly recorded White House conversation:

> GENERAL LEMAY: If we don't do anything to Cuba, then they're going to push on Berlin, and push real hard because they've got us on the run.... This blockade and political action, I see leading into war.... This is almost as bad as the appeasement at Munich....I just don't see any other solution except direct military action right now. A blockade, and political talk, would be considered by a lot of our friends and neutrals as being a pretty weak response to this. And I'm sure a lot of our own citizens would feel that way, too. You're in a pretty bad fix, Mr. President.
>
> PRESIDENT KENNEDY: What did you say?
>
> GENERAL LEMAY: You're in a pretty bad fix.
>
> PRESIDENT KENNEDY: Well, you're in it with me.

Given LeMay's habit of imprudent behavior, Stanley Kubrick's *Dr. Strangelove*, released in 1964, was on relatively solid ground picturing the commanding generals of the Air Force as maniacal sociopaths eager to instigate nuclear holocaust. Designed as dark satire, Kubrick's classic was inadvertently as faithful in its truth-telling as any documentary.

The plot of *Dr. Strangelove* is incited by the fully psychotic General Jack Ripper (Sterling Hayden). Certain that the communists are conspiring to pollute the "precious bodily fluids" of the American people through fluoridation, General Ripper personally authorizes his 843rd Bomb Wing at Burpelson Air Force Base to attack the Soviet Union. At the Pentagon's War Room, General Buck Turgidson (George C.

Scott) makes the case to President Merkin Muffley (Peter Sellers) that Ripper's lunacy has a silver lining, providing the United States with a golden opportunity to flatten the Soviets once and for all and to do so with only a few million dead. *Read the script slowly.* It is a wholly accurate rendering of the mind-set of the Cold War U.S. Air Force:

> GENERAL TURGIDSON: *One,* our hopes for recalling the 843rd Bomb Wing are quickly being reduced to a very low order of probability. *Two,* in less than fifteen minutes from now the Russkies will be making radar contact with the planes. *Three,* when they do, they are going to go absolutely ape, and they're gonna strike back with everything they've got. *Four,* if prior to this time, we have done nothing further to suppress their retaliatory capabilities, we will suffer virtual annihilation. Now, *five,* if on the other hand, we were to immediately launch an all-out and coordinated attack on all their airfields and missile bases we'd stand a damn good chance of catching them with their pants down. Hell, we got a five-to-one missile superiority as it is. We could easily assign three missiles to every target, and still have a very effective reserve force for any other contingency. Now, *six,* an unofficial study which we undertook of this eventuality, indicated that we would destroy ninety percent of their nuclear capabilities. We would therefore prevail, and suffer only modest and acceptable civilian casualties from their remaining force, which would be badly damaged and uncoordinated.

Indeed, there was little daylight between the intemperate warmongering as portrayed by the bomb-happy General Buck Turgidson and the principal model for the role, Curtis LeMay. More than any other Cold War figure, LeMay would modernize and normalize the concept of indiscriminate and catastrophic aerial destruction and, by doing so, put the world on notice that anyone could be a target—anytime, anyplace, anywhere.

CHAPTER 2

OPERATION PAPERCLIP

In early April 1945, as the sound of Soviet guns had become audible to the east, Wernher von Braun and his fellow rocket scientists at the Peenemünde production facility were told to evacuate. Before making his way south from the Baltic Sea location, von Braun, the chief science official, also made sure to plan for life after the Nazis. As leverage, he stashed away fourteen tons of V-2 documents in an abandoned salt mine.

Von Braun had been using the German army to pay for his dream of making space travel possible, and in return, he provided a working rocket with a bomb on top—the world's first ballistic missile. In this quid pro quo, he had joined the Nazi Party, in 1937, and in 1940 moved up to SS Untersturmführer (lieutenant). The relationship with the Fatherland had at times been testy.

In 1943, a female dentist working as an SS spy reported that von Braun was bitching about not getting to build a spaceship and had expressed a "defeatist" attitude about Germany's chances of winning the war. Heinrich Himmler, the head of the SS, added several fabrications to further implicate Lieutenant von Braun, claiming he was a communist sympathizer, had attempted to sabotage the Nazi rocket program, and, because he was a pilot with access to his own personal Messerschmitt, was all but ready to hop over to England. Von Braun was jailed for two weeks and only a direct appeal to Hitler attained his release.

By 1944, he and his team had developed the V–1 and V–2, the latter carrying a payload of two thousand pounds and flying at a velocity five times the speed of sound. It was the first man–made device to reach space. Ultimately, rockets by the thousands terrorized Brussels, Antwerp, and London, killing approximately eighteen thousand people, mostly civilians.

The backbone of the rocket program was slave labor from concentration camp inmates. Von Braun couldn't avoid visiting the hellish Mittelbau complex, which included Mittelwerk, an underground factory dug out of a mountain by the inmates; and Dora, a Buchenwald subcamp that supplied many of the laborers. Of the sixty thousand prisoners involved in the Nazi rocket program—captives from France, Poland, and the Soviet Union—it is estimated that twenty-five thousand died from starvation, illness, overwork, beatings, and executions. More people died making the rockets than were killed by them.

On April 11, 1945, American troops liberated the camp at Dora-Mittelbau, discovering half-built rockets and jet planes, unburied bodies, and several thousand starved and battered survivors. The stills and film recording the liberation were among the first images Americans saw of stunning, haunting Nazi genocide. In the meantime, von Braun was enjoying himself at one of the finest hotels in the Austrian Alps. "There I was," he'd tell the *New Yorker*, "living royally in the ski hotel on a mountain plateau. There were the French below us to the west, and the Americans to the south. But no one, of course, suspected we were there.... The hotel service was excellent."

In the first week of May, von Braun decided it was time to surrender, and he asked his brother Magnus to bicycle down the mountain and find American soldiers. On May 3, 1945, most of the Nazi rocket program was peacefully taken into custody. The moment is captured with a group photo that shows weary, puzzled American soldiers standing next to agreeable-looking male civilians. When von Braun chauvinistically detailed his rocketry heroics, an American GI became suspicious. "If we hadn't caught the biggest scientist in the Third Reich," the soldier said, "we had certainly caught the biggest liar."

"No, I wasn't afraid," said von Braun. "It all made sense. The V-2 was something [the Germans] had and [the Americans] didn't have. Naturally [the Americans] wanted to know all about it."

Von Braun had accurately judged his worth. America's military establishment had a deep and unreserved appetite for Nazi technology. "Occupation of German scientific and industrial establishments has revealed the fact that we have been alarmingly backward in many fields of research," Air Force major general Hugh Kerr wrote in a memo just after Germany's surrender. "If we do not take this opportunity to seize the apparatus and the brains that developed it . . . we will remain several years behind while we attempt to cover a field already exploited. Pride and face-saving have no place in national insurance."

There were dissenters from this view. U.S. Army officer Walter Jessel judged it problematic to be offering a second life to people who had no trouble supporting a diabolically criminal regime. Jessel had been born in a German Jewish family, in 1913, witnessed the rise of the Nazis, and was able to emigrate to the United States. At the start of World War II, he enlisted in the U.S. Army, became an intelligence officer under Patton, and, following the war, was assigned to a counterintelligence detachment screening members of Wernher von Braun's rocket team.

As a group, Jessel found the rocketeers to be a rather alarming bunch. They seemed to share a largely amoral, almost exclusively transactional worldview. They were indifferent to the devastation caused by their work, unrepentant about their attachment to the Nazi madness, and prepared to sell their secrets to anyone who would keep them from being detained or shot.

"Almost to a man these people are convinced that war between the U.S. and Russia is around the corner," Jessel said. "They shake

their heads in amazement and some contempt at our political ignorance and are impatient at our slowness in recognizing [the Nazis as]
the true savior of Western civilization from Asia's hordes."

———

Reconstituting Hitler's war room in America was also apparently
judged critical to national insurance. As part of the top-secret Hill
Project, members of the Wehrmacht high command were brought
to the United States on the SS *West Point* and stationed at Camp
Ritchie, located in a secluded spot on the Maryland–Pennsylvania
border, about sixty-five miles northwest of Baltimore. Waiting for
them was a library of captured German war records, publications,
periodicals, and intelligence reports, which had been conveniently
filed using the German *Einheitsaktenplan* system.

The principal goal of the Hill Project was to evaluate the German
experience fighting the Soviets and, by doing so, plan a winning U.S.
strategy for a future war with the Red Army. The staff of "hillbil-
lies" ultimately grew to two hundred POWs. In less than a year, they
would complete 3,647 pages of reports and studies. Historian Derek
R. Mallett wrote that "the reports these generals produced began to
play a highly influential role in the development of U.S. Army policy
in the late 1940s and early 1950s, particularly in planning to defend
Western Europe from a potential Soviet invasion."

As Camp Ritchie was hosting a committee of Hitler's war planners, Fort Hunt became the site of Hitler's reconstituted spy service.
General Reinhard Gehlen and his Nazi intelligence associates were
rechristened as the BOLERO group. Under Pentagon supervision,
they produced numerous wonky reports on Soviet military capabili-
ties. One was titled *Development of the Russian High Command and Its
Conception of Strategy During the Eastern Campaign*, another, *Fighting
Methods of the Russian Armies Based on Experience Gained from the Large-
Scale Russian Offensive in the Summer of 1944 and the Winter of 1945*.
The BOLERO team also produced studies on the Red Army order

of battle, and surveys of Red Army units, equipment, and command-ers. "The early courtship of Gehlen by American intelligence sug-gests that Washington was in a Cold War mode sooner than people realize," Mallett wrote. "The Gehlen gambit also belies the preva-lent Western notion that aggressive Soviet policies were primarily to blame for triggering the Cold War."

While in the United States, General Gehlen pitched himself as someone who could make a valuable contribution to the fight against communism. He claimed he could go back to Germany and reacti-vate his network of tested anticommunists inside the Soviet empire. Gehlen succeeded in winning sympathy from Americans in high places, such as Allen Dulles, the influential Wall Street lawyer who had been based in Bern, Switzerland, during the war as a top Ameri-can spy with the Office of Strategic Services (OSS).

Before the war, Allen and his brother John Foster Dulles had established deep ties to German industry while working on behalf of America's moneyed class at Sullivan & Cromwell; and as dyed-in-the-wool capitalists, both Dulles brothers were innately hostile to the Soviet concept of state-planned socialism and inclined to provide soft landings for knowledgeable Nazis.

However, it would slowly dawn on the U.S. intelligence com-munity that Gehlen had oversold and underdelivered. "The Agency loved Gehlen because he fed us what we wanted to hear," said an unnamed CIA source. "We used his stuff constantly, and we fed it to everyone else—the Pentagon, the White House, the newspapers. They loved it, too. But it was hyped-up Russian bogeymen junk, and it did a lot of damage to this country."

———

Accumulating the all-star technocrats of the Third Reich before they could be kidnapped by the Soviets, or charged at the Nuremberg trials, or smuggled by a ratline to South America, would soon be for-malized as Operation Paperclip. It was run by the Joint Intelligence

Community (JIC), a new entity established in the summer of 1945. The JIC had representatives from the intelligence divisions of the State Department, Army, Navy, and Air Force. The project was called "paperclip" because the Army bureaucrats doing the sorting were told to attach paperclips to the folders of the most desirable rocket experts, among the first groups taken into custody.

"To understand the mind-set of the Joint Intelligence Committee," Annie Jacobsen wrote in *Operation Paperclip*, "consider this: Within one year of the atomic bombing of Hiroshima and Nagasaki, the JIC warned the Joint Chiefs of Staff that the United States needed to prepare for 'total war' with the Soviets—to include atomic, chemical, and biological warfare—and they even set an estimated start date of 1952."

In September 1945, von Braun was flown by a military cargo plane to Wilmington, Delaware. "He cleared no customs and passed through no formal passport controls," wrote Matthew Brzezinski in *Red Moon Rising*. "The paper trail documenting his entry was sealed in an army vault, along with his incriminating war files; his Nazi Party ties, his depositions denying involvement in slave labor, and his three SS promotions remained classified until 1984, seven years after his death."

Dr. von Braun and other Paperclip rocketeers—enough to man a football team—were shipped, by design, to a hideaway smack on the southern border, Fort Bliss, on the outskirts of El Paso, where they occupied a former military hospital. "Brown, dusty plains stretched to the East as far as the eye could see," Brzezinski wrote. "The desert was unbroken save for the occasional tumbleweed, buzzard and cactus, and it baked at over 100 degrees most of the year." In Germany, the coddled scientists had regularly dined at the nearby four-star Schwabes Hotel, which had a wine cellar stuffed with exquisite vintages seized from occupied France. But there was nothing cosmopolitan about their new Texas milieu.

On June 25, 1946, a story by Virginia Strom in the *El Paso*

Herald-Post reported that at least one of the Nazis was finding Army grub truly appalling. The headline read: "American Cooking 'Tasteless,' Says German Rocket Scientist, Dislikes 'Rubberized' Chicken." "Everything is fried," chief design engineer Dr. Walther Riedel told Strom. "The bread, when you cut into it, looks like cotton. Then you serve what we call rubberized chicken, fried to a crisp.... Your green salads are tasteless."

Riedel wasn't entirely negative, adding, "Your banana sundaes are really something! As soon as my children arrive, a banana sundae is the first thing I want to get them."

The rubber chicken story out of El Paso was one of the first press reports about Operation Paperclip recruits, and, once unearthed, the program drew immediate criticism from Eleanor Roosevelt, Albert Einstein, and Rabbi Stephen S. Wise, of the American Jewish Congress. A Gallup poll indicated most Americans thought it was a "bad idea." The Society for the Prevention of World War III, an organization of thousands of writers, artists, and scholars, excoriated Operation Paperclip in its journal: "These German experts performed wonders for the German war effort. Can one forget their gas chambers, their skill in cremation, their meticulous methods used to extract gold from the teeth of their victims, their wizardry in looting and thieving?"

———

The rocket scientists hadn't been saved in order to build space stations and send astronauts on voyages of discovery—which wouldn't change until the launch of Sputnik, in 1957, when, almost overnight, an all-hands-on-deck space race erupted. And while star trekking was something von Braun was still fantasizing about, he knew what he was tasked to do in the meantime. As Daniel Lang's *New Yorker* feature on von Braun made clear, "There is nothing secret about the broad objective.... That objective is to build a guided missile capable of carrying an atomic warhead to any point on the face of the earth."

On the other side of the world, captured German manpower and machinery became an important additive to the Soviet nuclear program. Nazi scientists were shipped to Black Sea research sites tasked with uranium processing and isotope separation. (Alexander Solzhenitsyn called the relatively civilized scientific research centers staffed by well-educated political prisoners the "First Circle" of the Soviet prison system.) Pilfered German-made precision instruments—vaunted for their craftsmanship—permitted the Soviets to leap yet another technology gap. A Berlin factory used for producing pure uranium was dismantled and transported to the Soviet Union, rebuilt near Moscow, and renamed Elektrosal, becoming one of the first islands in a soon to be vast atomic infrastructure.

CHAPTER 3

FACE-TO-FACE

During World War II, U.S. and Soviet forces never fought side by side; Hitler—the common enemy—had been squeezed between two distinct fronts. On April 25, 1945, the U.S. and Soviet armies converged in southeast Germany at the River Elbe, about eighty miles south of Berlin. The Red Army troops arriving in Torgau had fought across Poland and what is now the Czech Republic. The American soldiers had crossed the Rhine, captured Frankfurt, and claimed the industrial Ruhr Valley.

As soldiers from both nations began pouring into Torgau, the two armies united like brothers in arms. There were hugs. There were kisses. American veteran Ben Casmere recalled, "I never kissed so many men in my life." The First Ukrainian Front broke out their accordions and balalaikas. The Russians hosted a feast, serving macaroni, salami, small raw fish, raw fat, meat covered with dough, black bread, hard-boiled eggs, hot chocolate, and cookies. Dancing commenced. Thousands of toasts were punctuated by swigs of beer and shots of vodka.

"Every time I took a drink from my glass, the fellow behind me would refill it," said H. W. (Bill) Shank, who was a first lieutenant in the 104th Mechanized Cavalry Reconnaissance Troop. "Wishing to appear equal to my Russian hosts, I kept pouring the stuff into my boot."

Added Lieutenant Shank, "Of all the experiences in my life, finding and meeting the Russians was the most memorable. The war made people love each other so much when it was finally over. If everyone intermingled—like we did when we linked up with the Russians—there could be no war."

Two weeks later, on May 9, 1945, less than four years after Hitler's forces had loomed within miles of the walls of the Kremlin, Soviet radio reported Germany's surrender at 1:10 a.m. Despite the hour, people flocked into the streets of Moscow by the millions. Searchlights panned the sky. Fireworks and cannon shells exploded above Red Square. A Soviet captain was overheard saying, *"Pora jit"* ("It's time to live"). Within twenty-four hours, there would not be a drop of vodka left in the Soviet capital.

With Soviet ambassador Averell Harriman out of the country, George Kennan was the ranking American diplomat in the city. To his amazement, a massive crowd gathered in the enormous square in front of the U.S. embassy. "They crowd up against our wall in thousands, waving and cheering—they cannot be induced to go anywhere else," Kennan later wrote. "After some hours of this, I, being in charge of the embassy at that moment, feel it necessary to acknowledge in some way this great demonstration of goodwill; and I go out onto one of the pedestals of the high pilasters on the front of the building and say a few simple words to the crowd in Russian, congratulating them on the common day of victory. They love it and roar their approval."

Later that same month, Dwight Eisenhower expressed confidence about maintaining a peaceful relationship with the Soviet Union. He noted how, in 1941, American and British forces had to work through an often heated culture clash. "As we dealt with each other, we learned the British ways and they learned ours," he wrote. "Now the Russians, who have had relatively little contact with the Americans and British, do not understand us, nor do we them. The more contact we have with the Russians, the more they will understand us and the greater will be the cooperation." Speaking a few months later before Congress, Eisenhower reasserted the opinion: "Russia has not the slightest thing to gain by a struggle with the United States."

It bears noting that the majority of Americans at the time shared

Ike's view. A poll taken in the summer of 1945 indicated that 60 percent expressed confidence about cooperation between Russia and the Western Allies. But even before the war against Japan had ended, prominent voices returned to framing the world as capitalism versus communism, the God-fearing versus the atheists, the forces of light battling the forces of darkness.

"The Soviet Union," *Life* cautioned, "is the number one problem for Americans because it is the only country in the world with the dynamic power to challenge our own conceptions of truth, justice, and the good life." The *Catholic Mind* warned its readers about "wishful thinking" regarding the possible transformation of the Soviet system. "The reality...remains unchanged," the publication maintained, "and the war has given the dictatorship a stronger, more penetrating grip on the country than it ever had before."

America's top spy was also alerting Harry Truman in a secret memo that was written just a week after Hitler's suicide. "The United States will be confronted with a situation potentially more dangerous than any preceding one," advised General "Wild Bill" Donovan, head of the OSS. "[Russia will] become a menace more formidable to the United States than any ever known."

———

On October 21, 1939, immigrant physicist Leo Szilard was in Washington, D.C., attending the first meeting of the Advisory Committee on Uranium. It didn't go well. An Army representative berated Szilard as naïve to think he could create an atomic bomb, advised him that it usually took two wars to find out whether a new weapon was any good, and, further, told him that "in the end it is not weapons which win wars but the morale of the troops."

You could say, or at least hypothesize, that we had a Cold War of lasting duration because powerful people in the U.S. government kept doubting Leo Szilard's wisdom. It happened again on Monday, May 28, 1945. It was one of the worst days of Szilard's life, because when he

failed to effectively educate a president's top advisor about a prospective doomsday, an immediate peace with the Soviet Union was all but
junked and humanity edged significantly closer to extinction.

The day before, Szilard had taken an overnight train from Washington to Spartanburg, South Carolina, to meet with Jimmy Byrnes,
who was about to conclude a microscopic retirement. Byrnes had just
left a job as head of the Office of War Mobilization under the recently
deceased Franklin Roosevelt and would soon formally accept a new
role as Harry Truman's secretary of state.

Secretly, Byrnes was already in the midst of another assignment
from Truman, as the head of the new Interim Committee, a body of
senior military and civilian experts charged with advising the president on the use of the atomic bomb. The sixty-three-year-old Byrnes
was about to become, effectively, the second most powerful man in
the country, if not the world.

When the native South Carolinian opened the door on the evening
of May 28, the visiting scientist in front of him was short and stout,
five foot six inches, with thick, curly dark hair, starting to recede. A
round face was highlighted by warm brown eyes advertising intensity
and intellect. Byrnes was about the same height, but decidedly thin-
ner, to the point of being wiry, with eyes small and deeply set, his nose
narrow and elongated, hair gray, sparse, closely trimmed.

The origins and mentalities of Jimmy Byrnes and Leo Szilard were
studies in opposition. Szilard, age forty-seven at the time, was a Jewish,
Hungarian-born peripatetic refugee who had recently made it his habit
to keep a packed suitcase on standby anywhere he landed. In 1933,
during a morning walk on the streets of London, he had understood
how neutrons could elude the electric barrier guarding the nucleus and
produce exponential mayhem, creating a chain reaction. It was Szilard
who in 1939 compelled Albert Einstein to send a letter to FDR warning that Germany had the capacity to build the kind of super weapon
that might provide Hitler with a rather swift route to world dominion.
As chief physicist of the Manhattan Project's Metallurgical Laboratory,

Szilard, along with colleague Enrico Fermi, demonstrated the world's first self-sustaining atomic chain reaction. As the Manhattan Project spread across the country—becoming a $20 billion experiment encompassing thirty-seven laboratories, with newly built production cities at Oak Ridge, Tennessee; Los Alamos, New Mexico; and Hanford, Washington—Szilard toured the facilities as a troubleshooter. "He is a man with an astounding amount of ideas," said Fermi.

Byrnes, in his fourth decade of continuous public service, was a classic American success story. Born in Charleston to a working single mother, he had left school at age fourteen to take a job as a runner in a law office, where he cleaned and performed errands. He would go on to serve in every branch of the federal government: Congress, the Supreme Court, and the White House. In 1942, becoming head of the Office of War Mobilization, Byrnes more or less ran the U.S. economy since the entire U.S. economy had mobilized for war. The press began calling him "assistant president."

Szilard had an innate distrust of the political and military class and had classified General Leslie Groves, the administrative head of the Manhattan Project, as pompous, rigid, imperialistic, and a very "big fool." Groves, who was openly anti-Semitic, thought of Szilard as a Jewish busybody and judged him the project's "biggest villain." The one-star brigadier general preferred "quiet, shy and modest" non-Jews, such as Fermi. Szilard's sparkling idea-a-minute intelligence unnerved him. So did Szilard's radical independence. Groves had determined that the fundamental problem with the Hungarian physicist was that he hadn't played baseball, and therefore had failed to learn the concept of teamwork. Eventually, Groves even suspected Szilard was a spy, and proposed having him locked up in an internment camp. The secretary of war judged otherwise.

Unable to imprison Szilard, Groves began keeping him under constant surveillance. The general knew exactly where Szilard was on May 28, 1945, because on May 27 an undercover agent had boarded the overnight train Szilard took to Spartanburg. Before the physicist arrived, Groves had also conveyed his decidedly negative view of Szilard to Byrnes.

After all but dreaming the atomic bomb into existence—acting as the prime mover, supplying the force of his genius and his bottomless persistence to shake an oblivious and at times obnoxious Pentagon hierarchy into action—Szilard believed the pretext for using the weapon had vanished. "Until recently," he wrote in a memo he gave to Byrnes, "we have had to fear that the United States might be attacked by atomic bombs during this war and that her only defense might lie in a counterattack by the same means.... With the defeat of Germany, this danger is averted."

Szilard had no issue with the bomb as a *defensive* weapon. However, he judged preemptive use immoral. In the third paragraph of the memo, Byrnes read: "Perhaps the greatest immediate danger which faces us is the probability that our 'demonstration' of atomic bombs will precipitate a race in the production of these devices between the United States and Russia and that if we continue to pursue the present course, our initial advantage may be lost very quickly in such a race."

On Monday, May 28, 1945, Leo Szilard was hoping to educate Jimmy Byrnes about the prospect of a different kind of chain reaction, one that could erupt on the timeline of history, leading to humanity's end. What he was asking Byrnes to envision was a future in which the United States, after detonating the first atomic bomb, would obtain only a short-lived monopoly on nuclear weapons. He made it clear to Byrnes that the Soviet Union had the wherewithal to rather quickly join the nuclear club, following which—in the absence of any controls, any agreements, any restraints—an arms race propelled by a natural paranoia would place all existence in the shadow of a prospective Armageddon.

But Byrnes had already decided to play atomic poker, counting up all the needs the bomb could serve: (a) to secure the unconditional surrender of Japan; (b) to limit Soviet territorial conquests in the Pacific; and (c) to intimidate Stalin into granting self-determination for Eastern Europe. Byrnes had his own reputation prejudicing the last of those objectives. He had been one of Roosevelt's chief advisors at Yalta, where an all-too-vague agreement on Poland's autonomy was being predictably abused by Stalin. With Roosevelt dead, Byrnes was suddenly receiving a greater share of the blame for Soviet suppression in Eastern Europe.

"I'm concerned about Russia's postwar behavior," Byrnes told Szilard. "Russian troops have moved into Hungary and Romania. I believe it will be very difficult to persuade Russia to withdraw her troops from these countries, and Russia might be more manageable if impressed by American military might."

Szilard responded, "I share your concern about Russia throwing her weight around in the postwar period, but I disagree that rattling the bomb might make Russia more manageable. I fail to see how sitting on a stockpile of bombs, which we could not possibly use, will have this effect. I think it's conceivable that doing so will even have the opposite effect."

"Well," said Byrnes, "you come from Hungary—you would not want Russia to stay in Hungary indefinitely."

Said Szilard, "I'm more concerned at this point that by demonstrating the bomb and using it in the war against Japan, we might start an atomic arms race between America and Russia, which might end with the destruction of both countries. I'm not disposed at this point to worry about what would happen to Hungary."

Groves, who was not a scientist, had badly misinformed Byrnes about the Soviet Union's potential to join the atomic age. The general had told him that the USSR did not have access to uranium (wrong), claimed that Stalin's regime didn't have the necessary technology (wrong), and predicted it would be decades before the country produced a nuclear weapon (wrong again). In 1948, a year before the Soviets detonated their first atomic bomb, Groves wrote a profoundly chauvinistic and inaccurate assessment in the *Saturday Evening Post*: "The Soviet Union simply does not have enough precision industry, technical skill, or scientific numerical strength to come even close to duplicating the magnificent achievement of American industries."

At the end of his visit with Byrnes, Szilard was fully aware that he had completely failed to slow the march toward a future piled high with nuclear weapons. Indeed, a political chain reaction on history's timeline was about to be set in motion, a Doomsday Clock about to be born and placed minutes to midnight, a new kind of dread unleashed, entrenched and universal. Szilard would later say he was rarely as depressed as when he left the house in Spartanburg and walked toward the train station: "I thought to myself how much better off the world might be had I been born in America and become influential in American politics, and had Byrnes been born in Hungary and studied physics. In all probability, there would have been no atom bomb, and no danger of an arms race between America and Russia."

———

On July 18, 1945, the first day of the eighth and final Allied summit, in the Berlin suburb of Potsdam, a cat-and-mouse game began. Who was the cat and who was the mouse became interchangeable.

This tragicomedy began with Joseph Stalin, general secretary of the Communist Party of the USSR, telling U.S. president Harry Truman about Japan's recent peace overtures.

But Stalin, from his spies, knew that Truman, from his spies, had already learned about the overtures.

Truman responded by telling Stalin to delay any talks with Japan—although Truman knew that Stalin had already decided to do that.

Stalin was making the fraternal gesture of sharing "confidential information" about the Japanese because he wanted to be part of a joint declaration at the end of the conference in which the Soviets would officially sever their neutrality with Japan. Stalin was anxious to grab a chunk of Asia. But Truman had no intention of fulfilling Joe's wish.

On July 24, during a recess at the Potsdam Conference, Truman nonchalantly approached Stalin and told him that "we have a new weapon of unusual destructive force."

Stalin replied that he was glad to hear it and hoped the United States would make good use of it against the Japanese. Speaking of the exchange, Manhattan Project science director Robert Oppenheimer said, "That was carrying casualness rather far."

Afterward, Truman suspected Stalin did not understand the significance of what he'd been told. But Stalin had.

Completely.

Here's what Truman didn't know:

Number one: Stalin's intelligence operatives had stolen virtually all the relevant classified documents related to the bombs about to be dropped on Hiroshima and Nagasaki. The amount of stolen data was, in total, a how-to manual enabling the Soviets to make duplicates of the American bombs.

Number two: The USSR possessed the necessary scientific elite to comprehend the cutting-edge physics contained in the pilfered documents.

Number three: Stalin was in command of an almost limitless supply of slave labor, which was incarcerated in a continent-wide network of prison camps. Stalin's U.S.-based spies had also made the dictator aware of the prodigious amount of men, money, and materials that would be required to match the Manhattan Project.

Number four: Logic dictated that Stalin assign the job of making an atomic bomb to the principal administrator of the gulags, Lavrentiy Beria, the head of internal security and a criminal genius. Beria was a serial rapist, an expert in the commission of mass murder, and a masterful organizer. As the new atomic czar, he had immediate access to tens of thousands of people who could be worked to death, if necessary, with tens of thousands more available as ready replacements. On their backs, new atomic cities would rise.

Most of Stalin's superstar atomic spies came by way of Britain, which had partnered with the United States on nuclear research.

In all, some ten thousand pages of stolen technical data about the U.S. atom bomb would be forwarded to Soviet physicists, including experiments and designs related to every aspect of development: the physiology of uranium, isotope separation, gaseous diffusion, centrifuges, the construction of reactors, and drawings of the custom-made machinery used to detonate the bomb.

One of Stalin's British moles was Alan Nunn May, who joined the British Communist Party in the 1930s. During the war, May was attached to the Manhattan Project as a physicist based in Canada, where the world's most powerful research reactor was built at Chalk River. He provided the Soviets with a clear overview of the functions of the key atomic sites: the University of Chicago (where Szilard, Fermi, and many of the Nobel Prize winners were clustered); Oak Ridge (the site of isotope separation units to enrich uranium); Hanford (plutonium processing); and Los Alamos (the bomb factory). May forwarded expert analysis of the July 16 Trinity test in New Mexico shortly after it took place. He even shared a sample of enriched uranium, shipped to the Soviet Union in a small glass tube.

Bruno Pontecorvo was an Italian theoretical physicist who had worked closely with Enrico Fermi. Unlike Fermi, Pontecorvo was a devoted communist. During World War II, he worked with May at Chalk River, and in that position, he also had full access to the entire scope of the Manhattan Project. He would defect to the Soviet Union in 1950 and continue his work on high-level nuclear research until his death, in 1993.

German-born Klaus Fuchs may have been the most valuable player of all the moles. He was the most accomplished physicist and had the greatest access to the most sensitive and valuable information. In 1943, Dr. Fuchs was the prime culprit in a gigantic security breach, informing the Soviets about plutonium, the new synthetically created substance that was more powerful than uranium. By 1944, Fuchs was on site at the Los Alamos Lab in New Mexico, where he had access to every document in the laboratory's archives, in particular the latest work being done by Edward Teller on the vastly more destructive hydrogen bomb.

———

On July 26, 1945, China, Great Britain, and the United States issued the Potsdam Declaration demanding unconditional surrender of all Japanese forces. The declaration warned that the alternative was prompt and utter destruction. Stalin was not invited to be a co-signer. Truman wrote in his diary, "I was not willing to let Russia reap the fruits of a long and bitter and gallant effort in which she had no part."

On August 6, in the first billionth of a second after the detonation of the Little Boy atomic bomb, the temperature at the burst point in Hiroshima was several million degrees, hotter than the surface of the sun. Spontaneous combustion occurred at a distance of over two thousand yards. Passengers in a tram near ground zero were reduced to a pile of black cinder. At a military base, the shadows of soldiers, literally evaporated, were etched on the training ground.

Hundreds who sought shelter in water basins were boiled alive. In a city of 260,000, a quarter were killed immediately: 66,000. Another 70,000 were injured, and 68,000 buildings were damaged or destroyed. Only three of the fifty-five hospitals and first aid stations remained operational. Out of 200 physicians in the city, 180 were either dead or injured.

The nuclear explosion triggered an enormous amount of gamma and neutron radiation. Less than two hours after the bomb exploded, a "black rain," dark in color and sticky, fell on the city for three hours. The precipitation was the product of the bomb's dust cloud, and was highly radioactive. There were reports that some survivors, desperately parched by the city's heat and fires, opened their mouths to the sky to drink this toxic rain.

An Associated Press bulletin introduced Americans to the reality of atomic warfare at 11:03 a.m. Eastern Time on August 6. That night, the bar at the Washington Press Club was offering a gin and

Pernod mix called the "Atomic Cocktail." In a matter of days, a Los Angeles burlesque establishment was promoting "Atom Bomb Dancers." A New York jewelry company began selling "atomic inspired pin and earring sets as daring to wear as it was to drop the first atom bomb." Kix cereal soon advertised an Atomic Bomb Ring for the price of 15 cents and a cereal box top.

While U.S. citizens were reading headlines of the Hiroshima attack, Stalin was certain that in displaying this new wonder weapon, the "noisy shopkeeper" who'd replaced FDR was *not* sending a message to Japan. Rather, the destruction of Hiroshima was directed *at him*. "Of course, the Soviet Union was moving troops to the Far East in order to enter the war with Japan," said David Holloway, author of *Stalin and the Bomb.* "So yes, it was seen very much as directed against the Soviet Union, not only in order to deprive the Soviet Union of gains in the Far East, but generally to intimidate the Soviet Union."

Stalin called a meeting with Boris Vannikov, people's commissar of munitions, and Igor Kurchatov, the director of the Soviet atomic bomb project. "A single demand of you comrades," he said. "Provide us with atomic weapons in the shortest possible time. You know that Hiroshima has shaken the whole world. The equilibrium has been destroyed. Provide the bomb—it will remove a great danger from us."

During the Cold War, leaders of both the Soviet Union and the United States could accurately be accused of failing to stop the insanity of stockpiling nuclear weapons capable of ending life on the planet. The era demanded more imaginative and sustained diplomacy from both sides. An often cowardly political class—demonizing the other side ignorantly and willfully, regularly claiming foul and fictional conspiracies—chose to enflame the threats posed by the rivalry. And, yes, any war, even a so-called cold war, requires at least two belligerents. But it's also important to understand who fired the first shot. And in the Cold War, that was Harry Truman and the United States of America.

In the view of the Soviet Union, the balance of power had been destabilized when the United States became the sole nuclear power. Ergo, there were only two ways for that to be corrected: Either (1) the United States disarmed, or (2) the Soviets caught up. But from the U.S. perspective, having an atomic monopoly provided significant leverage over the Kremlin, and unilateral disarmament could be disastrous if the Soviets, a genuinely untrustworthy bunch, introduced their own bomb after American denuclearization and therefore gained a destabilizing monopoly of their own.

Ultimately, the worst-case scenario took place. The United States would begin military testing of nuclear weapons soon after World War II, and, in the meantime, Stalin wasn't waiting for America to unilaterally disarm. When the Soviets shocked an all-too-complacent U.S. leadership by becoming a nuclear power much sooner than anticipated, the shaken Americans responded by fast-tracking development of an even bigger bomb.

The vicious circle that ensued had previously been identified as the "security dilemma" by Sir Edward Grey, the British foreign secretary at the start of World War I. "Fear," Grey wrote, "begets suspicion and distrust—and evil imaginings of all sorts—until each government feels it would be criminal and a betrayal of its own country not to take every precaution...while every other government regards every precaution by every other government as evidence of hostile intent."

On August 10, 1945, General Groves had informed Truman that a third atomic bomb could be dropped on Japan within a week. By that point, however, the previously gung-ho president had been sobered by the savagery and attendant moral implications of using the most indiscriminate weapon ever devised, which, like an irrepressible biblical plague, spared virtually no one, nor any structure, in the wake of its considerable blast radius. After the advisory from Groves, Truman told a cabinet meeting that he had ordered the atomic bombing stopped. The thought of wiping out another 100,000 people was "too horrible," he said, especially the idea of killing "all those kids."

But it seems he didn't ever ask himself: What happens when the next country gets the bomb? And then another? It was necessary for Truman, with a degree of urgency, to have sought more counsel about the implications of a frightening new dawn in science, to consider what it would mean if physicists were able to produce even more powerful bombs, already in development. He should have more fully considered how all of America's major metropolitan areas would be in the crosshairs of any adversary that could assemble as few as two or three dozen nuclear devices. Ultimately, the only equalizer the Soviets would ever have was their own nuclear arsenal.

Critically, the first person in charge of America's nuclear weaponry was a narrow-minded soldier, and that man, Leslie Groves, did his nation and the world a great disservice by sidelining such dissidents as Leo Szilard and he then magnified his lack of foresight by successfully suppressing the truth about the lingering and deadly effects of radioactive fallout at Hiroshima and Nagasaki. The world needed to immediately see and understand *all the gruesome effects* of a single bomb that was capable of not only vaporizing its victims, but also inexorably and fatally poisoning survivors at a cellular level. Humanity's scientists had gone too far. Instead, the full scope of that sin became the first big secret of a soon to be booming U.S. security establishment, thus further stifling accountability and debate.

Truman had a tool to reimagine the international world order, the new United Nations. Roosevelt had envisioned the UN carrying the flag for a grass-roots "Century of the Common Man," with an ethos encapsulated by the pursuit of "four freedoms": freedom of speech and worship, freedom from want and fear. In Roosevelt's robust conception, the UN had the chance to be a dynamic moral and humanitarian force that, with the backing of the entire world family, could, for the first time, vigorously challenge colonial masters, promote self-determination, and stifle the whims of solipsistic rulers, like Stalin. But, as Roger Morris observed, that version of the UN "was all over in April 1945 with [Roosevelt's] death. Into the

Oval Office moved the more typical American certainty of Harry Truman, a feisty, remorselessly compromised machine politician who would be led in the White House by bellicose, half-informed aides."

Stalin was presented the same blank slate. The existential threats to his society had also been defeated, and none were on the horizon. He too had the authority and freedom to reimagine the dynamic of global relations. But, predictably, he would choose the safety of isolation over the demands and risks of cooperation, spending his final years largely hidden from public view, sequestered in one of several custom-built sanctuaries across the Soviet empire, a pampered communist czar expecting people to show up and kiss his ring.

"The dynamic circularity of U.S.-Soviet relations gained in velocity," wrote Harold Evans. "Even statesmen of goodwill and imagination may attribute evil motives to an opponent while at the same time finding it hard, if not impossible, to recognize that their own actions might be seen as menacing. Truman had the goodwill, but not the imagination; and the odious Stalin had neither. He was truculent, ruthless, suspicious, mendacious, and xenophobic."

In the decade following the war, no face-to-face dialogue took place between the leaders of the superpowers. Truman would invite Stalin to come to the United States, and he received a no in reply. This pretty much ended any chance for summitry, since Truman had decided, after being repelled by Berlin's devastation during the Potsdam meeting, that he had no desire to ever go back to Europe. In fact, Truman would make only four other extended foreign junkets during the nearly eight years of his presidency, three of which were to neighboring Canada, Mexico, and Bermuda.

In short, world affairs in the first chapters of the Cold War would be shaped by very provincial men.

———

Although most Americans only participated in World War II vicariously, the nation *had* been attacked, and even if those attacks were in no way commensurate with withering clashes oceans away, a new vulnerability had been introduced. The shock of Pearl Harbor had cut to the bone and settled deep in the mind.

As the war progressed, readers of West Coast newspapers were repeatedly alerted to other chinks in the aura of invincibility, such as lurking Japanese submarines close enough for their shells to strike targets along the Pacific Coast Highway; a seaplane bombing an Oregon forest; and the arrival of menacing Japanese fire balloons, propelled across the Pacific by the jet stream, each packing fifty pounds of explosives. One balloon had killed six civilians, the only combat deaths on the U.S. mainland during the war.

On the East Coast, Nazi submarines had deposited saboteurs on beaches in both New York and Florida in the dead of night. The FBI claimed to have foiled the plot but in reality it was a saboteur who immediately had second thoughts and, intrepidly, showed up at FBI headquarters in Washington to rat out the operation. J. Edgar Hoover shamelessly took full credit for capturing the Germans who fell into his lap and spiked national anxiety with a chest-thumping press conference.

Finally, a new meme had been imprinted on the American psyche: a massive explosion reaching up into the sky to form a spreading cloud shaped like a mushroom, the signature of a super weapon out of science fiction negating every last trace of life.

In the wake of Japan's capitulation, Norman Cousins wrote a widely discussed editorial in the *Saturday Review* addressing the atomic attacks: "Whatever elation there is in the world today because of final victory in the war is severely tempered by fear. It is a primitive fear, the fear of the unknown, the fear of forces man can neither channel nor comprehend. The fear is not new; in its classical form, it is the fear of irrational death. But overnight it has become intensified, magnified. It has burst out of the subconscious and into the conscious, filling the mind with primordial apprehensions."

CBS broadcast titan Edward R. Murrow offered a similar view: "Seldom, if ever, has a war ended leaving the victors with such a sense of uncertainty and fear, with such a realization that the future is obscure and that survival is not assured."

On August 30, 1945, the U.S. military issued a top-secret document titled *A Strategic Chart of Certain Russian and Manchurian Urban Areas*. The chart established a priority target list for nuclear attacks on the USSR. For example, the chart indicated six atomic bombs would be necessary to destroy Moscow, and the same number to destroy Leningrad. When the memo was issued, the Red Army was still fighting Hirohito's Far East Command and the planned formal surrender of Japanese forces on USS *Missouri* was still days away.

Such future war gaming was daft. Wrote Morris: "As it happened, though few American experts seemed to realize it, the target had already been demolished as the Cold War began, a condition from which it never really recovered....Revolution, terror, civil war, purges, collectivization, famine, the horrors of the Gulag, World War II's carnage, still more postwar starvation" had left the people of the USSR, Morris continued, with "an inconceivable demography of national desolation."

In mid-October 1945, Robert Oppenheimer retired as director of the Los Alamos lab, saying: "If atomic bombs are to be added to the arsenals of the warring world then the time will come when mankind will curse the name of Los Alamos and Hiroshima."

A few days later, he was in Washington, D.C., and met with Truman in the Oval Office. "I feel we have blood on our hands," he told the president.

According to Oppenheimer, Truman replied, "Never mind, it'll come out in the wash."

Afterward, Truman told aides he hoped never to see the great physicist again and later wrote derisively about how the "crybaby scientist" came to his office "and spent most of the time wringing his hands."

Oppenheimer also met with Henry Wallace, who, after being supplanted as vice president by Truman in 1945, had accepted

Roosevelt's offer to stay on as commerce secretary. In his diary Wallace wrote of the meeting:

> I never saw a man in such an extremely nervous state as Oppenheimer. He seemed to feel that the destruction of the entire human race was imminent…He had been in charge of the scientists in New Mexico and says that the heart has completely gone out of them there; that all they think about now are the social and economic implications of the bomb and that they are no longer doing anything worthwhile on the scientific level…He says that Secretary Byrnes's attitude on the bomb has been very bad…He thinks the mishandling of the situation at Potsdam has prepared the way for the eventual slaughter of tens of millions or perhaps hundreds of millions of innocent people.

By the end of the year, a grumpy Truman was losing patience with Byrnes, finding him to be an egotistical, high-handed, and secretive figure scripting U.S. foreign policy all by himself. During a Moscow conference in December, the secretary of state had agreed to grant diplomatic recognition to Soviet-occupied Romania and Bulgaria in return for "democratic participation," and he also proposed that the UN control all atomic weapons. In reaction, a print report wondered if America's top diplomat was "communistically inclined," a criticism happily seconded by congressional Republicans.

On January 5, 1946, Truman would write Byrnes a scolding letter, which ended: "I'm tired of babying the Soviets.…Unless Russia is faced with an iron fist and strong language, another war is in the making,"

CHAPTER 4

COLD WAR BIBLES

George Orwell's *Animal Farm* was intended, first and foremost, to be an attack on the fundamental hypocrisy of the Soviet state. As Hitler hogged the spotlight, the less colorful Stalin had successfully and artfully perpetuated opposing realities. He was able to convince far too many outsiders, including leftist intellectuals in the West, that the Soviet Union was a big, happy commune of social progress, when in practice, everyone living under Soviet rule was deadly aware that freedom of thought could be hazardous to one's health.

The USSR wasn't *socialist*, it was *tyrannical*. The Soviet Communist Party was, more accurately, a stealthier version of the czarist Romanovs—missing panache, but similarly cruel, violent, insular, elitist, and contemptuous of the peasantry. As the nomenklatura in Moscow were co-opted by luxuries, treated like aristocracy, a giant confidence game was being played on the so-called proletariat, who, while thinking they were building a just, classless society, were instead tolerating the unbearable to ensure the comfort of a demented autocratic minority. The men in the Kremlin were running a bullshit factory at war with nature, history, and reality.

The subtleties of Stalin's Big Lie were lost on me when I was assigned to read *Animal Farm* in high school. As I recall, the book ended up confirming my understanding—or the one conveyed to me by a typical Cold War–era teacher—that communism was horrible, the Soviet Union was evil, the Russians were going to take over the world unless we stopped them, and George Orwell was a hero. I also remember noting that *Animal Farm* was blessedly short. But as I later learned, the only way I could have truly decoded the book was by having a clear grasp of the distinction Orwell was making between Marxism and Bolshevism.

He had made it his mission in life to champion the little people and, in principle, agreed with the stated purpose of the Russian Revolution—empowering the rise of the proletariat. Moreover, Orwell was hoping for a socialist revolution in England. "It is only by revolution that the native genius of the English people can be set free," he wrote in 1941. "Whether it happens with or without bloodshed is largely an accident of time and place." The tragedy expressed by *Animal Farm* is how ideals are crushed; the book's author was a disillusioned radical. In Russia, Bolshevism had cynically exploited a genuine Marxist uprising. Orwell, in fact, was not quite the Cold War hero he was served up to be.

Although I was required to read *Das Kapital* and *The Communist Manifesto* as part of Columbia's core curriculum, there was no chance either text was seeing the light of day at my Catholic high school, which was run in large part by Polish American priests who regularly prayed for Russia's salvation and viewed all communists as Satan's disciples. But without at least an introduction to the theory of the class struggle, or the argument for common ownership, I couldn't possibly appreciate the full meaning of the anthropomorphic characters in *Animal Farm*, such as the boar named Old Major, a stand-in for Karl Marx. The same ignorance also prevented a full understanding of all the main plot points.

When Old Major convinces his fellow farm animals to revolt, Farmer Jones (the czar) is aided by other farmers, a reference to the invasion of Russia by Western powers—an event unmentioned in our high school history classes. Nor did we study Russia's long predilection to terrorize its people with secret police thugs (represented by the loyal and fearsome dogs who guard the violent dictator pig

Napoleon). We also never discussed Stalin's collectivization, state-created famine, or Great Terror (referenced when the pigs snuff out a rebellion by the other animals with starvation and execution). I ended up with a shallow, dumbed-down appreciation of Orwell's story filtered by a biased black-and-white take on the Cold War rivalry. But *Animal Farm*'s moral truly is simple. The problem on the farm wasn't all of the animals. It was just the pigs. By extension, the problem with the Soviet Union wasn't all of its citizens. It was just the megalomaniacs in charge.

The spark for *Animal Farm* emerged from Orwell's experience in the Spanish Civil War, in the spring of 1937. This is a key bit of biographical information I wish I had had when I first read the book. Knowing the details of an author's life isn't always necessary. You don't really need to know very much about J. K. Rowling's bio to fully enjoy her wizarding world of Harry Potter. Fantasy can be plucked out of thin air anywhere. In Rowling's case, the initial moment of inspiration occurred when her train from Manchester to London was delayed by four hours. By contrast, Orwell's inspiration for *Animal Farm* was a bit more raw and relevant. It came out of nearly being killed, on two occasions, during the Spanish Civil War. More-over, the germ of *1984* comes from the same experience.

Seeking to join forces supporting the leftist government, Orwell, whose real name was Eric Blair, found an underground route from England to Barcelona, a major center of resistance against Franco's Fascist insurgency, and linked up with a far-left splinter group called the POUM (Partido Obrero de Unificación Marxista; in English, Workers' Party of Marxist Unification). The Marxist POUM were separatist Catalan militiamen and rogue communists who excoriated the show trials of Stalin's Great Terror. On May 20, 1937, as the sun was rising near the village of Siétamo, a sniper shot Orwell in the neck, barely missing the carotid artery.

After being treated in a hospital for bruised vocal cords and paralysis in one arm, Orwell traveled back to the relative safety of

Barcelona, intending to continue his recuperation. His wife, Eileen, who was staying at a hotel in the city, met him as soon as he entered the lobby and told him to turn around and find a place to hide. Spain's Soviet-controlled Communist Party, backed by Stalin's henchmen, were rounding up POUM supporters, labeling them as dangerous "Trotskyites, Fascists, traitors, murderers, cowards, and spies." Had Orwell not been tipped off by his wife, there was a reasonable chance he would have been tortured and killed.

After Orwell figured out how he would disarm the Soviet myth, a literary odyssey followed. The story of the making of *Animal Farm* would come to be intertwined with the book's message. Orwell survived another near miss in 1943, when a Nazi bombing attack destroyed his London residence. No one was hurt, but he had to rescue the manuscript of *Animal Farm* from the ruins. Then, as Orwell anticipated, the book generated zero heat in the world of British publishing. He'd write, "The English intelligentsia, or a great part of it, had developed a nationalist loyalty towards the USSR, and in their hearts they felt that to cast any doubt on the wisdom of Stalin was a kind of blasphemy." An even bigger problem for the fate of *Animal Farm* was the sparkling success of Stalin's spy network in England.

Jonathan Cape, publisher of James Joyce and T. E. Lawrence (and, later, Ian Fleming's James Bond series), was ready to buy the book, but he changed his mind after being contacted by an official from Britain's Ministry of Information.

"I must confess," Cape wrote to Orwell about the official's comments, "that this expression of opinion has given me seriously to think. I can see now that it might be regarded as something which is highly ill-advised to publish at the present time. If the fable were addressed generally to dictators and dictatorships at large then publication would be all right, but the fable does follow, I see now, so completely the progress of the Russian Soviets."

The official who spooked Cape was H. P. Smollett, a.k.a. Hans Peter Smolka, a refugee raised in a wealthy Austrian Jewish family that made a fortune producing a revolutionary ski binding. In the early 1930s, while publishing a short-lived leftist magazine called *The New Youth*, Smolka watched despairingly as Austria's parliamentary democracy morphed into a Nazi satellite. He judged communism as the only salvation for Europe's Jews. After fleeing to England, Hans Peter Smolka changed his name and became a Soviet spy, with the code name ABO.

He was anything but a clubbable, high-tea Brit, described by his grandson as "a bulky, buccaneering mercurial figure with a voice that boomed." But H. P. Smollett was adept at flattery and used it to seduce Brendan Bracken, Winston Churchill's closest advisor. H.P. turned this relationship into a job at the Ministry of Information that was a Kremlin fantasy in the flesh.

During World War II, the person assigned by the British to improve the image of ally Russia was an Austrian communist and Stalin plant dispensing propaganda via Moscow. Such a spot gave him license to legitimately police anti-Soviet literature, such as *Animal Farm*. As a member of Churchill's inner circle, H.P. was also able to convince British spymaster Sir Dick White that Stalin had no intention of dominating Eastern Europe when the war ended. This act of disinformation might have been Smollett's most significant. By the time Winston Churchill hatched the metaphor of an Iron Curtain, in 1946, the window for trying to derail the divide had already been closed.

After ten publishers in England and the United States rejected *Animal Farm*, tiny Secker & Warburg agreed to buy the book in October 1944 (although owner Frederic Warburg got shit from his pro-Russian wife and employees for doing so). Orwell's classic then confronted one more obstacle. Because Secker & Warburg had a limited share of rationed paper stock, publication was delayed for another seventeen months.

On the eve of the book's arrival, in the late summer of 1945, Orwell was a relative nobody and struggling financially, physically, and emotionally, at one of the lowest points of his life. He was a recent widower and suddenly a single father. A few months earlier, his wife, Eileen, had died during a hysterectomy at a London hospital. She was only thirty-nine, and he wasn't in England at the time, away in Europe reporting on the liberation of Paris and the push into Germany. Eileen had given her husband short notice about the operation because she had expected a speedy recovery.

After her death, Orwell's sister Avril became the surrogate mother to the couple's adopted son, Richard. Meantime, friends of the star-crossed writer noted his droopy mustache, skeletal body, generally grumpy demeanor, and how he'd wear the same rumpled tweed jacket all the time. In addition, the wound in his throat would produce an off-putting whistling sound, and though he was battling tuberculosis, he remained a habitual smoker and refused to even put on a hat in chilly weather.

So it was that, at age forty-two, when George Orwell was as sick as he looked and had less than five years to live, fame arrived in a rush. His riveting allegory skewering the hypocrisy and gangsterism of Stalin's Soviet Union was soon being bought faster than it could be printed by Secker & Warburg. Serendipity followed when a visiting American editor with Harcourt Brace, Frank Morley, found the book at a shop in Cambridge and rapidly negotiated the U.S. rights. *Animal Farm* would be chosen as a Book of the Month Club selection, leading to the printing of almost half a million copies.

"As communism in Russia and Eastern Europe took on more and more of the appearance of a 'New Class' system," Christopher Hitchens observed, "with grotesque privileges for the ruling elite and a grinding mediocrity of existence for the majority, the moral effect of Orwell's work—so simple to understand and to translate, precisely as he had hoped—became one of the many unquantifiable forces that eroded communism as a system and an ideology."

Although money was no longer an object, Orwell was lonely, in fast-fading health, and increasingly paranoid. He carried a gun for protection and began spending the bulk of his time on the remote Scottish island of Jura, where the wind knocked people flat, it could be freezing in August, and the closest telephone was twenty-seven miles away. Orwell wasn't crazy to think that someone might be out to get him. He had in fact narrowly escaped the bloody purge of Trotskyites in Spain and had now written a best-selling novel that compared Stalin to a vile pig. Moreover, a few recent Kremlin-sponsored wet jobs had been hard-to-forget tabloid spectaculars.

In 1940, a Stalin-authorized assassin had murdered the then sixty-year-old Leon Trotsky in Mexico. The killer had plunged a mountaineer's ice ax with a sawed-off handle into Trotsky's skull. In 1941, General Walter Krivitsky, a Soviet intelligence officer who had defected to the West, was found dead in room 532 of the Bellevue Hotel in Washington, D.C. Krivitsky had made himself a target by writing articles for the *Saturday Evening Post* in which he made clear that the USSR was a totalitarian enterprise and the show trials "were not trials at all, and were nothing but weapons of political warfare." A chambermaid discovered Krivitsky's body. His right temple had a bullet hole the size of a fist. A .38-caliber revolver was resting in his right hand. The police could not determine if the death was a suicide or murder.

Orwell also was of the mind to keep a detailed enemies list. In 1996, the British Foreign Office disclosed that he had shared some of the names in his notebook with a Cold War–era outfit called the Information Research Department. In *Slate*, Jacob Weisberg offered some context: "When World War II ended, Orwell became preoccupied with Stalin's power grab in Eastern Europe and the way those whom he saw as dishonest intellectuals in the West were abetting it. . . . In his notebook, Orwell listed 135 names . . . [He] was often not just correct but also uncanny. Peter Smollett, a journalist who headed the Russian Department of the British Ministry of Information during the war and whom Orwell described as 'almost certainly an agent of some kind,' was later revealed to be, in fact, a Soviet agent."

———

Orwell was one of the first to use the term "Cold War," and he definitely thought such a condition would be a very bad thing for humanity. The phrase appeared in an October 19, 1945, essay for the *Tribune*, a socialist publication associated with Britain's left-wing Labour Party. Under the headline YOU AND THE ATOMIC BOMB, Orwell wrote, "We may be heading not for general breakdown but for an epoch as horribly stable as slave empires of antiquity…that is, the kind of worldview, the kind of beliefs, and the social structure that would probably prevail in a state which was at once unconquerable and in a permanent state of cold war with its neighbors."

After the 1943 Tehran summit between Winston Churchill, Franklin Roosevelt, and Joseph Stalin, Orwell became haunted by the prospect of giant, insular, totalitarian empires chopping up the world into spheres of influence, wielding weapons of mass destruction, and subjugating their citizenry through fear and thought control. He assumed his native Britain and the United States were just as capable of squashing individual liberty as was the Soviet Union.

With the arrival of the atomic bomb, Orwell was all but certain that a tyrannical age was in the making. In the same *Tribune* essay, he wrote, "It is commonplace that the history of civilization is largely the history of weapons. Ages in which the dominant weapon is expensive or difficult to make will tend to be ages of despotism, whereas when the dominant weapon is cheap and simple, the common people have a chance."

These churning fears would act as the emotional spine of his next and last book, *1984*, which became the twentieth century's ultimate cautionary dystopia and the signature text for an age riven with paranoia. The novel described a shrinking world of instant communication, where it was possible to govern populations by constant psychological manipulation. The superstate in Orwell's fiction is ruled by a cult leader, remains constantly on the verge of war, outlaws privacy, and abuses language to enforce obedience. Stalin's Soviet Union was already halfway to the future of *1984*, but the novel also anticipated America's mania of McCarthyism, creeping Big Brother surveillance, and the creation of an unbridled military-industrial complex.

Orwell's darkening days are evident on almost every page of *1984*, which presents a world going to shit in the not-too-distant future. There are as yet no robots, or flying cars, or spaceships. Much of daily life appears stuck in a sorry impoverished past. The book's central character is a middle-aged Londoner named Winston Smith who drinks gin, smokes low-quality cigarettes, and lives in an apartment building that smells of "boiled cabbage and old rag mats." His England has been renamed Airstrip One, the province of a superstate named Oceania. A Cold War has been institutionalized: Oceania maintains a fabricated conflict in order to unite the citizenry against a shadowy foreign enemy.

Winston is a clerk in the Records Department at the Ministry of Truth, rewriting history to match the constantly changing party line. Truth is only what Big Brother says it is. At the edge of Winston's desk is the "memory hole," in which documents containing discarded facts are dropped. "The Party," Winston informs the reader, "told you to reject the evidence of your eyes and ears. It was their final, most essential command."

Orwell's last novel was a sequel, in some respects, to *Animal Farm*. The ubiquitous Big Brother was a barely disguised reference to the all-seeing godlike Joseph Stalin, whose eyes indeed watched every Soviet citizen always, using every possible means of reproduction, from pamphlets to statuary. As in Orwell's dystopia, the Soviet Communist Party also defined truth. "Just as the Soviet regime combined brutality and technology of the totalitarian state to leave behind tens of millions of corpses and a perverse social order," David Remnick wrote in *Lenin's Tomb*, "it also used the completeness of the state, the pervasiveness of every institution from the kindergarten to the secret police, to put an end to historical inquiry. Stalin was not the first leader to enforce the myth of history, only the most successful."

But, as was not conveyed to me in high school, Orwell also made a sincere effort to distance himself from those who thought that *Animal Farm* and *1984*, as takedowns of Stalinism, were therefore endorsements for conservatism and free enterprise. Believing it important to clarify his politics, Orwell made multiple attempts to do so before his death, such as his 1946 essay "Why I Write": "The Spanish war and other events in 1936–37 turned the scale and thereafter I knew where I stood. Every line of serious work that I have written since 1936 has been written, directly or indirectly, *against* totalitarianism and *for* democratic socialism, as I understand it."

Orwell never visited the United States. Journalist Thomas Ricks speculated that had he done so he "probably would have been repelled by much of it—the gargantuan size and what he would have seen as the conspicuous consumption and swaggering and smugness.... What he most liked about England was its strong sense of private community." Orwell, Ricks added, extolled the virtues of the pub, the football match, the back garden, the fireside, and the nice cup of tea. For this avowed socialist, the only thing that could have made such English delights better would have been a planned economy in which the state owned everything and everyone got paid the same wage.

"The danger," Orwell wrote shortly before his death in 1950, at age forty-seven, "lies in the structure imposed on Socialist and on liberal capitalist communities by the necessity to prepare for total war with the USSR and the new weapons, of which of course the atomic bomb is the most publicized. But danger also lies in the acceptance of a totalitarian outlook by intellectuals of all colours.... In the USA the phrase 'American' or 'hundred percent American'... is as totalitarian as any could wish."

CHAPTER 5

CONCEPTS OF CONTAINMENT

On February 6, 1946, Joseph Stalin spoke at Moscow's Bolshoi Theater. This rare public appearance was interrupted repeatedly by hysterical cheers. For the politicos with front-row seating, the sixty-seven-year-old man on the stage was an aging figure the size of a jockey, with discolored teeth, a withered arm, a pockmarked face, and a graying mustache. The occasion was a "meeting of voters of the Stalin Electoral District, Moscow," and the speech was tied to the election of the Supreme Soviet, in which the outcome was preordained. In short, the pretext was all bullshit. Stalin's words, beamed live by radio, were principally intended for internal consumption and his own edification. He had a keen interest in perpetuating his royal rule. Like many senior Communist Party officials, Stalin had many "jobs," and was paid for each of them. In Stalin's case, ten:

1. Chairman of the Council of Ministers
2. Secretary of the Central Committee
3. Member of the Politburo (the communist version of a board of directors)
4. Deputy of the Supreme Soviet of the USSR
5. Deputy of the Russian Republic
6. Deputy of the Moscow Soviet
7. Member of the Presidium of the USSR Supreme Soviet
8. Supreme Commander in Chief

9. Member of the Central Committee
10. Minister of Defense

Since Stalin was never required to pay for anything, he simply made it a habit of putting wads of cash into a nearby drawer or cupboard, as one would do with a paperclip, or staples, or pens. And, just as he had ten jobs, he was also known by just as many titles. These included:

1. Leader and Teacher of the Workers of the World
2. Father of the Peoples
3. Wise and Intelligent Chief of the Soviet People
4. The Greatest Genius of All Times and Peoples
5. The Greatest Military Leader of All Times and Peoples
6. Coryphaeus of the Sciences
7. Faithful Comrade-in-Arms of Lenin
8. Devoted Continuer of Lenin's Cause
9. The Mountain Eagle
10. Best Friend of All Children

During his Bolshoi speech, Stalin attempted to equate his sagacious rule with the Soviet victory in World War II. Otherwise, he painted a flattering picture of the Bolshevik experiment at odds with reality. He was speaking to an "electorate" living in ruins and poverty. For many listening, Stalin's words were rather depressing. He announced three more Five-Year Plans, which augured the return of nutty wish lists for impossible economic growth. For an utterly exhausted nation, the speech proclaimed there would be no respite. Withering hardships would continue. It would be the same old same old.

Amid the rhetoric, statistics, and flimflam, a couple of fragments from the Bolshoi speech generated an unreasonable level of panic from Soviet haters in Washington, D.C. In one paragraph, Stalin blamed the capitalist countries, accurately, for starting World Wars I and II: "The development of world capitalism in our times does not proceed smoothly and evenly, but through crises and catastrophic wars." He said the Soviet Union desired peace, but warned it would be ready for "all possible contingencies." At the close of his speech, Stalin promised a better future through technological progress: "I have no doubt that if we give our scientists proper assistance they will be able in the very near future not only to overtake but even outstrip the achievements of science beyond the borders of our country." What he was talking about was making an atomic bomb, which was much, much further along than the U.S. government suspected.

Supreme Court justice William O. Douglas, who had presidential aspirations, decided Stalin had made a "Declaration of World War III." Historian David Holloway noted, "That speech was taken in the West to mean that Stalin not only thought that war was inevitable... but also that he was kind of willing to engage in war. I think the interpretation of the speech in the West was actually more alarmist than was warranted. I think Stalin did not want war, but I think that people in the West read this as a sign of a very bellicose and potentially aggressive Soviet Union."

Following the speech, a telegram was sent by the U.S. State Department to the American embassy in Moscow. The query was for the then forty-two-year-old George Kennan, the deputy at the embassy and regarded by this juncture as the country's top Soviet analyst. He was asked to provide an assessment of Stalin's words and to explain Moscow's recent refusal to join the newly established World Bank and International Monetary Fund.

Deep in that Moscow winter, Kennan was feeling like crap and already fed up with stateside officials who, to that point, never seemed to pay attention to anything he produced. "I am ill in bed," he recalled, "with a severe sinus infection.... The department's telegram reflects bewilderment.... I am filled with impatience and disgust at this naiveté. For two years, I have been trying to persuade people in Washington that the Stalin regime is the same regime we knew in the prewar period....I have tried to persuade Washington that dreams of a happy postwar collaboration with this regime are quite unreal; that our problem is deeper than that; that Stalin and his associates are now elated with their recent military and political successes and think they see favorable prospects for extending their political influence over all of Europe through the devices of infiltration and subversion."

Kennan, a Wisconsinite, was a member of the well-off, well-schooled WASP elite. He was bookish and sensitive. His mother had died two months after he was born; his father, a somber Milwaukee tax lawyer, would remarry and act in his life like a semi-detached grandfather figure. Kennan's sister Jeannette recalled young George sitting silently at the kitchen table staring at his soup. He spent childhood summers at a rustic camp and was packed off to a boarding school, the austere St. John's Military Academy, in Delafield, Wisconsin, where students being groomed for West Point dropped snakes in Kennan's shirt and the yearbook reported his pet peeve as "the universe."

At Princeton, he joined an eating club, the established method of gaining friends and sharing frivolity, but soon withdrew, judging the decision to make socializing easier a weakness of character. While other young men of his breeding were regularly misspending portions of their youth submitting to outrageous bacchanalias, Kennan was doing graduate work at the University of Berlin, studying Russian history, and building fluency in multiple languages. He'd ultimately master Russian, German, French, Polish, Czech, Portuguese, and Norwegian. While overseas, he convinced Annelise Sorensen, a quiet young lady from Norway, to marry him.

In 1933, when the United States restored diplomatic relations with the USSR, Kennan had been a member of the first State Department team to land in Moscow. He stayed five years, was reassigned to other duties, and sent back to Moscow, in 1944, as second in charge. On

February 22, 1946, at 9 p.m., the frustrated, flu-ridden Sovietologist went to the code room of the U.S. embassy and sent his response to the State Department's annoying request for an assessment of Stalin's intentions. He'd later say that he wrote as if composing "a primer for schoolchildren" and therefore refreshed the recipients on the beginning of the Bolshevik enterprise, as if teaching a class to students who knew nothing about that history. It was a beautifully written treatise and became the policy outline for the conduct of the incipient Cold War against the Soviet Union

"After the establishment of the Bolshevist regime," he wrote, "Marxist dogma, rendered even more truculent and intolerant by Lenin's interpretation, became a perfect vehicle for [a] sense of insecurity with which Bolsheviks, even more than previous Russian rulers, were afflicted. In this dogma, with its basic altruism of purpose, they found justification for their instinctive fear of the outside world, for the dictatorship without which they did not know how to rule, for cruelties they did not dare to inflict, for sacrifice they felt bound to demand."

Kennan judged the Soviet regime delusional: "There is good reason to suspect that this Government is actually a conspiracy within a conspiracy; and I for one am reluctant to believe that Stalin himself receives anything like an objective picture of outside world." But he also made a glaring illogical turn, contending that the men in the Kremlin, even while fooling themselves, were nonetheless capable of alarming global influence: "The Soviet regime is a police regime par excellence.... It has an elaborate and far flung apparatus of amazing flexibility and versatility, managed by people whose experience and skill in underground methods are presumably without parallel in history."

One of the sentences that had the greatest impact in 1946 could have been written about Vladimir Putin's twenty-first-century Russia: "We have here a political force committed fanatically to the belief that with the U.S....it is desirable and necessary that the internal harmony of our society be disrupted, our traditional way of life be destroyed, the international authority of our state be broken, if Soviet power is to be secure."

Although Kennan did not use the word "containment"—the word that would define U.S. policy toward the Soviets appeared in a later slightly revised version of the telegram—the concept emerged out of this thinking: "Soviet power, unlike that of Hitlerite Germany, is neither schematic nor adventuristic. It does not work by fixed plans. It does not take unnecessary risks. Impervious to the logic of reason, it is highly sensitive to the logic of force. For this reason it can easily withdraw—and usually does—when strong resistance is encountered at any point."

Kennan suggested treating the Soviets the same way a doctor treats "an unruly and unreasonable individual" and provided bullet points for how to do so:

- Temper a history of hysterical anti-Sovietism by telling the American public that the United States had little skin in the day-to-day doings of the USSR: "We have here no investments to guard, no actual trade to lose, virtually no citizens to protect, few cultural contacts to preserve. Our only stake lies in what we hope rather than what we have."
- If the United States remained true to its ideals, the American way would win out: "Much depends on health and vigor of our own society. World communism is like a malignant parasite which feeds only on diseased tissue."
- Be a better neighbor to people we like: "We must formulate and put forward for other nations a much more positive and constructive picture of the sort of world we would like to see than we have put forward in the past."
- Don't start acting like the Soviets to beat them: "We must have courage and self-confidence to cling to our own methods and conceptions of human society."

Some eighteen months later, the July 1947 issue of *Foreign Affairs* published an essay by Kennan titled "The Sources of Soviet Conduct." It was similar to the 1946 telegram, but not quite a carbon copy. It contained that one essential word the telegram did not— containment. "It is clear," Kennan wrote, "that the main element of any United States policy toward the Soviet Union must be that of a long-term, patient but firm and vigilant containment of Russian expansive tendencies." Stalin received a darker interpretation of the policy. In the Russian version of the article, Kennan's "containment" was translated as "strangulation."

Kennan would come to have very mixed feelings about the policy he first formulated while cranky and battling some kind of illness in the middle of a Moscow winter: "I seem to have aroused a strain of emotional and self-righteous anti-Sovietism that in later years I wish I had not aroused." In a 1996 CNN interview, he'd say, "My thoughts about containment were of course distorted by the people who understood it and pursued it exclusively as a military concept; and I think that that, as much as any other cause, led to the forty years of unnecessary, fearfully expensive and disoriented process of the Cold War."

In March 1946, during a long train ride shortened by hands of poker and the swigging of scotch, Harry Truman proudly escorted former British prime minister Winston Churchill from Washington, D.C., to his home state of Missouri. The president had been born in the farm village of Lamar and maintained a comfy Victorian-style home in Independence. Churchill was making a major address at tiny Westminster College, a Presbyterian men's school in the little town of Fulton, located among rolling farmland twenty miles south of Jefferson City. The site for the speech had been arranged by Truman's military aide Harry Vaughan, who had once played center on the Westminster football team.

In his biography of Truman, David McCullough would write, "The setting and reception at Fulton were all Truman could have wished for. The day was sunny, the temperature in the high sixties, the little town spruced up and looking exactly as he wanted Churchill to see. Thousands of people, many in from the surrounding country, were waiting to cheer them as their motorcade rolled down the red-brick main thoroughfare."

The Soviet Union had made quick work of placing half of Europe under its control, and what the world long remembered from the day Churchill packed a gymnasium in Fulton, Missouri, were these words: "A shadow has fallen upon the scenes so lately lighted by the Allied victory.... From Stettin in the Baltic to Trieste in the Adriatic an iron curtain has descended across the Continent." In time, the remark was judged prescient. But that day, the wordsmithing was greeted by silence. The line receiving notable applause was Churchill saying, "I do not believe the Soviet Union wants war." Further, the next day's reaction to the speech was so negative, Truman ended up wishing he'd missed that train to Missouri.

Churchill had also pitched an Anglo-American imperium with hints of an Orwellian superstate: "If the population of the English-speaking Commonwealth be added to that of the United States, with all that such cooperation implies in the air, on the sea, and in science and industry, there will be no quivering precarious balance of power to offer its temptation to ambition or adventure."

Fact was, the United States and Britain were still technically allies with the Soviet Union, and a sizable portion of the American press derided Churchill for damaging already tender U.S.-Soviet relations. The *Wall Street Journal* was opposed to such an "Anglo-American alliance," or any alliance with any other nation. *The Nation* called the president "remarkably inept" for associating himself with the speech. Columnist Walter Lippmann judged the event a "catastrophic blunder." Senator Claude Pepper accused Churchill of being unable to divorce his thinking "from the roll of drums and the flutter of the flag of empire." Henry Wallace argued that "aside from our common language and common literary tradition, we have no more in common with Imperialistic England than with Communist Russia."

Eleanor Roosevelt was reportedly furious. She accused Churchill of "desecrating the ideals for which my husband gave his life.... Perhaps it's just as well that my husband is not alive today to see how [Mr. Churchill] has turned against his principles." Stalin judged it "a call to war." Truman backtracked, saying he hadn't read the speech beforehand. That was a fib.

———

Assembling the Iron Curtain required an extreme form of social engineering. As Anne Applebaum would write in her book *Iron Curtain*, the eight countries suddenly under Stalin's thumb had vastly different cultures, political traditions, and economic structures.

"The new territories," Applebaum instructed, "included formerly democratic Czechoslovakia and formerly fascist Germany, as well as monarchies, autocracies, and semi-feudal states. The inhabitants of the region were Catholic, Orthodox, Protestant, Jewish and Muslim. They spoke Slavic languages, Romance languages, Finno-Ugric languages, and German. They included Russophiles and Russophobes; industrialized Bohemia and rural Albania; cosmopolitan Berlin and tiny wooden villages in the Carpathian mountains. Among them were former subjects of the Austro-Hungarian, Prussian, and Ottoman empires, as well as the Russian empire." This was a conglomeration that was never a unified bloc and, to varying degrees, in constant rebellion.

The Soviet totalitarian playbook, as Applebaum summarized, had four key elements:

1. The Soviet NKVD, in collaboration with local communist parties, immediately created a Stalinist secret police.
2. Communists were put in charge of the national radio network.

3. Independent organizations of all kinds were banned, especially those attached to youth, such as the Boy Scouts and the Girl Scouts, and those related to Christian churches.

4. Ethnic cleansing was liberally used because the trauma from such events made everyone easier to control.

While testifying before a Senate subcommittee, an exiled member of Romania's royal family offered a succinct evaluation of how communism was imposed on her country. During questioning by the Senate, Princess Ileana related a conversation with Ana Pauker, who, as Romania's foreign minister, claimed the distinction of being the first woman to hold that position in modern world affairs. *Time* would put Pauker on its cover in 1948 and called her the most powerful woman alive.

The princess related a conversation in which she told Pauker that the communists were failing to win support.

"But we are not trying to change your point of view," Pauker replied.

"What are you trying to do?' the princess asked.

"We are trying to eliminate you," Pauker admitted, "but, as we can't shoot you all...and your generation cannot be convinced...the young generation can be taught our way of living. Therefore, you are going to be terrorized into silence, so that you cannot pass on any tradition or any thought out of the past to your children."

In *True Believer*, Kati Marton wrote, "By 1948, not one country had freely elected a Communist regime. A string of rigged elections forced Communist rule on Poland, Hungary, Czechoslovakia and East Germany. Instilling fear in their population was the only way for these unpopular regimes to hold power. Terror was their chief weapon. Vigilance against the invisible enemy was the order of the day. Every poster, rally, and trade union conference hammered a single message into a cowed people: the danger of foreign subversion is ever present; sometimes the enemy wears Communist clothes."

In 1970, Soviet dissident Andrei Amalrik titled his critique of Soviet power *Will the Soviet Union Survive Until 1984?* The book was written two years after 250,000 Warsaw Pact troops invaded Czechoslovakia to put down a liberalizing regime trying to establish "socialism with a human face." Red Army officers nearly lost control of their troops when, instead of being welcomed, as they had been told they would be, they were instead jeered on the streets of Prague.

"This isolation," Amalrik wrote, "has created for all—from the bureaucratic elite to the lowest social levels—an almost surrealistic picture of the world and of their place in it. Yet the longer this state of affairs helps to perpetuate the status quo, the more rapid and decisive will be its collapse when confrontation with reality becomes inevitable." Amalrik predicted, accurately, as it turned out, that "any state forced to devote so much of its energies to physically and psychologically controlling millions of its own subjects" couldn't possibly survive "indefinitely."

CHAPTER 6

SMALL AND DEVASTATING

On May 25, 1946, an article appeared in *Script*, a weekly literary film magazine based in Beverly Hills. It was titled "The Red Menace," and the author's goal was to get his readers to see how threatening America might seem *outside* America. "Sensible men all over the world," Dalton Trumbo wrote, were viewing "American military power with increasing apprehension." They were wondering "just how far geographically our legitimate defense needs may extend." They were beginning "to sense and dread the overwhelming pressure of American military might in every portion of the world."

In 1939, Trumbo had won a National Book Award—then called the American Booksellers Award—for *Johnny Got His Gun*. The story's main character is a totally incapacitated World War I veteran and was inspired by an article Trumbo had read about the Prince of Wales visiting a Canadian soldier who had lost all his limbs. A year later, Trumbo's screenplay of *Kitty Foyle*, about a feisty working-class Irish girl in a love triangle with wealthy suitors, received an Oscar nomination. As World War II began, Trumbo classified himself as an isolationist, and in 1943, he formally joined the Communist Party. By 1946, he was one of the highest-paid writers in Hollywood, earning around $100,000 annually—the equivalent of more than $1 million today.

"No Russian," he continued in the article for *Script*, "can turn his face east without being confronted with a solid wall of American air and naval power immediately contiguous to his country. He cannot turn his face south without encountering the iron curtain of British power from Singapore to the Red Sea and from Port Said to Gibraltar. He cannot turn his face west without running into the tremendous Atlantic power of the Anglo-American allies, including its complete domination of Africa and the Northwestern land masses."

Trumbo asked: What if America was faced with a Russia that truly matched the United States in war-making capacity?

> If the situation were reversed, I, as an American, would be alarmed....I would be alarmed if I was aware that the Russians had a navy greater than all the navies of the world combined, and the greatest air force in the world, and the most destructive bomb, and the most powerful allies, and the greatest industrial capacity, and twenty-seven years of concentrated hatred carefully built up by a gloriously free and hostile press. I would be alarmed, and I would petition my government to take measures at once against what would seem an almost certain blow aimed at my existence....That is how it must appear to a Russian today.

Such a perspective was about to be judged dangerously unpatriotic. A few weeks after the publication of "The Red Menace," Trumbo and several other alleged Soviet sympathizers were vilified by *Hollywood Reporter* publisher William R. Wilkerson in a column he titled "A Vote for Joe Stalin." In turn, "Billy's Blacklist" drew the attention of the House Un-American Activities Committee. Born in 1938 as a temporary body, the HUAC had been made permanent by conservative Representative J. Parnell Thomas. Eighty-four hearings into "communist subversion" were to follow over the next five years. One of the first was a new investigation into communist influence in Hollywood, the opening salvo of what would be a sweeping, politically motivated national paranoia.

Wrote Nicholas von Hoffman, "People were taken before boards, commissions, courts, grand juries, and other instruments of inquiry and asked the terrible question: 'Are you now or have you ever been a member of the Communist Party?'... The efforts to extirpate domestic American Communism entailed forcing people under oath and then questioning them about their beliefs; it led to the recrudescence of the employment blacklist of people who didn't give the right answers. None of these things were unprecedented in American history, but in the economically and politically centralized society which evolved out of the Second World War, the espousal of heresy, a dangerous occupation anywhere, any time, became doubly perilous."

On June 14, 1946, American Bernard Baruch, a seventy-five-year-old self-described advisor to the powerful, made a speech at the United Nations setting forth a U.S. plan for the international control of atomic energy. He began, "We are here to make a choice between the quick and the dead.... If we fail, then we have damned every man to be the slave of fear." At the same time, the U.S. military was preparing to test two atomic bombs at remote Bikini Atoll, in the middle of the Pacific Ocean. Noting the mixed message, an American radio commentator said at the time, "So we strive to save civilization, and we learn how to wreck it, all on the same weekend."

Operation Crossroads comprised two tests of 21-kiloton nuclear weapons. They were to be the first atomic detonations since the bombing of Nagasaki. William Blandy was the vice admiral in charge. As part of the pre-blast festivities, his wife was shown cutting a mushroom-cloud cake. Rumors that the weapons might end all life on the planet prompted a denial from Admiral Blandy:

The bomb will not start a chain reaction in the water, converting it all to gas, and letting the ships on all the oceans drop down to the bottom. It will not blow out the bottom of the sea and let all the water run down the hole. It will not destroy gravity. I am not an atomic playboy, as one of my critics labeled me, exploding these bombs to satisfy my personal whims.

———

Meantime, in France, the Bikini tests inspired the name of a new swimsuit. Louis Réard was a French automotive and mechanical engineer who also assisted with his mother's lingerie business in Paris. He had noticed women on the Saint-Tropez beaches rolling up the edges of their suits to get a better tan. It prompted him to produce a more minimal design, which he introduced on July 5, 1946, four days after the first Bikini test. "Like the bomb," Réard said, "the bikini is small and devastating."

The Frenchman first displayed the new garment at Piscine Molitor, a public pool in Paris; his model was Micheline Bernardini, an eighteen-year-old nude dancer. Afterward, Bernardini received fifty thousand fan letters. The suit, by revealing a woman's navel, shocked the world. American women claimed to be revolted. But by the time a bikini-clad Ursula Andress emerged dripping from the Caribbean in *Dr. No* (Bond film number one in 1962), the suit had been adopted by a burgeoning California surf culture defining the latest standards of cool.

———

The second of the two atomic tests took place on July 25, 1946. Code-named Baker, it was an underwater detonation and significantly more impressive than the first Bikini test, Able, in which the bomb dropped by a B-29 missed its target by half a mile. Baker sent a column of two million tons of water a mile high. The battleship *Arkansas*, being used as a target, was lifted into the air and dropped in a nearby lagoon. Nine ships, including another battleship and an aircraft carrier, eventually sank. The radioactive hazard produced by the spread of water made it too dangerous to inspect the target area. The Joint Chiefs of Staff Evaluation Board noted that "contaminated ships became radioactive stoves, and would have burned all living things aboard with invisible and painless but deadly radiation." Chemist Glenn Seaborg, a future Nobel Prize winner and future chairman of the Atomic Energy Commission, called the Baker test "the world's first nuclear disaster."

Observers from the UN Atomic Energy Commission viewed the tests from a U.S. ship, at a safe distance. Two were from the Soviet Union. According to recently declassified documents obtained by the National Security Archive at George Washington University, "one of the observers, Simon Peter Alexandrov, who was in charge of uranium for the Soviet nuclear project, told a U.S. scientist, Paul S. Galtsoff, that while the purpose of the Bikini test was 'to frighten the Soviets,' they were 'not afraid,' and that the Soviet Union had 'wonderful planes which could easily bomb U.S. cities.'"

The other Soviet observer, physicist Mikhail Meshcheryakov, reported back to Moscow that the Americans were already integrating nuclear weapons into their military doctrine, were not interested in disarmament, and, he concluded, the Soviet Union should therefore suspend any negotiations about international control. In short, Meshcheryakov decided the United States was far more interested in wrecking civilization than saving it.

———

The bomb soon began to poison democracy. Although Harry Truman had a sincere antipathy to secrecy, he'd fail to prevent the federal government from becoming a bureaucracy of fiefdoms habitually hiding deliberations and decisions central to the public welfare. The beginning of the darkness was August 1, 1946, when Truman signed the Atomic Energy Act, which created the Atomic Energy Commission to replace the Manhattan Project. The legislation placed even the president on a need-to-know basis about America's nuclear arsenal.

"For the first time in American history," Annie Jacobsen wrote, "a federal agency run by civilians, the Atomic Energy Commission, would maintain a body of secrets classified based on factors other than presidential executive orders. It is from the Atomic Energy Act of 1946 that the concept 'born classified' came to be, and it was the Atomic Energy Commission that would oversee the building of seventy thousand nuclear bombs in sixty-five different sizes and styles."

Wrote Senator Daniel Patrick Moynihan in 1998, "Secrecy had intangible costs in the erosion of public confidence in the government, because so much of the government secrecy served only to protect the careers and reputations of policy makers, without any clear justification in terms of national security.... Secrecy beguiled us into a new and expensive arms race when watchful waiting would have accomplished the same end at much less cost."

CHAPTER 7

COMMUNISM AND REPUBLICANISM

In large measure, the overriding narrative of the Cold War will be set in motion by America's right-wing counterrevolutionaries who unleash J. Edgar Hoover, back Richard Nixon, indulge McCarthyism, institutionalize a giant military-industrial complex, use an out-of-control CIA to overthrow democratically elected governments, employ racist and nativist dog whistles, slam the social safety net, and, in sum, stoke fear and division during an era when the United States had no serious external enemies and should have spent more dollars and effort in building a more perfect union. In this climate, as writer Talia Lavin neatly summarized, people could be viewed as socialists or communists for arguing that it was bad that Americans died broke because they got sick, or that poor people should eat, or that corporations shouldn't write laws.

Frustrated Republicans, long eclipsed by Franklin Roosevelt's appealing audacity of hope, would choose a contradictory counterattack engaging our primitive fight-or-flight response: telling voters that someone was out to get them. The new fact of a Cold War was seen as an opportunity, not a tragedy, and, like cynical movie producers who abuse proven plot lines, the GOP dusted off the Red Scare from a not-too-distant past. "Fearful people," media researcher George Gerbner told Congress, "are more dependent, more easily manipulated and controlled, more susceptible to deceptively simple, strong, tough measures and hard-line postures."

Starting with the midterm elections of 1946, the Republican Party repositioned Roosevelt's New Deal as a secret communist plot. This ideological cri de coeur even had a waiting manifesto. In a 1941 edition of *Life*, following a story about iceboating, publisher Henry Luce had written an incongruous editorial. It was incongruous because *Life* was the first all-photographic magazine in the United States, keyed to light entertainment, and Luce's nearly seven-thousand-word editorial, stretching across five pages, was all text... and deadly serious. The headline read THE AMERICAN CENTURY. Luce's screed urged America to wean itself from FDR's pinkish New Deal:

> The President of the United States has continually reached for more and more power, and he owes his continuation in office today largely to the coming of the war. Thus, the fear that the United States will be driven to a national socialism, as a result of cataclysmic circumstances and contrary to the free will of the American people, is an entirely justifiable fear.

In the simplest terms, Luce argued it was time for America to lead as top dog and the president of the United States, Franklin D. Roosevelt, was not yet managing that task adequately enough. Luce was giving voice to a battle under way between Republican internationalists like himself and the big-government, labor-friendly Roosevelt, who had just been elected to an unprecedented third term. Backing Luce was an oligarchy of old money that was becoming increasingly impatient with Roosevelt's popularity and populist impulses. Put another way: Wall Street was tired of being sublimated to Main Street.

Luce's worldview was of a piece with his upbringing: born in China to WASP missionaries who preached, to the alleged unenlightened of an ancient civilization, the virtuous trifecta of a Christian faith inside a democratic society powered by a free enterprise system. After attending Yale and Oxford, Luce had made a pulpit out of his new national magazines. In 1923, he published the first issue of *Time*. The business monthly *Fortune* followed in 1930, and in 1936, *Life* made its debut. Their print perspectives were married by Luce's muscular Christianity and vehement anticommunism. By 1941, *Life*'s pioneering photojournalism had made it the most successful of the three. It was estimated that some sixty million readers would look at a "passed-on" copy every month—at the barber shop, or the beauty salon, or in the periodicals section of the local library. That astonishing reach explains why Luce used *Life* to launch his vision of the American Century:

> Ours cannot come out of the vision of any one man. . . . It must be a sharing with all peoples of our Bill of Rights, our Declaration of Independence, our Constitution, our magnificent industrial products, our technical skills. It must be an internationalism of the people, by the people and for the people.

———

In 1946, one of the opening salvos against Truman and the Democrats came from Tennessee congressman B. Carroll Reece, chairman of the Republican National Committee. Reece argued that the America of 1946 confronted a choice between "Communism and Republicanism." Senator Robert Taft accused Harry Truman of seeking a Congress "dominated by a policy of appeasing the Russians abroad and fostering communism at home." Author Fred Cook would observe that such rhetoric was often a smokescreen. In *The Nightmare Decade*, Cook wrote, "The real foe was always the American liberal—the New Dealer, the innovator, the idealist who saw the injustices in American society and advocated the use of the instrumentalities of democratic government to effect reforms. To the emperors of the status quo, such shakers and movers were dangerous men."

During the 1946 election season, everything anyone would ever need to know about Richard Nixon, little of it laudatory, was fully evident in the way he conducted his very first campaign. Seeking a seat in the House of Representatives, Nixon had been handpicked by Old Guard Southern California ranchers and bankers who hated FDR, the New Deal, labor unions, and, within their own echo chamber, shared a conviction that America was headed to a disastrous socialism. Nixon's opponent was Jerry Voorhis, the five-time, liberal-minded incumbent in California's 12th District, which served an agricultural area in Orange County, on the eastern fringe of Los Angeles.

According to Nixon, he was summoned back to his home state of California in the fall of 1945 by a Whittier banker seeking to gauge his interest in running for Congress. At the time, the then thirty-two-year-old Duke Law graduate was in the final months of his Navy tour of duty, settling terminated war contracts on the East Coast. In reality, he received blanket support from all of the state's most powerful business leaders, including the archconservative Chandler family, who had built a fortune in railroads, held wide and diverse interests, and owned the state's biggest and most influential newspaper, the *Los Angeles Times*.

In an unpublished memoir, Voorhis would claim that Nixon's financial support was even deeper and wider, writing, "The Nixon campaign was a creature of big Eastern financial interests...the Bank of America, the big private utilities, the major oil companies." While Voorhis was spending the bulk of his time in Washington, D.C., serving his constituents, Nixon had the financial wherewithal to mount a ten-month campaign and was able to hire—or was "advised" to employ—Murray Chotiner, a campaign manager notorious for coloring outside the box.

Like all the campaigns to come, Nixon's 1946 race used unethical scheming and unsubstantiated attacks. His political bible appeared to be an old favorite, *The Prince*, by Niccolò Machiavelli. The sixteenth-century Italian diplomat, tutored by the Borgias, rationalized how unscrupulous tactics can be justified to achieve power. By 1946, being called Machiavellian was a bad thing. Nixon, however, really did believe that politics was a cutthroat survival of the fittest.

Nixon hammered the fiction that his opponent was a tool of the communists. In fact, during his five terms, Jerry Voorhis had put his loathing of communism very much on the record. For example, he had served on the House Un-American Activities Committee, and sponsored the eponymous 1940 Voorhis Act, which required communist organizations to register with the Justice Department. Nonetheless, in the last days of the election, voters were besieged by mystery callers saying, "Did you know that Jerry Voorhis is a Communist?" Much later, in an aside to White House counsel Leonard Garment, Nixon would admit that dishonesty was one of his central tenets: "You'll never make it in politics, Len. You just don't know how to lie."

As biographer Stephen Ambrose would write, Nixon "made the transition from nice Quaker boy to ruthless politician without even noticing." In *The Fifties*, David Halberstam observed, "If there was any politician in America who reflected the Cold War and what it did to the country, it was Richard Nixon—the man and the era were made for each other. The anger and the resentment that were a critical part of his temperament were not unlike the tensions running through the nation as its new anxieties grew. He himself had seized on the anti-communist issue earlier and more tenaciously than any other centrist politician in the country."

In the 1946 midterms, Nixon and his fellow Republicans enjoyed a substantial victory, gaining majorities in both houses of Congress for the first time since 1931. The Republicans picked up fifty-four seats in the House and eleven in the Senate. The *Chicago Tribune*—owned by isolationist and vociferous New Deal critic Robert "Colonel" McCormick—gushed that the results were the greatest victory for the country since Appomattox. The new arrivals in the 80th Congress also included Wisconsin's thirty-eight-year-old Joe McCarthy, elected to the Senate, and twenty-nine-year-old John Kennedy, of Boston, who joined Nixon in the House.

CHAPTER 8

DACHAU MODEL

At the first Nuremberg trial, an International Military Tribunal sentenced Hermann Goering and eleven other top Nazi officials to death. Twelve additional tribunals followed, known as the Subsequent Nuremberg Proceedings. In the first of those, the Doctors Trial, twenty-three leading German physicians and administrators were identified as war criminals.

One of the greatest examples of cognitive dissonance in the early stages of the Cold War was the contrasting U.S. policy of hiring and hanging Nazis at the same time. "Even before the verdicts were in," John Marks wrote about the Doctors Trial, "special U.S. investigating teams were sifting through the experimental records at Dachau for information of military value."

The Doctors Trial ran for 140 days, during which the court heard eighty-five witnesses testify to how Nazi doctors asphyxiated, burned, carved up, drowned, froze, and poisoned thousands of concentration camp prisoners, including children. None of the victims were volunteers. None had granted their consent. All the accused doctors had taken the Hippocratic Oath: "First, do no harm."

"This case and these defendants have created this gruesome question for the lexicographer," said Brigadier General Telford Taylor, the chief American war crimes prosecutor. "For the moment we will christen this macabre science 'thanatology,' the science of producing death." Dr. Leopold Alexander, one of the American investigators, later said, "It sometimes seems as if the Nazis had taken special pains in making practically every nightmare come true."

A gamut of experiments causing prolonged suffering—and often death—had been undertaken to explore ways of keeping German troops alive under extreme conditions. To investigate the limits of human endurance at extremely high altitudes, a subject of interest to the Luftwaffe, prisoners at Dachau were placed into a chamber that could duplicate altitudes as high as sixty-eight thousand feet—nearly thirteen miles above sea level, more than twice as high as Mount Everest. Many died from lack of oxygen. The Luftwaffe also wanted to protect their air crews from hypothermia. To that end, naked prisoners were immersed in tanks of ice water for hours, developing "extreme rigor." The German navy, along with the Luftwaffe, sought to make seawater drinkable. The subjects of this experiment were deprived of food and given only chemically processed seawater to drink.

Muscles and nerves were harvested to investigate regeneration; bone transplants were done from one person to another. Such mutilations produced agony and permanent disability. Concentration camp inmates were regularly used—and killed—during tests of hazardous chemicals and lethal biological agents. Of the prisoners at Buchenwald who were shot with poisoned bullets, prosecutor Taylor clarified that their purpose was not as "guinea pigs to test an antidote for the poison; their murderers really wanted to know how quickly the poison would kill."

Sixteen of the defendants in the Doctors Trial were found guilty, and seven were executed. One of the seven men acquitted was Dr. Kurt Blome. He had been the deputy surgeon general in the Third Reich—the Reichsgesundheitsführer—and headed its biological warfare program. The Nuremberg prosecution charged him with conducting deadly experiments using malaria, tuberculosis, bubonic plague, and mustard gas. Though not mentioned in the indictments, it was later reported that Blome had used aircraft to spray Auschwitz prisoners with tabun and sarin, highly lethal nerve agents. He was also linked to experiments with the hallucinogenic mescaline.

In its acquittal of Blome, the Nuremberg judges wrote, "It may well be that the defendant Blome was preparing to experiment on human beings in connection with bacteriological warfare, but the record fails to disclose that fact, or that he ever actually conducted the experiments."

It is strongly suspected that senior U.S. military officials intervened in Dr. Blome's case and may have managed to suppress incriminating evidence. This supposition is supported by what Blome did next. Almost immediately after being exonerated, he was hired by U.S. intelligence. His senior role in the largest and most horrendous science experiment on human beings ever attempted was apparently judged too good to pass up.

In the *Journal of the History of the Behavioral Sciences*, Alfred McCoy wrote, "In sum, medical science was repulsed by Dachau's inhumanity, but U.S. intelligence was intrigued. Consequently, Washington's postwar defense research was soon infected by the Dachau model, whose methods it mimed across a broad spectrum of Cold War experiments on, literally, tens of thousands of unwitting human subjects—from atomic, chemical, and biological warfare to psychological torture."

———

Shortly after Blome's acquittal, representatives from Fort Detrick in Maryland—the location of the Army's top bacteriologists and chemists—went to Europe and interviewed the Nuremberg-charged concentration camp doctor about germ warfare. He was then hired to work at Camp King, strategically situated in the village of Oberursel, eleven miles northwest of the U.S. European Command headquarters in Frankfurt.

Concealed by the rolling Taunus Hills, surrounded by barbed wire, Camp King had previously been the site of the Luftwaffe's famed Durchgangslager Luft interrogation center. As it turned out, little changed when new management took over. In the early part of the Cold War, the bulk of the staff at the secret compound was made up of ex-Gestapo officers, ex-Nazi doctors, and ex–German intelligence operatives, including General Reinhard Gehlen, who, after a long period of debriefing at Virginia's Fort Hunt, was sent back to Germany to work for U.S intelligence.

In an offshoot of Operation Paperclip, Camp King was reportedly used to resurrect Nazi experiments in torture and interrogation, a program identified as among the most nefarious and inhumane of the Cold War. "At the time," wrote Annie Jacobsen, "U.S. intelligence officials believed the Soviets were pursuing mind control programs—supposedly a means of getting captured spies to talk—and wanted to know what it would be up against if the Russians got hold of its American spies." As a so-called black site, Camp King was seen as a suitable spot for the testing of torture techniques that would be far more problematic if attempted inside the United States. In this German hideaway, as one official put it, "disposal of the body is not a problem."

Camp King's first chief medical doctor was Dr. Walter Schreiber, the surgeon general of the Third Reich. Dr. Schreiber would eventually join thirty-four other recruited Nazi doctors at a new School of Aviation Medicine at Randolph Field, Texas—"bringing," as McCoy wrote, "the Third Reich's scientific esprit into the heart of U.S. military medicine." In 1950, the U.S. Air Force effectively altered the historical record of these scientists—and unofficially expunged their war crimes—with the publication of a book titled *German Aviation Medicine: World War II*. It was a laudatory assessment, portraying the doctors as noble men who "showed great scientific understanding... and personal concern in aeromedical research." In spite of the con job, complaints about Dr. Schreiber's blotted résumé never ceased, and in 1952 he left the United States for Argentina.

Dr. Schreiber's successor at Camp King was an equally pernicious choice: Nuremberg-indicted Dr. Blome, the former deputy surgeon general of the Third Reich. Tainted by the very visible association with the Nuremberg trials, Blome had no chance of receiving a visa from the State Department to travel to the United States—more cognitive dissonance in action. However, this didn't prevent U.S. scientists from coming to him.

Blome would consult regularly with visitors from the Army Chemical Corps at Camp Detrick, where the highly classified and morally dubious work of researching biological and chemical warfare was assigned to a unit called the Special Operations Division. The work was based at a top-secret facility within Camp Detrick, designated Building No. 439, a drab one-story block of concrete that, by intention, was as forgettable-looking as the many other nondescript structures at the base. From 1950 to 1975, the Special Operations Division is believed to have conducted experiments on more than seven thousand soldiers. The experiments included the use of mind-altering drugs and the dangerous incapacitating chemical agents tabun and sarin, substances very familiar to Dr. Blome.

Dr. Blome also began an association with the U.S. Navy Medical Research Institute near Washington. Dr. Charles Savage, a U.S. physician hired by the Navy, had studied the mind-control experiments done at Dachau as a way to secure information during interrogations without using force. Dr. Savage began conducting experiments with mescaline under a program with the code name Chatter. Because Chatter showed little success, it was discontinued in 1953. Yet the U.S. government persisted in testing psychedelic substances, only to find out what Dr. Savage already knew by 1953. These kinds of drugs didn't control minds. They scrambled them.

CHAPTER 9

UNITED STATES OF SURVEILLANCE

Even before *1984* was published, the United States had an unelected, unchecked kleptocrat who ruled as a ubiquitous despot. If FBI director J. Edgar Hoover wasn't quite Big Brother, he was awfully close. Hoover claimed to be protecting an America of Boy Scouts and Camp Fire Girls using a squad of dedicated public servants who nabbed bank robbers, white-collar criminals, and Soviet spies. But no working-class stiff would have been able to identify with the corrupt, pampered, suspicious, attention-grabbing, narrow-minded, punctilious, unethical, unmarried, childless, pug-faced control freak operating behind the FBI-stoked cult of personality.

Following his mother's death, the extent of Hoover's family was a long and intimate relationship with another man. If it was love, Hoover could never say its name, and he found a way to punish anyone who publicly suggested that his attachment to top aide Clyde Tolson was anything other than collegial. The two were openly inseparable, however. They shared almost every meal, were regulars at New York nightclubs, trading gossip and dishing dirt with celebrated columnists, and every summer they trekked across country for the horse racing season in Del Mar, on the Pacific Ocean, where Edgar and Clyde rubbed elbows with the Hollywood A-list.

The cost of such leisure, by the way, was never an issue. It was all being billed to the American taxpayer. Hoover made a personal kingdom of the FBI. "He never paid for a meal," said John Dowd, a Justice

Department investigator. "He had beef flown in free by suppliers. It was the greatest shakedown in U.S. history going on behind the badge." The shakedown included his self-aggrandizement. Hoover would use agents to write his bestselling book about the communist threat, *Masters of Deceit*, which sold two million copies in paperback. The bulk of the proceeds went to the FBI director through a fake charity.

"Hoover engaged in a range of practices over the years that could have sent him to jail," wrote FBI historian Ronald Kessler, "from illegal wiretapping to use of government funds to refurbish and maintain his house. A Jekyll and Hyde, he built a superb organization but also presided over monumental abuses. Whether he was ignoring organized crime, hiding incriminating information from judges, blackmailing members of Congress, or spying on political adversaries of Presidents, preserving his job came first."

Hoover was also a racist and generally hateful of social progress. He viewed civil rights, gay rights, women's liberation, and the anti-war movement as communist plots. "He was very consistent through the years," said Bill Sullivan, an FBI assistant director. "The things he hated, he hated all his life. He hated liberalism, he hated blacks, he hated Jews—he had this great long list of hates."

While conflating liberalism with criminality, Hoover may have done more to stoke Cold War paranoia than any other American figure. Most famously, he amassed files with the overriding goal of using blackmail to keep himself in power. "In the endless estuarial mingling of paranoia and control, the dossier was an essential device," novelist Don DeLillo wrote in *Underworld*. "Edgar had many enemies-for-life and the way to deal with such was to compile massive dossiers. . . . It was a truth without authority and therefore incontestable. . . . The file was everything, the life nothing. And this was the essence of Edgar's revenge."

In the late 1930s, as war loomed in Europe and Asia, Hoover deftly used the pretext of homeland security to substantially increase

the size of the FBI and institutionalize extraordinary and unconstitutional powers. With Franklin Roosevelt's tacit encouragement—and
maximizing the distractions provided by a worldwide war—Hoover's
FBI conducted even more illegal surveillance while continuing to
target people whose only offense was a left-leaning political view or
a critical opinion of the easily offended FBI director. For looking the
other way, what Roosevelt received in return were hundreds of FBI-
created dossiers providing him with dirt on political opponents.

In 1932, at the start of FDR's first term, the FBI had less than a
thousand employees, and a budget of $2.8 million. By the end of
the war, Hoover had a staff of twelve thousand, with a budget of
$44.2 million. Unleashed and enlarged, Hoover reengaged his love
of subterfuge and voyeurism and began decades of illegal wiretapping, bugging, and break-ins.

The FBI got back into the business of identifying "enemies of
the people" by reestablishing a blast from the past: the General Intelligence Division. In 1924, the GID had been abolished by Attorney General Harlan Stone after the entity—guided by the young
but already overzealous Hoover—committed egregious civil rights
abuses during the Harding administration. Hoover's resurrected
GID began creating indexes "arranged not only alphabetically but
also geographically," therefore giving the FBI the ability "to go into
any community and identify individuals or groups who might be a
source of grave danger to the security of this country."

Hoover's agents also began reviewing virtually every communication with the outside world. Western Union, RCA, and ITT—
the country's top telegraph and cable companies—were required
to delay the transmission of all messages to selected countries for
twenty-four hours, so that they could be copied and examined by the
FBI. This practice continued until 1975. In a program code-named
"Z-coverage," the FBI laboratory received all mail entering or leaving the United States. The contents were photographed before being
returned for delivery. In connection with the procedure, British

spies were recruited to teach FBI agents the technique of "chamfering," a.k.a. mail opening. No postmaster general, attorney general, or president was ever informed of Z-coverage. It continued through most of the Cold War.

Surreptitious entries, also known as black bag jobs, became common. Break-ins were often used to place a concealed listening device. In the attic of the Department of Justice, where the main office of the FBI was located during Hoover's era, agent trainees practiced picking locks. Wiretapping and bugging were taught at the FBI's "Sound School."

American hotels provided ongoing assistance, assigning targeted FBI subjects to pre-bugged rooms. The Hilton Hotel and Holiday Inn chains cooperated, as did many prominent big-city hotels, including the Willard in Washington, the Waldorf in New York, the Blackstone in Chicago, and the St. Francis in San Francisco.

———

In anticipation of running for president in 1948, and seeking to quiet rabid Republican voices, Harry Truman began proving he wasn't going soft on homegrown communists. Two weeks after the 1946 midterms, before the new Republican Congress could even be seated, Truman established a Temporary Commission on Employee Loyalty. The commission's report, issued in February 1947, warned that the presence within the government of any disloyal or subversive person presented a problem of such importance that it compelled immediate and vigorous action. Following the commission's recommendation, Truman issued Executive Order 9835, which established the Federal Employees Loyalty and Security Program in order to provide the country "maximum protection...against infiltration of disloyal persons into the ranks of its employees."

The FBI won a turf battle with the Civil Service Commission to supervise any and all necessary investigations. Hoover's archive of gossip, the contents of which were in large measure illegally obtained, were now in play, to be accessed and used as necessary. Hearings were scheduled before Loyalty Review Boards comprising employees from the same agency as the accused. There was no provision for the accused to see evidence, no way for the accused to refute evidence, no stipulation that there be a record of any hearing.

Historian Henry Steele Commager called the boards "an invitation to precisely the kind of witch hunting which is repugnant to our constitutional system.... Here is the doctrine of guilt by association with a vengeance." In short order, the federal plan would become the model for newly established state and municipal loyalty programs. Universities and private industry followed suit. The National Education Association issued a decree that members of the Communist Party should not be employed in American schools.

The definition of "disloyalty" expanded almost infinitely. People were brought before loyalty boards for being on the wrong mailing list, for owning "suspect" books or records, for associating with relatives or friends who held unconventional political views. Those who were suspected of being gay or involved with civil rights efforts were disproportionately investigated. One department loyalty board chairman said, "Of course, the fact that a person believes in racial equality doesn't prove that he's a Communist, but it certainly makes you look twice, doesn't it? You can't get away from the fact that racial equality is part of the communist line."

Washington Post civil liberties reporter Alan Barth addressed the abuse resulting from the program: "As a rule only the unorthodox come before the loyalty boards. They come before the loyalty boards because someone has charged them with expressing the 'wrong' opinions, associating with the 'wrong' people, belonging to the 'wrong' organizations, and in general criticizing or seeking to change the existing patterns of American life."

Wrote David McCullough in his Truman biography, "The FBI would begin running 'name checks' on every one of the two million people on the federal payrolls, a monstrous, costly task. Over four years, by 1951, three million employees would be investigated and cleared by the Civil Service Commission, and another 14,000 by the FBI. Several thousand would resign, but only 212 would be dismissed as being of questionable loyalty. None would be indicted and no evidence of espionage would be found.... In private conversations with friends, [Truman] would concede it had been a bad mistake. 'Yes, it was terrible,' he said."

———

On March 12, 1947, speaking before a joint session of Congress and a national radio audience, Truman effectively endorsed Henry Luce's vision of the American Century—"an internationalism of the people, by the people and for the people." His eighteen-minute address would echo for the remaining forty-ish years of the Cold War. President Truman told his fellow Americans it was now their burden to beat back the threat of worldwide communism, starting with a $250 million aid package to the Greek government, which could no longer rely on the all but broke British and urgently needed American might to win a civil war against a communist guerrilla movement. A new Truman Doctrine was defined by these words:

> The peoples of a number of countries of the world have recently had totalitarian regimes forced upon them against their will.... I believe that it must be the policy of the United States to support free peoples who are resisting attempted subjugation by armed minorities or outsized pressures.

The Truman Doctrine produced the first iteration of what morphed into the tragically simplistic domino theory—a world that could either be with us or against us. Speaking about the threat of the communist insurgency in Greece, then under secretary of state Dean Acheson spoke of metaphorical fruit: "Like apples in a barrel corrupted by one rotten one, the corruption of Greece would infect Iran and all to the East. It would also carry infection to Africa through Asia Minor and Egypt, and to Europe through Italy and France, already threatened by the strongest communist parties in Europe." In *The American Century*, Harold Evans wrote, "This was containment with a halo—and a sword. The sweeping rhetoric ... underlined once again the American taste for moral absolutes."

According to biographer McCullough, Truman didn't care for the term "Cold War," calling it instead a "war of nerves." A month after the announcement of the massive aid to Greece, the president's simmering anxiety about the state of the world was reactivated when George Marshall returned from Moscow with a firsthand report that the Soviets only knew how to negotiate in bad faith and Joe Stalin wasn't planning to be part of the solution for a Europe on the verge of starvation and collapse. The Marshall Plan, the $13 billion effort to provide humanitarian and military aid to Europe, went into effect on April 3, 1948.

———

As a response to World War I, the United States established a cryptanalytic organization called the Cipher Bureau, also known, more mysteriously, as "the Black Chamber." The codebreakers continued their work until 1929, when the new secretary of state, Henry Stimson, closed the bureau. He later defended the decision with the rubric, "Gentlemen do not read each other's mail." Truman was more inclined to think like Henry Stimson when it came to spying on other people. He was already worried that Hoover had turned the FBI into a Gestapo, and in discussions about establishing a peacetime U.S. intelligence service, the president had made clear he didn't want anything more than a global news service.

But on June 27, 1947, Allen Dulles began making America's first civilian peacetime spy service into the version desired by Allen Dulles. Though technically a lawyer in private practice, he had been summoned by the empowered Republicans to a secret congressional hearing that would lead to the formal creation of the CIA. In Room 1501 of the Longworth Office Building, sealed off by guards, with all inside sworn to secrecy, Dulles described the kind of espionage operation he had in mind.

"Puffing away on his pipe," wrote Tim Weiner in *Legacy of Ashes: The History of the CIA*, "a tweedy headmaster instructing unruly schoolboys," Dulles described a CIA that was to be "directed by a relatively small but elite corps of men with a passion for anonymity" and a director of "judicial temperament in high degree" with "long experience and profound knowledge." It was apparent that Allen Dulles's definition of the ideal CIA director was Allen Dulles. Left unsaid was that he also wanted agents to have a license to kill and the liberty to remake the world.

Dulles and his brother John Foster were, like Henry Luce, active oligarchs who always found ways to pull strings in Washington. One front organization of this ghost leadership was the Council on Foreign Relations, which published the journal *Foreign Affairs*. Members of the council, including John Foster, regularly produced classified policy memos for the U.S. State Department. In the late 1930s, Allen Dulles joined an *actual* super-secret organization called The Room, a small ad hoc "forum for ideas and intelligence" based in a nondescript apartment on East 62nd Street in Manhattan.

The men in The Room—about three dozen bankers, businessmen, and corporate lawyers—met to exchange the most sensitive information they had gathered from their extensive travels. In 1941, Roosevelt appointed one of these secret sharers—war hero and Wall Street banker William Donovan—to plan and build what became the OSS. Donovan recruited Allen Dulles, who negotiated a posting to Switzerland, Germany's neutral neighbor. The Alpine hideaway, which famously obliged shady financial transactions, was an ideal location for exploiting in every possible way the many European friends, including Nazis, Dulles had made rich and happy as a lawyer for Sullivan & Cromwell.

Army colonel B. A. Dixon would describe the efforts of Wild Bill's boys as an achievement of style over substance: "The O.S.S. is the most fantastic damned organization in all of our armed forces. Its people do incredible things. They seduce German spies. They parachute into Sicily one day and two days later they're dancing on the St. Regis roof. They dynamite aqueducts, urinate in Luftwaffe gas tanks, and play games with I.G. Farben and Krupp, but ninety percent of this has not a goddamned thing to do with the war."

For many who worked for the OSS, returning to their day jobs was a profound letdown. Being American spies in Europe had been the most rewarding experience of their lives. It was not only electrifying, it was also *meaningful*, a unique high combining largely unchecked power with an ad hoc mission of attempting to sway the course of human events. "They were pining to get back," said Peter Sichel, who lunched with Dulles at the exclusive Down Town Association on Wall Street. "They were boy scouts who were bored in their law jobs. They were like fighter pilots in England after the Battle of Britain. They couldn't adjust. They were ... great romantics who saw themselves as saviors of the world."

Dulles's secret congressional testimony in Room 1501 would inform a piece of legislation that became the National Security Act, which Truman signed into law on July 26, 1947. It contained, as Stephen Kinzer wrote, "a tantalizing clause worded to allow endlessly elastic speculation. The CIA was to perform not only duties spelled out by the new law—which were 'to correlate, evaluate and disseminate intelligence'—but also 'such other functions and duties related to intelligence affecting the national security as the National Security Council may from time to time direct.'" This gave the agency legal cover, albeit debatable, to take any action, including regime change, anywhere in the world, as long as the president approved. The executive branch had usurped a new secret authority to make policy decisions that the president never needed to disclose or, if convenient, could plausibly deny knowledge of, especially if the decisions resulted in negative consequences. Truman's second-term secretary of state, Dean Acheson, later said, "I had the gravest forebodings about this organization and warned the President that as set up neither he, nor the National Security Council, nor anyone else, would be in a position to know what it was doing or to control it."

———

Inside the newly ordained U.S. spy shop, it was feared the Kremlin would soon be able to compel Italy to adopt communism just by "picking up the phone." James Jesus Angleton, at the time the CIA station chief in Rome, assessed he would need $10 million to defeat the surging Italian Communist Party in the upcoming 1948 general election. Angleton was an OSS agent in Italy during the war, described by journalist Thomas Powers as "a tall, thin, unapproachable man" whose "true calling was counterintelligence," which, Powers wrote, was "an exotic discipline which [Angleton] was to practice the way other men play chess." One immediate need, Angleton stressed, was foiling a scheme by the communists to buy up all the cheap paper stock used for newsprint, which, if successful, would ensure that the bulk of what Italians read would favor the Communist Party and attack the Christian Democrats, the leading opposition.

The CIA, brand-new and without an independent budget, didn't have easy access to large sums of money. Allen Dulles came to the rescue, taking a leave of absence from Sullivan & Cromwell. He began by soliciting the eastern financial elite at various Wall Street social clubs, such as the Brook, the Links, and the Knickerbocker. Eventually, his covert work became so conspicuous that the *Boston Globe* ran a story about his involvement under the headline DULLES MASTERS NEW "COLD WAR" PLAN UNDER SECRET AGENTS.

More cash was required—and found. A little-known pot of money was controlled by Treasury Secretary John Snyder, a top Truman ally. Something called the Exchange Stabilization Fund was stocked with $200 million taken from the Nazis. Laundering the money to conceal the source came next.

The Treasury sent checks to wealthy Americans, the majority of Italian ancestry, who in turn forwarded the money to CIA front organizations working in Italy. The recipients of the checks were instructed to use a special code when tallying charitable contributions on their next income tax forms. Meanwhile, in Rome, the five-star Hassler Hotel, at the top of the Spanish Steps, was the luxury setting for relaying buckets of cash to Italian politicians, priests, labor officials, and newspaper editors. "We would have liked to have done this in a more sophisticated manner," said CIA agent F. Mark Wyatt. "Passing black bags to affect a political election is not really a terribly attractive thing."

The CIA supplemented the rampant bribery by flooding Italy with letters, pamphlets, books, and posters warning of the communist danger. Powers noted how "the brutality of the Russian Army occupation in Germany, notorious for its looting and raping, was vividly evoked in anonymous publications, and the fates of Poland and Czechoslovakia...were projected for Italy in a campaign based on fear."

The skullduggery was supplemented by visible actions. The United States supplied wheat and other commodities to alleviate food shortages, and Truman threatened to withhold money from any Italian government that included communists. "Threats of this sort," Powers wrote, "are a heavy-handed form of psychological warfare." On election night, the communists suffered a sizable defeat.

CHAPTER 10

UNIDENTIFIED OBJECTS

On June 24, 1947, pilot Kenneth Arnold was searching Washington's Cascade Mountains for a downed Marine Corps C-46 transport plane that had been missing for several days. The thirty-two-year-old Arnold was an Idaho businessman who had founded Great Western Fire Control Supply, a company that sold and installed fire suppression systems. The job took him around the Pacific Northwest, which he traveled by air, specifically a CallAir Model A-2, a two-seat, low-wing monoplane with fixed landing gear that had been introduced only the year before, in 1946. He was a skilled pilot and had flown thousands of hours. Half of those hours were logged for search-and-rescue efforts as a Mercy Flyer. Arnold was a deputy U.S. marshal as well.

On the afternoon of July 24, Arnold was on his way to Yakima, but in his role as a Mercy Flyer he had agreed to make a slight diversion in his flight plan in order to look for the C-46. After circling the canyons southwest of Mount Rainier and not seeing any wreckage, he climbed and turned east toward Yakima. Minutes later, according to an account he would later provide to reporters, Arnold was startled by a bright flash that lit up the surface of his aircraft. Scanning the sky to the north, he observed a chain of nine peculiar-looking objects, in loose formation, flying close to the mountaintops at tremendous speed. At first he thought they were jet planes, but as they approached Mount Rainier he was able to see their outlines against the snow. He could not distinguish a tail, and they did not fly like aircraft he had ever seen before.

Upon landing at Yakima, Arnold told the ground crew what he had seen. At his next stop, Pendleton, Washington, the word had spread and newsmen were waiting. Arnold searched for the right image to describe an event for which he didn't have a good explanation. He told the reporters the objects flew "like speed boats on rough water or similar to the tail of a Chinese kite that I once saw blowing in the wind. Or maybe it would be best to describe their flight characteristics as very similar to a formation of geese, in a rather diagonal chain-like line, as if they were linked together." This was the analogy that stuck: "They flew like a saucer would if you skipped it across the water."

On June 25, 1947, this Associated Press report appeared in some 150 American newspapers:

PENDLETON, Ore., June 25 (AP)—Kenneth Arnold, with the fire control at Boise and who was flying in southern Washington yesterday afternoon in search of a missing marine plane, stopped here en route to Boise today with an unusual story—which he doesn't expect people to believe but which he declared was true.

He said he sighted nine saucer-like aircraft flying in formation at 3 p.m. yesterday, extremely bright—as if they were nickel plated—and flying at an immense rate of speed. He estimated they were at an altitude between 9,500 and 10,000 feet and clocked them from Mt. Rainier to Mt. Adams, arriving at the amazing speed of about 1,200 miles an hour.

"It seemed impossible," he said, "but there it is—I must believe my eyes."

In *Close Encounters of the Fourth Kind*, C. D. B. Bryan wrote, "Arnold's was by no means the first sighting of unidentified flying objects...but the wide publicity he received and the credibility and courage in speaking out about what he had witnessed encouraged others.... More important, perhaps, is the fact that Arnold's story gave birth to the term 'flying saucer' as a means of describing something strange and anomalous that was clearly artificial, machinelike, and possibly otherworldly."

Arnold's courage was not rewarded. What immediately followed his sighting in 1947 were various suggestions that he had hallucinated the whole thing. The June 27, 1947, issue of the *San Francisco Chronicle* published a roundup of possible explanations for the Mount Rainier incident. A United Airlines pilot believed that Arnold had seen reflections of his instrument panel; a meteorologist suggested that Arnold had experienced snow blindness; and a University of Oregon astronomer said that Arnold's sighting was a result of persistence of vision, often experienced after staring at the sun for long periods of time.

Arnold became annoyed: "Call me Einstein or Flash Gordon or just a screwball, I'm absolutely certain of what I saw! But, believe me, if I ever see again a phenomenon of that sort in the sky, even if it's a one-story building, I won't say a word about it."

———

The Cold War vocabulary had another unsettling addition. As the mushroom cloud and Doomsday Clock would serve as shorthand for the prospective termination of the species, the flying saucer—or wingless craft—would come to be viewed as the established mode of travel for alien visitors of an apparently superior civilization. There was also a spiritual, if not a moral, reaction to the unidentified flying objects, or UFOs: Their arrival came to be seen as a warning of some kind connected to the birth of the atomic age and our reckless stewardship of the planet. In the *New York Times*, psychology professor Clay Routledge wrote, "As with traditional religious beliefs, many of these paranormal beliefs involve powerful beings watching over humans and the hope that they will rescue us from death and destruction."

On January 7, 1948, a Kentucky Air National Guard pilot, Thomas Mantell, died in a crash after blacking out at high altitude while pursuing an alleged flying saucer, raising the prospect that extraterrestrial visitors could be hostile. Three years later, the Navy revealed that a secret, high-altitude Skyhook reconnaissance balloon was in the area, and that Mantell had likely died trying to reach it.

As the reports of unidentified flying objects mounted, the Air Force would authorize three different studies of UFOs—projects Sign, Grudge, and Blue Book—which collectively had the effect of supplying the phenomenon with greater credibility, an unintended and undesired consequence, but which ultimately satisfied no one when the investigations determined that these objects could not be chased down, nabbed, or verified by any known science. A fourth study by the CIA essentially recommended ignoring the whole subject. Suspicion of a massive government cover-up was stoked when the U.S. government rejected calls to make the UFO investigations available to the public. By 1956, a former Marine pilot named Donald Keyhoe had cofounded the National Investigations Committee on Aerial Phenomena (NICAP)—an organization born out of the conviction that the Air Force was lying about UFOs.

Dan Barry, a reporter for the *New York Times*, wrote about a devoted NICAP member, his father, Gene: "Through the 1960s and 1970s, he joined many others in monitoring reports of aerial anomalies, tracking down reams of redacted official reports and swapping theories about credible sightings and cover-ups.... He was no astronomer or physicist. Just a working stiff who endured the anonymous drudgery of a daily commute but then, at night, often felt connected to something larger than himself, larger than all of us."

———

Stories of extraterrestrial visitors became a staple of Cold War cinema. This theme was generally exploited in two different ways: The aliens had come to either kill us or save us. *The Thing from Another World* (1951, produced by Howard Hughes's RKO Pictures) was the former. The Thing of the title is the pilot of an alien ship that has crashed near an American Arctic research station. Found frozen, and then accidentally thawed out, the alien visitor turns out to be a plant version of Frankenstein. When the grunting creature loses a limb, he grows another. Even more disturbing, the severed limb begins sprouting little Things. The film concludes with an ominous radio message from the survivors of the encounter: "Watch the skies, everywhere, keep looking, and keep watching the skies."

War of the Worlds (1953), the H. G. Wells classic, was reproduced in vivid Technicolor and updated for the atomic age. As the film opens, we meet Dr. Clayton Forrester (Gene Barry), a scientist who had worked on the Manhattan Project. He is fishing with colleagues when a large object crashes nearby. The Martians have arrived, and, it turns out, even our nukes are no match! The film would go on to win an Academy Award for Special Effects. *Variety* raved, "It's a socko science-fiction feature, as fearsome as a film as was the Orson Welles 1938 radio interpretation.... What starring honors there are go strictly to the special effects, which create an atmosphere of soul-chilling apprehension so effectively that audiences will actually take alarm at the danger posed in the picture."

———

A merger of law and order with science fiction produced Ronald Reagan's first success as an actor. Shortly after being signed by Warner Brothers, in 1937, he starred in four Brass Bancroft movies. The character was a "rough and tumble" pilot cum agent for the Secret Service Division of the U.S. Treasury. Lieutenant Bancroft foiled plots by counterfeiters, plus whatever other evildoers came his way. These were low budget B-movies, action-packed thrillers tailored for children attending Saturday matinees.

The plot of *Murder in the Air* (1940), the fourth in the Bancroft oeuvre, would bubble up in Reagan's subsequent political career. The script was ripped from the headlines, when the scourge of Fascism in Europe was at its peak. As Reagan biographer Edmund Morris summarized, Reagan as Bancroft "heroically pursued a Lindbergh-like pacifist bent on preserving American neutrality, and Public Enemy Number One, a saboteur who bore the *mitteleuropaisch* name of Swenko." Spoiler alert: Bancroft foils the foes of freedom by liquidating them with a secret weapon called an "Inertia Projector." This is your basic airplane-mounted atomic laser cannon capable of blasting enemy planes out of the sky.

Such weapons remained in the realm of fantasy until a group of people walked into the Oval Office during President Reagan's first term and told him they could build something like the Inertia Projector used for *Murder in the Air.* When Edward Teller, the father of the hydrogen bomb, pitched space-based lasers that could zap incoming missiles, Reagan was ecstatic. It was exactly what he had been waiting for.

Reagan had long wondered why the United States only had offensive weapons, especially since it would be morally more acceptable if all the nukes were *defensive.* Teller's lasers had the potential of altering America's military strategy from *destruction* to *protection.* The Strategic Defense Initiative would be derisively dubbed "Star Wars" by Democrat Ted Kennedy, and the less generous in the press would begin referring to the president as "Ronald Ray Gun." But for Reagan, such mockery was easily dismissed. He didn't think Teller's SDI was silly at all.

———

Although he was not part of its cast, Reagan's political life was also influenced by the Cold War sci-fi classic *The Day the Earth Stood Still* (1951), which presented technologically superior aliens in a paternal role. After a flying saucer lands in Washington, D.C., containing a humanoid named Klaatu and his menacing eight-foot-tall robot, Gort, we learn that Klaatu is an emissary from planets concerned about humanity's development of rockets and atomic weapons. Producer Julian Blaustein freely admitted that the film was intended to have a dovish political message, telling the press it was an argument in favor of a "strong United Nations." Hollywood's foreign press later awarded the movie a special Golden Globe for "promoting international understanding."

As J. Hoberman wrote in the *New York Times*, there were several other pointed references to the Cold War landscape: "Klaatu makes contact with Dr. Barnhardt, the smartest man on earth, played by a wide-eyed, wild-haired Sam Jaffe as an obvious stand-in for Albert Einstein. This was not an innocent choice. America's most famous brain was a proponent of world government and opponent of loyalty oaths, reviled as a Communist fellow-traveler for being a co-sponsor of the Cultural and Scientific Conference for World Peace held at the Waldorf-Astoria in 1949. Encouraged by Klaatu, Dr. Barnhardt organizes an international peace conference similar to the Waldorf conclave."

The film concludes with Klaatu encouraging humans to join the other planets in peace while also warning that if our violence is extended into space, "this Earth of yours will be reduced to a burned-out cinder. . . . We shall be waiting for your answer."

America's actor turned politician found the movie's message consistent with his own philosophy. Following World War II, Reagan joined a peace-oriented society called the United World Federalists, and he was an ardent booster of the newly established United Nations. He also supported the views of another new postwar organization, the American Veterans Committee, which called for peaceful coexistence with the Soviet Union and urged the United States to cede nuclear power to the UN. Like Einstein, Reagan hoped the world would one day shed all its nuclear weaponry and join together for peace. His lifelong foreboding about the prospect of nuclear holocaust, not apparent when he was first elected to the presidency, became evident at the start of his second term, when he told the country that "my dream is to see the day when nuclear weapons will be banished from the face of the Earth."

In November 1985, during his first face-to-face meeting with Mikhail Gorbachev, in Geneva, Reagan apparently referenced science-fiction films about alien visitations, including the storyline of *The Day the Earth Stood Still*. As Gorbachev was pleased to discover, Reagan still remained something of a United World Federalist.

According to Gorbachev, Reagan asked him, "What would you do if the United States were suddenly attacked by someone from outer space? Would you help us?"

Gorbachev said he replied, "No doubt about it.'"

Reagan then apparently said, "We too!"

CHAPTER 11

HOLLYWOOD ON TRIAL

Louis B. Mayer's MGM made the pro-Soviet *Song of Russia* in 1943. The love story is set on the eve of Hitler's invasion. While on a forty-city tour of the Soviet Union, an American conductor named John Meredith (played by Robert Taylor) meets a beautiful Soviet pianist named Nadya Stepanova (Susan Peters). Their romance is rudely interrupted by Hitler's Operation Barbarossa.

As production was getting started, the then thirty-one-year-old Taylor, a staunch conservative, was desperate to join the war. "He wanted no part of a film he considered pro-communist propaganda," wrote Margarita Landazuri for TCM.com. "Mayer insisted that the government wanted the film made, and brought in a representative of the Office of War Information to help 'persuade' Taylor. The implication was that Taylor's naval orders would be held up until he made the film."

In 1947, Taylor made sure that *Song of Russia* would be a topic of conversation when the House Un-American Activities Committee began investigating rumors of communist subversion in Hollywood. "Far from objecting to the witch hunt," Landazuri wrote, "Taylor went on a witch hunt of his own. He contacted the committee, and suggested that the Roosevelt administration had delayed his induction into the Navy" so he could make the film. Taylor would be among forty-one "friendly" witnesses subpoenaed to testify, as was author Ayn Rand, who gave a thumbs-down to MGM's Russian romance.

"The poor, sweet Russians were unprepared," said Rand of the moment in *Song of Russia* when the Nazis attack. "Now, realize—and that was a great shock to me—that the border that was being shown was the border of Poland. That was the border of an occupied, destroyed, enslaved country which Hitler and Stalin destroyed together....Also realize that when all this sweetness and light was going on in the first part of the picture, with all these happy, free people, there was not a [secret police] agent among them, with no food lines, no persecution— complete freedom and happiness, with everybody smiling."

Wrote Otto Friedrich in *City of Nets*, "What Miss Rand could not seem to understand, what the House Committee could not seem to understand, was that *Song of Russia* was rubbish not because of any political purpose, subversive or otherwise, but because MGM was in the business of producing rubbish....MGM was the home of Andy Hardy, of Judy Garland and Esther Williams, and no Communist ideology could ever penetrate or take root in such a playland."

Rand was in vogue after the success of *The Fountainhead* (1943), a novel about a young architect named Howard Roark who bucks the establishment and embodies Rand's assertion that hearty individualism is superior to all forms of collectivism. This philosophy emerged from the trauma of her firsthand experience with Bolshevism. Rand had left Russia in 1926, at age twenty-one. "In my time," she told the HUAC, "we were a bunch of ragged, starved, dirty, miserable people who had only two thoughts in our mind. That was our complete terror—afraid to look at one another, afraid to say anything for fear of who is listening and would report us—and where to get the next meal."

Prior to her testimony, the FBI consulted Rand for a humongous, forest-shredding 13,533-page report entitled *Communist Infiltration of the Motion Picture Industry*, which quoted from a pamphlet she had written for the Motion Picture Alliance for the Preservation of American Ideals. "The purpose of the Communists in Hollywood," Rand wrote, "is to corrupt non-political movies—by introducing small, casual bits of propaganda into innocent stories and to make people absorb the basic principles of Collectivism by indirection and implication. Few people would take Communism straight, but a constant stream of hints, lines, touches, and suggestions battering the public from the screen will act like drops of water that split a rock if continued long enough. The rock they are trying to split is Americanism."

Rand believed it was necessary to issue several commandments to scriptwriters, directors, and producers. To quote:

- Don't Smear Industrialists.
- Don't Smear the Free Enterprise System.
- Don't Smear Success.
- Don't give to your characters—as a sign of villainy, as a damning characteristic—a desire to make money.
- Don't ever use any lines about "the common man" or "the little people." It is not the American idea to be "common" or "little."
- Don't tell people that man is a helpless, twisted, drooling, sniveling, neurotic weakling....
- It is the moral duty of every decent man in the motion picture industry to throw into the ash can, where it belongs, every story that smears industrialists as such.

In keeping with Rand's analysis, the FBI report saw a communist plot behind the apparent celebration of small-town American values in Frank Capra's classic *It's a Wonderful Life.* The film's real purpose, according to the FBI, was to instigate class warfare by maligning the upper class. In particular, according to the FBI, the portrayal of banker Henry F. Potter, a Scrooge as played by Lionel Barrymore, was a "common trick used by Communists." The FBI also claimed that the film's screenwriters, Frances Goodrich and Albert Hackett, were communist sympathizers because they "practically lived with known Communists and were observed eating luncheon daily with such Communists as Lester Cole, screenwriter, and Earl Robinson."

Walt Disney, who testified before the HUAC on the same day as Rand, had been called by the committee to highlight another alleged cause for national concern: communist infiltration of American labor. Disney was eager to provide his insight after enduring a workers' revolt at his studio.

On May 29, 1941, two hundred Disney animators had gone on strike for the right to join the Screen Cartoonists Guild. The strike would last for nine weeks. On July 2, 1941, while several hundred picketers were still making a noisy scene outside the animation studio in Burbank—holding such signs as ONE GENIUS VS. 600 GUINEA PIGS and LEONARDO, MICHELANGELO AND TITIAN WERE UNION MEN—Disney took out an ad in *Variety* claiming communists were behind the effort: "I am positively convinced that communistic agitation, leadership, and activities have brought about the strike." But the facts proved otherwise.

Walt Disney Studios, which had literally started in a storefront, had become a major Hollywood institution by the 1940s, with nearly thirteen hundred employees. As the studio grew, Disney made a habit of plowing his profits back into new facilities and better technology while many of his artists were working six days a week for low wages, only given raises or bonuses at the whim of management, and not entitled to screen credits. The only name on any Disney picture was Walt's.

Herb Sorrell, a leading Hollywood labor organizer, and Art Babbitt, a well-compensated senior Disney animator who was sympathetic to the conditions of the lower-paid, overworked staffers, met with Disney and his attorneys to ask for union recognition. Feeling betrayed, bleeding cash like always, Disney angrily refused and shortly fired Babbitt and sixteen other pro-union artists, a violation of federal labor law. That action sparked the strike.

As it dragged on into a third month, Disney's financiers at the Bank of America and brother Roy Disney, the studio's business manager, successfully pushed Walt to recognize the guild. A federal mediator ruled in the union's favor on every issue. Salaries were doubled, a forty-hour workweek was established, and, for the first time, all the animators were eligible for screen credits.

In 1947, questioned at the HUAC hearings by investigator H. A. Smith, Disney was prompted to push communism's role in the labor confrontation:

SMITH: Have you had at any time, in your opinion, in the past, have you at any time in the past had any Communists employed at your studio?

DISNEY: Yes; in the past I had some people that I definitely feel were Communists.

SMITH: As a matter of fact, Mr. Disney, you experienced a strike at your studio, did you not?

DISNEY: Yes.

SMITH: And is it your opinion that that strike was instituted by members of the Communist Party to serve their purposes?

DISNEY: Well, it proved itself so with time, and I definitely feel it was a Communist group trying to take over my artists and they did take them over.

Disney willingly named names and smeared reputations without a second thought.

SMITH: Can you name...individuals that were active at the time of the strike that you believe in your opinion are Communists?

DISNEY: Well, I feel that there is one artist in my plant that came in there, he came in about 1938, and he sort of stayed in the background, he wasn't too active, but he was the real brains of this, and I believe he is a Communist. His name is David Hilberman.

SMITH: How is it spelled?

DISNEY: H-i-l-b-e-r-m-a-n, I believe. I looked into his record and I found that, No. 1, that he had no religion and, No. 2, that he had considerable time at the Moscow Art Theater studying art direction, or something.

SMITH: Any others, Mr. Disney?

DISNEY: Well, I think Sorrell is sure tied up with them. If he isn't a Communist, he sure should be one.

Yahoo Entertainment writer Ken Tucker observed that Walt Disney tried to present himself as a "paternal operator," but that idealization of himself was the man "he wished-upon-a-star he was." Tucker continued, "What he *really* was, was a relentless businessman, one who felt his employees owed him gratitude, and when they rose up, he began to tap into deeper darknesses in his personality. This manifested itself as an angry paranoia: Disney convinced himself, with no real proof, that these men (and they were by far mostly men)—who wanted nothing more than to draw cute animals and put food on the table for their families—were manipulated by Communists, their demands contributing to Disney's pile of debt."

Ronald Reagan's obsessive anticommunism emerged after he assumed the presidency of the Screen Actors Guild, in 1947. Reagan was a successful and well-liked SAG president who had been targeted, unfairly, by the Conference of Studio Unions, a newly established craft union representing set designers and other crew members working behind the camera. During a strike by the CSU that turned violent, Reagan received a death threat, began carrying a gun, and was assigned a security detail by his studio, Warner Brothers.

The CSU had been founded by the hard-charging Herb Sorrell after his success unionizing Disney. Sorrell was not a communist, but, as he later confessed, had no trouble accepting financial aid from the party. "American Communism had a discipline when they worked in unions, civic, student, and cultural organizations that gave them a power and an influence wildly out of proportion to their small numbers," Nick von Hoffman wrote. "The fact that these smart, tough men and women often did not identify themselves as Communists gave non-Communists a permanent case of the jitters. A constant, unpleasant premonition pervaded much of the nation's political life that someone at the meeting was operating with a secret agenda in collusion with other unidentified people on the floor."

Reagan's first major political test was navigating the response by the Screen Actors Guild to the labor civil war Sorrel had started with IATSE—the International Alliance of Theatrical Stage Employees. To win attention for the newly created CSU and demonstrate that it could deliver for its members, Sorrell called a strike against all the studios. The SAG actors, desperate to work after the lean years of the war, overwhelmingly decided to cross the CSU's picket line. Reagan himself had just signed a seven-year deal with Warner Brothers that was going to pay him $150,000 annually—the equivalent of $2.3 million today. But natural avarice wasn't the only consideration.

The Hollywood unions generally abided by an unspoken code. Solidarity was demanded when a strike was pitting workers against owners. However, Sorrell's strike was a stunt, an upstart union taking a whack at a more powerful one serving the same members, a situation that allowed SAG to exercise its discretion not to support the CSU. "It wasn't meant to improve the wages and working conditions of its members," Reagan later said of Sorrell's strike, "but to grab something from another union that was rightfully theirs."

During the strike, Warner Brothers took the precaution of busing their actors to the studio. Calls would be made each morning to identify off-studio meeting sites. The locations were changed daily to thwart CSU spies. Buses, with guards, drove through the studio gates with all the windows closed and the high-priced passengers told to crouch out of sight. One morning, Reagan showed up late for a bus pickup and had to take a cab. The bus he'd missed was lit on fire by the strikers and, according to Reagan, "was still burning when I got there."

One night, Reagan picked up the phone to hear, "There's a group being formed to deal with you. They're going to fix you so you'll never act again." He assumed it was one of Sorrell's goons threatening to splash his face with acid. Informed of the call, Warner Brothers paid for a security detail to be posted at his home and also arranged for Reagan to be licensed for a .32 Smith & Wesson. "Thereafter," Reagan said, "I mounted the holstered gun religiously every morning and took it off the last thing at night."

Such events made Reagan, like Disney, the kind of witness the HUAC could exploit to bolster the tie between communism and labor activism—however tentative and thin that association might be. On October 23, 1947, Reagan was one of several actors summoned to the Old House Office Building. The hearing room was jammed. Even the jaded Washington establishment wasn't immune to the glamour of Hollywood star power. Flashbulbs popped, a forest of newsreel cameras whirred, and most of the veteran performers played the role their audience desired.

Adolphe Menjou told the House members, "This is a foul philosophy, this Communist thing. I would move to the state of Texas if it ever came here, because I think the Texans would kill it on sight." Robert Taylor said, "If I had my way about it, they'd be sent back to Russia, or some other unpleasant place." His remark generated immediate applause.

Reagan wore a light tan suit, white shirt, and blue knit tie. After he sat down, he put on glasses, a rare occasion. Reagan had 20/200 vision, but never wore glasses or contact lenses when he performed, or, for that matter, almost ever. Daughter Patti later complained that her father didn't know who she was half the time.

The HUAC's lead investigator, Robert Stripling, questioned Reagan, whose answers were more measured than most of the Hollywood invitees. He conceded there might be a small clique within the Screen Actors Guild who used communist-style tactics, but when asked if they were members of the Communist Party, Reagan said he didn't know. The lasting impression he gave those listening to him in the Old House Office Building, including Richard Nixon, was that whatever threat communism posed to the United States, it would always be overmatched. Reagan concluded by saying of communists, "I detest, I abhor their philosophy, but I detest more than that their tactics, which are those of the fifth column and are dishonest. But at the same time, I never, as a citizen, want to see our country become urged, by either fear or resentment of this group, [to] compromise with any of our democratic principles. . . . I still think that democracy can do it."

Reagan's deep devotion to SAG, and a compulsion to wrestle with the nation's larger political issues, would be cited by his first wife, Jane Wyman, as one of the reasons for their divorce. During a party where Reagan was lecturing everyone in the room about communism, Wyman reportedly whispered to a friend, "I'm so bored with him, I'll either kill him or kill myself." Later, Reagan would lament, "I should have let someone else save the world and saved my own home."

———

While testifying before the HUAC, eleven Hollywood figures, including Dalton Trumbo and German-born writer Bertolt Brecht, refused to answer questions about their associations with communism. They also denounced the proceedings. Being a communist or not wanting to talk about being a communist was, in theory, protected by the First Amendment. But by refusing to clearly answer questions about their political orientation, Trumbo and Co. walked into a different trap. Instead, on November 27, 1947, all were cited for contempt. Congress merely sidestepped any claims to freedom of speech and used its power to punish a perceived lack of cooperation. By that point, the pragmatic Brecht had fled, resettling in communist East Berlin.

On December 3, 1947, there was a closed-door meeting at New York's Waldorf Astoria with forty-nine movie executives, including Jack Warner and Louis B. Mayer. The blacklist of the "Hollywood Ten" emerged from the meeting. Their statement concluded by saying, "We will not re-employ any of the 10 until such time as he is acquitted or has purged himself of contempt and declares under oath that he is not a Communist." After the Supreme Court refused to reverse their contempt citations, the "Hollywood Ten" all served brief prison terms.

CHAPTER 12

CULTURAL CONTENT

Following the congressional colonoscopy, officially called the hearings on "Communist Infiltration of the Motion Picture Business,"
Hollywood covered its ass and made enough films with anti-Soviet
messages to stay out of any further significant trouble. As Daniel J.
Leab wrote in the *Journal of Contemporary History*, "Even Westerns
were not immune to the cultural politics of the day. *California Conquest*, a 1952 Columbia release set in early nineteenth-century California, touched on Russian endeavors to seize the territory; this
effort, spearheaded by disloyal citizens, was aborted when Spanish
and American settlers banded together to save California from the
subversive pro-Russian group." The story had no basis in fact.

The studio bosses made such films with gritted teeth and in
the hope that the fever would pass. Such men were hardly socialists. However, they were box-office realists and keenly aware that
moviegoers didn't like paying for propaganda. Predictably, such films
as *The Iron Curtain* (20th Century Fox), *The Red Menace* (Republic),
I Was a Communist for the FBI (Warner Brothers), and *The Girl in the
Kremlin* (Universal) didn't make anyone rich, nor enhance anyone's
artistic careers.

My Son John was produced, directed, and scripted by Leo McCa-
rey, who, like Reagan and Disney, was one of the favored witnesses
at the HUAC hearings. Leab offered this summary of the film:
"John is a prissy, quirky, possibly homosexual Federal government

functionary who is exposed as a communist tied to a Soviet espionage ring, thanks to the patience and fortitude of an FBI agent who, working through John's devoted mother, gets him to repent before he is murdered by his comrades at the foot of the Lincoln Memorial."

More successful, artistically and financially, were subtler mash-ups of science fiction with an intimation of the anti-Soviet dread and paranoia being steadily pumped out of Washington, D.C. One example was *Them*, released by Warner Brothers. The *Them* are giant mutant ants, which, after rising out of the Los Angeles sewer system, get beaten back by the police, the FBI, and the U.S. armed forces. One critic said the film was "a vicious allegory calling for the extermination not of giant ants but of communists."

In this darkening era, American moviegoers were ready for shadier themes, as long as productions were delivered with a sufficient panache and a suspenseful punch. *Citizen Kane* (1941) set the photographic template for American noir with succulent expressionistic photography, the composition of the images deepening the story of a tycoon's corruption—style and meaning intertwined. *Double Indemnity* (1944) adapted a James M. Cain story of an insurance agent who is seduced by a sultry wife and joins a murderous plot to stage the death of her husband as an accident in order to activate the double indemnity clause of a life insurance policy, twice the payout. *Sunset Boulevard* (1950) charts the ultimate Hollywood tragedy, in which a failing scriptwriter, played by William Holden, becomes a gigolo to a possessive, faded actress from the silent film era, played by Gloria Swanson.

The Third Man (1949) is one of the first classics of Cold War cinema, a film noir set in the postwar moment, when broken, stumbling European nations were enduring survival-of-the-fittest economies. If *Casablanca* conveyed the heroism and righteousness behind the resistance against Nazi nihilism—exemplified by the scene in Rick's Café when French patrons silence obnoxious Nazis singing "Die Wacht am Rhein" by tearfully belting "La Marseillaise"—*The Third Man* portrays a far more ambiguous geopolitical reality.

An uneasy peace exists between the Western powers and the Russians. Postwar Vienna is on the unsettled frontier of an intensifying Cold War, somewhere between anarchy and order. We experience a city that seems starved of light yet somehow energized by silken blacks and towering shadows. Anxiety simmers, violence awaits. British director Carol Reed and Australian cinematographer Robert Krasker accentuated the noir milieu of menace by occasionally tilting the camera—a technique known as a Dutch angle.

The film's title is made clear early in the story. Holly Martins, played by Joseph Cotten, is informed that his friend Harry Lime has been killed by a truck in a hit-and-run accident. Martins seeks details and hears conflicting versions of the accident. He's first made to understand that two men picked up Lime's body from the road. This minor detail becomes sinister when the porter at Lime's apartment suggests a cover-up. "There was a third man," he tells Martins. Shortly, in a plot that delightfully thickens, the porter is murdered.

Holly Martins is cynical and flawed—a penniless pulp fiction writer of westerns, and a drunk. However, there is a basic goodness about him, a moral core, as he searches to find the truth about his friend. The sultry femme fatale—Italian actress Alida Valli, playing a brooding, fatalistic Czech refugee named Anna Schmidt—is tenuously protected by a forged Austrian passport. Being able to remain west of the Iron Curtain is, for Anna, perhaps a matter of life and death. If discovered by the Russians, she can be repatriated with unknown and possibly terrible consequences—as it was in the real world. In *The Third Man*, Schmidt's trembling paranoia is ever present, as she tries to avoid notice and remain alert for what the city's shadows and alleys may be hiding. Anna also proves to be hopelessly in love with Lime, even after discovering he's guilty of peddling diluted black market penicillin that has sickened and killed the city's children.

The scandal attached to Lime—selling fake penicillin—wasn't a fiction. In 1946, American and British intelligence agents arrested ten members of a ring that filled used penicillin bottles with face powder and crushed antimalarial tablets, selling each for $300, the equivalent of $4,000 today. Among the ten were two former American infantry soldiers and an American doctor. In another case, Zane Todd, who served in postwar Vienna as a criminal investigator for the U.S. military, arrested two American medical officers for stealing and selling penicillin on the black market. They were assisted by a former Miss Austria, with whom both officers were reported to be romantically involved. Meanwhile, the real drug was used as bait in a U.S. espionage mission called Operation Claptrap. Red Army soldiers who'd contracted syphilis or gonorrhea were provided penicillin in return for secrets or agreeing to defect. For Soviet forces, contracting venereal disease was a court-martial offense.

———

The making of *The Third Man* began in January 1948, when British film producer Sir Alexander Korda, head of British Lion Films and London Film Productions, commissioned novelist Graham Greene to write and research "an original postwar continental story to be based on either or both of the following territories: Vienna, Rome." Korda and Greene brought a unique shared perspective to the project: Both had worked for British intelligence. This past provided Greene with two tremendous research sources for a tale about Vienna. One was Kim Philby, at the time the head of counterintelligence for MI6. Greene's other key contact was Philby buddy H. P. Smollett, who had tried to snuff Orwell's *Animal Farm*. Greene likely knew, or at least suspected, that both men were Soviet assets.

When Greene went to Vienna to soak up the atmosphere, he had already imagined a character called Harry who was apparently dead and then suddenly resurrected. It would appear that many other elements in the story were provided by Smollett, who had returned to Vienna after World War II and served as Greene's tourist guide. Smollett told Greene about a scandal involving diluted antibiotics at a local children's hospital. He was also likely the source for using the city's sewers as an important location in the movie's plot.

Greene almost certainly learned of how Smollett and Philby, in their younger days, had joined together as members of a communist front organization called the Committee for Aiding Refugees from Fascism. The two had chaperoned escaping socialists through Vienna's relatively civilized, capacious, and accessible sewer system. Greene carefully translated these real and murky strands into his fictional screenplay. The movie also included an artfully conceived "special thanks" to the Austrian spy: One of the scenes in *The Third Man* takes place at a bar called Smolka, H.P.'s birth name.

———

As the film proceeds, Holly Martins inevitably becomes smitten with Anna Schmidt. He's rebuffed with a polished contemptuousness. The brush-off is a detour. The key relationship in the film is a friendship steadily sundered, especially after the third-act discovery that Harry, played by Orson Welles, is alive. On a desolate winter night, while hiding in a tall, darkened doorway, Lime is suddenly revealed when a window on the opposite side of the street is thrown open and a shock of light unmasks him. Discovered, Welles's Lime greets us with an impish smile. In his ten minutes of screen time, Welles rapidly shades and deepens Harry Lime into one of the Cold War's quintessential film villains. Welles's Lime is loathsome. But he's also charming, cocksure, and worldly. We're captivated, even as Lime proves to be irredeemable, prepared to sacrifice anyone to avoid capture.

Holly and Harry have a climactic conversation while riding a Ferris wheel. Glimpsing at the city below, Holly inquires about those who thought they were going to be saved by Lime's phony penicillin:

HOLLY: Have you ever seen any of your victims?
HARRY: ... Victims? Don't be melodramatic. Look down there. Tell me. Would you really feel any pity if one of those dots stopped

moving forever? If I offered you twenty thousand pounds for every dot that stopped, would you really, old man, tell me to keep my money, or would you calculate how many dots you could afford to spare? Free of income tax, old man. Free of income tax—the only way you can save money nowadays.

Harry's departing words, the most quoted lines in the film, were written not by Greene but Welles:

HARRY: Don't be so gloomy. After all it's not that awful. Like the fella says, in Italy for thirty years under the Borgias they had warfare, terror, murder, and bloodshed, but they produced Michelangelo, Leonardo da Vinci, and the Renaissance. In Switzerland they had brotherly love—they had five hundred years of democracy and peace, and what did that produce? The cuckoo clock.

"While most noir films are about betrayal, *The Third Man* is one of the few that lays that betrayal at the feet of an old and dear friend and not a woman," Madeline Ashby wrote on the culture site Tor .com. "Stories about conniving femme fatales, like *Double Indemnity* or *The Postman Always Rings Twice*, are easy to tell....But *The Third Man* gets at the unspoken core of male friendship and pries the lid off the dishonesty that occurs when one person is carefully, tactically blind to the flaws of another."

CHAPTER 13

INSANE ERA

By the time he was twenty-five years old, Howard Hughes had already made an Oscar-winning film, *Two Arabian Nights* (1927). Three years later, in *Hell's Angels*—a tribute to World War I combat pilots—Hughes dazzled theatergoers with astonishing aerial photography. He had designed the dogfights himself and directed them airborne, by radio. When his pilots balked at an especially dangerous scene, Hughes switched from the director's seat to the cockpit and, predictably, crashed his plane, requiring facial surgery.

Hell's Angels was a critical and financial success, earning $8 million—the equivalent of about $120 million today. Hughes had two more hits with *The Front Page* (1931), a screwball comedy of newspaper life based on the Broadway play by Ben Hecht and Charles MacArthur, and *Scarface* (1932), a thinly veiled version of the life of Al Capone and his Chicago mob, directed by the esteemed Howard Hawks. Various censorship entities had found the screening cut of *Scarface* immensely objectionable, due to a liberal amount of bloodshed and overtones of incest. Hughes, a gifted manipulator of public opinion, successfully fought back, calling these entities "self-styled guardians" who were "a serious threat to the freedom of honest expression."

Hughes had inherited a lifetime fountain of liquidity from his father, who patented a revolutionary bit for oil drilling that could bore through solid rock. This invention was the basis for the formation of the eternally profitable Houston-based Hughes Tool Company. When Howard Hughes Sr. died in 1923, Junior was only eighteen years old, but he took over ownership of Hughes Tool, which made him instantly a millionaire. Hollywood immediately beckoned.

In their biography of Hughes, Donald L. Barlett and James B. Steele write, "Hughes cast himself into a life-role that he was ill-equipped to play. On the one hand he aspired to greatness. But on the other, as one who hated to make decisions, who lived in fear of making a mistake, who agonized over options to the point of exhaustion, he did not have the mental and emotional toughness necessary to survive in his chosen areas."

Attempting to be a legend in his own lifetime, Hughes sensibly determined that he could make a quick splash in the sexy worlds of movies and aviation. In 1935, as was his habit, he courted disaster in the air. Hughes set a world airspeed record of 352 miles per hour in his H-1 racer while willfully oblivious to his gas gauge. The plane conked out, but he was able to make a serviceable landing in a beet field. In 1938, Hughes flew around the world in a record three days and nineteen hours and, after landing in New York, received a ticker tape parade attended by a million people. He had become legendary by age thirty-three.

What mostly followed, however, were gargantuan failures. Counterbalancing this record, his very able public relations machine made sure that in large measure the media kept printing the legend for the rest of his life.

As World War II began, Hughes said he would build a seven-hundred-passenger flying boat called the Hercules—nicknamed the "Spruce Goose." It was meant to be an alternative to transporting troops and armaments by ships, which were highly vulnerable to German U-boats. Only one example was completed, and it wasn't capable of sustained flight. Hughes also told the Air Force he could mass produce photoreconnaissance planes, but the war ended before he had finished even one.

On July 7, 1946, Hughes was piloting a prototype of the XF-11, the high-speed twin-engine spy plane he had been promising the Air Force. The plane experienced engine failure and crashed into a Beverly Hills neighborhood, slicing through the roof of a home and breaking apart on impact, littering a lawn with chunks of twisted metal. Newsreel viewers saw black-and-white imagery of the scattered wreckage. The only person injured was Hughes. He had a lacerated scalp, a broken nose, his collarbone had been crushed, his ribs were cracked, one lung had collapsed, his heart was moved to the right side of his chest cavity, and he had numerous third-degree burns. Hughes was still young at the time, in his early forties, but following the crash he was irretrievably broken, beginning a steady decline, beyond the capacity to even ask for the psychiatric help he had always needed, now ever more desperately so.

During his recovery, Hughes became addicted to Valium, Demerol, and codeine. He was left with lasting nerve damage. Eventually, he remained nude on most days. It has been theorized that even wearing clothes may have been painful to him. Already beset by a raging case of obsessive-compulsive disorder and a militant germophobe, Hughes eventually vanished altogether from public view and began a vagabond existence hiding in the biggest rooms on the top floors of various hotels around the world. As Barlett and Steele note in their biography, he would create "his own asylum." He let his hair, fingernails, and toenails grow for months, refused to bathe, urinated in jars, and lived in mortal fear of infection. Doors and windows had to be sealed with masking tape. Papers or objects handed to him had to be wrapped in layers of Kleenex. Layers of paper towels were used to "insulate" his bed, chairs, and bathroom floors. Though impossibly moody, incredibly capricious, terribly malnourished, and eventually a complete shut-in—called eccentric, but more accurately psychotic—Hughes nonetheless was relatively coherent often enough to regularly insert himself into the ongoing Cold War narrative.

When Hughes took over RKO Pictures in 1948, the studio ranked third in total receipts behind MGM and 20th Century Fox. RKO had been the home of such film treasures as *King Kong*, *Citizen Kane*, and *Notorious*. But in the three years following its purchase by Hughes, during what the authors of *The RKO Story* would call "the most insane era in the company's history," this Hollywood mainstay—one of the "Big Five" production shops—would be run into the ground. The gutting of RKO would also coincide with Hughes becoming a very outspoken anticommunist.

Many who knew Hughes doubted he had any ideology. One associate said he was apolitical and "cared nothing about candidates or issues—unless they had some effect on Howard Hughes." He never voted, and in all likelihood used anticommunism as a convenient distraction. Mary McCall Jr., at the time the president of the Screen Writers Guild, said, "Howard Hughes [threw] a mantle of Americanism over his own ragged production record."

One of his first projects was highly personal. It was a bid to re-create the wow factor achieved by *Hell's Angels*. Hughes acquired the rights to a story called *Jet Pilot* and signed John Wayne, one of Hollywood's most outspoken anticommunists, to play the pilot who chases a female character who checks all the Cold War boxes as (a) a fellow test pilot, (b) a Soviet, and (c) a spy. While Hughes obsessively waited for the cloud patterns he desired, a repeat of the demand he made during the filming of *Hell's Angels*, production was repeatedly delayed, 150,000 feet of film was shot (about twenty-five hours), and *Jet Pilot* wasn't released until 1957. Wayne had aged a decade during the shooting, turning fifty, and most of the aerial sequences had to be cut because the planes used in the film were so clearly obsolete. *Jet Pilot* lost millions. A critic called it "silly and sorry."

In RKO's originally titled *I Married a Communist*, "society girl"

Nan Lowry unwittingly marries a secret communist, shipping executive Brad Collins. The plot thickens when Brad is pressed by the party to use his job at the docks as a cover to commit acts of sabotage. In an effort to exploit the temperature of the late 1940s, Hughes considered having the film introduced by Elizabeth Bentley, "the Red Spy Queen," who had turned informant and during the HUAC hearings was fingering other alleged U.S.-based spies. In the same vein, Hughes asked J. Edgar Hoover for permission to use newsreel footage of the FBI director saying, "I hate communism because it is the enemy of all liberty, all religion, and all humanity." Hoover said no.

When *I Married a Communist* began shooting, Hughes screened all the footage and supplied a stream of notes. He was dissatisfied with two kissing sequences, noticed something on the nose of an actress, and thought two of the actors needed to be sent to a target range because they flinched when they shot their guns. A fan of explicit violence, Hughes also wanted a real actual person to be used in a scene where a Communist Party member is tossed off a wharf. Actor Paul Lukas was signed to play the lead, paid $50,000, and not used. One RKO veteran said that working for Hughes was like "taking the ball in the football game and running four feet only to find the coach was tackling you from behind."

Audience Research Inc., used by RKO to calculate "the national want to see" of upcoming films, reported a lukewarm rating for *I Married a Communist*. Preview audiences told RKO that the picture was mediocre. First released only in Los Angeles and San Francisco, the film grossed about 50 percent below average. The notion that Hughes was using anticommunism only when it suited his purposes is supported by what happened next. On October 14, 1949, he announced a delay in the national release, a search began for a new title, and on January 16, 1950, *I Married a Communist* became *The Woman on Pier 13*. However, the film remained, as Daniel Leab writes, "crude, lewd, simplistic, and formulaic." It lost an estimated $700,000.

In 1951, RKO hired Paul Jarrico to write the screenplay for *The Las Vegas Story*, in which Jane Russell was to play a sultry nightclub singer whose life is at a crossroads. On March 23, 1951, before completing all the work on the script, Jarrico was subpoenaed to testify at the second round of HUAC hearings on subversion in Hollywood. His Communist Party membership had been revealed to the HUAC by his cowriter on *Song of Russia*, Richard Collins, a fellow party member. Hughes fired Jarrico immediately and barred him from the studio.

On April 12, 1951, in Washington, Jarrico invoked the Fifth Amendment when asked at the hearings if he was ever a member of the Communist Party. He took the Fifth because of the experience of the "Hollywood Ten," who, by refusing to answer on First Amendment grounds, left themselves open to contempt of Congress charges. Asked if he would help uncover anyone who was "subversive in their attitude toward the constitutional form of government in our nation," Jarrico replied that he considered the Committee on Un-American Activities to be one such subversive organization. When California Democrat Clyde Doyle asked Jarrico if he had any suggestions for legislation to help the committee be more effective in finding subversives, Jarrico said to Doyle, "You might revise your guide to subversive organizations and publications issued by this committee. It includes, for instance, the Hollywood Democratic Committee, and, without wishing to embarrass you, Congressman Doyle, perhaps you remember that that committee contributed to your campaign and wrote speeches for your campaign. It is listed here as a subversive organization."

Ten months later, a gala premiere was held for *The Las Vegas Story*, in Las Vegas. As the credits rolled, Jarrico's name was missing, as Hughes had commanded. Since the final script had used a substantial amount of Jarrico's work, the Screen Writers Guild objected. As per the agreement between the guild and the studios, the issue went to arbitration. Hughes intensified the battle. On March 17, 1952, he filed a lawsuit in Los Angeles Superior Court claiming Jarrico had violated the standard morals clause in his contract by refusing to answer the HUAC's questions. Hughes also announced that he would ignore the result of any arbitration.

Hedda Hopper, Hearst's influential Hollywood gossip columnist, immediately lined up to support the hardball tactics of the RKO studio chief. In the lead of her next column, she wrote, "I applaud the stand of Howard Hughes in his refusing to submit to any more pressure from Paul Jarrico or any other sympathizer of the Communist creed.... I have said for many years, let's stand up and fight instead of coddling them, let's clean them out... let's get rid of every one of them. One rotten apple in the barrel can affect the other apples." The *Los Angeles Times* praised Hughes for "showing a spirit too seldom exhibited in Hollywood." Richard Nixon—who by this point had artfully maximized his anticommunist zeal to win a Senate seat— said Hughes had "shown the way for all industry to stamp out subversion and reaffirm the principles of American free enterprise."

As the Screen Writers Guild contemplated a strike against RKO, Hughes taunted them openly in a statement: "My determination that I will not yield to Jarrico or anyone else guilty of this conduct is based on principle, belief and conscience.... All I want is a simple answer to a simple question: Are you going to strike or aren't you?"

Hughes continued to drive the news cycle, even if it meant sending his film studio over a cliff. He told a Hearst columnist that it was necessary to have "everyone in a creative position or executive capacity" screened for communist sympathies. While this screening was taking place, Hughes said it would be necessary to suspend production "until the Communism problem is solved." With the studio effectively shut down, he decided to lay off a hundred RKO employees.

Although Hughes was now rarely making public appearances, he agreed to be honored by American Legion Post 43, where he gave a speech claiming that "there were a substantial number of people in the motion picture industry who follow the Communist Party line." He left his cocoon again to testify in his case against Jarrico. Superior Court judge Orlando Rhodes ruled that anyone taking the Fifth Amendment when asked about communism was disgraceful and therefore no other contractual rights mattered. The judge also dismissed a $350,000 damage suit Jarrico had filed against Hughes.

As all this was taking place, RKO was in free fall. It lost $10,178,003 in 1952, which brought the cumulative losses in the four years of Hughes's control to $22,324,538, a stunning total and testimony to his relentlessly horrific management. Next, an attempt by Hughes to sell the studio turned into a gigantic scandal.

A deal had been made with what turned out to be an outrageously corrupt syndicate headed by a sleazy Chicago businessman named Ralph E. Stolkin. Not long after Stolkin's group signed an agreement of sale in Hughes's bungalow at the Beverly Hills Hotel, on September 23, 1952, the *Wall Street Journal* informed the world that Stolkin and his associates had been selling fraudulent mail-order games, called punchboards, which promised prizes to winners that were rarely or never delivered. The *Journal* cited Better Business Bureau reports in which parents told of their children being cheated by the scam. The paper also looked at the books of a Stolkin-run charity called the National Kids' Day Foundation. The charity had raised $650,626.50, but administrative costs were $652,585.32. The *Journal* did the math before its readers had to: "The public had chipped in nearly two-thirds of a million dollars, but the foundation appeared $1,958.82 poorer."

The sale to the Stolkin group went poof. Hughes wouldn't be able to get rid of RKO Pictures until 1955, when General Tire and Rubber Company agreed to make the largest cash purchase in Hollywood history: $25 million. Production at RKO ceased altogether in 1957.

As Hughes cashed out of the movie business, he also removed himself from any further role in the Cold War military-industrial complex. In 1955, the Internal Revenue Service had denied him tax-exempt status for the Howard Hughes Medical Institute (HHMI), a bogus charity born of a fantastical press release that was a hysterically obvious multimillion-dollar tax dodge. But following a $205,000 loan made by Hughes to Donald Nixon, brother of the then vice president, the IRS had a change of heart. As a result of the byzantine maneuvering concocting the charity, the Hughes Aircraft Company was "donated" to the new medical institute, which severed the weapons-making arm of Hughes's empire from his personal portfolio.

Absent any regular input from its maniacal namesake, Hughes Aircraft began to soar, becoming one of the nation's top ten defense contractors, eventually employing the largest workforce in California (peaking at eighty-four thousand) and reliably earning billions. The company supplied surveillance systems for the North American Aerospace Defense Command (NORAD), the multilayered early warning system against Soviet attack, established in 1957, and also developed guided missiles, communications satellites, the first laser, and, in 1966, the first U.S. spacecraft to achieve a soft landing on the moon, Surveyor 1.

———

As the workaround for his self-imposed seclusion, Hughes hired a front man, Robert Maheu, who ran an independent investigation agency. One of Maheu's clients was the CIA, which hired him for cutout jobs—missions involving illegal activity that were best handled by people not directly affiliated with the U.S. government. Maheu's first assignment for the world's richest recluse was spying on movie star Ava Gardner, who'd had a tempestuous relationship with Hughes, including a brawl during which Gardner's jaw was dislocated and she knocked him out cold with an ashtray.

More than two decades after Gardner's death, more details about the incident emerged in a 2013 book by Peter Evans, *Ava Gardner:*

The Secret Conversations. Fearing she'd killed Hughes that night, with blood on the walls and the furniture, the actress made a panicked call. "[MGM boss] Louis Mayer nearly had kittens," Gardner told Evans. "He was convinced I'd whacked the bastard. His boys got me out of there so fucking fast, my feet didn't touch the Orientals." After the knockout, and suitably recovered, Hughes proposed. Gardner said no thanks—but she then became one of many ex-girlfriends he routinely surveilled, another perverse compulsion.

Hughes was soon a complete hermit, stuck in a nest atop the Desert Inn in Las Vegas, curtains drawn shut, his six-foot-one body dwindling to a hundred pounds. In addition to his unaddressed psychological issues and long-standing addiction to painkillers, Hughes was battling the effects of tooth decay, hearing loss, arthritis, constipation, and hemorrhoids. Although Maheu only communicated with him by phone and they never met in person, he nonetheless assisted Hughes with a never-ending torrent of wheeling and dealing— acquiring gold and silver mines, a regional airline, and a fifth of the real estate in Las Vegas, including a half dozen "mobbed up" hotels on the Strip. Maheu also arranged for the purchase of the local Las Vegas TV station, KLAS, so Hughes could dictate which of his favorite films should be programmed.

"We knew when Hughes was in town," wrote singer and songwriter Paul Anka, one of the first pop stars to perform at the Las Vegas casinos. "You'd get back to your room, turn on the TV at 2 a.m. and the movie *Ice Station Zebra* would be playing. At 5 a.m., it would start all over again. It was on almost every night. Hughes loved that movie."

The film was a Cold War thriller starring Rock Hudson that was based on the real story of an experimental satellite that went missing in the Arctic. It was estimated Hughes watched *Ice Station Zebra* 150 times.

CHAPTER 14

IMPOSSIBLE MISSIONS

On September 17, 1966, at 9 p.m., CBS introduced *Mission: Impossible*. Before Peter Graves took over as mission leader, in seasons two through seven, the role was first played by Steven Hill, as Dan Briggs. In the cold open of the pilot, we meet Briggs exiting the freight elevator of a nondescript warehouse. Stepping into a small office, he asks for a particular classical recording—the code for the warehouse supervisor to dip into a desk drawer and produce a box with a vinyl record. Briggs is left alone and sits down at an inexpensive phonograph, opens a vacuum-sealed plastic envelope containing the customized record, and places it on the turntable. He hears an authoritative male voice: "Mr. Briggs, your mission, should you choose to accept it…" The recording concludes with these words: "As always, should you or any member of your IM Force be caught or killed, the Secretary will disavow any knowledge of your actions."

On June 18, 1948, under national security memorandum NSC 10/2, an actual Mission: Impossible operation was created. By intention, it had a vanilla name that no TV producer would ever entertain. America's impossible mission force was called the Office of Policy Coordination, or OPC. The man in charge was thirty-nine-year-old Wall Street lawyer turned spy Frank Wisner, who, becoming ever more roundish from an appreciation of fine wines and martinis, was not exactly leading man material.

Wisner was from a wealthy Mississippi family, and spoke in the verbose and oracular fashion of a southern patrician, the kind one might find in the stories of Truman Capote and the plays of Tennessee Williams. His family ran a lumber yard in the town of Laurel and was known for their generosity, building the local schools, churches, parks, bank, museum, golf course, and cemetery. The Wisners had no plantation roots and were known to have enlightened views about their African American neighbors. The family thought of themselves as being from Mississippi, but not *Mississippian*.

However, Wisner's childhood bore no resemblance to the down-and-dirty, ragtag world of Hal Roach's popular delinquents, *The Little Rascals*. A maid dressed him every morning. Small and sickly, he lifted weights like his hero Teddy Roosevelt. As a rule, if he was in motion he was running. He became fiercely competitive at every game he played. Chivalry was celebrated when he was a student at the Woodberry Forest School, in Orange, Virginia. This was the school prayer: "Give me clean hands, clean words, and clean thoughts. Help me stand for the hard right against the easy wrong."

At the University of Virginia, he was tapped for a Dixie version of Yale's Skull and Bones called the Seven Society, which by tradition did not reveal the names of its members until after their deaths. A terrific sprinter and hurdler, Wisner was eligible to compete at the U.S. Olympic Trials before the 1936 Berlin Games. His father vetoed the opportunity. He wanted his son to work a "character-building job" at a Coca-Cola bottling plant. At Carter, Ledyard & Milburn, FDR's old law firm, he became deeply irritated with the condescension served up by the snotty Ivy League old boys network.

In 1944, at age thirty-five, after a stint as a censor with the U.S. Navy, Wisner became the new OSS station chief in Bucharest, Romania. He requisitioned the thirty-room mansion of a beer baron, built a spy network, and, as the Nazi puppet regime fled the advancing Red Army, was instrumental in putting Romania's twenty-three-year-old King Michael in charge of the government, a move that was well received inside the country. The king's advisors were so young, they were known as "the Nursery." On August 29, 1944, with the Wehrmacht and Luftwaffe still in the vicinity, Wisner and King Michael arranged for seventeen hundred American prisoners to be liberated from nearby Nazi camps and flown out of Bucharest, using twelve B-17s.

When Wisner went to his first party with the Russians, he was told to coat his stomach with olive oil for the vodka toasts. He often visited the king and the queen mother at their castle. He was known for his dancing, his magic tricks, and his skill at backgammon. Some members of his unit, exhausted by the partying, moved out of the beer baron's mansion to a quieter location. One reported, "Eating, working, sleeping, drinking, and loving other men's wives all under one roof while husbands and enlisted men were around was just a bit too much for some of us."

On January 6, 1945, with British and U.S. armies still far to the west, Joseph Stalin began ethnic cleansing in Romania. He ordered the Red Army to round up all young adults of German ethnic origin, regardless of citizenship. Men aged seventeen to forty-five and women eighteen to thirty were to be deported to the Soviet Union and mobilized for work. In *The Very Best Men*, Evan Thomas writes about the appalling scene: "Wisner knew many of these *Volksdeutsche* from Princess Caradja's soirees.... The desperate wife of her architect called him in the middle of the night. They were taking away her husband....He drove around the city in his jeep, personally trying to stop Russian soldiers from pulling Romanians from their beds.... But Wisner was unable to save the architect; by the time [he] arrived at the train station, the man had already vanished, like thousands of others. Wisner could only watch as the Romanians, weeping and begging for help, were herded onto boxcars."

Wisner's agents had penetrated the Romanian Communist Party. This allowed him to read cables from Moscow and learn that Stalin was ordering his Red Army commanders to impose a "broad democratic basis" on all of Eastern Europe. He reported this information to Washington. He also reported that the Soviets had permitted two trapped Nazi divisions to escape in order to attack American units fighting in the Battle of the Bulge.

"He was in a state of anger that seemed to go beyond the normal frustrations of the job," said James Jesus Angleton, a close colleague at the CIA. "What Frank witnessed out there made him a vehement anti-Communist. It really affected him."

———

Under the OPC's secret charter, which Wisner kept locked in his office safe, the essential mission was "countering the vicious covert activities of the USSR." This would be done with imitative covert operations "in threatened countries of the free world," actions that were broadly defined and included the use of propaganda, economic warfare, sabotage, demolitions, evacuations, subversive campaigns against hostile states, and assistance to underground resistance groups and indigenous anticommunist elements. The missions were to be planned and conducted so that "any U.S. government responsibility for them is not evident to unauthorized persons and that if uncovered, the U.S. government can plausibly disclaim any responsibility for them." One of the people who worked for Wisner summarized NSC 10/2 this way: "They do it, and therefore we have to do it, too."

George Kennan, back in the United States and in a senior role at the State Department, was the first to suggest a "Mission: Impossible" team, or what he called a "guerrilla warfare corps" that would "fight fire with fire." It was another brainstorm he'd come to regret as ill-conceived American-sponsored guerrilla actions sprouted like weeds across the world. Secretary of State George Marshall was also a booster, which is why Wisner found himself with access to stacks of cash when the OPC went into action. The generous funding was a clandestine codicil of the Marshall Plan, which directed that 5 percent of the allotted $13.7 billion would be used for intelligence work and political warfare. As for oversight, Wisner had none. The

OPC was attached to the CIA, but only for administrative support—housing and salaries.

Wisner's goal was as maniacal as his work pace. The purpose of his OPC was to do nothing less than free Eastern Europe of Soviet domination, and he was prepared to surrender virtually every waking hour to bring this to fruition, a regimen he expected everyone around him to emulate. Given Wisner's zealous and obsessive nature, one of his closest colleagues expected the job would eventually kill him. It did.

The OPC's operations were secret, and the OPC itself was secret. According to James McCargar, one of Wisner's first hires, the agency "was the most secret thing in the U.S. government after nuclear weapons." Wrote Tim Weiner in *Legacy of Ashes*, "The CIA's stated mission had been to provide the President with secret information essential to the national security of the United States. But Wisner had no patience for espionage, no time for sifting and weighing secrets. Far easier to plot a coup or pay off a politician than to penetrate the Politburo—and for Wisner, far more urgent."

Wisner focused first on recruiting in occupied Germany, where there were some seven hundred thousand displaced persons still living in camps. Many had worn a German uniform, fought against the Soviets, and despised communism. A portion had certainly committed war crimes. They were Albanians, Ukrainians, Czechs, Poles, Hungarians, Romanians, and even disgruntled Russians. Wisner had hoped to create an elite unit of shock troops who could penetrate the Iron Curtain and activate resistance. According to Weiner, Wisner had hopes of identifying a thousand suitable candidates, but at first found only seventeen.

A steady stream of failures didn't discourage him, or force him to reevaluate why they happened. His method was as heedlessly scattershot as the new splatter of abstract expressionism Jackson Pollock was producing contemporaneously inside an East Hampton cottage. In addition to recruiting anticommunist insurgents, Wisner was hatching schemes to subvert the Soviet economy by counterfeiting money and manipulating markets. Expecting to ignite multiple mutinies and revolutions, he started stockpiling arms in secret caches all over Europe and the Middle East. The Air Force asked him to steal a Soviet fighter, preferably with the pilot, and sabotage every military runway in the USSR. No problem, said Wisner.

He began building a multinational media conglomerate for propaganda with a panoply of fronts. All of sudden, the best of American culture was being touted by a Congress for Cultural Freedom and a high-minded monthly magazine called *Encounter*. Perhaps the most successful scheme of them all was the establishment of round-the-clock anticommunist radio stations. Wisner was the executive producer of Radio Free Europe (targeted to Eastern Europe), Radio Liberty (for Soviet consumption), and the Voice of America (which transmitted worldwide).

No American ambassador—or covert operative—may have been more effective or more popular than VOA DJ Willis Conover, host of a daily show called *Voice of America Jazz Hour* and known for his soothing deep voice and unhurried delivery. Conover's show religiously began with the opening notes of Duke Ellington's "Take the A Train." At its peak, the *Jazz Hour* had thirty million daily listeners.

When he was in the Czech army, Jan Zappner, later a jazz accordion player, navigated a clandestine route to hear Conover. "Private radios were not allowed," he'd explain, "so every night at ten o'clock, I sneaked through the toilet window into the communications building, where there was a shortwave radio on which I tuned in the *Voice of America*.... There it was, 'The A Train,' and the great voice of Willis Conover. I will never forget that feeling of sweet conspiracy. While the barracks, the country, indeed, the whole socialist camp was asleep, I...found out that over the trenches of the Cold War there was normal life, with great music."

Wisner created a front group ostensibly to raise money for Radio Free Europe. It was called the National Committee for a Free Europe and each year it ran a fund-raising campaign in the United States called the Crusade for Freedom. "Advertisements appeared on every TV network, on radio stations across the country and in hundreds of newspapers," wrote historian Kenneth Osgood. "The campaign may have been the largest and most consistent source of political advertising in American history. Every president from Harry Truman to Richard Nixon endorsed the campaign. So did hundreds of governors, mayors, celebrities, editors and executives."

Donations were even solicited by newspaper delivery boys, and media kingpins became willing co-conspirators to ensure message saturation. The value of the TV advertising provided free of charge was in the billions. One of the spots, scored with ominous music, showed a map of Europe split in half. On the western portion, a giant transmitter can be seen sending beams eastward over the half stamped with a giant hammer and sickle. In another ad, the Drifters singing "On Broadway" was the hip music used to introduce a Hungarian refugee hosting a pop music show. The spot ended with this tag: "For uncensored news and music, millions of East Europeans switch on Radio Free Europe, the in sound from outside." Typically, the annual appeal would raise about a million dollars, which was $29 million short of what it cost to keep the station on the air. But fund-raising was never the point.

"Declassified documents," Osgood wrote, "reveal that almost from the start, the CIA saw that it could exploit the fund-raising campaign as a conduit for domestic propaganda. It was a way to rally public support for the Cold War by dramatizing Communist repression and stoking fears of a worldwide menace. The plight of Eastern Europe brought moral clarity to the Cold War, and it cemented the region as a vital national interest in American domestic politics."

Wisner used Howard Hunt—later embroiled in the Watergate break-in—to secure the film rights to *Animal Farm* from Orwell's widow, Sonia, who had married the author just months before his death. Thinking she was dealing with Hollywood producers, Sonia said yes, provided a meeting could be arranged with Clark Gable.

In 1951, the CIA backed the production of a lavish animated version of *Animal Farm*, which employed eighty cartoonists. It wasn't a faithful adaptation. Orwell's book concludes with the animals outside the house watching forlornly as the pigs are playing cards with the humans—Bolsheviks indistinguishable from capitalists. In the CIA version, there are no humans mixing with pigs at the end of the tale, and the animals mount a counterrevolution by storming the farmhouse. The communists lose! "The great enemy of propaganda," wrote Louis Menand of Orwell, "was subjected, after his death, to the deceptions and evasions of propaganda—and by the very people, American Cold Warriors, who would canonize him as the great enemy of propaganda."

———

Wisner's OPC staffed up at lightning speed. Professors and coaches at Harvard, Yale, and Princeton were paid to spot prospective agents. Within a year, a staff of ten had become five hundred. Within three years, there were several thousand employees, manning forty-seven overseas stations.

One of the early covert military operations involved a resurrected World War II German force that the Nazis had named the Bataillon Ukrainische Gruppe Nachtigall, or the Ukrainian Nightingale Battalion. These were volunteer Ukrainian nationalists who had been part of a decades-long underground insurgency, based in the Carpathian Mountains, which had managed to regularly mount terrorist operations against the Soviets. In his memoir, Nikita Khrushchev noted that when he was Stalin's top lieutenant in Ukraine, the Carpathian alpine forests were "literally out of bounds for us" because "from behind every tree, at every turn of the road" there lurked an attack.

As the Nazis retreated, some members of the Nightingale Battalion went with them to Germany. Wisner located these fighters in refugee camps, and hatched a plan to have them parachuted back into Ukraine in order to supplement the ongoing anti-Soviet resistance with sabotage and assassination. Wisner was not dissuaded by the general profile of Nightingale Battalion members. The majority were homicidal anti-Semitic Fascists who had been implicated in the mass murder of Jews and the execution of families associated with the Red Army. One intelligence officer noted yet another example of the ongoing Cold War cognitive dissonance: As one wing of the CIA was identifying Ukrainian Nazis for the Nuremberg trials, another wing was trying to recruit them.

According to an unclassified CIA report, "[The agency] had few methods of collecting intelligence on the Soviet Union, and felt compelled to exploit every opportunity, however slim the possibility of success or unsavory the agent. Émigré groups, even those with dubious pasts, were often the only alternative to doing nothing. So the sometimes brutal war record of many émigré groups became blurred as they became valuable to the CIA."

Starting in 1949, Wisner's Office of Policy Coordination began sending armed Nightingale Battalion operatives into Ukraine. At first, the results seemed encouraging. The men indicated all was well and requested more men, more guns, and more money. But eventually it became clear that these return messages were being sent by the Soviets, who had immediately captured all the operatives and were sending the fake communications to lure more Nightingale commandos to their deaths. "In the long run," a CIA report concluded, "the agency's effort to penetrate the Iron Curtain using Ukrainian agents was ill-fated and tragic."

CHAPTER 15

CHARMING BETRAYAL

During the early portion of the Cold War, the greatest threat to American national security was not from internal communist subversion, the fear that would beget McCarthyism, nor from a Soviet defense establishment said to be prepping for World War III, a scare tactic liberally used by the Republican Party, U.S. generals, and a growing American weapons industry. The greatest danger, as it turned out, emanated from the land of Big Ben, Beefeaters, and good old Winston Churchill. As British-linked physicists were providing the Soviets with a blow-by-blow account of the Manhattan Project, virtually every other consequential U.S. secret was being fed to Moscow by Cambridge's Magnificent Five—the superlative Soviet moles Anthony Blunt, Guy Burgess, John Cairncross, Donald Maclean, and Kim Philby.

None of the five were as dashing as 007, or as vividly evil as a SMERSH villain, but they were nonetheless cinematic, in an arthouse sort of way. Several of the Cambridge-educated lads loved men not women, at least one went both ways, and all teetered at the edge of sanity. As raging drunks in states of breakdown, their alcoholic consumption wasn't a matter of quality but quantity, typically sustained until obliteration, or injury, or both. Given this predilection, none gave a shit whether their martinis were shaken or stirred.

They had all crossed paths at elite and exclusive Cambridge University, which, with Oxford, prepared its students for an almost seamless entry into Britain's ruling establishment. "The violent ideological currents sweeping Cambridge in the 1930s had created a vortex that quickly swept up...clever, angry, alienated young men," Ben Macintyre wrote in *A Spy Among Friends*. "Late at night, over copious drinks, in paneled rooms, young students argued, debated, tried on one ideological outfit or another, and, in a small handful of cases, embraced violent revolution."

Harold "Kim" Philby was the prime mover—the first to take a leap of faith. He was the kind of man capable of entrancing and influencing his peers. Macintyre described his "intoxicating, beguiling" charm: "He looked out at the world with alert, gentle blue eyes from under an unruly forelock. His manners were exceptional: he was always the first to offer you a drink, to ask after your sick mother and remember your children's names. He loved to laugh, and he loved to drink—and to listen, with deep sincerity and rapt curiosity."

While at Cambridge, Guy Burgess was intimately involved with two other members of the "Mag Five"—Anthony Blunt, a budding art historian, and Donald Maclean, the son of Liberal politician Sir Donald Maclean. Blunt was exclusively gay; Maclean was bisexual. Therefore, as Richard Rhodes wrote, "the majority of the group were homosexual or bisexual in a society that branded homosexual acts as felony crimes; sexual orientation contributed to affiliation even as it taught the young conspirators double standards and a double life." The other schoolmate in this quintuplet, John Cairncross, a rangy Scotsman, wasn't gay, but it was Burgess, upon the advice of Blunt, who verbally seduced him into betraying his country.

All the Cambridge kids had the same handler, Arnold Deutsch, an Austrian communist refugee who had to flee Vienna because of his association with a German sexologist who equated sexual repression with Fascist authoritarianism. Deutsch anointed some of the five with German code names: Philby was Söhnchen ("Sonny"); Burgess was Mädchen ("Girl"), in reference to his evident homosexuality; Maclean—donnish, athletic, aloof—was Waise ("Orphan");

Blunt—the art connoisseur—was "Poet"; Cairncross, who had studied at the Sorbonne before coming to Cambridge, was "Molière."

Soon, the Cantabrigians began to seem too good to be true. As Macintyre wrote, "Their very productivity posed a conundrum. In the insanely distrustful world of Soviet espionage, the quality, quantity and consistency of this information rendered it suspect. A misgiving began to take root in Moscow that British intelligence must be mounting an elaborate, multi-layered deception through Philby and his friends; they must all be double agents."

Philby acquired the post that would ultimately be of the greatest value to the USSR. He became head of MI6 counterintelligence—meaning he was in charge of making sure that the British version of the CIA wasn't loaded with Soviet spies like him. As Macintyre concluded, "The fox was not merely guarding the henhouse but building it, running it, assessing its strengths and frailties, and planning its future construction." In the estimation of Robert Cecil, a member of the British Foreign Office, "Philby at one stroke...ensured that the whole post-war effort to counter communist espionage would be known in the Kremlin. The history of espionage records few, if any comparable masterstrokes." Philby's double game was so crafty, he managed to emerge from World War II with enough regard to be tabbed as a possible future head of MI6, the man known as "C," for chief.

———

In September 1945, a senior Soviet intelligence officer in Turkey was ready to defect in return for safe haven in the West, and a payment equivalent today of $500,000. Konstantin Volkov had told British diplomats in Istanbul that he could provide detailed information about the NKVD's Moscow headquarters, and furnish the names of hundreds of Soviet agents, including 250 in Britain. Volkov had specifically mentioned that there was a Soviet agent "fulfilling the functions of the head of a Section of the British Counter-Espionage Service in London"—the post held by Philby.

Frantic about being exposed, Philby rushed to set up a meeting with his Soviet masters in London to report on Volkov's betrayal, and then, after arranging to be the agent tasked with collecting Volkov, conveniently dawdled for days before getting on a plane. By the time he arrived in Istanbul, Moscow had already dispatched operatives to put a sedated and bandaged Volkov—and his sedated and bandaged wife—on a transport back to the USSR, where, shortly, the couple was shot in the Lubyanka basement.

Returning from Turkey empty-handed, Philby suggested that Volkov had betrayed himself—gotten drunk and talked too much, or perhaps simply changed his mind. The head of MI6, Sir Stewart Menzies, the epitome of insular English aristocracy, ruled out an investigation as "impracticable and invidious." Many more people would meet Volkov's fate because, due to the blithering incompetence of MI6, the Magnificent Five fellows weren't caught in 1945, when Philby arranged Volkov's death sentence.

Between 1944 and 1951, the Cambridge conspiracy would also jump the pond. Maclean, Burgess, and Philby were all rotated to the United States, where they provided Moscow with a wonderful bonus—access to some of the most sensitive topics being discussed at the White House, the State Department, the Pentagon, the CIA, the Army signals intelligence unit, and the Atomic Energy Commission. However, the setting for what may have been Philby's finest hours as a Soviet asset was not inside any of those halls of government. Where he truly excelled was at Harvey's Oyster Saloon, the most famous, most exclusive, and most expensive restaurant in Washington, D.C.

From 1949 to 1951, the man who was often sitting across from Harold Kim Philby at Harvey's was James Jesus Angleton of the CIA, who was perfectly suited to be utterly smitten by Philby's act. Angleton had been born in Idaho, raised in Italy, and sent to a prep school in England. While at Malvern College, governed by the dictates of the Victorian era, he acquired a hint of a British accent, a cultivated eccentricity, and a fondness for handmade clothes, strong drinks, and smoky clubs.

After Malvern came Yale, where Angleton ran a literary magazine, wrote unremarkable poetry, and became convinced of the superiority of Western civilization and the irretrievable evil of communism.

Through two recommendations—one from his father, a wealthy businessman with deep ties to the Mafia in Italy, the other from a Yale professor—Angleton secured a wartime assignment with the Ivy-League-laden OSS. The first post was London, where Soviet mole Kim Philby had been asked by the still naïve Americans to provide new recruits with a final stage of grooming in the dark arts of espionage. Off duty, Philby provided Angleton a tutorial in the practice of droll banter and surviving copious alcoholic consumption.

Angleton's star was on the rise after he had successfully run the operation that flooded Italy with enough cash to keep the country from going communist. In May 1949, then thirty-one, he was named head of Staff A of the CIA's Office of Special Operations, responsible for the collection of foreign intelligence and liaison with the CIA's counterpart organizations.

Philby had been stationed in America to more fully introduce himself to the Yanks. This posting appeared to be a logical step in his apparent advance toward the top job in British intelligence. What was logical for Philby the Soviet spy, however, was bamboozling Angleton as regularly as possible.

Lunches between the two at Harvey's became routine. They typically started with bourbon on the rocks, proceeded into lobsters and wine, and concluded with brandy and cigars. Angleton and Philby had by this juncture in their lives trained their bodies to function effectively with blood alcohol levels that would have left others retching or comatose. For Angleton, the food, the booze, and the conversation—shared with a man who was a mentor, a truly proper Englishman, and a member of the small, elite brotherhood of spooks—was the very definition of fun. But during these long boozy lunches, Philby was prying loose many of the CIA's most sensitive topics and plans.

"The privately educated Englishman is the greatest dissembler on Earth," said British spy turned novelist John le Carré. "No one will charm you so glibly, disguise his feelings from you better, cover his tracks more skillfully, or find it harder to confess that he's been a damned fool. No one acts braver when he's frightened stiff or happier when he's miserable. And nobody can flatter you better when he hates you."

After every lunch with Angleton, Philby would file two reports, for two different audiences. The one for MI6 solidified the notion that he was being well received in the United States and taken into the confidence of top U.S. intelligence officials, which was accurate. The other report, for Moscow, was devastating to Western intelligence efforts.

At Harvey's, Angleton updated Philby on the latest activity by Germany's anti-Soviet spy network being run by ex-Nazi Reinhard Gehlen. He told Philby about blueprints for Allied cooperation in the event of war with the Soviet Union. Told him about the CIA's activity in Greece and Turkey; shared the details of covert operations in the Baltics, Iran, and Central America; gabbed about the Nightingale Battalion members being dropped into Ukraine's Carpathian Mountains. Every secret Angleton shared was potentially lethal to far-flung CIA operatives about to infiltrate hostile countries.

Frank Wisner, the king of covert operations at the Office of Policy Coordination, regularly communicated with Angleton, the unwitting missing link to a significant portion of intelligence disasters. As Wisner kept taking the fight to the Soviets, somehow the Soviets kept winning. The Nightingale scheme was a disaster. Money and arms sent to an anticommunist resistance group in Poland was almost immediately intercepted. Wisner flew anticommunist Lithuanians, Estonians, and Armenians into their homelands and all of them rapidly disappeared. In Germany, the NKVD penetrated all the anti-Stalin Soviet exile groups.

Operation Valuable was mounted to spur regime change in small, backward Albania. Angleton provided Philby with every CIA drop zone. All the guerrillas were swiftly located, and for every operative captured, forty relatives were shot or thrown in prison. Show trials were held with captured survivors and milked for maximum propaganda. Between one hundred and two hundred guerrillas died, as did thousands of others linked to the "freedom fighters."

———

Philby's rise in His Majesty's Secret Service was clipped when Burgess and Maclean suddenly vanished in May 1951, ultimately surfacing in Russia. This occurred shortly after American cryptographers had uncovered Maclean's treason. The more clear-eyed proletarians at the FBI assumed that the two men had been tipped off in a rather timely fashion. Their Cambridge confrere Philby, high enough in the food chain to be trusted with America's top secrets, including the super-top-secret VENONA intercepts of Soviet diplomatic traffic, looked to be the most logical tipster.

Philby was rather gently booted from MI6, remained on the loose, and continued to work as a Soviet agent. Fed up with British obliviousness, J. Edgar Hoover would leak damning details about Philby to the press, which would colorfully identify him as the presumed "Third Man" in the defection story of Burgess and Maclean. Even so, the Philby spy saga persisted in a kind of limbo, his treachery never fully resolved, until he jumped on a Soviet freighter out of Beirut in 1963 and left no doubt.

Between embarrassing defection number one (by Mclean and Burgess) and embarrassing defection number two (by Philby), all too many gullible figures in London and Washington couldn't bring themselves to believe that Philby, seen as the ultimate evocation of the English aristocrat, would ever betray his friends, his family, his school, his club, and his queen. These same people also deceived themselves into thinking that no one in their right mind would ever willingly choose communism.

The dastardly deeds of the Cambridge traitors resonated for the remainder of the Cold War. U.S. intelligence had its trust in British intelligence shattered. Repair would require years. American haughtiness didn't help. The British were greatly put off by lectures from the colonial upstarts. "In the U.S. State Department," the Brits were instructed, for example, "repeated drunkenness, recurrent nervous breakdowns, sexual deviations and other human frailties are considered security hazards and persons showing any one or more of them are summarily dismissed."

CIA agent Miles Copeland made this assessment: "What it comes to is, when you look at the whole period from 1944 to 1951, the entire Western intelligence effort, which was pretty big, was what you might call minus advantage. We'd have been better off doing nothing."

Philby's betrayal had an especially profound effect on James Jesus Angleton. Philby had been the kind of man Angleton aspired to be. The depth of the charade was both emotionally and intellectually devastating. Angleton would never again be able to fully trust his assessment of any other human being. This incident became a national security matter in 1954 when the CIA named Angleton head of counterintelligence, in charge of finding moles inside the CIA. He may have been the worst possible person for the job. Burnt so badly by Philby, having surrendered so much in so many lunches at Harvey's, and, for that matter, through all manner of regular contact, Angleton reacted by crippling the CIA with a poisonous paranoia, trusting no one, suspecting everyone, believing in the wildest conspiracies.

In the 1960s, Angleton was deceived yet again when KGB defector Anatoliy Golitsyn, a manipulative conspiracist, successfully sold a series of alternative realities. According to Golitsyn, the Sino–Soviet split in the 1950s and Nikita Khrushchev's proposal for peaceful coexistence with the West were slick KGB disinformation campaigns. He was wrong on both counts. The Chinese had indeed grown to hate the Soviets, and Khrushchev did want détente.

In 1964, when career KGB agent Yuri Nosenko defected to the United States, Golitsyn told Angleton that Nosenko was "a provocateur" on a mission from the KGB to protect a mole inside the CIA. Angleton refused to pay Nosenko a promised $50,000 and ordered him incarcerated at a secret CIA detention facility in southern Maryland. Nosenko would be held in solitary confinement for four years before the CIA overruled Angleton and released him.

"There was never an honest effort at the time to establish NOSENKO's bona fides," CIA Soviet specialist John Hart wrote as part of a 180-page report on the episode, titled *The Monster Plot*. "There was only a determined effort to prove NOSENKO was mala fide, and part of a KGB deception operation meant to mislead the CIA into believing it was not penetrated." As a result of Angleton's incompetence, Hart recommended that the CIA institute more rigorous psychological assessments of defectors.

At different points, Angleton believed that the leaders of Britain, Sweden, and Germany were Soviet operatives. Like Hoover, he illegally spied on perceived enemies, assembling a private collection of ten thousand dossiers. As a way to rationalize being so fully duped by Philby, Angleton put him on an even higher pedestal. Philby, he told others, was the leader of the orchestra, the key player in the KGB's master plan to one day rule the world.

"Angleton is clinically mad," an Italian intelligence officer serving in Washington informed his senior leadership in Rome, "and his madness has only gotten worse.... This is a madness that is all the more dangerous because it is sustained by an intelligence that has about it elements of the monstrous and that rests on a hallucinatory logical construction. The whole is unified by a pride that imposes a refusal to recognize his own errors."

In 1974, CIA director William Colby fired Angleton after the *New York Times* revealed that he had overseen a massive domestic spying program on Americans involved in the antiwar and black nationalist movements, acts illegal under the CIA's charter.

Angleton liked to say the spy trade was "a wilderness of mirrors." He claimed to have invented the phrase, but it's from T. S. Eliot's 1920 poem "Gerontion." The metaphor, Angleton once wrote, accurately expressed the "myriad of stratagems, deceptions, artifices, and all the other devices of disinformation which the Soviet bloc and its coordinated intelligence services use to confuse and split the West... an ever fluid landscape where fact and illusion merge."

Meanwhile, the Russia Philby found when he defected was a pit, a result of what author Ron Rosenbaum called Leonid Brezhnev's "slow-motion Stalinism." According to KGB agent Mikhail Lyubimov, Philby was utterly disillusioned with Soviet reality: "He saw all the defects—the people who are afraid of everything.... That had nothing to do with any Communism or Marxism which he had a perception of...the romantic Marxism of the Comintern agents of the 1930's." Living in a small three-room apartment, deeply distrusted by Russia's knee-jerk paranoid spy culture, which suspected he might be a plant, Philby spent much of the remainder of his days in a crawl toward oblivion loaded on whiskey.

CHAPTER 16

TRAGIC CLIMAX

The first man to hold the title of secretary of defense killed himself on May 22, 1949. The reasons behind the suicide of James Forrestal seem rather clear. His final moments, however, may always be shrouded in mystery.

In the early hours of May 22, a Sunday, Forrestal was awake in his spartan room at Bethesda Naval Hospital, where he had been admitted in early April for the treatment of severe depression. Upon his admittance, news reports had described him as "worn out" and battling "operational fatigue." His room was on the sixteenth floor of the hospital. It had three windows, securely locked, a narrow bed, and an uncomfortable chair. There was an oriental carpet on a dark tile floor, and a rotating fan on the wall. Just before his death, which took place around 2 a.m. on that Sunday, Forrestal was writing on a piece of paper, copying lines of Greek verse from a book titled *The Anthology of World Poetry*.

The verse was from *Ajax*, the ancient Greek tragedy by Sophocles. The play tracks a series of humiliations experienced by one of the greatest Greek fighters in the Trojan War. Ajax's first humiliation occurs when the shield and sword of the dead Achilles—armor made invulnerable by the gods—is awarded by Agamemnon and Menelaus to Odysseus. Enraged, Ajax heads to the tents of the two kings to kill them in their sleep. But he is prevented from doing so when the goddess Athena afflicts him with madness. Deluded, Ajax instead attacks

bulls, rams, and their herdsmen, the spoils of the Trojan War, mistakenly thinking he is taking vengeance on his enemies. Recovering his
sanity, he is ashamed by what he has done and falls on his sword.

The verse Forrestal was copying comes from the lines of the chorus of sailors who underscore how the gods have punished Ajax for
his pride, his rigid code, and his inability to recognize his own weak-
nesses. Forrestal wrote out two complete lines of verse from the chorus, but did not complete the final word of a third line:

> *"Woe, woe!" will be the cry—*
> *No quiet murmur like the tremulous wail*
> *Of the lone bird, the querulous night...*

The lone bird, from the play, is the querulous *nightingale*. Before
completing the line, Forrestal had put the paper back in *The Anthology of World Poetry* and set it aside. He then dismissed the young naval
corpsman assigned to guard his room and went across the corridor to
a small kitchen. He was able to open a window, pulled out a screen,
stepped onto the sill, and leaped.

———

Forrestal's path to success allowed him to enjoy the fizzy, decadent
Jazz Age evoked by fellow Princetonian F. Scott Fitzgerald in *The
Great Gatsby*. Like Jay Gatsby, Forrestal forced his way into privilege.
He was raised in a lower-middle-class Irish Catholic family, not far
from Franklin Roosevelt's home in Hyde Park, New York, became
a Navy aviator in World War I, and rocketed to a partnership at the
investment bank Dillon Read by age thirty-one. He didn't hide his
affluence, buying bespoke suits from London, attending the opera,
and dating debutantes. In 1926, at age thirty-four, he married a tall,
slender, photogenic woman who would gradually lose her mind.

Josephine Ogden was a columnist for *Vogue* when she met James
Forrestal at a cocktail party on Paris's Left Bank. Mr. and Mrs.

Forrestal had a five-story Georgian-style town house in Manhattan, and a thirty-acre estate on the North Shore of Long Island. Mrs. Forrestal soon became known for holding court at the Persian Room of the Plaza Hotel, where she began drinking too much. Hallucinations and paranoia emerged. She never fully regained her health.

In the 1930s, Forrestal played a leading role in brokering an oil deal of gigantic importance. Dillon Read negotiated the merger of Standard Oil of California (Socal) with Texaco, forming Caltex, which in turn negotiated an exclusive sixty-year deal with Saudi Arabian ruler Ibn Saud to explore and exploit the country's substantial oil assets. This was the beginning of what would become the Arabian-American Oil Company (Aramco). The U.S. State Department would later classify Aramco as the richest commercial prize in the history of the planet.

In 1940, as the Nazis occupied France, FDR recruited Forrestal to be an economic advisor. He concluded the war as secretary of the navy, overseeing a fleet that grew from eleven hundred vessels to fifty thousand. When hostilities ceased, Forrestal opposed Harry Truman's draconian postwar budget cutting because he was sure the Soviets were already gearing up to rule the world. His assessment of the communist threat was all too simple and, nonetheless, generally accepted. Forrestal, as Walter Isaacson and Evan Thomas write in *The Wise Men*, "was plagued by neither nuances nor doubts. Marxist-Lenin dogma, treacherous and insidious and evil, was dedicated to the destruction of the capitalist world and would do so unless forcefully checked."

In 1947, Truman insisted that Forrestal accept the mighty task of unifying America's military forces as the very first secretary of defense. As a senator, Truman had overseen military expenditures and was appalled by the waste and inefficiencies created by an Army, Navy, and Air Force operating like warring kingdoms incapable of sharing resources—or even communicating with each other. "We must never fight another war the way we fought the last two," Truman told advisor Clark Clifford. "I have the feeling that if the Army and the Navy fought our enemies as hard as they fought each other, the war would have ended much sooner."

Forrestal not only fought Truman's attempts to trim defense costs, he also vehemently resisted the concept of the services reporting up to one cabinet member. Truman ignored the objections because he had already determined that Forrestal possessed the necessary force of personality and administrative skills to reorganize the Pentagon from top to bottom. Under Forrestal's watch, the U.S. Navy had shone, winning the toughest and most important battles in the war against Japan. Said Clifford, "If Forrestal had remained Secretary of the Navy, he would have made life unbearable for the Secretary of Defense. If, on the other hand, he was the Secretary [of Defense], he would have to try to make the system work."

To no one's surprise, Forrestal became everyone's enemy at the Pentagon, where a bureaucratic civil war immediately erupted. When Truman established a secretary of defense, he also made the Air Force fully independent from the Army. Following liberation, Air Force generals tried to maximize the leverage they'd obtained by having, at the time, the only method of delivering a nuclear weapon: the B-29 bomber. But neither the Army nor the Navy were ready to concede to the Air Force exclusive access to atomic weapons. The Navy already had plans for its own carrier-based nuclear-capable planes. A nasty spat ensued.

On July 17, 1948, Air Force secretary Stuart Symington departed from preapproved remarks in a speech in Los Angeles and criticized Forrestal for supporting the maintenance of aviation wings in the Army and Navy. Forrestal's anger was intensified by a sense of betrayal. Symington had become a good friend, a regular golf and tennis partner. "If the account of your speech in Los Angeles...as reported in *The New York Times*...is accurate, it was an act of official disobedience and personal disloyalty. I shall await your explanation." Accounts differ about what came next. It seems Forrestal was reluctant to fire Symington lest he be accused of anti–Air Force bias. Symington had also been a prominent businessman in Truman's home state of Missouri, running Emerson Electric in St. Louis, and had been tapped to join the administration by Truman himself.

Inside this maelstrom, Forrestal bonded with perhaps the only man in Washington, D.C., who was even more certain that a Soviet attack was imminent: FBI director J. Edgar Hoover. This relationship was not good for Forrestal's teetering health. Hoover seethed with doom. Shortly after taking the top job at the Pentagon, the secretary of defense received a terrifying letter from the FBI director warning about "the smuggling into the United States of an atomic bomb, or parts thereof, which could be later assembled in this country." As Tim Weiner wrote in *Enemies: A History of the FBI*, "Over the next decade [Hoover] issued a steady stream of alerts against the threat of terrorists and spies wielding atomic, biological, and chemical weapons against American cities, a nightmare that still haunts the nation's leaders. Forrestal convened a secret group he called the War Council, comprising the uniformed and civilian chiefs of the American military, to respond to Hoover's alarm."

But the tortures of Forrestal were many. Some were self-inflicted. He fought Truman's support of a new Jewish state in Palestine. As the Arab world reacted with vehement hostility to such a step, Forrestal reminded the president that in World War II, the U.S. Army, Navy, and Air Force relied on cheap Arab oil; by the 1940s, U.S. oil production could no longer meet domestic demand. As part of a tenacious campaign opposing Israel's creation, Forrestal would take his case to Brewster Jennings, the head of Socony-Vacuum Oil Company (later Mobil), telling the businessman he "was deeply concerned with the future supply of oil . . . not merely for the possible use in war but for the needs of peace and unless [the United States] had access to Middle East oil, American motorcar companies would have to design a four-cylinder engine motorcar within the next five years." At the time, the six-cylinder engine was about to be replaced by the V-8, a muscular gas guzzler with marketable masculine appeal.

Truman fully grasped the connection between national security and warm relations with Arab countries, but as the president, he felt compelled—and was determined—to take a much wider and fuller view. Though it was good politics for Democrats to court the Jewish urban vote in the Northeast, there was also overwhelming national support for a Jewish homeland. Above all, the issue had a moral and humanitarian dimension for Truman. As the Arab states claimed it was wrong to make them pay for the crimes of Hitler, the horror of the Holocaust was for Truman sufficient justification to find a safe haven for Jewish refugees. "Everyone else who's been dragged from their country has someplace to go back to," he told Clark Clifford. "But the Jews have no place to go."

Forrestal didn't let up. He told Rhode Island senator J. Howard McGrath that "no group in this country should be permitted to influence our policy to the point it could endanger our national security." To Clifford, Forrestal said, "You just don't understand. There are four hundred thousand Jews and forty million Arabs. Forty million Arabs are going to push four hundred thousand Jews into the sea. And that's all there is to it. Oil—that is the side we ought to be on."

Within the Truman administration, Forrestal had plenty of company for his take on the Palestine question. Virtually all of Truman's top foreign policy advisors, including Secretary of State George Marshall, thought it was a mistake to support a new Jewish state. Wearied by the view, Truman said the situation would be handled in the light of justice, not oil. The state of Israel, backed by the full support of the U.S. government, was proclaimed on May 14, 1948.

As the 1948 election approached, Forrestal secretly met with Republican Tom Dewey to explore the possibility of being retained in a Republican cabinet. Like much of official Washington, he was all but certain Truman wouldn't be reelected. In the meantime, the increasingly lukewarm relationship between the president and his secretary of defense, leavened by rumors of Forrestal conspiring with Dewey, was perfect gossipy fodder for the highly opinionated, completely partisan, vaguely factual, and often libelous columns and radio broadcasts of Walter Winchell and Drew Pearson.

Winchell, who was Jewish and a vocal supporter of Israel, found Forrestal's strident anti-Zionism unforgivable. The liberal Pearson classified the Pentagon chief as a Wall Street tool, a shill for the oil companies, a dangerous warmonger, and, by encouraging the Red Scare, complicit in the ongoing assault on civil rights. Pearson was reported to have told his protégé Jack Anderson that Forrestal was "the most dangerous man in America" and if not removed from office would "cause another world war."

Though rivals, Winchell and Pearson joined forces in a withering and sustained effort to get Forrestal canned. Pearson raised the question of Forrestal's loyalty to Truman by publishing an exposé of the preelection meetings between Forrestal and Republican contender Dewey. Both columnists reminded their readers and radio listeners that Forrestal had been called before the Senate in 1933 to explain a lucrative tax shelter, although there was nothing illegal about what he had done. More hurtful was how Winchell and Pearson twisted the story of a 1937 robbery, claiming that while his wife was being accosted by jewel thieves in front of their Beekman Place home in Manhattan, Forrestal had fled out the back door. The truth was, he had been asleep when the robbery occurred.

Others piled on. A guest on an NBC radio show claimed that the IG Farben works in Frankfurt had not been bombed because Forrestal owned stock in the company. It was a stinging charge. In 1943, Senator Homer Bone had put it simply: "Farben was Hitler and Hitler was Farben." Moreover, as part of the Nuremberg trials, twenty-four IG Farben executives had been charged with "enslavement, plunder and murder" for using slave labor drawn from concentration camps to construct, at the cost of twenty-five thousand lives, a giant complex at Auschwitz, which supplied the German war machine with fuel and synthetic rubber. The company also industrialized its Zyklon B gas for the Nazi extermination program.

In early 1949, close friend Dwight Eisenhower described Forrestal as "looking badly. . . . He gives his mind no recess, and he works
hours that would kill a horse." Forrestal began battling insomnia,
lost his appetite, dropped twenty pounds, looked drawn and aged.
It was noticed at meetings how he unconsciously scratched a patch
of psoriasis on his scalp until it bled. Forrestal began telling friends
his phone was being tapped. He claimed Zionist agents were chasing him, a statement that had a basis in fact. During the very heated
debate over Israel, Washington police had stopped a sedan following
Forrestal's official limousine. The two men in the car told the police
they were photographers employed by a Zionist organization. They
had been tailing Forrestal's limo in the hopes of snapping a photo of
him entering or leaving an Arab embassy.

Forrestal began calling friends at 2 a.m. In long conversations with
Hoover, he brooded about subversion. Truman eventually found his
secretary of defense incapable of making a decision, and on March 2,
1949, he asked for his resignation. At the time, a longtime friend and
Princeton classmate who visited Forrestal at home found him bab-
bling anxiously that his house was wiretapped, strangers were watching him from the street corner, and communists were after him.

Forrestal was admitted to Bethesda Naval Hospital on April
2, 1949. On April 9, during his Sunday radio broadcast, Pearson
reported that Forrestal was experiencing "temporary insanity," had
made three suicide attempts, and been seen rushing into the street
screaming, "The Russians are attacking!" These were all lies.

After Forrestal's suicide, *Time* would accuse both Winchell and
Pearson of "overstepping the bounds of accuracy and decency."
Westbrook Pegler would blame his fellow columnists for Forrestal's
death. The Navy doctor who treated Forrestal, Captain George
Raines, concurred with Pegler. Dr. Raines did not find it coinci-
dental that Forrestal had killed himself on a Sunday, the day both
Winchell and Pearson had their national radio shows. In the *New
York Times*, columnist Arthur Krock asked his readers to consider

what part Winchell and Pearson had played in the "tragic climax" by attacking "Forrestal's official record, his courage, his character, and his motives while he was Secretary of Defense and followed him to the sick room with every fragment of gossip that could nullify the treatment his doctors hoped would restore him."

After Forrestal jumped from the hospital's sixteenth floor, his body landed on a passageway. He died instantly. The news rocked Washington. "Suicide among high-ranking government figures was unknown," David McCullough wrote. "As time went on, and fear of Communist conspiracy spread in Washington, it would be rumored that pages from Forrestal's diary had been secretly removed on orders from the White House—that Forrestal, the most ardent anti-Soviet voice in the administration, had in fact been driven to his death as part of a Communist plot and the evidence destroyed by 'secret Communists' on Truman's staff."

———

In 1999, fifty years after the suicide, Alexander Wooley assessed Forrestal's tragic demise in a piece for the *Washington Post*: "Why would a man about to kill himself copy an ancient Greek poem, but not complete it? Was there any connection between the words he copied and his last, desperate act?" Wooley made reference to speculation that the reason why Forrestal had completed only half of the word *nightingale* related to "the recruitment of members of former Ukrainian death squads, who had worked for the Nazis exterminating Jews and Red Army supporters.... The name of the group was Nachtigall, or Nightingale.... The secret program, which Forrestal almost undoubtedly helped bring about, failed, however." One Forrestal biography suggested that a shock of guilt about the dead Nightingale operatives may have triggered suicide.

But Wooley offered an alternate theory: "Perhaps there is another, less strained connection between Sophocles' verse and Forrestal's tragic end. Perhaps the key was in the verse that immediately followed the one containing the word 'nightingale.'" Wooley speculated that this might have been the verse Forrestal could not bring himself to copy:

Oh! when the pride of Graecia's noblest race
Wanders, as now, in darkness and disgrace,
When Reason's day
Sets rayless—joyless—quenched in cold decay,
Better to die, and sleep
The never-waking sleep, than linger on
And dare to live, when the soul's life is gone.

CHAPTER 17

APPROACHING MIDNIGHT

On August 29, 1949, the Soviets secretly tested their first atomic bomb. That same day, a long-range American reconnaissance plane, which was used to sample the stratosphere, showed an unusually high level of radioactivity. A similar flight two days later confirmed the results. When Truman was told that the Soviets had likely joined the nuclear club, he kept asking, "Are you sure?" He then speculated that captured German scientists must have been responsible. Even as late as 1953, Truman was saying he was not convinced that the Soviets "had the know-how to make an A-bomb work."

On September 23, 1949, the president announced to the nation, "We have evidence an atomic explosion occurred in the USSR." Curtis LeMay said the Soviet bomb, dubbed Joe One, had ended "the era when we might have destroyed Russia completely and not even skinned our elbows doing it." With the Soviets testing their first nuclear device, the *Bulletin of the Atomic Scientists* moved the Doomsday Clock from seven minutes to midnight to three.

"It was really quite a difficult time," *Bulletin* advisor Kennette Benedict recalled. "The Soviet Union and the United States weren't speaking to one another, really, except through their weapons, so it was really a time of great fear on the part of the scientists here. I think many people around the country began to see that we were really headed towards, if not an active war, certainly increasing hostility with the Soviet Union."

On October 1, after the American-backed Chiang Kai-shek and his loyalists fled across the Taiwan Strait, Mao Zedong declared the birth of the People's Republic of China, therefore claiming communist control of about a third of the world's population. Arthur Miller testified to the shock in America: "How could this mucky peasant horde have won fairly and squarely against a real general like Chiang Kai-shek, whose wife, moreover, was the graduate of an American college and so beautiful besides? It could only be that worming their ways through our State Department were concealed traitors who had 'given' the country to the Reds."

On January 13, 1950, the Soviets began a UN boycott after the United States refused to allow the new People's Republic of China to be seated. Rather incredibly, and in defiance of reality, the United States would prevent the PRC—the legitimate government of nearly a billion people—from gaining UN recognition until 1971.

In early 1950, George Kennan wrote a top-secret memo to Truman trying to stop him from endorsing the development of the next generation of nuclear weaponry: a fusion device, or hydrogen bomb. He argued that nuclear weapons simply defied any reasonable use: "They reach backward beyond the frontiers of western civilization, to the concepts of warfare which were once familiar to the Asiatic hordes. They cannot really be reconciled with political purpose directed to shaping, rather than destroying, the lives of the adversary. They fail to take into account the ultimate responsibility of men for one another, and even for each other's errors and mistakes. They imply the admission that man not only can be but is his own worst and most terrible enemy."

Truman was not persuaded. On January 31, 1950, he held a meeting at the White House to discuss pursuing the H-bomb, also known as the Super.

"Can the Russians do it?" he asked.

"Yes, they can," he was told.

"In that case," Truman responded, "we have no choice. We'll go ahead."

The meeting lasted seven minutes.

On April 7, 1950, State Department policy planner Paul Nitze made paranoia about a Soviet invasion official U.S. policy. He authored a confidential National Security Council paper—NSC-68—which, as scholar Ernest May summarized, "provided the blueprint for the militarization of the Cold War from 1950 to the collapse of the Soviet Union in the 1990s."

NSC-68 was raw and biblical, written to please Truman, who, according to an aide, "liked it with the bark off." The document described the Soviets as believers in "a new fanatic faith, antithetical to our own," and warned of an evil Kremlin design for world domination. "The integrity of our system," Nitze wrote, "*will not be jeopardized* by any measures, covert or overt, violent or non-violent, which *serve the purpose of frustrating Kremlin design*, nor does the necessity for conducting ourselves so as to affirm our values in actions as well as words *forbid such measures*" (emphasis added).

NSC-68 justified any and all means of militarization and mayhem if the end result was defeating the mortally dangerous Soviets, an amoral viewpoint that paved the way for embracing dictators and overthrowing foreign governments; motivated a gigantic increase in defense spending; and justified the rapid development of the hydrogen bomb. Kennan's concept of containment was transformed into an excuse to create a military large enough to police the entire world.

Nitze's policy paper truly terrified its readers by warning that the Soviets were quickly headed to clear military superiority and would be tempted to attack the United States in 1954, the year of so-called maximum danger. This was a preposterous fantasy. Joseph Stalin was a megalomaniacal, psychopathic sadist and had killed more people than Hitler, but he was not inherently suicidal.

After the German surrender in 1945, Dwight Eisenhower had seen the reality up close and personal when he traveled to Moscow at the invitation of his fellow commander Marshal Georgy Zhukov. As Eisenhower later recorded, "[Zhukov] told me with the utmost

frankness that the standard of living in Russia today was deplorably
low, and that it was his conviction that even the present standard in
Germany was at least as high as it is in Russia." It's worth emphasizing Zhukov's assessment: *Germany had lost a war during which it was
attacked and bombed from all sides but was still better off than the USSR.*

Two years later, in January 1947, British field marshal Bernard
Montgomery toured the USSR and wrote to Eisenhower, "The
Soviet Union is very, very tired. Devastation in Russia is appalling and
the country is in no fit state to go to war.... It will be 15 to 20 years
before Russia will be able to remedy her various defects and be in a
position to fight a major world war with a good chance of success."

Compounding the misery was famine in Ukraine in 1946 and
again in 1947. The region produced 25 percent of the USSR's agricultural output. Nikita Khrushchev, who was then the top Communist Party official in Ukraine, later recounted an indelible and
shocking scene he had witnessed in postwar Odessa: a woman who
"had the corpse of her own child on the table, and was cutting it up."

"Particularly powerful," wrote Kennan, "seems to have been the
temptation to leap to the conclusion that since the Soviet leaders of
the Stalin period were antagonistic toward us, since they were heav-
ily armed, and since they were seriously challenging our world leadership, they were just like the Nazis of recent memory: they wanted,
and intended, that is, to make war against us."

NSC-68 was the first of many Nitze products that overstated the
strength of the Soviet military. For example, the report claimed that
the Soviets had 175 combat-ready divisions, but as Nitze himself later
admitted, in 1997, it turned out only a third were at full strength,
another third at half strength, and the rest were only skeletal.

In noting that NSC-68 was classified until 1975, and thus its faulty
conclusions never openly debated, Daniel Moynihan wrote, "Policy
planners moved about in a fog of secrecy so thick that they did not
entirely recognize when they had changed directions. Thus, by the
time of the Nixon Administration, the movement from containment

to détente was based on an assumption of the Soviet regime's permanence and power. American government had lost touch with the concept that the Soviet Union was bound to self-destruct in time."

———

In 1945, the then thirty-eight-year-old Nitze—a wealthy former investment banker—had traveled to Japan as vice chairman of the U.S. Strategic Bombing Survey. For Nitze, the moral equation of atomic warfare was a minor consideration and too fuzzy to quantify. "Paul was in one sense like a child," said colleague Kennan. "He was willing to believe only what he could see before him. . . . He loved anything that could be reduced to numbers. He was mesmerized by them. . . . He'd have a pad before him, and when he wrote down the numbers, it was with such passion and intensity that his pen would sometimes drive right through the paper."

The bomb was "not supernatural or incomprehensible," Nitze wrote for the Bombing Survey report. "The effects," he added, "were not infinite, they were finite." In *The Hawk and the Dove*, Nicholas Thompson told of how Nitze "would remember a story of a train passing through Hiroshima when the bomb fell. People sitting near open windows were not cut by flying glass, but they died of radiation exposure. People sitting by closed windows were bloodied by the glass, but protected from the radiation." In Nagasaki, Nitze discovered that residents who reached bomb shelters had survived. "When he returned to New York," Thompson wrote, "Nitze tried to convince the city planner Robert Moses to require bomb shelters in all the new big buildings going up in New York City."

Nitze, however, only told half of the story about atomic destruction. What the world also needed to learn—and what neither Nitze nor the U.S. government wanted to publicize—was that the bomb had two ways of killing: fast and slow. The consequences of radioactive fallout had immediately become a titanic and ongoing disaster in Hiroshima and Nagasaki. In the *Asia-Pacific Journal*, Richard Tanter

portrayed the human costs Nitze's numbers ignored: "Patients...
on filthy tatami mats among the rubble, were being ravaged by the
effects of massive blast and primary and secondary burn trauma combined with advanced stages of radiation illnesses, resulting in fever,
nausea, hemorrhagic stools and diathesis (spontaneous bleeding,
from mouth, rectum, urethra and lungs), epilation (loss of hair), livid
purpura on the skin, and gingivitis and tonsillitis leading to swelling,
and eventually hemorrhaging of gums and soft membranes."

On September 19, 1945, General Douglas MacArthur imposed
sweeping censorship rules on the flow of information within Japan.
In *Hiroshima in America*, Robert Jay Lifton and Greg Mitchell wrote
that "Japanese scientists studying the effects of the atomic bomb also
had to submit their papers to the censorship board for review." The
papers would be held indefinitely, discouraging vital research. Lifton and Mitchell noted that radiation expert Dr. [Masao] Tsuzuki
"called it 'unforgivable' to restrict scientific investigation and publications while people were dying from a mysterious new disease....
Censorship would not end until 1949, and scientific papers could not
be freely published for two years after that. During this period, the
atomic bomb was virtually a forbidden subject in Japan."

On August 31, 1946, the *New Yorker* devoted its entire edition to
John Hersey's exhaustive reporting from Hiroshima, which provided
the first comprehensive account of the chilling and grotesque effects
of the atom bomb on civilians. After reading the Hersey article, Norman Cousins wrote an editorial for the *Saturday Review*. He posed
several rhetorical questions to encourage nuclear literacy:

> Do we know, for example, that many thousands of human
> beings in Japan will die of cancer during the next few years
> because of radioactivity released by the bomb? Do we know
> that the atomic bomb is in reality a death ray, and that the
> damage by blast and fire may be secondary to the damage
> caused by the radiological assault upon human tissue?... Have

we attempted to press our leaders for an answer concerning the refusal to heed the pleas of the scientists against the use of the bomb without demonstration?...And now that we have learned from a Navy spokesman that Japan was ready to quit even before Hiroshima, what happens to the argument that numberless thousands of American lives were saved?

Cousins was never going to get a straight answer to any of those questions from Harry Truman, who for the rest of his life (1) did his best to conceal how American nuclear policy began with a failed political power play and (2) served up a whopping red herring to cover up that failure, which (3) perpetuated a dangerous myth about the efficacy of the atomic bomb and, by doing so, (4) played a role in the proliferation of such weapons beyond the point of reason, (5) ultimately putting the planet in peril on a moment-to-moment basis. In the early part of the Cold War, the "red herring" that came to be viewed as fact was this: Harry Truman had dropped the atomic bombs to save the lives of up to one million American soldiers who, without the atomic bombs, would have died during a necessary invasion of the Japanese mainland. No one was more central to cooking up this red herring than James Conant, one of the chief advisors on the Manhattan Project.

As FDR was well aware, Conant had a fitting résumé for a role with the world's biggest military science experiment. He possessed previous experience—and professed no moral qualms—with weapons of mass destruction, having produced poison gas during World War I, a valuable chemist in a war that was fought between chemists. Subsequently named Harvard President, Conant then demonstrated a relevant aptitude for wrangling and even bamboozling superior intellects, a dime a dozen on the Manhattan Project.

After reading Hersey's *New Yorker* piece and the *Saturday Review* editorial by Cousins, Conant went into overdrive to form a counterattack. "A characteristic feature of James Conant's role in defending the Hiroshima decision in the autumn of 1946," Lifton and Mitchell wrote, "was his capacity to channel and transform his anger over the rise of a counter-narrative into a carefully crafted plan that included the idea of an article, the ideal person to write it, and much of the content of the essay, as well as its tone and style. Never had Conant's talent for manipulating history been more on display."

On September 23, 1946, Conant wrote to the then seventy-nine-year-old Henry Stimson, secretary of war at the time of the atomic bombings, saying it was of "great importance" that someone of Stimson's authority issue a "statement of fact." Put another way: The president of Harvard, the head of the country's most prestigious institution of learning, was floating, as he knew, a fraudulent claim that history was being distorted, when the reverse was occurring. And in order to manufacture a version of history that would enhance his legacy and Harry Truman's, President Conant was hell-bent on falsifying the truth of how the most important single decision of the war had been made.

Conant's machinations yielded a cover story in the February 1947 issue of the venerable *Harper's Magazine*, America's oldest general-interest monthly, established in 1850. The magazine was patronized by elite educators likely to evangelize the desired message on the Hiroshima rationale to the next generation of students. *Harper's* had also agreed to allow other publications to reprint the article without charge.

The headline on the cover trumpeted: "Henry L. Stimson explains Why We Used the Atomic Bomb." In truth, a committee of like-minded individuals seeking to justify the use of the weapon, including Conant and General Leslie Groves, ghostwrote the article. It might as well have been a White House press release. Before publication, Stimson confided his doubts about what had been hatched in his name: "I think the full enumeration of the steps in the tragedy will excite horror among friends who heretofore thought me a kindly minded Christian gentleman, but who, after reading this, will feel I am cold blooded and cruel."

There was no mention in the article of pre-Hiroshima attempts by Stimson and others to modify the unconditional surrender demand and allow Japan to keep its emperor. The article did not disclose that managing Stalin in the postwar world played a role in the decision to use the atomic bombs. Stimson did not admit to his own misgivings about the human carnage from the firebombing of cities, which would have highlighted Curtis LeMay's virtually unchecked civilian slaughter and muddled the article's argument that the decision about the bomb had a moral basis: *saving lives.* The article asserted, incorrectly, that there were no important voices inside the Manhattan Project opposing the bomb's use (such as Leo Szilard). It also claimed, incorrectly, that a demonstration of the bomb had been judged by all the top scientists as impractical.

The key argument of the *Harper's* piece was that the bomb had kept the United States from having to invade the Japanese mainland. Stimson wrote, "We estimated that if we should be forced to carry this invasion plan to its conclusion, the major fighting would not end until the latter part of 1946, at the earliest. I was informed that such an operation might be expected to cost over a million casualties, in American forces alone." But there was no such casualty estimate by any official.

Career diplomat Joseph Grew wrote to Stimson disheartened that the article had fudged the pre-Hiroshima debate. He told Stimson that he "and a good many others" would always feel that if Truman had assured the Japanese earlier about the status of the emperor, "the atom bomb might never have had to be used at all…and the world would have been the gainer." The United Press story about the article highlighted Stimson's assertion about how many American lives were saved, but inflated it. In the UP report, Stimson's one million casualties became one million *killed.*

By the time I was taking high school history, in the 1970s, this red herring had been made gospel in textbooks. A Harris poll taken around the same time found that 64 percent of Americans supported using the bomb on Hiroshima, with just 21 percent opposed. These were the dividends of a propaganda campaign authored by a Harvard president who had successfully mythologized, justified, and sanctified America's inauguration of the nuclear era.

———

Presuming the Soviets were preparing for World War III, the Truman administration judged it necessary to maintain a large military presence in still occupied Japan as a buffer against another Pearl Harbor. In reaction, Stalin reassessed the balance of power. "If Japan... was to remain indefinitely a bastion of American military power," Kennan explained, "if there was to be no agreed peace settlement for Japan, and if Moscow was to have no look-in on the Japanese situation, then Moscow wanted, by way of compensation, to consolidate its military-political position in Korea—an area we appeared not to care too much about in any case."

In 1949, the United States had appeared to signal its apathy about South Korea by withdrawing eight thousand troops, leaving a small force of five hundred. When North Korean ground forces, backed by 150 Soviet T-34 tanks, flowed across the border on June 25, 1950, at 3:30 a.m., there was only one American who witnessed it, a suddenly awakened U.S. Army captain named Joseph Darrigo. As the CIA later concluded, "The United States was caught by surprise because, within political and military leadership circles in Washington, the perception existed that only the Soviets could order an invasion by a 'client state' and that such an act would be a prelude to a world war. Washington was confident that the Soviets were not ready to take such a step, and, therefore, that no invasion would occur."

Truman learned of the North Korean attack while spending a weekend with family at his home in Independence, Missouri. Sitting on a porch off the kitchen, he engaged in more fatally flawed logic. He recalled how World War II was preceded by the strong attacking the weak, by Japan invading Manchuria in 1931, by Mussolini storming Ethiopia in 1935, by Hitler attacking Poland in 1939—which, in Truman's thinking, eventually led to the sneak attack on Pearl Harbor. Truman would write, "I remembered how each time the democracies failed to act it encouraged the aggressors to keep going ahead.... If this was allowed to go unchallenged, it would mean a third world war, just as similar incidents had brought on the second world war."

By October 1950, following a daring amphibious landing at Inchon, the United States was on the verge of winning the Korean War and unifying the Korean peninsula. But as Allied troops approached the Chinese border at the Yalu River, Mao Zedong had as many as 300,000 troops ready to emerge en masse from North Korea's rugged terrain. MacArthur, who had authored the brilliant amphibious attack, ignored intelligence reports about the gathering Chinese forces and remained clueless about the likely impact even after they attacked.

Suddenly facing an influx of thirty fresh divisions, the U.S. Eighth Army was forced into the longest retreat in American history, falling back 120 miles. "Mao had dealt an enormous psychological blow to the U.S.A.," wrote Jung Chang and Jon Halliday in their Mao biography. "Truman went on the radio to declare a State of National Emergency, something that did not happen in either World War II or the Vietnam War." Truman's rhetoric was dire: "If aggression is successful in Korea, we can expect it to spread throughout Asia and Europe to this hemisphere. We are fighting in Korea for our own national security and survival." *But we weren't.*

"Victory in World War II brought no sense of security, therefore, to the victors," Cold War expert John Lewis Gaddis wrote. "Neither the United States, nor the Soviet Union at the end of 1950 could regard the lives and treasure they had expended in defeating Germany and Japan as having made them safer: the members of the Grand Alliance were now Cold War adversaries.... Fears of surprise attack continued to haunt the military establishments in Washington, London and Moscow. A contest that had begun over the fate of postwar Europe had now spread to Asia."

———

America's failure to anticipate the North Korean attack was also related to one other key factor: A highly reliable intelligence instrument was no longer functioning. The Pentagon's line into the thinking of the Kremlin had gone dead. There was at least one Cold War competition where the Soviets enjoyed a sizable lead: the game of spy versus spy.

By 1948, genius U.S. codebreakers, led by Meredith Gardner, had found the secret to deciphering coded Soviet communications. Ultimately, the VENONA intercepts—the name for the operation was randomly chosen—would lead to the discovery of some two hundred Soviet spies working within the United States. The intercepts also enabled the U.S. military to read encrypted communications involving Soviet military, police, and industry, providing a rather accurate assessment of Stalin's national security posture. But in 1948, on a day that came to be known as "Black Friday," the Soviets changed their system. Nothing could be read.

It was later learned that the Armed Forces Security Agency had been penetrated. The spy was William Wolf Weisband, a gregarious Russian linguist who translated broken messages into English at Arlington Hall, AFSA's nerve center. Weisband was born in Russia and likely trained at Comintern's Lenin Hall in Moscow. By 1936, he was in New York working as a courier for Soviet intelligence. He became a U.S. citizen in 1938, joined the Army, and served with signals intelligence during World War II in England, Italy, and North Africa.

At Arlington Hall, Weisband had the reputation "as a stroller," according to a government report. "He wandered around, chatting and picking up pieces of gossip.... His postwar wedding party was talked about as a who's who of Army cryptology." The Weisband case instilled a long-lasting paranoia within the national security community and would be called "perhaps the most significant intelligence loss in U.S. history."

Truman ordered a thorough investigation. In addition to the Weisband disaster, U.S forces in the Korean War had been unable to decode critical communications between the Chinese and North Koreans.

"Gone was the well-oiled machine that had helped win World War II," James Bamford wrote in *Body of Secrets*. "In its place was a confusing assortment of special-interest groups, each looking upon the other as the enemy; no one had the power to bring them together." The blueprint for a new "global monitoring" agency was created.

On October 24, 1952, during a small off-the-record Oval Office meeting, Truman signed a highly secret seven-page memorandum that acted as the charter of the new National Security Agency. The memo was classified. A new federal agency had been born without the knowledge of Congress. Even its name was classified. Almost immediately, NSA computers, devices, and personnel began monitoring every overseas cable sent or received by Americans. The practice wasn't stopped until 1975. Eventually, the NSA's top-secret Crypto-City in suburban Maryland would grow to sixty buildings, with more than sixty thousand employees. The super high-tech agency became, as Bamford wrote, "home to the largest collection of hyperpowerful computers, advanced mathematicians, and language experts on the planet," where time would soon be "measured by the femtosecond— one millionth billionth of a second—and scientists [worked] in secret to develop computers capable of performing more than one septillion (1,000,000,000,000,000,000,000,000) operations every second."

During the Cold War, the United States would create, in total, thirteen new intelligence agencies to gather and interpret information from around the world and, often illegally, from within the United States. This represented, as national security expert Loch Johnson noted, "the largest cluster of information gathering organizations [ever established] in American history...rivaled in world history only by the intelligence apparatus of the Soviet Union."

———

On November 1, 1952, America tested the first megaton-scale hydrogen bomb in the Marshall Islands, three thousand miles west of Hawaii. The device was a thousand times more powerful than an atomic bomb. Detonated from a ship thirty miles away, the H-bomb vaporized the entire island of Elugelab and created a radioactive cloud a hundred miles wide. Less than a year later, on August 12, 1953, the Soviets tested their first thermonuclear device at the Semipalatinsk test site in Kazakhstan. The blast left a massive crater and scattered the area with "yellow lumpy glass."

After the tests, the *Bulletin of the Atomic Scientists* put the little hand of the Doomsday Clock at two minutes to midnight, writing: "The hands of the Clock of Doom have moved again. Only a few more swings of the pendulum and, from Moscow to Chicago, atomic explosions will strike midnight for Western civilization."

In *Foreign Affairs*, Robert Oppenheimer wrote, "We may anticipate a state of affairs in which two Great Powers will each be in a position to put an end to the civilization and the life of the other, though not without risking its own. We may be likened to two scorpions in a bottle, each capable of killing the other, but only at the risk of his own life."

As the Cold War rivals amassed greater amounts of nuclear firepower, each new global conflict became shadowed by *omnicide*, a word coined in 1959 by philosopher John Sommerville, who explained to the *Los Angeles Times* how the scale of destruction from the use of thermonuclear weapons required an entirely new word. "With two superpowers having the capability of destroying every human on the face of the earth a dozen times over, the word 'war' is an inappropriate... use of language," Sommerville said. "Since the beginning of time, war has been based on the notion that one side would win. But no matter how destructive the war was, you could always count on the fact that most of the human race would still be alive. The planet would still be livable. . . . War can even be 'just,' but how can any war that destroys all humankind be *just*?"

CHAPTER 18

ABSENT EVIDENCE

Trial by congressional committees was where J. Edgar Hoover excelled. Trial by judge and jury, not so much. Take the case of Judith Coplon, a twenty-eight-year-old Barnard graduate and a no-doubt-about-it Soviet spy. What should have been a layup for Hoover became an epic fuckup. Actually, there was a fuckup that preceded the fuckup that wasn't entirely Hoover's fault.

At fashionably leftist Barnard, where half the students were spending some period of time toying with anarchism, communism, or socialism, Coplon was an active member of the Young Communist League who had published pro-Soviet articles in the school newspaper. Here's the first fuckup: Although an FBI background check had discovered her support for communism, which at the time meant there was a 50/50 chance you were a cultish Stalinist, she had been hired anyway by the Justice Department, in 1944, and as of 1949 had been promoted to a high-level job in Washington, D.C., as a political analyst in the Foreign Agents Registration Section, which gave her access to the names of known or suspected Soviet intelligence agents.

This made Coplon a version of Kim Philby. She was a Soviet agent who could tell the Soviets what the FBI knew about Soviet agents working in the United States, one of whom was her. Coplon's code name was SIMA. Her KGB recruiter said of SIMA, "She treats very seriously and honestly our task and considers our work the main thing in her life. Her serious attitude is demonstrated by her decision not to marry her former fiancé because, otherwise, she couldn't continue working with us." Mother Russia, or Comrade Stalin, was her one true love.

Here was the layup: Through the VENONA decrypts, the FBI learned, somewhat belatedly, that Soviet spy SIMA was an elevator ride away. Hoover could have brought Coplon a coffee to her desk over at the Justice Department and it would have still been hot when she received it. Hoover's first instinct was to quietly dismiss her to limit the embarrassment to his organization—she had been literally spying for the Soviets under his nose. *Image was everything.* Moreover, with the VENONA operation unearthing Soviet spies everywhere, most notably inside the Manhattan Project, it was becoming evident that the FBI's wartime counterintelligence efforts had been at best mediocre. Ultimately, Hoover was somehow persuaded that it might be a good idea to find out the identity of Coplon's Soviet contact. A sting operation was mounted.

On March 3, 1949, Coplon told her supervisor she was leaving for New York the next day. Before she left the office on March 3, her supervisor handed her a document from the Atomic Energy Commission, which he described to her as "quite hot and interesting." Anything with the word "atomic" in it automatically made it tantalizing for a Soviet mole. On March 4, in New York, FBI agents described "the most remarkable conduct" on the part of Coplon and the man who turned out to be her handler, Valentin Gubitchev, a Soviet national working at the United Nations.

According to a court filing, "They met, separated, met again; they travelled on foot, by subway and by bus, sometimes together and sometimes separately. At all times the two acted in a furtive manner.... They wandered from as far uptown as Broadway and 193rd Street to a point on Third Avenue between 15th and 16th Streets. There they were arrested by an FBI agent at 9:35 p.m."

The "quite hot and interesting" Atomic Energy Commission document was found in Coplon's purse, as were twenty-two FBI "data slips," and an incredibly incriminating letter written by Coplon apologizing to her Russian handlers for not being able to obtain a 115-page "top secret FBI report" on Soviet and Communist activities in the United States going back fifteen years. Judith Coplon, cum laude graduate of Barnard College, class of 1943, had been caught in the act with the goods.

A month after her arrest, Coplon went on trial in Washington, D.C., charged with stealing government documents. But when the prosecution introduced the "data slips" into evidence, Coplon's defense attorney requested the introduction of the documents that formed the basis for all this data—the raw files. The judge ruled in favor of the defense. "It was a historic moment," wrote Curt Gentry in *J. Edgar Hoover: The Man and the Secrets*, "the first time anyone outside the government had seen copies of raw FBI files. And both the press and the defense made the most of it. One report identified the Hollywood actors Frederic March, Helen Hayes, John Garfield, Canada Lee and Paul Muni as 'Reds.'" There was also a report, stamped SECRET, involving a Bronx man who claimed to have spied a neighbor walking around naked in his house. "It was clear," Gentry wrote, "that the FBI employed a vacuum cleaner approach, collecting everything on anyone and filing, rather than discarding, the dirt."

The revelation that Hoover was invading privacy and collecting gossip did not keep Judith Coplon from being found guilty and sentenced to ten years in prison. But when Coplon faced a second trial in New York for conspiring to transmit documents to a foreign power, her new defense team learned a new piece of information: Illegal wiretaps had been used to help convict their client in the first case, and, moreover, an FBI agent at that trial had lied when asked if wiretapping had taken place. Coplon's defense also noted that the FBI had arrested their client without getting a search warrant.

Although Coplon was convicted, again, in the New York trial, as was handler Gubitchev, with both receiving fifteen-year sentences, her defense had raised enough malfeasance by the FBI for

Judge Learned Hand of the U.S. Circuit Court of Appeals to reverse both convictions, along with Coplon's cumulative twenty-five years of jail time. The Washington conviction was ultimately overturned because the FBI had wiretapped privileged conversations between Coplon and her attorney, and the New York conviction was set aside on two grounds: the lack of a search warrant, and the government's refusal to turn over the products of illegal wiretapping.

Judge Hand delivered Hoover a public and stinging rebuke, telling the country that the nation's top cop often operated lawlessly. Hand reminded the FBI that the Supreme Court's ban on wiretapping was still in force, warrants were still required before arrests, and evidence obtained by unlawful methods—"fruit of the poison tree"—was still inadmissible in court. The judge also wrote that the defendant had the right to know the FBI's original confidential informant. This was the VENONA decrypts identifying SIMA as a Soviet agent.

—

The Army bureaucracy, topped by Omar Nelson Bradley, chairman of the Joint Chiefs of Staff, permitted the VENONA decrypts to be shared with J. Edgar Hoover. But according to several sources, they were *not* shared with President Harry S. Truman, who as commander in chief and head of the executive branch was technically in charge of the Army and the FBI. Bradley was concerned that the White House would leak the information. In retrospect, leaking the decrypts would have been a much lesser evil.

By sharing VENONA with Hoover, Bradley gave the clearest account of Soviet espionage in the United States to a distrustful and divisive figure. Hoover's bureaucracy of secrets was more problematic than any White House leak because Hoover's bureaucracy was principally charged with fluffing Hoover and serving his goal of inflating the Soviet threat. As George Kennan summarized, the truth about Soviet espionage was not trivial, but it was never *overwhelming*. Hoover, however, saw that the clear path to further empowerment—and lavish funding—was by making the threat overwhelming. Similarly, Republican opportunists, greatly aided by Hoover's selective leaking, seized the chance to tar Truman and the Democrats by blaming them for having made the overwhelming possible, even though virtually all of them knew this was baloney.

"Had Truman been able to draw on the secret stash," Jack Shafer wrote in the *Columbia Journalism Review*, "he could have arrested America's paranoia about the internal communist threat by speaking the truth about the pitiful weakness of Soviet spies. But because he was in the dark, too, he couldn't directly refute the alarmists."

Here is another unfortunate miscalculation made by General Bradley: Although VENONA was the biggest secret in the government, it wasn't *that big a deal*. Due to the able work of U.S.-based Soviet spies, such as the garrulous William Weisband and the aristocratic Kim Philby, it's likely that Joseph Stalin was better informed about VENONA than was Harry Truman. As a result, the only people being protected by concealing VENONA were the spies who had been outed by the decrypts, which were the best evidence of their crimes. In the trial of Judith Coplon, for example, the prosecution could have simply read the jury decrypted Soviet messages detailing how Coplon—agent SIMA—was doing wonderful work on behalf of the Kremlin.

"In the void created by absent or withheld information," Daniel Moynihan wrote, "decisions are either made poorly or not at all. What decisions would Truman have made had the information in the VENONA intercepts not been withheld from him? The question tantalizes, for the President was hardly a passive figure."

———

Instead of coolheaded clarity about the communist menace, or a caution about the menace of overreaction, the way was paved for Richard Nixon and Joseph McCarthy, and many others, to abuse the truth, inflame paranoia, destroy lives, and climb the ladder of fame.

Backed by the full and stout cooperation of Hoover, Nixon used his perch on the House Un-American Activities Committee to stage a show trial of Alger Hiss and did his darnedest to first convict him in the court of public opinion. When the effort was made to *actually convict* Hiss in an *actual court*, a process that began with grand jury indictments in 1948, it required two attempts and nearly three years. The extent of the FBI's involvement in the investigation of Hiss was revealed in 1976, when the agency was forced by a court order to release 15,376 pages of Hiss-related records. As with Judith Coplon, two or three decrypted VENONA cables were really all that was necessary to make the case.

Alger Hiss was charged with two counts of perjury. The government said he had lied in denying he had passed government documents to admitted spy Whittaker Chambers, and that he had lied about having never seen Chambers after January 1, 1937. He could not be charged with espionage because the statute of limitations had run out.

Chambers was supposed to be the star witness. Claiming to be part of Hiss's D.C.-based spy cell, he had come in from the cold in 1939, and as of 1940 the FBI was aware that he had been chirping about spying for the Soviets and working with Hiss, who at the time had a high-level spot at the State Department. However, the FBI didn't bother to interview Chambers until 1942, after which the agency took no action. But seven years later, between January and April 1949 alone, Chambers would be "interviewed" thirty-nine separate times by FBI agents.

Chambers was "interviewed" thirty-nine times in that period in order to "prepare him" to be a witness in the first Hiss trial, which began on May 31, 1949. During these repeated interviews, the FBI was spoon-feeding him information that the bureau had illegally obtained by recording virtually every conversation Hiss had been having, going back years. The best way for Chambers to prove that he knew really intimate things about Alger Hiss after January 1, 1937, and thus convince the jury of Hiss's perjury, was by testifying to details about Alger Hiss's life after that date—the kind of details the FBI was learning by listening to everything Hiss was saying, every waking hour, of every day.

The FBI had no fix for human nature, however. The defense was able to convincingly portray Chambers as a moral leper and a psychopathic liar. This is from a review of the case by the CIA:

> Chambers was an admitted Communist and spy...had denied that Hiss had engaged in espionage...was a troubled man with a record of homosexual activities during the 1920s and 1930s. Moreover, numerous details of his story had turned out to be inaccurate, largely because his memory had become hazy during the decade since his desertion. Nor was Chambers the kind of witness who would win a jury's sympathy, for he was dumpy, unattractive, and had a melancholy air. In contrast, the defense presented the slender, handsome, well-connected Hiss as a model American who would never stoop to treason.

Like Kim Philby, Hiss reeked of establishment credentials. He was Phi Beta Kappa at Johns Hopkins, graduated Harvard Law, became a clerk at the Supreme Court, and rose to be one of Roosevelt's senior foreign policy officials. He played a pivotal role in the creation of the United Nations, and was in line to become the UN's first secretary-general. If Hiss had ascended to that role, it is logical to wonder if he might have taken orders from Stalin.

A quiet radicalization may have occurred when he was at Harvard. At the time, the robbery-murder trial of shoemaker Nicola Sacco and fishmonger Bartolomeo Vanzetti was taking place in a Boston court. The event attracted worldwide attention and, subsequently, condemnation, when the men were found guilty and in 1927 electrocuted. Sacco and Vanzetti, credibly suspected of belonging to an anarchist ring of lethal bomb makers, had been scapegoated, attached to crimes they didn't commit. Hiss was not alone in having his confidence in American fairness shattered by the execution of the Italian immigrants.

———

On July 7, 1949, Hiss's first trial concluded in a hung jury, four members voting for acquittal, eight for conviction. Hoover had a conniption and censured four FBI agents attached to the case. Nixon attacked the judge and threatened to use Congress's subpoena power to drag the dissenting jurors before the HUAC. Hiss, who had a very high opinion of his ability to fool people, was stunned that eight fellow citizens were ready to put him in jail.

On November 17, 1949, Hiss was retried on the same two charges. The prosecution had a more convincing key witness the second time around, ex-communist operative Hede Massing, who had been the top recruiter in America for the NKVD, the Soviet secret police, in the 1930s. Hiss, allegedly, belonged to the competing spy network run by the GRU, Soviet military intelligence. Massing testified how in 1935 she had sparred at length with Hiss over gaining the services of two Americans, Noel Field and Larry Duggan. Duggan's name was still top of mind when Massing testified—in a chilling way. On December 21, 1948, after being named as a Soviet spy by HUAC investigators, Duggan became a consummate tabloid headline—and appeared to confirm his guilt—by jumping out a window at his Manhattan office and plunging sixteen floors to his death, landing on the southwest corner of Fifth Avenue and 45th Street. In one of many grisly news photos, a priest was seen delivering last rites over Duggan's crumpled body.

On January 21, 1950, the jury found Hiss guilty of both counts of perjury and he was sentenced to five years in jail. Hiss's appeal was denied, and he went to prison on March 22, 1951.

"The actual damage to U.S. interests by Hiss's spying often gets lost amid the rhetorical heat of the cultural and political wars surrounding the Hiss-Chambers case," wrote Kati Marton in *True Believer.* "A high-ranking State Department official and close FDR friend, Sumner Welles, when shown the documents Hiss gave his courier, Whittaker Chambers, summed up the real harm. It was not so much the cables' *content*, Welles testified, but the clues they provided Soviet cryptanalysts that would have provided code breakers with texts that could be matched against intercepted telegrams."

Wrote Moynihan, "Belief in the guilt or innocence of Alger Hiss became a defining issue in American intellectual life. Parts of the American government had conclusive evidence of his guilt, but they never told." American liberals, Moynihan continued, "were left to rant on about 'scoundrel time' and witch-hunts and blacklists. In an odd way, government stayed out of the most heated political argument of the time."

Here are the top four things that appear to be true about the Alger Hiss case:

1. Hiss was indeed a Soviet spy who was incapable of admitting it.
2. Nixon and the FBI used scummy and illegal tactics to put Hiss in jail.
3. The result of these two competing narratives is that Hiss was able to exploit left-wing outrage about the dubious tactics used to nail him as a way to maintain his innocence and marinate in his martyrdom, and Nixon was able to exploit right-wing fears about an epidemic of communist infiltration in order to become a national political figure.
4. In short, the Nixon-Hiss battle was a contest between two fundamentally dishonest men who were able to fog up the Cold War debate to the detriment of all sides.

Nixon's doggedness in gaining Hiss's conviction would pay off. Elected to the Senate in 1950, he would be selected as Dwight Eisenhower's vice president in 1952, at age thirty-nine. Hiss would serve forty-four months in prison and, following his release, vigorously maintained his innocence until his death, in 1996.

CHAPTER 19

CRIME OF THE CENTURY

Ethel Greenglass graduated from Seward High School on the Lower East Side of Manhattan and became a secretary in a shipping company. She was a committed communist and labor activist. Ethel met Julius Rosenberg at the Young Communist League, and they married in 1939 and had two sons, Michael and Robert. Julius had a degree in electrical engineering from CCNY and ran a very productive spy ring for the Soviet Union, which passed thousands of classified documents to the Soviets, including bleeding-edge U.S. military developments in guided missiles and jet engines.

One of the people Julius had recruited into his network was Ethel's brother and fellow Young Communist David Greenglass, who worked as a machinist at Los Alamos and shared information on the atom bomb's detonation device with a Soviet courier. It was Greenglass, after being arrested and interrogated in June 1950, who fingered Julius as his recruiter. During questioning by the FBI, he made clear that his sister Ethel had *no involvement* in the atomic spying.

The VENONA decrypts had found numerous references to Julius. One of his code names was LIBERAL. Ethel was mentioned in the Soviet spy traffic, but as "Ethel." She had no official code name, indicating she likely had no formal espionage role. Nonetheless, in the summer of 1950, she was arrested along with her husband. The couple was not charged with treason, nor espionage, but the vague offense of conspiracy to commit espionage. This placed a lesser burden of proof on the prosecution because conviction did not require tangible evidence that the Rosenbergs had either stolen anything sensitive or, if they had, given it to anybody.

When all of the VENONA intercepts and grand jury testimony was finally declassified and released, which took until 2015, this was the extent of the case for the prosecution in *United States v. Rosenberg et al.*: Julius Rosenberg had engaged in espionage for the Soviets, but there was no evidence he had traded atomic secrets; his wife, Ethel, was not an espionage agent, although, as a still zealous communist, she had knowingly played a support role in her husband's spy ring: concealing money and equipment, facilitating contacts with Soviet intelligence, and appraising potential recruits. All the relevant parties knew the bulk of these details in the summer of 1950, and in a more reasonable, less-heated age, prosecutors would have likely sought no more than substantial jail time for Julius and perhaps a lighter sentence for Ethel. However, with the VENONA road map and a country in the throes of losing its mind over what seemed like out-of-control communist subversion, J. Edgar Hoover, with plenty of company in the Justice Department, became greedy and, figuratively, rolled the dice.

After Julius's arrest, more than half a dozen of his known associates had fled the country. One of them, Morton Sobell, was soon located by the Mexican police and dumped at the border in Laredo, Texas. Gambling for a bigger score—that is, a full confession from Julius Rosenberg providing all the details of what seemed like a large nest of spies, the smashing of which could be trumpeted as an intelligence coup worthy of the boldest headlines—Hoover, along with the Justice Department, looked for a way to squeeze both Ethel and Julius into giving up the names of all of Julius's associates.

Hoover had the support of senior players in Washington and New York. At a secret session of the Joint Congressional Committee on Atomic Energy, Myles Lane, from the Justice Department, said "the prospect of the death penalty or getting the chair" was about "the only thing you can use against these people." Gordon Dean, chairman of the Atomic Energy Commission, offered, "It looks as though Rosenberg is the kingpin of a very large ring, and if there is any way of breaking him by having the shadow of a death penalty over him, we want to do it."

A miscarriage of justice was intentionally set in motion—and, inadvertently, a corollary public relations disaster—during which there would be multiple improper ex parte communications between judge and prosecution, concluding with the execution of a mother of two boys for a crime that could only be proven by suborning perjury.

The attempt to gain Julius's cooperation began by effectively holding his wife hostage. Bail was set at a sum the couple couldn't possibly raise, a total of $200,000—$100,000 for each. Their sons, ages seven and three, ended up at the Jewish Children's Home in the Bronx. Next was finding a so-called hanging judge. Forty-year-old Irving S. Kaufman, who was eyeing an appointment to the Supreme Court, was all but jumping up and down and saying, *Pick me!* In a pretrial discussion, he confirmed a willingness to impose the death penalty as a lever to break Julius Rosenberg, "if the evidence warrants."

This was when a coiled, heavy-lidded, snarling, Hobbit-like figure made his entrance on the Cold War timeline. In 1950, Roy Cohn was a twenty-three-year-old assistant prosecutor for the Southern District of New York who had been assigned to the Rosenberg case. He had graduated from Columbia Law at age twenty, and gained notice in 1949 during a raucous and often ridiculous ten-month trial known as the Battle of Foley Square, when eleven members of the U.S. Communist Party leadership were dubiously convicted for "conspiring to overthrow the U.S. government," a violation of the 1940 Smith Act.

The son of a New York state supreme court judge, Cohn was precociously introduced to the ways and means of exploiting the city's invisible but very real Favor Bank. As a high school student, he had already figured out how to fix a parking ticket for a teacher. The Favor Bank also had various hubs, one of them being the Stork Club, where Cohn became a regular, deftly retailing gossip, hearsay, and scandal with Hoover, Walter Winchell, and other adherents of the destruction-by-salacious-headline gang.

Cohn would claim to have played matchmaker in getting Judge Kaufman assigned to the high-profile Rosenberg trial, and it is alleged he was a key participant in fabricating a case against Ethel Rosenberg. Ten days before the start of the trial, on February 23, 1951, Greenglass and his wife, Ruth, were suspiciously *reinterviewed* by the FBI. After those interviews, Ethel was suddenly implicated in the conspiracy. The new story was that Ethel had typed up David Greenglass's Los Alamos secrets on a folding bridge table in the Rosenberg living room, as witnessed by both David and Ruth.

Like Ethel, Ruth was the mother of two young children, but unlike Ethel, she was *demonstrably guilty*, enough of a party to her husband's espionage to be given the code name OSA ("Wasp") by Soviet intelligence. Both David and Ruth had provided atomic bomb secrets to a Soviet courier, but *never* through either Julius or Ethel. Ruth Greenglass was made to understand that if she wasn't willing to commit perjury, she too would be indicted.

The trial began on March 6, 1951, and lasted for three weeks. Under questioning by Cohn, David and Ruth Greenglass repeated the fiction of Ethel's direct complicity. Ethel's brother and his wife provided the only testimony incriminating either Julius or Ethel in the passing of atomic secrets. Chief prosecutor Irving H. Saypol told the jurors that when Ethel Rosenberg was at her typewriter, striking the keys, "blow by blow" she was betraying her own country "in the interests of the Soviets." The jury took less than a day to reach a guilty verdict.

———

No one in the FBI hierarchy favored the death penalty for Ethel. However, Roy Cohn would claim he had had ex parte phone communications with Kaufman urging the judge to sentence both Ethel and Julius to the electric chair. Later, Cohn would say of Ethel:

I think she was the stronger of the two. She was the one who got her brother, David, into the Young Communist League to start with. She was the one who kept drilling him full of propaganda until she had him sufficiently hyped up that when it was put to him concerning the stealing and making of those sketches and turning over secret information in the name of the Soviet Union and all of that, he was totally acclimated to what he was supposed to do. Ethel was the strong one, not the weak one.... I never had any doubt about her guilt, but I feel she was the strong one among the two of them and belonged in that case as much as he did, if not more.

This was Cohn's "communist den mother" theory of why Ethel Rosenberg deserved to die. But from the statement above, and many other statements Roy Cohn made about the case, what you learn from the protestations are that Roy Cohn understood that he was a willing participant in a lynch mob—and was uneasy about that fact. For justification, he would hint at the existence of the VENONA decrypts, which had indeed clearly identified Julius Rosenberg as a Kremlin agent—*but not Ethel.* However, since the VENONA information was never revealed as evidence in any of the trials involving the era's Soviet spies, Cohn could claim that the VENONA decrypts also incriminated Santa Claus and the Easter Bunny.

By hiding the VENONA evidence, investigations were being constructed backwards. Proof of guilt existed, but that proof was judged too sensitive to be used in court. Therefore, other evidence had to be found, whether real or invented. Cohn had no qualms about participating in a kangaroo court. He was in the protean stage of contorting and corrupting and abusing the American legal system for his own gain, daring disbarment, becoming a man so lacking in scruples that many would judge him to be the most evil person they had ever known.

In 1973, Cohn would become a mentor to the then twenty-seven-year-old Donald Trump after the two met at a New York nightspot known for a clientele of "models, fashionistas, and Eurotrash." Trump and his father, Fred, had just been sued by the Civil Rights

Division of the Department of Justice for not renting to blacks at their thirty-nine apartment buildings, a violation of the Fair Housing Act. Cohn told Donald he should tell the government to "go to hell and fight the thing in court and let them prove you discriminated."

The Trumps took the advice and held a press conference to announce a $100 million countersuit against the Justice Department for defamation.

———

The young Roy Cohn was ready to let Ethel Rosenberg die because he enjoyed the buzz accrued from being an anticommunist champion in the age of the Red Menace. He was also a Jewish anti-Semite who saw an opportunity to proclaim his patriotism in full view of America's generally anti-Semitic WASP establishment, which often blackballed Jewish Americans from their schools, clubs, and businesses. By seeking vengeance on the Rosenbergs, Cohn was proving that his background did not keep him from punishing Jews who took their orders from the Kremlin.

"Not all Jews are Communists," Cohn would later say, "but most communists are Jews. I did resent very much the idea of associating Jews with a sympathy toward communism. And I do admit that this is something that has always bothered me, and I've tried every way I can to make it clear that the fact that my name is Cohn and the fact of my religion [is perfectly compatible] with my love for America and my dislike for communism."

On April 5, 1951, Judge Kaufman sentenced the spy captured in Mexico, Martin Sobell, to thirty years. For cooperating, Greenglass received a lesser sentence of fifteen years. Announcing his reasons for putting Julius and Ethel Rosenberg to death, Kaufman produced what might have been the most dishonest, ignorant, and hyperbolic statement of the entire Cold War:

I believe your conduct in putting into the hands of the Russians the A-bomb, years before our best scientists predicted

Russia would perfect the bomb, has already caused…the Communist aggression in Korea, with the resultant casualties exceeding 50,000, and who knows what millions more innocent people may pay the price of your treason.

Kaufman also added:

Let no mistake be made about the role which his wife, Ethel Rosenberg, played in this conspiracy.…She was a full-fledged partner in this crime.

The wife and mother standing before Kaufman was not a passive participant. She had helped recruit her brother and, as historians Ronald Radosh and Steven T. Ushin noted in 2015, "declassified Soviet intelligence documents [later revealed] that Ethel was present at meetings with Soviet intelligence officers and American spies for the Soviet Union, and that she actively participated in the crime for which [the Rosenbergs] were convicted, conspiracy to commit espionage." But she had no more than a high school degree, no expertise in military technology, was at best a minor Soviet asset, and the prosecution had contrived her guilt. Her husband had betrayed his nation, but he did not do so from inside the Manhattan Project, like his brother-in-law, who would serve only nine years of his sentence and get out of jail in 1960.

As it was, even David Greenglass—a low-level worker bee at Los Alamos—was a tiny cog in Stalin's formidable atomic spy network. According to convicted Rosenberg accomplice Martin Sobell, "What [Greenglass] gave them was junk." Meanwhile, two of the featured players in the A-bomb espionage story had already been quietly rushed to judgment across the Atlantic.

Prior to the arrest of the Rosenbergs, Soviet spies Alan Nunn May and Klaus Fuchs—world-class physicists who were tasked with actually *making the bomb work*—had been efficiently convicted by the British and sentenced to ten and fifteen years, respectively. This was done without any prolonged media melodrama or showboating prosecutors. Like David Greenglass, the two were released early—Nunn May in 1952, Fuchs in 1959. Along with Bruno Pontecorvo, who escaped Western justice altogether by defecting to the Soviet Union, the three British-hired scientists were far, far more significant actors in the contours of the Cold War contest than Julius and Ethel Rosenberg. Likewise, Cambridge moles Donald Maclean (defected), Guy Burgess (defected), and Kim Philby (fired) also escaped serious punishment for acting as Stalin's critical eyes and ears on virtually every step of Western nuclear research.

———

Kaufman had scheduled the executions for the week of May 21, 1951. Appeals took two years. Worldwide protests began. "It is worth remembering," wrote Harvard Cold War historian Mark Kramer, "that the Rosenberg case prompted the first major Soviet propaganda and disinformation campaign after Stalin's death, when Soviet officials in the spring of 1953 provided funding and backing to groups around the world that were demanding the release of the Rosenbergs." Wittingly or unwittingly, two prominent fellow travelers piped up. Marxist and existentialist Jean-Paul Sartre said, "Your country is sick with fear...you are afraid of your own bomb." In the communist *L'Humanité*, Pablo Picasso wrote, "The hours count. The minutes count. Do not let this crime against humanity take place."

Pope Pius XII appealed to President Dwight D. Eisenhower to spare the couple, as did Ethel's brother David, writing to the president, "If these two die, I shall live the rest of my life with a very dark shadow on my conscience.... Here I had to take the choice of hurting someone dear to me, and I took it deliberately. I could not believe that this would be the outcome. May God in His mercy change that awful sentence."

Ike was unmoved. He told son David, who was serving in Korea, that if Ethel were spared it would only encourage the Soviets to establish an all-female spy corps.

Meanwhile, Roy Cohn became convinced that the communists were after him. He asked the FBI to check if his phones were tapped and if his office contained hidden microphones. Hoover ignored Cohn's jitters.

On the morning of the execution, June 19, 1953, the FBI director sent six field agents to Sing Sing prison in Ossining, New York. One was a stenographer capable of transcribing 170 words per minute. At the prison, the agents turned two cells on death row into offices. The FBI team waited to see if after three years behind bars, and moments before their electrocutions, Julius and Ethel Rosenberg would at last relent and confess.

The following day, newspapers around the world carried the story of the executions of thirty-five-year-old Julius Rosenberg and his thirty-seven-year-old wife, Ethel. Because the leather cap containing the electrodes was too large for Ethel's head, the executioner had to throw the switch multiple times to kill her. The United Press wire service account provided unsparing, minute-by-minute detail:

> When the first electric shock was applied, a thick white stream of smoke curled upward from the football-type helmet on her head. The juice went off and the burned body relaxed. Then came the second shock . . . the third . . . the fourth.

When attending physicians discovered Ethel Rosenberg was still alive, a final fifth shock was required.

The Rosenbergs were the first American civilians to die for spying—and the only ones executed during the Cold War.

In 2001, Greenglass told author Sam Roberts that he had lied on the witness stand about his sister's involvement. Wrote Roberts, "Without that testimony, Ethel Rosenberg might never have been convicted, much less executed." In 2003, Greenglass gave an interview to *60 Minutes*. He claimed that Roy Cohn had pressured him to make up the story about Ethel and the typewriter. He also said, "I would not sacrifice my wife and my children for my sister. How do you like that?" Asked why he thought Julius and Ethel maintained their silence to the end, he replied, "One word: stupidity."

CHAPTER 20

THIRD-RATE SPEAKER

On Thursday, February 9, 1950, Joe McCarthy went to the first stop on a brief speaking tour. It was in Wheeling, West Virginia, a city of fifty-eight thousand on the Ohio River, in the foothills of the Appalachian Mountains. This was, as Curt Gentry notes, a "third-rate speech stop" and therefore required no more than a "third-rate speaker." The freshman junior senator from Wisconsin fit the bill. McCarthy was disappointed that he had no national profile whatsoever, but he didn't have any idea of how to change that.

McCarthy's office had given him two different speeches to choose from for the Wheeling appearance. One was on housing, the other on communists in the government. McCarthy was so completely dispassionate about both topics that he left the choice of which one to use to the local Republican operative who met him at the airport. That night, McCarthy told the Ohio County Women's Republican Club that he had a list of Communist Party members working in the State Department, and he even knew exactly how many:

> While I cannot take the time to name all the men in the State Department who have been named as members of a spy ring, I have here in my hand a list of 205 that were known to the Secretary of State as being members of the Communist Party and who nevertheless are still working and shaping the policy of the State Department.

Except there was no list. There were no names. There were no spies. Joe McCarthy did not foresee any consequences for making a rather inflammatory charge based on a lie. After all, he was only a third-rate speaker in a third-rate town.

McCarthy flew the next day for a speech in Salt Lake City. When he made a stopover in Denver, reporters confronted him. He failed to offer more details, claiming that the list of 205 names was in a suit still on the plane. By the time McCarthy returned to the Senate, on February 20, 1950, it seemed like his list of communists in the State Department had gone from 205 to 57 to 4, although the more he spoke about the whole thing the vaguer he became. "Talking to Joe was like putting your hands in a bowl of mush," said United Press reporter George Ready.

In a panic, because the State Department and the Truman White House and hundreds of reporters were demanding actual details about the 205 or 57 or 4 communists engaged in traitorous acts on the public dime, McCarthy reached out to people who might be able to provide him with some kind of cover. He called Jack Anderson, who, as Drew Pearson's legman, was learning the fine art of muckraking from Washington's muck master. "I have hit the jackpot," McCarthy told Anderson, "and have gotten hold of one hell of an issue." Anderson shared a potentially damaging but unverified tidbit with McCarthy while also making clear that more research was required. That was the last time Anderson helped McCarthy. The senator did not verify the allegations and destroyed the career of a person who was likely innocent. It would not be the last travesty by any means.

McCarthy also called J. Edgar Hoover, to whom he admitted that the numbers about communists in the State Department were all made up. Hoover told McCarthy that using specific figures was always a bad idea. He also told the senator he would be glad to assist. McCarthy had already found a way into Hoover's heart: flattery. "No one need erect a monument to you," McCarthy wrote in one tribute. "You have built your own monument in the form of the FBI—for the FBI is J. Edgar Hoover and I think we can rest assured that it always will be."

Hoover instructed his senior aides to "review the files and get anything you can for [McCarthy]." Bill Sullivan protested that the FBI didn't have enough evidence to show there was even a single communist in the State Department. "We gave McCarthy everything we had," Sullivan said, "but all we had were fragments, nothing that could prove his accusations."

FBI agents spent hundreds of hours reading bureau files and making abstracts for McCarthy. The FBI supplied speechwriters. FBI press chief Lou Nichols served as McCarthy's PR guru, advising the senator on the wordsmithing of witch hunting. Nichols told him to avoid the phrase "card-carrying communists," since it was often hard to prove. It was better to say "communist sympathizer" or "loyalty risks." When McCarthy exploited his lightning in a bottle to secure the chairmanship of a Senate committee with investigative powers, Hoover selected staff investigators for him, to the point that McCarthy's office was dubbed "the little FBI."

———

The phenomenon of McCarthyism, inaugurated on February 9, 1950, would last for four-plus years, as the previously unsung Wisconsin senator held the Capitol in thrall to his destructive political theater of frightening rhetoric and meritless attacks. One of the first people smeared was Dorothy Kenyon, a liberal New York City lawyer and judge who had been a U.S. delegate to the United Nations Commission on the Status of Women.

The sixty-two-year-old Kenyon had once been loosely associated with leftist organizations that had been designated as communist fronts by the less-than-reliable House Un-American Activities Committee, which was sufficient for McCarthy to identify her as a full-fledged communist, of which there was no evidence. Kenyon promptly denied that she was a communist, called McCarthy "an unmitigated liar," demanded to appear before Congress, and, in eloquent testimony, noted how "literally overnight whatever personal and professional reputation and standing I may have acquired after many years in private practice and some in public office [has been] seriously jeopardized, if not destroyed, by the widespread dissemination of charges of Communistic leanings or proclivities that are utterly false."

McCarthy made no effort to further support his slanderous claims about Kenyon and moved on, next charging that Dr. Philip Jessup, the State Department's ambassador at large, had an "unusual affinity for Communist causes." Jessup denounced McCarthy for demonstrating a "shocking disregard" for U.S. national interests, and in short order the ambassador's loyalty was certified by strong letters of support from Dwight Eisenhower and George C. Marshall.

On March 21, 1950, McCarthy told reporters that he had "the name of a man—connected with the State Department—whom I consider the top Russian espionage agent in the country." This man was revealed to be Dr. Owen Lattimore, a prominent authority on Far Eastern affairs. McCarthy claimed that Dr. Lattimore was "one of the principal architects of our far eastern policy [whose] record as a pro-Communist goes back many years." Five years earlier, Lattimore had worked for four months in a freelance advisory capacity for the State Department. He had never been an employee. He was not a spy. He was not a communist. And until McCarthy put Lattimore's name in the headlines, he was even unknown to Secretary of State Dean Acheson.

McCarthy insisted that an FBI file would back up his innuendos about Lattimore. During a Senate session, Connecticut Democrat Brien McMahon asked a logical question.

McMAHON: Have you seen the FBI files?
McCARTHY: I think I know what is in them.
McMAHON: That is not the question. Have you seen them?
McCARTHY: I will tell you, Senator McMahon, do not worry about whether I have seen them or not.

McMAHON: You refuse to answer?

McCARTHY: No, I don't refuse to answer.

McMAHON: The original FBI files. Have you seen a copy of them?

McCARTHY: Let me say this. To the best of my knowledge...the FBI file will show in detail not the case merely of a man who happens to favor Russia, not the case of a man who may disagree with what we think about Russia, but a man who is definitely an espionage agent.

A year after the speech in Wheeling, Joe McCarthy believed he had the leverage to slay giants, such as George Marshall, the five-star general who had been the chief architect of the victory in World War II and was about to win the Nobel Peace Prize for his European Recovery Program. Speaking in the Senate on June 14, 1951, McCarthy would read part of a speech that, when it was submitted in full to the *Congressional Record*, was seventy-two thousand words and turned into a book: *America's Retreat from Victory: The Story of George Catlett Marshall*. This would be the most noted excerpt: "How can we account for our present situation unless we believe that men high in this Government are concerting to deliver us to disaster? This must be the product of a great conspiracy, a conspiracy on a scale so immense as to dwarf any previous such venture in the history of man."

McCarthy did not know how to be anything other than a polarizing figure. In *Modern Times*, Paul Johnson called him "an adventurer who treated politics as a game." According to McCarthy biographer Richard Rovere, the senator "faked it all, and could not understand anyone who didn't."

———

Importantly, a sizable portion of one large voting bloc was oblivious to the senator's dangerous flaws. In a flash, Catholic culture merged the fight against communism with hosannas to McCarthy, who was a loud and proud member of St. Mary's Parish in Appleton,

Wisconsin. Brave "Tailgunner Joe," battling a sinister, atheistic ideology, was praised in thousands of Catholic school classrooms, during Sunday sermons, in the weekly parish bulletin, at nine-day novenas, the monthly Prayer Breakfast, and by armies called the Knights of Columbus, the Catholic War Veterans, and the Holy Name Society.

The church's holy war against communism was already a century-old battle, torched by the unsettling thought of Karl Marx, who in 1844 famously wrote that religion "is the opium of the people." Marx also endorsed the kind of radical change that discomfited clerics, who, in spite of vows of poverty and a Gospel elevating Good Samaritans, liked being cozy with capitalists and tacitly blessed the cruel economics of haves and have-nots.

Troubling political theory became murderous political reality when Marx disciple Vladimir Lenin took charge at the Kremlin and made slaughtering the clergy a top priority. "All modern religions and churches," Lenin wrote, are "the organs of bourgeois reaction used for the protection of the exploitation and the stupefaction of the working class."

In 1917, the year of the Russian Revolution, an apparition of Mary was reported to have appeared to a group of children at Fatima, Portugal. Mary was said to have told the children, "If my requests are heard, and the world is consecrated to my Immaculate Heart, Russia will be converted and the world will have peace," but "if my requests are not heard, the evil doctrines of atheistic Russia will spread over the whole world." For decades to come, novenas to pray for the conversion of the Russians were common in American dioceses. Members of the Blue Army honored the Fatima visionaries and circulated *Soul* magazine to seventy thousand anticommunist enthusiasts.

The new fact of an Iron Curtain was an especially tragic event for U.S. Catholics of Eastern European descent—and further enflamed opposition to the Soviet Union. Large Catholic populations in Poland, Hungary, Czechoslovakia, and Yugoslavia all suddenly confronted religious oppression, and the persecution of Hungarian cardinal József Mindszenty had incited outrage across the Catholic world.

As Anne Applebaum notes in *Iron Curtain*, Mindszenty demanded that the state "restore the Church's confiscated buildings and funds, revive the disbanded associations, and establish diplomatic relations with the Vatican." In response, the communist puppet regime resorted to gangsterism. After the cardinal was arrested during the Christmas holiday period in 1948, he was stripped of his robes, interrogated, and tortured for weeks. "Eventually," Applebaum writes, "he was forced to undergo a humiliating show trial, during which he publicly 'confessed' to a series of ludicrous crimes, including plotting the theft of Hungary's crown jewels and conspiring to return Archduke Otto von Habsburg to the Hungarian throne."

On February 12, 1949, Pope Pius announced the excommunication of all persons involved in the conviction of Mindszenty. Around the same time, Hungarian handwriting experts Laszlo and Hanna Sulner surfaced in Vienna and displayed microfilm of the forged documents they'd been forced to create in order to frame Mindszenty. Laszlo Sulner died the following year in Paris, at age thirty, and his wife was convinced he had been poisoned by Soviet agents.

For American Catholics, the defiant, courageous Hungarian prelate became a living martyr and a source of inspiration. Hungarian refugees formed "Mindszenty societies," groups that studied communist techniques in order to combat them. A Catholic church in New Brunswick, New Jersey, even erected a statue of Mindszenty. Two films were made of the Cardinal's trial, *Guilty of Treason* (1950) and *The Prisoner* (1955, starring Alec Guinness). The story was still resonant in 1966, when, in a two-part *Mission: Impossible* episode titled "Old Man Out," the stylish covert team rescues an imprisoned Catholic cardinal in Eastern Europe before he can be executed.

On August 15, 1950, as a froth of fear, fever, and faith continued, an estimated hundred thousand people made a pilgrimage to a farm in Necedah, Wisconsin. Mary Ann Van Hoof, a forty-one-year-old mother of eight, had promised the Virgin Mary would appear. The date coincided with the Feast of the Assumption, a holy day in the Roman Catholic calendar celebrating the belief that Mary was assumed bodily into heaven.

Just before noon, Van Hoof knelt in front of a statue of Mary and then used a microphone to convey her revelation. She said the Virgin Mary told her that "the Enemy of God is all over America," and "the black clouds are coming," and that "Alaska is the first stepping stone." According to a report by the Associated Press, "the faithful went away satisfied, many of them firmly believing the Virgin had been in their midst."

"At Necedah, and in her subsequent apparitions in the United States," Notre Dame professor Thomas Kselman wrote, "[The Virgin] Mary took on the role of a Cold Warrior, responding to the frightening course of events that had occurred in the aftermath of World War II."

Said religious scholar Joseph Laycock, "Van Hoof was trying to firmly frame Catholics as American long before Kennedy was elected president. People were saying you can't be a true American and follow the pope. She was saying Catholics are truly American because they are fighting communists."

In 1951, Tuesday nights at 8 p.m. became must-see viewing in Catholic living rooms as Archbishop Fulton J. Sheen launched his weekly show, *Life Is Worth Living*, broadcast by the DuMont Television Network (rival to CBS and NBC until folding in 1956). Sheen's overt support for measures to root out communist sympathizers in government and schools validated McCarthy's crusading ways. In one broadcast, Sheen advised, "Communism is to the social body what leprosy is to the physical body; in fact it is more serious, for Communism affects personality directly, while disease affects the mind and soul only indirectly. In moral language, Communism is intrinsically evil. It is evil because it submerges and destroys personality to the status of an ant in an anthill."

Sheen did his show without pay, without a script or cue cards, in front of a live audience. His only regular prop was a chalkboard. Soon, *Life Is Worth Living* was racking up weekly totals of thirty million viewers. There were four times as many requests for tickets as could be fulfilled. Every show would generate ten thousand letters. *Time* called Sheen "the first televangelist."

TV maker Admiral, the sponsor, paid the production costs in return for a one-minute commercial at the opening of the show and another minute at the close. The sponsorship was a good fit. The company was one of America's top TV manufacturers, with sets ranging in cost from $179.95 to $695, the equivalent today of about $500 to nearly $7,000, and Sheen had made it almost doctrine that millions of Catholics needed to buy a TV to patronize *Life Is Worth Living*.

In 1952, Sheen won an Emmy. Upon accepting the award, he said, "I feel it is time I pay tribute to my four writers—Matthew, Mark, Luke and John." In a February 1953 show, the archbishop equated Stalin's Soviet Union with Roman tyranny by giving a dramatic reading of the burial scene from Shakespeare's *Julius Caesar*. In place of Caesar, Cassius, Marc Antony, and Brutus, he substituted the names of Stalin, Lavrentiy Beria (head of the KGB), Georgy Malenkov (Stalin's apprentice and presumed successor), and Andrey Vyshinsky (top executioner). He concluded by saying, "Stalin must one day meet his judgment."

The dictator died within a week.

———

Joe McCarthy was also fully and regularly embraced by the most glamorous Catholic family of all: the Kennedys of Boston and Hyannis Port, Massachusetts. Joe Kennedy, the king of the clan, was a close friend and also an unabashed anticommunist. He thought of McCarthy as a kind of political experiment. In 1928, when Catholic Al Smith ran for president, his faith was a huge liability. Kennedy Sr.

saw McCarthy paving the way for Jack, the son he was hoping might soon run for the nation's highest office. As the designated guinea pig, Joe McCarthy enjoyed access to Joe Kennedy's money and his national network of contacts, providing the Wisconsinite with added national credibility and power.

As the relationship with the Kennedy family intensified, McCarthy reportedly dated two of Joe's daughters, Patricia and Eunice. He also hired Robert Kennedy to be one of his Senate staff attorneys. In 1952, when Jack ran for the Senate, McCarthy refused to campaign for Kennedy's Republican opponent, incumbent Henry Cabot Lodge Jr. In the 1952 presidential election, Eisenhower easily carried Massachusetts by a margin of 208,000 votes, but Democrat Kennedy flipped the state, defeating Lodge to win the seat. Kennedy, grateful for McCarthy's gesture, was one of the few Democratic senators who never attacked McCarthy. It was both a cynical and a smart stand. Asked by Arthur M. Schlesinger Jr. why he avoided criticism of McCarthy, Kennedy said, "Hell, half my voters in Massachusetts look on McCarthy as a hero."

———

In *McCarthy and His Enemies* (1953), rising Catholic conservatives William F. Buckley and L. Brent Bozell dared to defend McCarthy's attack on General Marshall, writing, "Marshall's loyalty is not doubted in any reasonable quarter. On the other hand, Marshall no longer rides as high as he once did in the esteem of his countrymen.... To the extent that McCarthy, through his careful analysis of Marshall's record, has contributed to cutting Marshall down to size he has performed a valuable service."

The authors envisioned McCarthy leading a movement toward a "new conformity" that would exclude communism and perhaps even liberals. "Someday the patience of America may at last be exhausted," the twenty-eight-year-old Buckley and twenty-seven-year-old Bozell wrote, "and we will strike out against the Liberals.

Not because they are treacherous like Communists, but because, with James Burnham, we will conclude 'they are mistaken in their predictions, wrong in their advice, and through the results of their actions injurious to the interests of the nation.'"

Civil libertarians were less enamored of the tie between the church and McCarthyism. Paul Blanchard, described as an anti-Catholic polemicist, assessed "deadly parallels" between Catholicism and communism in his book *Communism, Democracy and Catholic Power* (1951). Blanchard told his readers that Stalin and the pope were each running immoral, tyrannical systems threatening democratic freedoms.

In 1953, Arthur Miller debuted *The Crucible*, resurrecting the Salem witch trials of 1692 to address the hysteria and madness of the McCarthy era. "In the early Fifties," Miller recalled, "a Catholic university survey asked me why I thought there were so few of the faith in the arts or the contentions of social debate. I wrote back that Irish Catholicism and Yankee Puritanism had combined in this country to sink the inquiring mind without a trace."

CHAPTER 21

NOTORIOUSLY DISGRACEFUL CONDUCT

After Dwight Eisenhower's election, a day in the life of America began to contain more references to God and country. Ike asked Congress to add the words "under God" to the Pledge of Allegiance. A joint resolution of Congress, approved by Eisenhower, declared that "In God We Trust" had to appear on U.S. currency. Virtually all schools began the day with a prayer. In the wee hours of the morning, TV broadcasters typically signed off with the sound of "The Star-Spangled Banner" and the image of a flapping American flag. Simultaneously, the conservative class was becoming more intolerant of difference, in particular of people who weren't white, or Christian, or straight. Brewing social change justified new outbreaks of paranoia.

On April 27, 1953, Eisenhower determined that gays in government were dangerous to national security because they were judged likely to be blackmailed into traitorous activities. He issued Executive Order 10450, which authorized federal agencies to examine employees for "notoriously disgraceful conduct," such as "sexual perversion." The action, which followed the start of the Sex Deviates Program by the FBI, supplied a "Lavender Scare" to go along with the Red Scare.

"Many assumptions about Communists mirrored common beliefs about homosexuals," said Judith Atkins, an archivist at the National Archives. "Both were thought to be morally weak or psychologically disturbed, both were seen as godless, both purportedly undermined the traditional family, both were assumed to recruit, and both were shadowy figures with a secret subculture."

As McCarthyism peaked, homosexuals were also suspected of subverting U.S. foreign policy. In the New York *Daily News*, John O'Donnell wrote, "The primary issue is…that the foreign policy of the U.S., even before World War II, was dominated by an all-powerful, super-secret inner circle of highly educated, socially highly placed sexual misfits in the State Department, all easy to blackmail, all susceptible to blandishments by homosexuals in foreign nations."

O'Donnell's unsupported contention mimicked the fabricated and belabored charge by Republicans that Roosevelt and Truman had allowed a gay cabal at the State Department to sell out the country. It was Democrats at the State Department who had hired communist Alger Hiss; State Department Democrats who had sent Hiss to Yalta in order to hand Eastern Europe over to Joe Stalin; Harry Truman's State Department that had lost China to Mao and caused the Korean War. During the 1952 presidential campaign, Senator Everett Dirksen had said that a Republican victory in the November elections would mean, at last, the removal of the State Department's "lavender lads."

Senator Kenneth Wherry—a licensed undertaker who often identified Vietnam as "Indigo China"—invented a gay conspiracy that was a kitchen sink of demons, demagoguery, and lunacy. Senator Wherry explained that Adolf Hitler had made a "world list" of homosexuals who could be enlisted for espionage, sabotage, and terrorism. Hitler's list, Wherry claimed, had then fallen into the hands of the Soviets when the Red Army captured Berlin. Stalin had since added to the count of gay Manchurian Candidates and was already activating them.

"You can't separate homosexuals from subversives," Senator Wherry said. "Mind you, I don't say every homosexual is a subversive, and I don't say every subversive is a homosexual. But a man of low morality is a menace in the government, whatever he is, and they are tied up together."

Joe McCarthy told reporters, scatologically, "If you want to be against McCarthy, boys, you've got to be either a Communist or a cocksucker."

When Eisenhower signed Executive Order 10450 and codified "sexual perversion" as a security risk, it was interpreted as a ban on all homosexual employees. A wave of repression followed. In *Stonewall: The Riots That Sparked the Gay Revolution*, David Carter wrote of how "the Civil Service Commission and the FBI complied by initiating an intense campaign to ferret out homosexuals by, for instance, correlating morals arrests across the United States with lists of government employees and checking fingerprints of job applicants against the FBI's fingerprint files." Investigators also looked for supposed "indicators" of homosexuality, such as being unmarried, or having certain stereotypically gay mannerisms or dress.

The FBI pressured suspected gay employees to resign. The State Department, under Eisenhower, encouraged its staff to report suspected homosexuals. As many as five thousand gay individuals would lose their government jobs. The sudden loss of income and reputation, devastating and humiliating, caused some to choose suicide.

States followed the example of the federal government, writing new antisodomy laws and increasing sentences for homosexual activity. California convened a special session of the state legislature, which, as Carter noted, "invented a new crime: loitering in a public toilet." Those convicted were added to a state register. "Twenty-nine states enacted new sexual psychopath laws," Carter wrote, and "in almost all states, professional licenses could be revoked or denied on the basis of homosexuality, so that professionals could lose their livelihoods."

Tougher sentences were instituted for even the act of consensual gay sex by adults in the privacy of a home. Prison sentences for sodomy ranged up to twenty years. "In Pennsylvania and California," Carter added, "sex offenders could be locked in a mental institution for life, and in seven states they could be castrated.... At

California's Atascadero State Hospital, known soon after its opening as 'Dachau for Queers,' men convicted of consensual sodomy were... given electrical and pharmacological shock therapy, castrated and lobotomized."

———

Homosexuality became the inescapable subtext of the final act of Joe McCarthy's reign of terror, starting with the question: Was the senator himself gay? In 1952, *Las Vegas Sun* publisher Hank Greenspun—who would be described as one of McCarthy's "apoplectic haters"—ran a series of stories that said the answer was yes.

"Joe McCarthy is a bachelor of 43 years," wrote the *Sun*. "He seldom dates girls and if he does he laughingly describes it as window dressing. It is common talk among homosexuals in Milwaukee who rendezvous in the White Horse Inn that Senator Joe McCarthy has often engaged in homosexual activities." Another Greenspun story reported that "Young Republicans held a state convention in Wasau, Wis., at which Sen. McCarthy was an honored guest. During the convention, McCarthy spent the night with William McMahon, formerly an official of the Milwaukee County Young Republicans, in a Wasau hotel room, at which time McCarthy and McMahon engaged in illicit acts with each other."

When McCarthy married his thirty-year-old staff researcher, Jean Kerr, in 1953, the less generous view was that he did it to stifle the gossip. Whatever the truth about the senator's sexual preference—and a wide range of other possibilities have been offered by biographers—it does seem there was a measure of karmic payback in McCarthy being gay-baited since he was doing more gay-baiting than anyone else in Washington, D.C.

Although he was ostensibly uncovering communists, this was a smokescreen. McCarthy's primary goal in life was seeing his name in the paper. As one reporter put it, "Joe couldn't find a Communist in Red Square—he didn't know Karl Marx from Groucho." But

McCarthy did need to collect skins to validate his hunt and identifying a government figure as gay, or as having gay associates, or as acting like a typical gay individual, was a very reliable way to pick off a target in the gathering crusade to sweep the capital of all alleged pinkish perversions.

In March 1953, Dwight Eisenhower nominated forty-nine-year-old Chip Bohlen to be the U.S. ambassador to the Soviet Union. Bohlen was a highly respected, pragmatic career diplomat. In 1933, he and George Kennan were part of the staff that opened the U.S. mission in Moscow, when the United States resumed diplomatic relations with Russia. The two men became close friends and intellectual partners, and established themselves as the nation's top Soviet experts. Basic party loyalty dictated that a worthy selection nominated by a Republican president should have the complete backing of Republican senators. But the egomaniacal McCarthy saw a way to put his picture on the front page with an attack on a prominent name whom he could contrive to be a Soviet appeaser.

He judged Bohlen vulnerable because Bohlen had been Roosevelt's essential Russian-speaking advisor at Yalta, which therefore made him complicit in the galling surrender of Eastern Europe to Stalin. As usual, McCarthy's first call was to Hoover looking for dirt. Aware that Ike was anxious to get Bohlen confirmed, the FBI director was stingy with what he'd share. Hoover informed McCarthy that Bohlen had a number of homosexual associates. Asked by McCarthy if Bohlen was a homosexual, Hoover said he didn't know and "had no evidence to show any overt act," but "Bohlen had certainly used bad judgement in associating with homosexuals."

"On March 21," Walter Isaacson and Evan Thomas wrote in *The Wise Men*, "McCarthy rose to say that he had obtained sixteen 'closely-typed pages' of damning allegations from the [FBI] file, though he declined to offer any specifics. The rumors picked up. From his farm in Pennsylvania, George Kennan had already felt compelled to write his sister Jeannette on March 20, 'No matter what you read or hear on the radio, you can take it from me that Bohlen is not a homosexual, nor is he disloyal. That these things can be seriously suggested fills me with horror and foreboding.'...McCarthy ranted and raved, whined that Bohlen's is 'an ugly record of Great Betrayal.'"

In a preview of the crash ahead, the senator's usual demagoguery rang hollow. When senior Republicans asked to see Bohlen's FBI file, it was mostly stuffed with testimonials praising his honor and morals. He was confirmed by a vote of 74 to 13.

———

Roy Cohn's work on the Rosenberg trial brought him to Joe McCarthy's attention, and he became the senator's chief counsel in January 1953. "Not yet quite twenty-six," journalist Fred Cook wrote, "Roy Cohn was like a whirling dervish, avid to strike out in all directions at enemies of the republic, real or fancied. It soon became obvious that, brilliant as he was, he lacked those very qualities that his unstable boss most needed in an assistant—balance, a sense of restraint, and scrupulousness in the preparation of his cases. The union of McCarthy and Cohn was the partnership of kindred souls, each fueling the excesses of the other."

Cohn, like McCarthy, was also a pathological liar, and the biggest lies were the ones he told himself. A Jewish anti–Semite, he was also a draft-dodging patriot and a homosexual homophobe—in all, a confused and combustible muddle of horrible hypocrisies. In *The Paranoid Style in American Politics*, Richard Hofstadter wrote, "The real frustration of the Great Inquisition of the 1950s was not anything so simply rational as to turn up spies or prevent espionage, but to discharge resentments and frustrations, to punish, to satisfy enmities whose roots lay elsewhere than in the Communist issue itself."

Cohn long claimed he couldn't possibly be gay because he didn't act effeminately. "Anybody who knows me and knows anything about me or who knows the way my mind works or knows the way I function...would have an awfully hard time reconciling that...with any kind of homosexuality," he told Ken Auletta in 1979. "Every facet of my personality...of my aggressiveness, of my toughness, of everything along those lines, is just totally incompatible with anything like that."

In 1985, when Cohn had used his clout to get to the head of the line for treatment with AZT, the new experimental drug to fight AIDS, he told the press he had liver cancer. After Cohn's death, boyfriend Jay Taylor said, "Roy had to have sex every night, and no matter what the cost....If it weren't me, it was someone else...but no matter what, he had to have it every night."

It was also Roy Cohn's close attachment to another young man that played a central role in Joe McCarthy's undoing. G. David Schine was the handsome son of hotel and theater magnate J. Myer Schine, and had published a six-page anticommunist pamphlet titled *Definition of Communism*, a copy of which was placed in every room of his family's chain of hotels. Cohn had seen the pamphlet and hired Schine as an unpaid consultant on McCarthy's Senate staff. The relationship became notorious when the two twenty-six-year-olds went on a European junket to investigate the free libraries being run by the U.S. Information Agency. Their mission, as they very publicly announced, was to purge books by "communists, fellow travelers and unwitting promoters of the Soviet cause." U.S. Foreign officials with allegedly leftist and homosexual leanings were also being identified and tarred.

From the start, Cohn and Schine acted like they were on an extended honeymoon—although there was never an admission of a sexual relationship by either party, nor was there any proof of it. "This was no joke, but the trip was," wrote Richard Rovere. "In the basic circumstance, there was the ready-made plot for a gorgeous farce: two young Americans—a study in contrasts, like Laurel and Hardy or Rosencrantz and Guildenstern...preposterously bent on the ideological purification of the greatest government on earth. The pair spent forty hours in Paris, sixteen in Bonn, nineteen in Frankfurt, sixty in Munich, forty-one in Vienna, twenty-three in Belgrade, twenty-four in Athens, twenty in Rome, and six in London."

In the *New York Herald Tribune*, Stewart Alsop wrote, "What is going on here, in short, is less a reign of terror than a reign of stupidity.... Yet an almost incalculable amount of damage has already been done. The United States has been made to look ridiculous by such incidents as the book burning mess and the Cohn-Schine spy hunt.... One sometimes wonders what a Hiss, or a Fuchs, or a Rosenberg could have done to harm America more."

After Schine was drafted into the Army, in November 1953, Cohn campaigned to obtain special privileges for his "good friend." Harassing senior military officials, Cohn pushed for Schine to be given a commission, light duties, and extended leave, and that he be allowed to fulfill his duties in the United States, not overseas. At one point, Cohn was alleged to have said he would "wreck the Army" if his demands weren't met.

The Army issued a report on the aggressive pressure tactics, and filed charges against both Cohn and McCarthy for seeking special treatment for Private G. David Schine. McCarthy reciprocated with the countercharge that the Army was acting in bad faith. The Senate decided that the conflicting charges should be investigated by the Senate Permanent Subcommittee on Investigations. Since McCarthy was both the chairman of the subcommittee and a target of the investigation, South Dakota senator Karl Mundt replaced him temporarily as chairman. Upstart network ABC made the decision to cover the Army-McCarthy hearings live, gavel to gavel, for thirty-six days. An estimated eighty million people saw at least a portion of the TV coverage.

———

Edward R. Murrow's prime-time torching of McCarthy took place on the March 9, 1954, episode of *See It Now*. By then, the senator's political viability was in jeopardy. His net favorable rating had dropped 37 points, from a +21 to a −15. Even so, Bill Paley and CBS erred on the side of business. Neither Paley nor any of the brass at the network wanted to see the McCarthy show before the broadcast, therefore allowing them to claim ignorance if the presentation was a debacle. Murrow and his producer Fred Friendly also had to pay out of their own pockets to advertise the show in the *New York Times*.

By the early fifties, Paley's CBS had become the largest carrier of commercial advertising in the world. The sponsors of CBS programs, generally cautious and conservative, did not have much in common with the generally liberal Murrow Boys of the news division. In December 1950, Paley had demanded that all employees fill out a short questionnaire asking if they had ever been members of the Communist Party, or any other subversive group. In 1951, CBS hired its own witch hunter, a lawyer named Daniel O'Shea, whose job was to root out communist sympathizers. His title was vice president of security; inside CBS, he was called "Vice President in charge of treason."

Hoover's FBI had begun a file on Murrow in 1950. A right-wing booklet, *Red Channels*, listed two of the Murrow Boys—Howard K. Smith and Alexander Kendrick—among 151 entertainers and broadcast journalists said to be communist sympathizers. After his criticism of McCarthy's tactics, CBS's Eric Sevareid was labeled "Eric the Red" and Metropolitan Life Insurance canceled its sponsorship of his nightly radio broadcast.

Sevareid was among several at CBS News who were disappointed that Murrow had waited until 1954 to finally address McCarthyism. In 1978, after retiring, he told Charles Kuralt, "Youngsters read back and they think only one person in broadcasting and the press stood up to McCarthy, and this has made a lot of people feel very upset, including me, because that [Murrow] program came awfully late. But in the meantime, the place was strewn with the walking wounded and the bodies of journalists who'd been under fire from McCarthy."

It was the winter of 1950 when McCarthy had launched himself into prominence with a speech in a midsized West Virginia city. Four years later, in the winter of 1954, Murrow's staff spent two months editing film clips of McCarthy, a highlight package of intemperate speeches and surly behavior with congressional witnesses. As Stanley Cloud and Lynne Olson write in *The Murrow Boys*, the archival footage revealed the Wisconsin senator as "a sniggering, browbeating bully.... The program was electrifying. Not 'balanced' in the accepted sense of the word, it tested the outer limits of advocacy journalism on commercial television.... Murrow had agonized weeks beforehand about whether he was right to mount such a one-sided assault. He finally went ahead because he had come to believe about McCarthy, as he had about Hitler, that there was no 'other side' to present."

This is a portion of Murrow's close:

> We must not confuse dissent with disloyalty. We must remember always that accusation is not proof and that conviction depends upon evidence and due process of law.... We proclaim ourselves, as indeed we are, the defenders of freedom, wherever it continues to exist in the world, but we cannot defend freedom abroad by deserting it at home.... The actions of the junior Senator from Wisconsin have caused alarm and dismay amongst our allies abroad, and given considerable comfort to our enemies. And whose fault is that? Not really his. He didn't create this situation of fear; he merely exploited it—and rather successfully. Cassius was right. "The fault, dear Brutus, is not in our stars, but in ourselves."

On December 2, 1954, by a vote of 67–22, the Senate passed a measure condemning McCarthy. Senator John Kennedy abstained from voting on the motion. Already an alcoholic, McCarthy became addicted to heroin, and in 1957, he died a complete physical wreck, age forty-eight. He had used people as pawns in his phony drama, and grievously harmed America's standing in the world. But the Catholic Church invested his passing with pomp and circumstance. At Washington's St. Matthew's Cathedral, a Solemn Pontifical Requiem Mass was celebrated with more than a hundred priests. McCarthy was later buried at his parish cemetery in Appleton, where more than seventeen thousand filed through St. Mary's Church to pay their last respects. Robert F. Kennedy was among them.

CHAPTER 22

CROSS OF IRON

The essential tragedy of the Cold War was the unconscionable waste of a heedless arms race. Weapons of astonishing destruction and mountainous costs were developed, produced, and, not long after, tossed away, replaced by bombs with bigger bang, better aim, and quicker delivery. Dwight Eisenhower fully understood the implications of this state of affairs. Raised to be frugal and schooled in the terrible cost of war and its weaponry, he had made peace the closing message of his 1952 campaign—an issue that helped seal his victory—and then he genuinely attempted to make disarmament one of the first goals of his presidency, which turned into a hopeless Sisyphean struggle.

In 1953, just weeks into his first term, Eisenhower met with speechwriter Emmet Hughes to prepare for an April appearance before a group of newspaper editors. "Here is what I would like to say," he told Hughes. "The jet plane that roars over your head costs three quarters of a million dollars. That is more money than a man earning ten thousand dollars every year is going to make in a lifetime. What world can afford this sort of thing for long?...We are in an armaments race: everyone is wearing himself out to build up his defenses. Where is it going to lead us?...Now here's the other choice before us, the other road to take—the road of disarmament. What does that *mean*? It means for everybody in the world: butter, bread, clothes, hospitals, schools—good and necessary things for a decent living."

On April 16, 1953, as he spoke to the American Society of Newspaper Editors, Eisenhower's polished thoughts on the subject had him
sounding more like a liberal Democrat:

> Every gun that is made, every warship launched, every rocket
> fired signifies, in the final sense, a theft from those who hunger
> and are not fed, those who are cold and are not clothed. . . . This
> is not a way of life at all, in any true sense. Under the cloud of
> threatening war, it is humanity hanging from a cross of iron.

When Eisenhower was elected, America's nuclear arsenal contained a total of 841 bombs, and the United States was producing
around 600 more every year. By comparison, the Soviets had 50
atomic weapons. When Eisenhower left office, in 1961, America's
nuclear stockpile contained approximately 20,000 nuclear weapons
and the total megatonnage, or explosive power, of the U.S. arsenal
was equivalent to 1,366,000 Hiroshima-sized bombs (the "Little
Boy" bomb dropped on Hiroshima had a yield of 15 kilotons, or
15,000 tons of TNT). By comparison, the Soviet nuclear stockpile in
1960 was about one-tenth the size, with 1,600 weapons.

On January 17, 1961, Eisenhower made his final televised address
to the nation. Humanity was still hanging on a cross of iron:

> [The] conjunction of an immense military establishment and
> a large arms industry is new in the American experience.
> The total influence—economic, political, even spiritual—is
> felt in every city, every State house, every office of the Fed-
> eral government. . . . We must guard against the acquisition of
> unwarranted influence, whether sought or unsought, by the
> military-industrial complex.

So the president who had begun his administration making a
passionate speech about controlling defense spending concluded his

second term by, in effect, telling the nation how horribly he had failed to do so.

On January 12, 1954, Secretary of State John Foster Dulles announced a "New Look" nuclear policy at the Council on Foreign Relations in New York. In the familiar, crusty epicenter of Christian corporatist globalism, Dulles said the United States would contain "the mighty landpower of the Communist world" by doubling down on atomic diplomacy. The "New Look" was kind of like the "Old Look," except even more terrifying.

"The most chilling line in Dulles's speech," Evan Thomas wrote in *Ike's Bluff*, "was his perhaps overly succinct summation of the administration's impetus behind the New Look: 'The basic decision was to depend primarily upon a great capacity to retaliate, instantly, by means, and at places of our own choosing.' Delivered in Jehovah-like manner, the line seemed ghoulish, as if the Christian avenger Dulles relished having an apocalyptic hair trigger on his finger. The press immediately announced Dulles's policy of 'massive retaliation' and the label stuck."

"We are at a curious juncture in the history of human insanity," C. Wright Mills wrote in *The Causes of World War III*. "In the name of realism, men are quite mad, and precisely what they call utopian is now the condition of human survival.... Practical actions are now the actions of madmen and idiots. And yet these men decide; these men are honored, each in his closed-up nation, as the wise and responsible leaders of our time who are doing the best they can under trying circumstances."

The New Look posited that nuclear weapons were more cost-effective than conventional ones because pound for pound they could deliver more "killing power." The concept could be made to seem logical. In theory, if a smaller number of nuclear weapons would be *replacing* a larger number of conventional weapons, money would be saved while still deterring war. Ike in fact gave everyone a tax cut right away, in 1955. But for a number of reasons, nuclear weapons ended up *supplementing* conventional weapons and the United States developed enormous arsenals of both, wiping out any potential savings envisioned by the New Look's nuke buildup. A legion of other unforeseen consequences also emerged.

Because the Army, Navy, and Air Force each ferociously pursued nuclear weaponry, to the point of absurdity, billion-dollar redundancies and wrongheaded armaments became rampant. For example, the Army developed nuclear artillery that would have likely killed U.S. soldiers from radioactive fallout. The military services also began to discover that nuclear weapons had large add-on costs: They required sizable technical support, elaborate command-and-control centers, and extraordinary security measures.

Rival corporations and laboratories attached to nuclear R&D also competed ruthlessly, like enemy combatants, and together became yet another well-financed special interest group. For Congress, and especially representatives of poor and rural communities, the nuclear weapons infrastructure turned into pork-barrel jackpots. And once McCarthy-era Republicans convinced voters that the Soviets presented a daily existential menace to the American way of life, even Democrats decided it was politically correct to give the Pentagon a blank check. In 1959, for example, Missouri Democratic senator and presidential hopeful Stuart Symington charged that Eisenhower was choosing a balanced budget over national security. "What do you do with a government," he said, "which decides that money is more important than security?"

Behind the irrational exuberance was an inadvertent economic irony. Taking a page, unwittingly, from Karl Marx, if not Joseph Stalin, the American defense establishment observed the principles of state socialism with a heaping of totalitarianism. Mirroring the Soviet way, decisions and spending related to the U.S. nuclear arsenal were centrally planned, in secret, without consideration of market forces or budgetary oversight, and absent any kind of public disclosure.

Estimates of how much firepower was enough also depended on which general you asked. Admiral Arleigh Burke, chief of naval operations, estimated in 1957 that 720 warheads aboard 45 Polaris submarines were sufficient to achieve deterrence—*by themselves.* This figure took into account the possibility that some weapons would not work and others would be destroyed in a Soviet attack. If all went according to plan, Burke said only 232 warheads were actually required to destroy the Soviet Union. However, that same year, General James Gavin, head of Army research and development, told Congress that his branch of the service would require 151,000 nuclear warheads. General Gavin envisioned the use of as many as 423 warheads in a single day of "intense combat." And when ballistic missiles were introduced, a gluttonous Air Force absurdly demanded 10,000.

"During the Kennedy and Johnson Administrations," nuclear arms expert Eric Schlosser wrote in the *New Yorker*, "Secretary of Defense Robert McNamara concluded that the United States should have enough nuclear weapons to fulfill two objectives: deter a Soviet attack and limit the damage of such an attack by destroying Soviet nuclear forces....McNamara believed the United States should always be able to kill at least a quarter of the Soviet population and eliminate at least two-thirds of its industrial capacity."

Curtis LeMay secretly tasked Air Force think tank RAND (short for **R**esearch **AN**d **D**evelopment) with establishing the targets for a full-scale nuclear blitz. It came to be called the Single Integrated Operational Plan (SIOP). Neither the secretary of defense nor any of the civilians at the Pentagon was shown or informed about it. "The reasons for this secrecy," Thomas Powers wrote, "had to do with service rivalries, technical complexities...and the personality of LeMay, who had made up his mind that he would know and decide when nuclear attack on Russia was necessary, and what ought to be on the list.... The first SIOP in December 1960 planned an overwhelming knockout blow. Moscow alone was targeted with at least eighty nuclear weapons, and every Russian city with a population greater than 25,000 would be hit by at least one. China would get the same, for no particular reason.... [The planners] estimated that about half the population of Russia and China would die of radiation effects alone—a total of about 380 million people."

Edward Teller, the inventor of the hydrogen bomb, eventually realized that there was a limit to the destructiveness of even thermonuclear explosions. He estimated that at somewhere around 100 megatons, an H-bomb "would lift a chunk of the atmosphere—ten miles in diameter, something of that kind—lift it into space. Then you make it a thousand times bigger still. You know what would happen? You lift the same chunk into space with thirty times the velocity."

The United States would ultimately build a total of 70,000 warheads during the Cold War. We would also establish military alliances with 50 nations and have as many as 1.5 million soldiers posted in 117 countries. Between 1946 and 1991, the United States spent an estimated $20 trillion on defense. (According to one source, it would take you 31,709 years to count to a trillion at the rate of one dollar a second.) Defense costs never dipped below 20 percent of the federal budget, with spikes during the Korean War (consuming about 70 percent of all government spending) and Vietnam (approximately 50 percent). At the height of the Cold War, our military industrial complex represented about 10 percent of the gross domestic product.

As for the Soviet Union, it was estimated that defense-related activities employed one out of five citizens. But all statistics on Cold War Soviet arms spending are unreliable since the Kremlin shaded or outright lied about the costs. Writing for the Hoover Institution, Soviet specialist Mark Harrison explained the thinking of Marshal Sergei Akhromeev, who was chief of the general staff in the 1980s and opposed to transparency.

"First," Harrison wrote, "Akhromeev feared that honesty would do more damage to Soviet credibility than continuing to lie. A truthful figure would come out too low." The Kremlin had long claimed strategic parity with the United States, and the CIA had conveniently supported this fiction. A sudden confession to budget inflation, Akhromeev reasoned, would immediately expose what had been a super-successful bluff and also supply an already skeptical Soviet citizenry with more confirmation that the leadership was always deceiving them. "Full disclosure," Harrison continued, "would also complicate the market position of the Soviet Union in the global arms trade." In the USSR, labor and equipment were cheap, and if buyers knew about the low production costs, it could undermine prices on the world market. "Finally," Harrison wrote, "Akhromeev saw a significant ideological advantage in continued secrecy: It was useful to encourage 'myths about large outlays of the USSR's on military purposes' because they 'provided a justification... of the low standard of living of people in the USSR.'"

———

On March 1, 1954, a U.S. thermonuclear test was staged on a coral island at Bikini Atoll. The bomb went off at 6:45 a.m. The makers of the top-secret Castle Bravo device had estimated that it would yield five to six megatons. However, the lithium deuteride used as an ingredient of the fusion fuel proved far more combustible than anticipated, and tripled the size of the explosion to *15 megatons*. This was five times the power of all the bombs dropped during World War II, including Hiroshima and Nagasaki.

Navy weathermen stationed 155 miles to the east saw the flash of the explosion. As the force of the bomb disintegrated the island that had served as its platform, a cloud of radioactive pulverized coral billowed menacingly, ultimately becoming 40 miles wide and 220 miles long. Some of the scientists observing the test wondered if the atmosphere was indeed catching on fire. The worst radiological disaster in history was under way.

A Japanese fishing trawler called the *Lucky Dragon*, with a crew of twenty-three, was ninety miles east of Bikini, and forty miles outside the designated danger zone. When the radioactive cloud reached the boat, a white coral dust fell from the sky. "It was so dense," Daniel Lang wrote in a 1955 piece for the *New Yorker*, "one of the crew later reported that it was faintly audible as it landed on the deck. The strange downpour continued until about noon, and by the time it let up, the dust had covered the boat, the men, and their catch like a white sheet; it lay so thick on the deck that the men left footprints when they walked on it."

The U.S. military had to evacuate residents of Pacific islands as far as three hundred miles from the explosion. Covering up the disaster was the immediate knee-jerk U.S. response. The Atomic Energy Commission ordered a news blackout. That proved futile. When the *Lucky Dragon* arrived back in Japan, on March 14, Lang wrote of how "practically every one of the fishermen was ridden with nausea, blisters, lesions, fever, conjunctivitis, abdominal pains, and other symptoms of overexposure to radiation." The incident received massive and prolonged press attention in Japan and around the world.

Stonewalling continued nonetheless. Ike didn't even want to acknowledge the existence of a new and more destructive nuclear weapon.

"Mr. President," reporter Merriman Smith began at a March 17 White House press conference, "the Joint Congressional Atomic Energy Commission said last night that we now have a hydrogen bomb and can deliver it anywhere in the world. I wonder if you could discuss that?"

"No," Eisenhower answered. "I wouldn't want to discuss that."

A few months later, a thirty-nine-year-old member of the *Lucky Dragon* crew, Aikichi Kuboyama, was hospitalized with hepatitis—a symptom related to the Castle Bravo accident. Before dying on September 23, 1954, Kuboyama said, "I pray that I am the last victim of an atomic or hydrogen bomb." The Japanese public called for an end to thermonuclear testing. The U.S. State Department would eventually pay Japan $15 million in reparations.

—

As the travails of the *Lucky Dragon* were making headlines, Tomoyuki Tanaka, a forty-four-year-old Japanese film producer, was flying back to Tokyo from Jakarta, Indonesia. He was scrambling for a new idea because Indonesian financing had collapsed just before his latest project was about to start filming. In the *Virginia Quarterly Review*, Steve Ryfle explained what happened next: "Nervous and sweating, [Tanaka] looked out the window at the ocean below, and a light went on in his head. Inspired by the anti-nuke clamor surrounding *The Lucky Dragon*'s misfortune, Tanaka approached his boss, Toho's powerful production chief Iwao Mori, and said he wanted to make Japan's first-ever giant monster movie. Tanaka had no story and no idea what the monster would look like, but he had a premise: what if a nuclear explosion stirred a monster from an eons-long sleep on the ocean floor and that monster vented its wrath on Japan?"

The film resulting from Tanaka's airborne inspiration premiered in Japan on November 3, 1954. It was titled *Gojira*—a portmanteau of the Japanese words for gorilla (*gorira*) and whale (*kujira*). Toho's foreign sales department would anglicize the title as *Godzilla*.

The film's first audio would be a series of primal shrieks, which for children raised during the Cold War became a chilling reminder of the constant prospect of being erased by a hail of city-smashing nukes. This sound effect was the invention of composer Akira Ifukube, who rubbed a leather glove coated in pine-tar resin against the strings of a double bass. The first scenes of the film reference the fate of the *Lucky Dragon*. As crew members of a fishing vessel are relaxing to a song being played on a harmonica and a guitar, the ocean around them begins to bubble. Following a flash, the ship is swallowed by an explosion.

About ten minutes into the film, Gojira—Godzilla—emerges from a roiling ocean during a typhoon, flattens a fishing village, and leaves behind immense radioactive footprints. The actor inside the monster reptile was Haruo Nakajima, wearing a two-hundred-pound suit made of rubber and latex. Nakajima would recall how Eiji Tsu-buraya, the special effects director, struggled to find enough material for the costume amid Japan's postwar shortages and rationing. Under the hot lights of the sound stage, Nakajima would sweat so much that he could wring enough perspiration from his undershirt to fill half a bucket.

As Gojira proves impervious to standard military weaponry, we learn that there is only one way to stop him: the Oxygen Destroyer, invented by a character named Dr. Serizawa, who wears an eye patch from a World War II injury. In the climax of the film, Serizawa ago-nizes about using his weapon, fearing that it will ignite another arms race. Ultimately, he allows the Oxygen Destroyer to be used, but he destroys his research papers so the weapon cannot be rebuilt.

In his *Study of the Effects of the Atomic Bomb on Japanese Culture*, John Rocco Roberto wrote how "in producing *Gojira*, special effects master Eiji Tsuburaya, producer Tomoyuki Tanaka, and director Ishiro Honda accomplished a feat unequaled at the time. In the guise of a typical Hollywood-style 'monster movie,' they made Japan, and ultimately the world, experience the bombings of Hiroshima and Nagasaki all over again."

CHAPTER 23

CIVIL DEFENSE

"The Shelter," a signature *Twilight Zone* episode, speculated on the moral quandary resulting from what might happen in a neighborhood where those who hadn't prepared for the worst appealed to someone who had. After a Civil Defense alert of a possible attack, the Stockton family of three—Dr. Bill, wife Grace, son Paul—retreat to their bomb shelter. When neighbors without their own shelters seek to join the Stocktons, Dr. Bill explains that there is only sufficient air and provisions for three people. Ugly emotions and prejudices emerge along with a mounting hysteria.

The neighbors ultimately break down the shelter door with an improvised battering ram. As the episode concludes, we learn that the attack is a false alarm. The neighbors attempt to apologize to Dr. Stockton—but the hatreds exposed by the incident make repairing the relationships impossible. In the closing narration, *Twilight Zone* creator Rod Serling tells us, "No moral, no message, no prophetic tract, just a simple statement of fact: for civilization to survive, the human race has to remain civilized. Tonight's very small exercise in logic from *The Twilight Zone*." The show was a sensation, generating thirteen hundred pieces of mail inside of two days.

Meanwhile, unknown to most Americans, the country's leadership was making sure they had a place to hide in the event of a nuclear attack—just like Dr. Bill Stockton in *The Twilight Zone*. Advised by captured Nazi engineers who'd expertly constructed Hitler's impermeable Berlin bunker, and using a workforce of miners who'd successfully dug out the Lincoln Tunnel, Civil Defense authorities established vast subterranean lairs in the mountains of rural Pennsylvania, Virginia, and West Virginia.

- The Raven Rock complex was the designated escape site for the Pentagon hierarchy. It was buried under a quarter mile of granite, had thirty-four-ton blast doors, and was positioned on coiled springs to ease swaying from an attack.
- Mount Weather, located in the Blue Ridge Mountains about forty-eight miles from Washington, was to serve as the emergency location for the president, key members of the executive branch, and the Supreme Court. It was an underground city with room for thousands, reservoirs for drinking water, and its own police and fire departments.
- Congress was to be housed in a bunker underneath the stately Greenbrier Hotel in West Virginia. The facility had its own power plant, a medical clinic, a dentist's office, and a four-hundred-seat cafeteria.
- Peters Mountain, in the Appalachians, was one of several underground sites for the intelligence community.
- The Federal Reserve built a bunker in Mount Pony, Virginia, to squirrel away $2 billion in emergency cash.

As these facilities were being built, the Cold War adversaries were producing missiles that could reach targets in the space of thirty minutes or less, which in all likelihood made all this mountain burrowing moot since it wasn't possible to move the entire guts of the federal government to safety in such a short period of time. But even had officials been able to reach such sites as Raven Rock, Mount Weather, and the Greenbrier, it rather quickly became clear to senior U.S. leadership that there wouldn't be much of a country left to govern in the wake of a nuclear holocaust.

After the 1954 Castle Bravo test, Eisenhower's scientific advisors showed him a top-secret map of the fallout pattern of the new multi-megaton hydrogen bomb. A vast swath of the far-flung Marshall Islands was littered with lethal levels of radiation. "The scientists then superimposed that same fallout pattern onto a map of the East Coast of the United States," Annie Jacobsen wrote in *The Pentagon's Brain*. "If ground zero had been Washington, D.C., instead of Bikini Atoll, every resident of the greater Washington-Baltimore area would be dead....Even in Philadelphia, 150 miles away, the majority of the inhabitants would have been exposed to radiation levels that would have killed them within the hour. In New York City, 225 miles away, half the population would have died by nightfall. All the way to the Canadian border, inhabitants would have been exposed to 100 roentgens or more, their suffering similar to what the fisherman on the *Lucky Dragon* had endured."

The fallout map would remain classified for decades, although Eisenhower would begin to tell his advisors that the concept of civil defense was laughable. In 1956, the president received a study from the U.S. military that confirmed his view. It determined that in the event of a thermonuclear war, the United States would experience total economic collapse, the federal government would be wiped out, and 65 percent of the population would require some kind of medical care. "You couldn't have this kind of war," he told intimates. "There just aren't enough bulldozers to scrape bodies off the streets....You might as well go out and shoot everyone you see and then shoot yourself."

At the same time, Pentagon planners kept thinking about how to win a nuclear war, and once the Soviets began regular nuclear tests with matching megabombs, it became politically hazardous to urge disarmament. In 1953, persistent H-bomb opponent Robert Oppenheimer had dared write that more wasn't really *more*: "The very least we can say is that, looking ten years ahead, it is likely to be small comfort that the Soviet Union is four years behind us, and small comfort that they are only half as big as we are. The very least we can conclude is that our twenty-thousandth bomb, useful as it may be in filling the vast munitions pipeline of a great war, will not in any deep strategic sense offset their two-thousandth." Before the end of 1953, Oppenheimer would have his security clearance revoked, the case against him greatly helped by Hoover's FBI, which had been shadowing the Manhattan Project head for years and discovered evidence that Oppenheimer's wife and brother were at one point members of the Communist Party.

An unfounded fear of falling behind the Soviets in the arms race also soon emerged, which made Western officials highly vulnerable to Kremlin optical trickery in 1955. On Soviet Aviation Day, the same ten Bison jet-powered strategic bombers flew past the reviewing stand six times, which created the illusion that the Soviets had at least sixty of these planes. The fictional sixty bombers were used as the basis for speculating that the Soviets would have six hundred in a few short years. As GlobalSecurity.org reported, "This show, combined with the introduction of the smaller Badger jet-powered bomber the year before, resulted in the perception in the United States of a *bomber gap*."

But there would never be six hundred Bison bombers, nor could even a single Bison hit any American targets because it only had a combat radius of 5,000 miles, too limited to reach either U.S. coast from the nearest point on Soviet territory. By contrast, the first generation of U.S. B-52 bombers, delivered in 1955, were able to fly 7,343 miles when refueled, and some of them didn't even need to travel that far to strike the Soviet landmass, because the Air Force assigned a sizable portion of the bombers to twenty-five overseas bases.

After touring SAC facilities across the world, Mississippi senator John Stennis told a colleague, "I was tremendously impressed and encouraged at the enormous striking power that we could put into action on many fronts in a matter of hours should we be attacked. This is not power on paper; it is actual, real, and to an extent, ready. Russia is rimmed by lines of bases three deep."

By the conclusion of Eisenhower's presidency, LeMay's Strategic Air Command was reaching peak strength, with 2,921 bombers and tankers. In the meantime, the USSR's balky turbojet Bison bomber was a total bust, phased out in favor of the turboprop Bear, which was capable of flying 9,000 miles on its own internal fuel. Technologically, the Soviets had gone backward to go forward: jet to propeller. They were also shifting to missiles as the chief method of delivering their nuclear arsenal. Almost inevitably, this strategic switch prompted talk from U.S. hawks about a "missile gap," which, like the "bomber gap," was also an illusion.

Overall, the U.S. military-industrial complex never fell behind the Soviet Union in the development of nuclear weaponry. "The United States," said physicist Herb York, "cannot maintain its qualitative edge without having an aggressive R&D establishment that pushes against the technological frontiers without waiting to be asked, and that, in turn, creates a faster paced arms race."

After testing the first atomic bomb, in 1945, the United States developed the first intercontinental nuclear bomber, the B-47, which began flying in 1951. A year later, the United States tested the first H-bomb. In 1954, USS *Nautilus* became the first nuclear submarine. The high-altitude U-2 spy plane, for which the Soviets had no answer, began operating in 1955. A year later, the United States was the first to air drop a live hydrogen bomb. In 1957, the United States began developing the first tactical nuclear weapons. The W-54 "Davy Crockett" rifle, a portable forty-eight pounds, was set on a tripod and fired a nuclear projectile that had the same yield as the bomb dropped on Hiroshima. USS *George Washington*, launched in 1959, was the world's first operational nuclear-powered ballistic missile submarine, armed with sixteen Polaris A-1 missiles, each carrying a one-megaton warhead that was a thousand times more powerful than

the atomic bombs dropped on Japan. The *Washington* and its succes-
sors gave the United States a hidden, mobile nuclear platform lurking
in the coastal waters around the Soviet Union. If you were the Kremlin leadership, this was like having a gun perpetually resting against
your temple.

———

As it turned out, the inevitability of species suicide from an atomic
exchange discouraged the start of a World War III. But the fates were
regularly tempted and proved awfully kind. As the superpowers
intensified the complexity of their nuclear arsenals, they simultaneously increased the probability of error, failure, or simple fuckups.
Predictably, machinery broke, accidents happened. Countdowns
were activated to answer incoming warheads nowhere to be found.
False alarms were caused by a faulty 46-cent computer chip, a moon
rising over Norway, the launch of a weather rocket, a solar storm, and
sunlight reflecting off clouds. Nuclear bombs were lost on land, on
the seas, and in midair.

As nuclear accidents became common, a classification system was
created based on Native American terminology:

- **Empty quiver**: loss, theft, or seizure of a nuclear weapon.
- **Bent spear**: damage to a weapon without any harm to the
  public or risk of detonation.
- **Broken arrow**: an accident that caused the unauthorized
  launch or jettison of a weapon, a fire, an explosion, a release of
  radioactivity, or a full-scale detonation.

One of the most serious "broken arrows" occurred on January 31,
1958, at a Strategic Air Command base in Sidi Slimane, Morocco.
A tire on a B-47 blew out while the nuclear bomber was taxiing
on a runway. It was carrying one of America's most powerful weapons, a 10-megaton Mark 36 hydrogen bomb. After the blowout, a

fire started in the wheel well and spread to the fuselage. The B-47 became engulfed in flames and split in two. Firefighters began spraying the wreckage, but after ten minutes, with the fire still out of control, the commanding general at Sidi Slimane ordered the base evacuated. As Schlosser wrote in *Command and Control*, "cars full of airmen and their families sped into the Moroccan desert, fearing a nuclear disaster." Explosives in the Mark 36 burned but didn't detonate. The accident report indicated that the hydrogen bomb and the jet bomber melted into a radioactive slab of slag weighing four tons. A jackhammer was used to break the slag into pieces. The most lethal chunks were sealed in cans. The rest was buried next to the runway. The Department of Defense decided to keep the incident secret, but told the king of Morocco.

On March 11, 1958, a B-47 accidentally dropped a Mark 6 nuclear bomb on a children's playhouse in Mars Bluff, South Carolina. The incident began when the pilot encountered a fault light indicating the bomb's locking pin had not engaged. Air Force captain Bruce Kulka, navigator and bombardier, went to check and mistakenly grabbed the emergency release pin. The Mark 6, with Kulka on top of it, suddenly dropped onto the bomb bay doors. Kulka was able to slide off before the weight of the nearly eight-thousand-pound nuclear device forced the doors open and the bomb plummeted fifteen thousand feet.

Below, on what was a Tuesday afternoon, six-year-old Helen Gregg, her nine-year-old sister Frances, and their nine-year-old cousin Ella Davies were about two hundred feet away when the Mark 6 hit their playhouse. The conventional explosives in the bomb detonated, which replaced the playhouse with a crater seventy-five feet wide and thirty-five feet deep. The Mark 6, however, did not yet contain its fissile core, so there was no atomic blast. The three girls suffered minor injuries, as did the other three members of the Gregg household: mother Effie, who was inside the house sewing, and Walter Sr. and Jr., who were in the toolshed. In addition to leaving a crater, the blast wave from the explosion, as Schlosser delineated, "knocked the doors off the Gregg house, blew out the windows, collapsed the roof, riddled the walls with holes, destroyed the new Chevrolet parked in the driveway, and killed half a dozen chickens." Seven other nearby buildings were also damaged, including a church. Walls and windows were cracked as far as five miles away. Cousin Ella Davies ultimately required thirty-one stitches for her wounds. The Greggs later sued the Air Force and received $54,000, the equivalent of about a half million dollars today.

Unlike the incident at Sidi Slimane, a secure military base in a cloistered kingdom, it was impossible to hide the Mars Bluff blunder from the press. Worldwide coverage followed. The *New York Times* asked, "Are We Safe from Our Own Atomic Bombs?" The Soviets claimed that South Carolina had been contaminated by radioactive fallout. Within weeks, the newly established Campaign for Nuclear Disarmament, one of the first major global antinuclear movements, staged a four-day protest march from London's Trafalgar Square to the British nuclear weapons factory at Aldermaston. In preparation for the march, artist Gerald Holton designed what would be an iconic image. "I drew myself," Holton said, "the representative of an individual in despair, with palms outstretched outwards and downwards in the manner of Goya's peasant before the firing squad." Holton's finished product was a stick figure inside a circle: the peace sign.

CHAPTER 24

SERVING MONEY

Together, CIA director Allen Dulles and Secretary of State John Foster Dulles formed a ready-reaction team to protect exploitive American mercantilism endangered by a global surge of self-determination. Eisenhower's intelligence establishment, according to Tim Weiner, "undertook 170 new major covert actions in 48 nations—political, psychological, and paramilitary warfare missions in countries where American spies knew little of the culture or the language or the history of the people." The problematic reverberations from this spasm of naked imperialism would last for decades.

In the 1950s, American foreign policy was often interchangeable with the Dulles family business history at the Wall Street law firm of Sullivan & Cromwell. "This was not a law firm like any other," said journalist Stephen Kinzer. "It had its specialty. Its specialty was helping big American companies pressure foreign governments into doing what they wanted. Virtually every large American multinational corporation retained Sullivan & Cromwell. Every time those companies had trouble in some other country they would turn to Sullivan & Cromwell."

In 1911, former secretary of state John Watson Foster used his influence to get grandson and recent law graduate John Foster Dulles a job at Sullivan & Cromwell. Allen joined his brother at the firm in 1926, and proved to be a master in the art of the revolving door. He rapidly used far-flung contacts he had obtained at the State

Department to facilitate bank loans of $13 million to Bolivia, $10 million to Colombia, and $50 million to Germany. In 1930, Allen was made a partner at the firm, and in the same year was accused by columnist Drew Pearson of fixing the Colombian election to protect a client's oil concession.

"Sullivan & Cromwell found ways to make offers to...countries that they couldn't refuse," Kinzer said. "It means that the Dulles brothers understood the world from the perspective of their Wall Street clients. It also means that at an early age they became experienced in the technique of pressuring foreign governments." What the brothers did on Wall Street for *the* biggest, and *the* most powerful, and *the* most globally active of all the Wall Street law firms would not be all that different from what they ended up doing in Washington, D.C. The Dulles boys seemed to abide by a commandment of their own making: *Government should serve money.*

In 1951, the new, democratically elected Iranian leader Mohammed Mossadegh had the audacity to nationalize the British-owned holdings of the Anglo-Iranian Oil Company, later known as British Petroleum, or BP. At Sullivan & Cromwell, the Dulles brothers had represented London's J. Henry Schroder Banking Corporation, which served as the financial agent for Britain's Iranian petroleum interests and had much to lose by anti-imperialist decolonization. Iran had also squelched a $650 million infrastructure development deal brokered by Allen Dulles just before he'd left Sullivan & Cromwell for the CIA. The contract—worth about $6 billion in today's money—would have been at the time the largest overseas development project in modern history.

The shah had approved the deal, but after he was stripped of power, Mossadegh's parliament killed it. The people's rebellion that neutered his royal highness was also unwelcome news to another longtime Sullivan & Cromwell client, the Rockefeller family, which was seeking a larger profile in the Iranian market for two Rockefeller holdings, Standard Oil and Chase Manhattan Bank. John Foster

Dulles had been one of the Rockefeller family's principal Wall Street lawyers and served on the board of the Rockefeller Foundation.

On August 19, 1953, in a coup staged by the CIA, Mossadegh was jailed and the shah returned to the throne. The shah declared martial law and became a supplicant to American interests. Guided by the CIA, his first priority was preventing another people's rebellion. In 1955, career CIA officers who were specialists in covert operations, intelligence analysis, and counterintelligence, including Major General Herbert Norman Schwarzkopf, built Iran's secret police unit, which would be called the SAVAK (Sāzemān-e Ettelā'āt va Amniyat-e Keshvar, or Organization of National Intelligence and Security). This tactic was a carbon copy of the Soviet playbook.

In the meantime, Secretary of State Dulles used his associates at Sullivan & Cromwell to handle the "re-colonialization" of Iranian oil. A new consortium required the British to share the spoils with American oil interests. Ownership in the new Iranian Oil Participants Company (IOP) was divided among BP (40 percent), Royal Dutch Shell (20 percent), and the five major American oil companies, which evenly split the remaining 40 percent. Those five were Standard Oil of New Jersey (later Exxon), Standard Oil of California (later Chevron), Socony-Vacuum Oil Company (later Mobil), the Texas Company (later Texaco), and Gulf Oil. Small independent U.S. oil companies were prevented from participation. Until the oil crisis in 1973, the seven companies participating in the Iranian oil deal—a group that would come to be known as the "Seven Sisters"—controlled approximately 85 percent of the world's known oil reserves.

Iran would also be a participant in the soon-to-be-established U.S. Overseas Internal Security Program, run by the CIA, in concert with the Pentagon and the State Department. Ultimately, the United States provided training for 771,217 foreign military and police officers. The program's facilities would include an international police academy in Panama and a school for bomb training in Texas. In addition to members of SAVAK, an organization soon reviled world-wide for torturing and killing Iranian dissidents, alumni of the Over-seas Internal Security Program included representatives from the secret police units of Cambodia, Iraq, Laos, the Philippines, South Korea, South Vietnam, and Thailand. Graduates also included the future leaders of death squads in El Salvador and Honduras.

—

As the CIA's covert action in Iran was taking place, Guatema-lan leader Jacobo Árbenz Guzmán, freely elected like Mossadegh, attempted to undo decades of exploitation by U.S. business inter-ests. He nationalized 234,000 acres of uncultivated land owned by the nation's largest landholder, the American-owned United Fruit Company, and announced plans to seize another 173,000 acres of idle company property along the Guatemalan coast.

United Fruit, also known as UFCO, exported bananas out of Costa Rica, Honduras, Panama, and Guatemala. In the 1920s and '30s, it was the world's largest banana production and marketing company, controlling 70 percent of the global banana trade. UFCO's relationship with Central American governments produced the term "banana republic," the pejorative for poor, unstable, corrupt coun-tries reliant on a single crop and submissive to American business and political interests.

In nationalizing United Fruit's property, Árbenz was in effect voiding a ridiculous one-sided agreement negotiated by Secretary of State Dulles while he was at Sullivan & Cromwell. The deal had granted United Fruit a ninety-nine-year lease on one-seventh of the country's arable land. In 1950, UFCO reported a profit of $65 million, which was twice the total revenue of the Guatemalan gov-ernment. At the same time, workers on the banana plantations were striking to raise their pay from $1.50 per day.

Though separated from Sullivan & Cromwell, both Dulles broth-ers had an ongoing interest in the financial welfare of UFCO. They had spots on the company's board of directors, and were believed to own substantial blocks of stock. Eisenhower's secretary at the White House, Ann Whitman, also had a direct tie to UFCO. Her husband, Ed, was the company's spokesman. In that role, Whitman brought journalists to Guatemala on all-expenses-paid junkets, an initiative that yielded puff pieces on the banana giant in the *New York Times*, the *Christian Science Monitor*, and the *Herald Tribune*. Whitman's PR efforts also included the production of a propaganda film, *Why the Kremlin Hates Bananas*, a fairy tale of how United Fruit was acting as a bulwark against creeping communism.

———

After the successful covert action in Iran, President Eisenhower didn't need much convincing to authorize a CIA-backed military coup to get rid of Árbenz. As it was, Ike had a business-friendly outlook and a firm belief that the world's poor were prime targets for exploitation by the Kremlin. But Operation Success got off to a rough start.

As Árbenz's successor, the CIA had picked a cashiered Guate-malan colonel, Carlos Castillo Armas. On June 18, 1954, Castillo Armas launched an assault from Honduras. Wearing a leather jacket and driving a battered station wagon, he tried to occupy three small villages with a force of a hundred men. Half of them were killed or captured in a matter of days. A CIA P-38 also accidentally dropped napalm on a British cargo ship being loaded with cotton and coffee. The incident would cost U.S. taxpayers $1 million in compensation.

Operation Success was being supplemented by psychological warfare conducted through the airwaves, which turned the tide. The CIA had established a pirate radio station, the Voice of Libera-tion. Announcer David Atlee Phillips, a Spanish-speaking agency freelancer with an acting background, told his listeners about a war that never was in which government troops were being pushed back or refusing to fight. On June 27, 1954, Phillips reported that Cas-tillo Armas and two huge columns of his men were just outside the capital preparing for the final battle. Árbenz, drunk and despondent, resigned to a force that didn't exist.

When Guatemala's newly installed leader, Castillo Armas, was summoned to Washington, D.C., he received a twenty-one-gun salute, and a state dinner at the White House. Richard Nixon, then Eisenhower's vice president, offered a toast. It was a giant load of horseshit:

> We in the United States have watched the people of Guate-mala record an episode in their history deeply significant to all peoples. Led by the courageous soldier who is our guest this evening, the Guatemalan people revolted against communist rule, which in collapsing bore graphic witness to its own shal-lowness, falsity and corruption.

As Tim Weiner wrote in *Legacy of Ashes*, "Guatemala was at the beginning of forty years of military rule, death squads, and armed repression."

One of the witnesses to the American-directed coup was twenty-five-year-old Ernesto Guevara. The middle-class Argentine medi-cal school graduate had made Guatemala City the last stop on a months-long cross-continental motorcycle trip. In Guatemala, Gue-vara hooked up with Cuban insurgents who had been exiled after the failed Moncada Barracks assault led by Fidel Castro. It was these Cubans who first began calling him "Che," after noticing how he often used the word, an Argentinian colloquialism that means "mate." Guevara would also meet his future wife in Guatemala City, a Peruvian Marxist named Hilda Gadea.

The experience of seeing a democratically elected government unseated, with U.S. warplanes strafing and bombing Guatemalan civilian areas, convinced Guevara to become a full-fledged socialist revolutionary, prepared to dedicate his life to liberating Third World countries from capitalist exploitation. "Whether consciously or not,"

Lucía Álvarez de Toledo wrote in *The Story of Che Guevara*, "from then on he was on a quest for a people ready to rise up in arms so that he could throw in his lot with them."

———

In the spring of 1954, the French were making a disastrous last stand against Ho Chi Minh's Vietminh forces at Dien Bien Phu. This was a fight that the French had welcomed. They had dropped twelve thousand paratroopers into the remote mountain outpost and created a fort in a valley with a series of strongholds. The French expected General Vo Nguyen Giap, head of the People's Army, to take the bait and suffer a devastating defeat because, it was assumed, his guerrilla fighters were unfamiliar with traditional warfare. This arrogance produced a French slaughter. Giap marched fifty thousand men and heavy artillery over the mountains, perched his army on the high ground, and rained a barrage of shells on the fort. The French soon began calling Dien Bien Phu *le Pot de Chambre*—"the Chamber Pot."

John Foster Dulles had decided, incorrectly, that the war was being conducted from Beijing, but Mao was never Ho's master. On April 7, 1954, Eisenhower introduced another wrongheaded notion. Discussing the surrounded French garrison with members of the press, and raising fear about a spreading communist hegemony, Ike formally introduced the horribly simplistic and fundamentally flawed domino theory, explaining, "You have a row of dominoes set up, you knock over the first one, and what will happen to the last one is the certainty that it will go over very quickly. So you could have the beginning of a disintegration that would have the most profound consequences." The loss of Dien Bien Phu, Eisenhower said, imperiled Australia, New Zealand, and Japan. *But it didn't.*

Around the same time, Eisenhower wrote a letter to Winston Churchill seeking to have the British join with the Americans to save the French. Both Truman and Eisenhower were stuck seeing World War III—and the clash of big powers—on every horizon. "If I may refer again to history," Eisenhower wrote to Churchill, "we failed to halt Hirohito, Mussolini, and Hitler by not acting in unity and in time. That marked the beginning of many years of stark tragedy and desperate peril. May it not be that our nations may have learned something from that lesson?"

What Ike, like his secretary of state, failed to fully understand or accept was that Ho Chi Minh's insurgency was, principally, a unitary fight for independence, consistent with a wider anticolonial struggle. Amid this disruption, overseers in Moscow, Beijing, and Washington were certainly picking sides and providing support, but the spark for these liberations and the path of their revolutions was being driven by internal militant movements. During the Cold War, the UN would grow from the original 51 members to 159. This explosion largely came from a so-called Third World of nonaligned nations achieving independence from colonial masters. "The most agonizing problems of recent American foreign policy," historian Marilyn Young would write in 1971, "have concerned not our ability to reach accommodation with acknowledged big powers, but our persistent refusal to allow revolutionary change and self-determination in smaller nations."

On May 7, 1954, with their refuge reduced to the size of a baseball field, the remaining French force surrendered at Dien Bien Phu. Of thirteen thousand French troops, all were either killed or taken prisoner. In July, at a peace conference in Geneva, Vietnam was divided in half. The communists claimed the North; the South became a U.S. client state. The peace conference also encouraged an election in 1956 in order to unify the country under a single leader.

"Of what . . . revolutionary war had done to Vietnam, of the fateful future political alignments it had produced, Americans had no comprehension," David Halberstam wrote. "We had given nearly $3 billion in aid to the French, yet it might as well have gone into a black hole. . . . We had come to see the struggle in Vietnam through the prism of the Cold War and had, in effect, already begun the process of making a commitment to a small, artificial country, where the other side held complete title to nationalism."

———

In July 1954, Ike asked General Jimmy Doolittle to conduct a classified study on the performance of the still relatively new CIA. Doolittle recommended even more constant conflict against the forces of communism and argued that there should be no code of conduct in the execution of that aim. "It is now clear that we are facing an implacable enemy whose avowed objective is world domination by whatever means and at whatever cost," Doolittle wrote. "There are no rules in such a game. Hitherto acceptable norms of human conduct do not apply. If the United States is to survive, longstanding American concepts of 'fair play' must be reconsidered. We must... learn to subvert, sabotage and destroy our enemies by more clever, more sophisticated and more effective methods than those used against us. It may become necessary that the American people be made acquainted with, understand and support this fundamentally repugnant philosophy."

Eisenhower concurred with repugnance as policy—*but without notice to the American people.* He next tasked the CIA with finding a political figure in South Vietnam who could rival Ho Chi Minh. The job fell to Edward Lansdale, a former West Coast advertising executive who in 1955 became the chief political and military operative for Ngo Dinh Diem, a portly, out-of-touch devout Catholic anointed by the United States to assume the presidency. French prime minister Pierre Mendès-France immediately made clear to John Foster Dulles that Diem was the wrong man for the job.

"Number one," the French PM explained, "he is a man from the north...so the people in this South Vietnam country don't feel he belongs, you understand? Number two, he is Catholic....Here is something which again doesn't belong in that country [which was 90 percent Buddhist]. Number three, he is connected with very reactionary military circles, and I don't think he is able to make any democratic reforms. You cannot count on him for agrarian reform, for example, because he has too many landlords in his entourage.... Number four, he is a man having too much confidence in the police, in some kind of government which is always treading toward a fascist conception."

In order to consolidate power for Diem, Lansdale and his fellow CIA agents spread millions of dollars in bribes to gain the support of military leaders and wealthy landowners. The agency also convinced the Army to crush a powerful organized crime family in Saigon. In 1955, ignoring the stipulation in the Geneva Accords calling for a unity election, Diem staged a fake presidential race in the fake country of South Vietnam. The total number of votes exceeded the number of voters by almost four hundred thousand. After claiming to have won with 98 percent of the vote, Diem indulged in shameless nepotism. His younger brother, Ngo Dinh Nhu, was put in charge of supervising the secret police, and his brother's wife, Madame Nhu, would come to be known as "the Dragon Lady" for her "unwelcome advice, public threats, and subtle manipulations."

———

In 1955, Graham Greene published *The Quiet American*. It would have improved the world's future had it expanded Dwight Eisenhower's thinking. Greene's anti-imperialist novel is about a U.S. official in Vietnam so blinded by American exceptionalism that he can't see its destructive consequences. "The Americans are prosperous and spiritually blank-eyed," wrote Arthur Miller of *The Quiet American*, "they walk with the best of intentions in the impenetrable delusion that theirs is the only civilized way to live; in this book they walk in a closed circle outside of which the alien millions of the world, especially the poor, lead a life unknown and unknowable to them, and they are forced, the Americans are in the book, finally to rely upon devious policies of political opportunism and terroristic force."

The novel was inspired by Greene's experience as a newspaper correspondent in French Indochina, where he met an American CIA agent working undercover who lectured him about finding a "third force" in Vietnam—neither communism nor colonialism, but a combination of traditions. It is believed that Greene's central character, Alden Pyle, was based on actual CIA agent Edward Lansdale. Greene's fictional version of Lansdale is a Harvard graduate who is thoughtful, soft-spoken, intellectual, serious, and idealistic. He has had no real experience in Southeast Asia and bases his foreign policy opinions on books and periodicals. Justifying his actions, Pyle—the quiet American of the novel—offers the domino theory.

"If Indochina goes—" he says. Thomas Fowler, the stand-in for Greene, interrupts:

"I know that record. Siam goes. Malaya goes. Indonesia goes. What does 'go' mean?"

"They'll be forced to believe what they're told, they won't be allowed to think for themselves."

Fowler responds, "Do you think the peasant thinks of God and Democracy when he gets inside his mud hut at night? I know the harm liberals do.... I've no particular desire to see you win."

When *The Quiet American* was made into a film, in 1958, director Joseph L. Mankiewicz turned the cautionary tale about American foreign intervention into American anticommunist propaganda. "Working with the American Friends of Vietnam, a lobby group connected to the CIA," Stephen Kinzer explained, "Mankiewicz bought the screen rights to *The Quiet American*. He told friends he would completely change the book's message and he did. His film starred the war hero Audie Murphy as the American in Vietnam, now portrayed as the selfless defender of freedom rather than a deluded imperialist. Lansdale, who helped write the screenplay, praised it as 'an excellent change from Mr. Greene's novel of despair.' Greene was appalled."

———

Indonesia's leader, Sukarno, had placed himself at the forefront of the nonaligned movement. In keeping with this orientation, he invited *both* the U.S. president and the Soviet leader for a visit, took a tour behind the Iron Curtain, and was in the midst of nationalizing industries attached to the country's many attractive resources: oil, coal, rubber, gold, nickel, and bauxite. Such behavior made him another monster in the eyes of the Dulles brothers, who convinced Eisenhower to use the CIA to get rid of him.

One scheme in Operation Archipelago drew upon Sukarno's reputation as a womanizer. The CIA produced and distributed a pornographic film entitled *Happy Days*, in which an actor impersonated the Indonesian leader by wearing a latex mask made by the agency's Technical Services Division. If anything, the film enhanced Sukarno's standing.

On January 8, 1958, the United States launched a "pseudo" covert war against Indonesia. An actual U.S. Navy ship (USS *Thomaston*) based at an actual U.S. Navy base (Subic Bay in the Philippines) delivered machine guns, rifles, rocket launchers, mortars, hand grenades, land mines, and ammunition to an inexperienced and ambivalent rebel force in the northern Sumatran port of Padang. A very short civil war ensued. The pro-American Indonesian military—who called themselves the "Sons of Eisenhower," and did not know about the CIA's involvement—crushed the rebellion in a matter of months.

In April 1958, Dulles authorized CIA pilots to bomb and strafe Indonesia's outer islands. By doing so, the CIA director was defying Eisenhower's order that no Americans were to be directly involved. The agency's bombers flew out of Clark Air Base in the Philippines and hit civilian and military targets in the villages and harbors of northwestern Indonesia. Hundreds of civilians were killed.

One of the CIA pilots was Florida-born Allen Pope. Over several missions, he had bombed military bases, ships, warehouses, a bridge, and, by accident, a church, resulting in heavy casualties and the worst U.S. atrocity of the covert campaign. On May 18, 1958, the Indonesian Air Force shot down his B-26. After parachuting into a coconut grove, Pope was captured. He had not flown "sterile." Inside his flight suit were some thirty documents, including his Clark Air Base ID, secret orders assigning him to the CIA operation, and a flight log documenting his past missions. Sukarno was infuriated. Allen Dulles terminated Archipelago.

"In their eagerness," Kinzer wrote of the Dulles brothers, "they oversimplified the complex political landscape of a newly independent nation, embarked on a major operation without a clear goal, underestimated the army's determination to prevent Indonesia from breaking apart, and misunderstood their clients, who despite receiving much weaponry did not want to fight."

In a 1959 *Commentary* essay, H. Stuart Hughes would serve up this critique of America's foreign policy: "A secretary of state like Dulles has become a kind of general busybody, always ready to set forth on his Sisyphean labors of propping up and plastering over. It never seems to occur to him that some of the ills toward which he rushes off to apply his questionable nostrums are by their very nature incurable. The idea has apparently never dawned on him that certain situations simply have to be let alone—that there are some places where no visible American interest is at stake, and where the only sensible policy is to 'sit this one out.' More and more, it seems to me, an attitude of benevolent detachment...should be the guiding principle of American policy toward the fast-growing segment of mankind that chooses to remain neutral in the power struggle."

CHAPTER 25

DRY THE GRASS

After Graham Greene's *Quiet American* picked apart the folly of U.S. involvement in Southeast Asia, *The Ugly American* presented the view that, with a bit of humility and humanity, American foreign policy in the region could be fixed. The book was written by Eugene Burdick and William Lederer. Burdick, a political scientist, would also write the Cold War classic *Fail Safe* (1962), about a nuclear crisis that arises when American bombers are mistakenly scrambled to erase Moscow, a not at all far-fetched premise. Burdick's coauthor, William Lederer, was a Navy captain who had served in Asia.

Though the term "ugly American" has since become strictly pejorative, often assigned to obnoxious American tourists, the titular character is one of the book's heroes. Homer Atkins is a plain-looking engineer with dirt on his hands who lives among the local people, helps improve rice production, and is a positive contrast to the clean-pressed but ignorant and condescending U.S. diplomatic corps. The real ugly American in the book is the U.S. ambassador, "Lucky" Lou Sears. He doesn't speak the language, nor understand the culture, and spends the majority of his time holed up in the embassy compound.

Someone very much like CIA agent Edward Lansdale appears in *The Ugly American* as the harmonica-playing, perspicacious Colonel Edwin Barnum Hillendale, and the same qualities and ideas that made Greene's Alden Pyle a destructive force are given a positive spin by Burdick and Lederer. Lansdale was known for pitching the idea of winning hearts and minds in Vietnam by mounting an anticommunist counterinsurgency—embedding soldiers in villages, where they would play a double role, providing safety and improving the general welfare. It was a theory that appealed to can-do types like John Kennedy and came to be called "Strategic Hamlets," but it had no chance of success. The South Vietnamese military never had any interest in attempting anticommunist evangelism among the peasantry. On a more basic level, the Diem government had been born illegitimate and chose to rule by thuggery and terror.

In 2009, the CIA declassified a study of covert action in South Vietnam entitled *CIA and the House of Ngo*. Among the findings was that the unequivocally negative 1954 assessment of Diem by French prime minister Pierre Mendès-France was 100 percent correct. "To succeed," the CIA study said, "Diem would of course have had to attract the loyalty of the non-Communist nationalists who had earlier cooperated with the Viet Minh against the French. Then, he would have faced the need to transform the ossified colonial bureaucracy into a functioning servant of his political and economic agenda. But Diem never tested this approach. Instead, he chose an essentially repressive strategy for the consolidation and expansion of his government's control. Its effect was to 'dry the grass,' as Mao had put it, intensifying peasant alienation from the government while it built for Diem the image of a reactionary mandarin dependent on foreign support for the survival of his nepotistic government."

The CIA also essentially confirmed that their own Edward Lansdale was the fundamentally flawed character fictionalized by Graham Greene. "Although constantly frustrated by Diem's intransigence," the CIA wrote, "Edward Lansdale neither wavered in his support, nor entertained the idea that the President might be simply incapable of meeting the challenge. It is difficult to avoid the inference that this loyalty represented an emotional commitment to the success of his own project to turn Diem into the revered father of his country, rather than the fruit of detached analysis.... This emotional commitment contained the seeds of a serious distortion of the intelligence process."

The CIA report offered another reminder that in viewing everything through a Cold War prism, the complexity of unique national cultures was overlooked: "U.S. judgement of the balance of forces . . . was perpetually flawed by the assumption that Diem's citizenry saw the alternatives in much the same terms as the Americans did—either the Southern insurgents and their masters in Hanoi or the Diem regime and its benevolent U.S. sponsors. . . . But up to 1963, at least, few Vietnamese of the Buddhist-Confucian majority appear to have regarded the conflict as one between Communism and freedom, or between Communism and democracy. The politically active among them had other concerns, among these nationalism tinged with xenophobia, social reform—skillfully if cynically exploited by the Viet Cong—and, even for non-Communists among the veterans of the war against the French, simple protection from Diem's police. CIA and other U.S. officials' preoccupation with Communism allowed them to underestimate the power of these concerns and thus to dismiss the Buddhist dissidence, peasant resistance to Strategic Hamlets, and the pervasive incompetence of the regime as either irrelevant or as remediable by a program of military and police repression."

Finally, the most logical assessment of the situation in Vietnam was a notion no one was prepared to consider: *Get out.* "As the insurgency advanced after 1959," the CIA noted, "American officials looking for a response to it framed their discussions almost exclusively in disjunctive terms. One side insisted that Diem's continued tenure doomed the South to absorption by the Communists. The other saw his continuation in office as indispensable to the defeat of the insurgency. Nowhere in the records examined for this study do any of the participating U.S. officials acknowledge, up to 1963, that these propositions might both be valid. Whatever the possibilities in 1955, it is possible by 1963 the conflict could not be won either with Diem or without him."

Had the United States supported a national election in 1956, therefore abiding by an international agreement, it would likely have allowed (1) communist Ho Chi Minh to unify the country and (2) erased the circumstances that produced a two-decade Cold War proxy battle that spread to Laos and Cambodia, killing millions, including nearly sixty thousand U.S. soldiers, with another three hundred thousand wounded. As it was, Diem, the autocrat installed by the CIA, ultimately became so problematic, the United States conspired with South Vietnamese generals to have him removed.

The predawn coup d'état that ended in Diem's killing took place on November 2, 1963. The coup leaders reported that Diem and his despised brother, Ngo Dinh Nhu, had committed suicide while taking sanctuary in a Catholic church. However, a few days later, *Time* and media outlets around the world acquired a photo proving this assertion a lie. The brothers were seen lying face-up inside an armored personnel carrier, dressed in the robes of Roman Catholic priests, clearly bruised and bloodied, with their hands tied behind their backs. The caption below the photo in *Time* read: *Suicide with no hands.*

———

When International Telephone & Telegraph (ITT) had asked Cuban dictator Fulgencio Batista for a steep rate hike, John Foster Dulles gently pressured Batista to agree. In 1957, with American ambassador Arthur Gardner in attendance, ITT staged a "thank-you" event honoring Batista, during which the company presented the Cuban leader with a golden telephone. Gardner, who had been lying to the State Department about the strength of Fidel Castro's insurgency, was sacked after showing up for the golden phone presentation—an appearance that put a giant exclamation point on America's crass imperialism. (By the way, you can see the phone today at Havana's Museum of the Revolution.)

The golden phone is referenced in *Godfather II* (1974), during a scene at Cuba's Presidential Palace. It is Christmas 1958. An actor portraying Batista sits at the head of a gigantic table. Those in attendance include a mix of corporate and Mafia chieftains. Batista shows the gathering a sparkling golden rotary phone and passes it around the table for inspection. In the Oscar-winning screenplay, written by Francis Ford Coppola and Mario Puzo, the corporations are identified as the General Fruit Company, United Telephone and Telegraph, Pan-American Mining, and South American Sugar. Michael Corleone, played by Al Pacino, is said to be representing Nevada associates in "tourism and leisure activities."

The Cuban economy had long been indistinguishable from U.S. private enterprise, legal and illegal. American businesses and mob families were tied to virtually every sector: entertainment, tourism, alcohol, drugs, oil, railroads, utilities, mining, sugar, and cattle ranching. Organized American crime figures ran a massive empire of hotels, casinos, clubs, and brothels. An estimated hundred thousand Cubans worked as prostitutes. Havana was also the base for exporting heroin and cocaine into the United States. Meyer Lansky, the *capo di tutti capi* in Cuba, had various business interests with a value of about $100 million, which would translate to about a billion dollars today.

"At the beginning of 1959," John F. Kennedy would explain in the Senate, "United States companies owned about 40 percent of the Cuban sugar lands, almost all the cattle ranches, 90 percent of the mines and mineral concessions, 80 percent of the utilities, practically all the oil industry and supplied two-thirds of Cuba's imports." At Sullivan & Cromwell, the Dulles brothers had represented several American companies operating on the island.

On January 1, 1959, as the rebels were about to claim victory, Batista fled to the Dominican Republic. In one of his first acts as Cuba's new leader, Castro began confiscating American properties. On May 13, 1960, Eisenhower told his national security team he wanted Castro "sawed off." By the summer of 1960, the CIA had hatched two assassination plots, one using the Mafia, the other a CIA sniper. In August, Eisenhower approved $10 million to train Cuban exiles for an invasion.

On December 21, 1960, Allen Dulles—in his role as the director of CIA—attended a meeting in New York with American corporations doing business in Cuba. Although the location wasn't Havana, the pow-wow had the aura of the "golden telephone" scene in *Godfather II*. The head of the CIA met with representatives from Standard Oil of New Jersey, Texaco, the American Sugar Refining Company, the American & Foreign Power Company, the Freeport Sulphur Company, and ITT. They expressed the urgency of unseating Castro. Less than six months later, an amphibious U.S.-backed assault was launched at the Bay of Pigs.

———

In a desperate pursuit of perceived advantage, the Cold War super-powers enflamed hundreds of violent mutinies by picking sides and demanding fealty. Often peace never had a chance. A table in a 1991 paper prepared for the World Bank by Robert McNamara, "The Post–Cold War World: Implications for Military Expenditure in the Developing Countries," calculated a total of approximately forty million killed in wars and conflicts from 1945 to 1990.

In Vietnam, Cambodia, and Laos, the United States deservedly lost the battle for hearts and minds with an orgy of indiscriminate bombing that killed thousands of women and children and destroyed vast areas of jungle. A quarter of Laotian residents became refugees. The secret Cambodia bombing campaign was even more horrific:

> "Three F-111s bombed right center in my village, killing eleven of my family members," one Cambodian eyewitness testified. "My father was wounded but survived. At that time there was not a single soldier in the village, or in the area around the village. 27 other villagers were also killed. They had run into a ditch to hide and then two bombs fell right into it."

The 2.7 million tons of bombs used on Cambodia exceeded the amount of *all Allied bombing* during World War II, including Hiroshima and Nagasaki. As many as 150,000 Cambodian civilians were killed. The attacks also destabilized the country. As a way to avenge the deaths of their families, previously apolitical peasants joined Pol Pot's communist insurgency, the Khmer Rouge. At the beginning of Nixon's air war, in 1969, the Khmer Rouge had 10,000 fighters. When the bombing concluded, in 1973, the communists had a force of 200,000.

In 1975, Pol Pot took charge of the country and reestablished Cambodia as Democratic Kampuchea. The new regime reset the clock to "Year Zero," commanded urban residents to move to the countryside, and mounted a genocidal "purification" campaign to purge intellectuals and minorities. An era of the so-called killing fields continued until 1979, when Vietnam invaded and removed Pol Pot from power. During the reign of terror by the Khmer Rouge, 1.7 million people—21 percent of the population—were murdered.

When the Vietnam Veterans Memorial was dedicated on December 13, 1982, thousands of veterans marched down Constitution Avenue. "It was a day of flags and tears and stirring music," the *Washington Post* wrote, "of marching Green Berets in jungle fatigues and Gold Star Mothers in cream-colored capes." Etched in the memorial's V-shaped black granite wall were the names of 57,939 dead or missing in action.

Essayist Christopher Hitchens attended the dedication. "I was present for the extremely affecting moment," he wrote, "and noticed that the list of nearly 60,000 names is incised in the wall not by alphabet but by date. The first few names appear in 1954, and the last few in 1975. The more historically minded visitors can sometimes be heard to say that they didn't know the United States was engaged in Vietnam as early or as late as that. Nor were the public supposed to know. The first names are of the covert operatives sent in by Colonel Lansdale without congressional approval to support French colonialism before Dien Bien Phu." The final names on the wall are of eighteen U.S. servicemen killed on May 15, 1975, in the attempt to rescue crew members of the *Mayaguez*, a U.S. merchant ship that had been seized by Pol Pot's Khmer Rouge.

CHAPTER 26

BURYING HISTORY

Joseph Stalin may have had a stroke in 1945 and another in 1947. He was a habitual smoker and drinker, like Franklin Roosevelt, and, like FDR, had progressive arteriosclerosis. It would kill him in 1953. During his final years, the aging tyrant became more isolated, lonelier, increasingly bitter, and, if possible, even more paranoid. He began conducting the bulk of his business outside the Kremlin, at one of his many homes.

His primary Moscow residence was a dacha in the middle of a forest tract in the Kuntsevo district, about a fifteen-minute drive from the Kremlin. The dacha had twenty rooms, with a greenhouse, solarium, and a Russian *banya*, or steam bath. There was a separate building for a library, which had twenty thousand volumes and was staffed by a full-time librarian. Several pavilions, with tables, were built on the grounds for Stalin's walks in the surrounding parkland. There were large auxiliary accommodations for guards and a domestic staff.

In his later years, Stalin also took extended vacations, often for months at a time. For rest and relaxation, custom-made homes were built for him in Crimea, on the Black Sea, and astride Lake Ritsa, in the mountains of Abkhazia. The retreats were hidden by thick forests, their exteriors painted green for camouflage. In all the homes, there were rooms designated for billiards and film screenings. All the walls were made of wood and left unpainted. Stalin believed air quality was improved by wood vapors.

Like all kings who make it a habit of killing their rivals, Stalin was in perpetual fear of assassination. He banned carpet from his homes because it could muffle the sound of intruders. For the same reason, he didn't want fountains anywhere. None of his food was served until someone else had first tasted it.

In the postwar period, he often held late-night meetings in one of his residences with the core members of the Politburo. Top aides, such as Nikita Khrushchev, would often be expected to first watch a film, which would be followed by eating and drinking into the early hours of the morning. Khrushchev called the post-film dinners "frightening, interminable, agonizing." As Stalin sipped Georgian wine, he all but demanded that his guests drink themselves into a stupor. Said Khrushchev, "He found it entertaining to watch the people around him get themselves into embarrassing and even disgraceful situations. For some reason, he found the humiliation of others very amusing."

As for his film tastes, Stalin had long favored American westerns. In *Stalin: The Court of the Red Tsar*, Simon Montefiore observed, "Stalin the solitary, pitiless and Messianic egocentric seemed to associate himself with the lone cowboy riding shotgun into town to deal out brutal justice. Hence, he liked director John Ford's work—and John Wayne."

This positive assessment would sour when Stalin learned that Wayne had become one of Hollywood's most outspoken anticommunists. After becoming president of the Motion Picture Alliance for the Preservation of American Ideals, and vocally supporting the investigation of communist influence in Hollywood, Wayne would also play a HUAC investigator in *Big Jim McLain* (1952), a bald example of Red Scare propaganda. Stalin not only "withdrew" from the John Wayne Fan Club, he also reportedly put out a hit on "Duke."

British author Michael Munn claimed that the FBI learned of the plot, and when two KGB hit men showed up at Wayne's office on the Warner Brothers lot, agents were waiting, guns drawn, to arrest them. According to Munn, the Soviet assassins were so afraid of telling Stalin about their failure, they asked for—and received—asylum in return for sharing intelligence.

Later, when Khrushchev traveled to the West Coast as part of his busy two-week tour of America, in 1959, Munn alleges he had the opportunity to meet Wayne and tell him how he'd saved the actor's life. "That was the decision of Stalin in his last mad years," he explained. "I rescinded the order."

———

In 1955, when Khrushchev quietly took power without anyone in the West noticing, he began undoing the worst aspects of Stalinism and indicated he was ready to begin an era of "peaceful coexistence" with the United States. The Soviet Union, in his estimation, desperately needed a break from the Cold War treadmill. The gap between the two countries—military and economic—was vast and Soviet communism had become a sclerotic, bureaucratic hell. Although Khrushchev boasted about rapidly catching up to Western standards, his true ambitions were much more modest: providing adequate food, shelter, and clothing for a struggling, fraying empire.

In the late fifties, Max Frankel was assigned to the Moscow Bureau of the *New York Times*. Having been forced to flee from Nazi Germany as a boy, Frankel was especially attuned to the dehumanization endemic to dictatorships. But he came to have a largely favorable opinion of the "squat, paunchy, and steely-eyed" Khrushchev, who, Frankel wrote, "sprang from the circle of Stalin's henchmen to rule with a peasant's wit, cunning, and vigor. Rash and belligerent, he struggled to lead a long-suffering people out of slavery and toward the Marxist promise of prosperity. He really believed that he could reform and rescue the communist system by exorcising the ghosts of Stalin, serving goulash to his people, and turning sputniks into swords....Behind his mask of bluster, I thought I saw a face of decency."

The USSR was a feeble empire mired in desperate poverty and further depressed by ubiquitous alcoholism. Each new day involved the same old struggles. To buy food, one waited on an interminable line, and once inside a grocery, the few choices available would typically include, as a 2016 *Pravda* article put it, "diluted sour cream spooned out of huge, dirty aluminum cans; bitter herring wrapped in newspaper; thin bluish whole chickens; brick-like bread; and tasteless birch-tree juice." Such basics as footwear, if available, were said to be "terribly hot to wear in summer, cold in winter, and wet in spring and autumn." At best, housing was a tiny, bleak, overcrowded apartment, with one bathroom shared by an entire floor. Toilet paper was a rare treasure. Sarcasm became a source of sanity. "We pretend to work," went one popular joke, "and they pretend to pay."

Khrushchev's top priority was, in fact, feeding his citizens, and he was not too embarrassed to seek help from the United States. "At the height of the Cold War," writes Khrushchev biographer William Taubman, "when not many Americans dared to provide it, his main American supplier turned out to be the shrewd, earthy Iowa farmer Roswell Garst, who was as interested in easing East-West tensions as in selling hybrid seed corn." Garst traveled to the Soviet Union in the fall of 1955 and spent a day with Khrushchev at his dacha in Yalta. After the visit, the Soviets ordered five thousand tons of American hybrid corn seeds.

Six months later, Khrushchev did something at least as bold as Mikhail Gorbachev's calls for glasnost and perestroika. On February 26, 1956, he stunned the entire communist world with a speech at the Twentieth Congress of the Soviet Communist Party. On the final day of the Congress, speaking for four hours in a closed session, Khrushchev ripped the "cult of personality" Stalin had created. He accused the late dictator of "grave abuses of power" and said that Stalin's reign of "mass arrests and deportation of thousands and thousands of people, and executions without trial or normal investigation, created insecurity, fear and desperation."

"Khrushchev's speech," wrote Frankel, "branded much of Soviet history a lie, Soviet law a sham, and Soviet theory a fraud."

The Polish leader Bolesław Bierut was in a Kremlin hospital with pneumonia when he was given a copy of the speech. While reading it, he had a heart attack and died. In Stalin's native Georgia, there were four days of protest and demands that the republic secede from the USSR. In Tbilisi, marchers tried to storm the radio station. Troops and tanks were summoned. Twenty were killed, and at least sixty wounded.

Radio Free Europe, one of the chief tools in the CIA's multimillion-dollar media empire, beamed the contents of Khrushchev's secret indictment across the Eastern Bloc. In Poland, not long after announcers began hyping the takedown of Stalinism, there were riots. Fifty-three were killed. On October 23, 1956, a student-led protest in Hungary rapidly gained popular support. A new prime minister, Imre Nagy, formed a coalition government, abolished one-party rule, and announced that a neutral Hungary was going to quit the Warsaw Pact. "Khrushchev's days may well be numbered," CIA director Allen Dulles told Eisenhower.

As Hungary lurched toward democracy, Frank Wisner was in Europe on a prescheduled trip. He had invested much of the past decade of his life to liberating the countries behind the Iron Curtain, charged by such memories as the night in Romania during the winter of 1945 when he witnessed the Red Army kidnapping thousands of ethnic Germans and shipping them by freight train to the gulags. But after relentless mania and plotting, Wisner's Office of Policy Coordination remained a fundamentally toothless operation that could do little more than feed Hungarian rage. As Eisenhower later noted, Hungary was "as inaccessible to us as Tibet." Frank Wisner had overpromised and underdelivered.

On November 4, 1956, Radio Free Europe's Hungarian announcer, Zoltan Thurry, became yet another CIA-paid voice encouraging the Hungarian resistance, proclaiming that "the pressure upon the U.S.

government to send military help to the freedom fighters will become irresistible." That same day, the Soviets sent two hundred thousand troops and twenty-five hundred pieces of armor into Hungary. On November 7, Wisner flew to Vienna, where a river of bloodied refugees testified to human slaughter. A final message from the partisans was sent from the Associated Press office in Budapest: WE ARE UNDER HEAVY MACHINE GUN FIRE. . . . GOODBYE FRIEND. GOD SAVE OUR SOULS.

As the body count in Hungary rose into the thousands, and Imre Nagy was executed, Wisner began to come apart. His colleague Richard Bissell said he "was profoundly moved, distressed, and depressed. . . . He felt we had done a lot to inspire and encourage the event." In 1958, diagnosed with manic depression, Wisner consented to months of shock treatment. Never able to fully recover, he would leave the CIA in 1961, and, in 1965, after another breakdown, killed himself with a shotgun. He was fifty-six.

———

After the Hungarian rebellion, the Kremlin shuddered. "We were scared," Khrushchev would write in his memoirs. "We were afraid the thaw might unleash a flood, which we wouldn't be able to control, and which would drown us." Khrushchev's coming policy gyrations would be the product of a man walking a tightrope. Wrote Frankel, "Most clearly among Stalin's heirs, [Khrushchev] understood that terror could no longer hold the empire or stimulate a modern economy. Jet planes and radio broadcasts were penetrating the frontiers of totalitarian societies, bearing news and ideas of western freedom and prosperity. Post-war industries needed an ever more educated, sophisticated workforce, not the slave labor that had once dug the mines, and felled the forests of Siberia."

Khrushchev liberated nearly two million prisoners from Stalin's Gulag (an acronym for Glavnoe Upravlenie Lagerei, or Main Administration of Corrective Labor camps). The system comprised 476 complexes, each containing thousands of individual camps, the majority located in the country's most inhospitable areas, the Arctic, Siberia, and the Central Asian deserts. A new legal framework was enacted, theoretically giving rights to the accused. Censorship was relaxed. Between 1955 and 1957, the USSR reduced troop strength by more than two million. Under Khrushchev, the annual rate of housing construction nearly doubled. Between 1956 and 1965, about 108 million people would move into new apartments. He personally approved the publication of *One Day in the Life of Ivan Denisovich*, a searing account of one of Stalin's camps. The book brought Alexander Solzhenitsyn to worldwide attention.

As this political earthquake was taking place inside the Soviet Union, the CIA had desperately few Soviet citizens on the payroll. The twenty or so controlled agents included a low-ranking naval engineering officer; the wife of a guided missile research scientist; a laborer; a telephone repairman; a garage manager; a veterinarian; a high school teacher; a locksmith; and a restaurant worker. None of them could have had any pertinent information about the thinking of the Kremlin leadership. Similarly, the Kremlin failed to secure an enlightened take on the thinking inside the White House.

Looking back on the Cold War for a piece in *The Guardian*, Peter Preston wrote, "Did the CIA, with all its billions of dollars spent, have one good spy near the top of the Soviet tree? No: not one. Did [the Soviets] have the intelligence feedback from the US that might have produced moments of calm reflection rather than convulsions? Yet again, no.... The brutal fact is that... neither of the superpowers either understood or had any meaningful contacts with the other.... This war was not so much cold as deep frozen."

CHAPTER 27

SPACE RACE

On Friday, October 4, 1957, as *Leave It to Beaver* premiered on American TV, the Soviet Union officially opened the "space race" by launching into orbit a 184-pound satellite called Sputnik, which means "fellow traveler" in Russian. Tom Wolfe explained the instant overreaction in America: "During the Cold War period, small-scale competitions once again took on the magical aura of a 'testing of fate,' of a fateful prediction of what would inevitably happen if total nuclear war did take place. This, of course, was precisely the impact of Sputnik I.... It dramatized the entire technological and intellectual capabilities of the two nations and the strengths of the national wills and spirits."

The hyperventilation overran the reality. Sputnik wasn't very intelligent technology. It was an aluminum sphere the size of a beach ball that circled the earth every ninety-two minutes in a steadily degrading orbit. The only function it had was to send out a beep, which was in A-flat. Naturally, it was immediately speculated that Sputnik was sending encrypted messages to Soviet agents, but that would have been news to the KGB. On October 5, an NBC radio broadcaster introduced a recording of the beeps with these portentous words: "Listen now for the sound that will forever separate the old from the new." After a few weeks, the satellite's battery died, the beeping stopped, and the hunk of aluminum burned up on reentry.

At the time, neither Nikita Khrushchev nor Dwight Eisenhower had been planning to start a space race. It is instructive to note that there was no advance publicity by the Soviet Union before the launch. That was because chief Soviet rocket designer Sergei Korolev had previously failed five times to achieve a successful liftoff at the Tyuratam test site in Soviet Central Asia. Moreover, until Sputnik became *the greatest threat to America ever,* it was officially part of a cooperative bilateral science project. In 1955, rocketeers in the United States and USSR had agreed they would celebrate the International Geophysical Year of 1957 by putting an object into space. In fact, they were all meeting in Washington, D.C., when Moscow radio broadcast news of Sputnik's launch.

Khrushchev's real interest in space was, in a sense, on the ground. Rocketry was the means by which the Soviets were hoping to even the balance of power with the Americans, who had hundreds of intercontinental nuclear bombers while the Soviets had zero. Rocketry offered a way to catch up quickly and less expensively, and to that end, Sputnik had ridden into orbit on top of a prototype R-7 intercontinental ballistic missile.

Senate majority leader Lyndon Johnson was down on his Texas ranch when the news about Sputnik was reported on TV. As biographer Robert Caro wrote, "He was to recall that when, after dinner, he, Lady Bird, and their guests...took their evening walk on the dirt road next to the Pedernales, they peered up at the dark Hill Country sky, unsuccessfully 'straining to catch a glimpse of that alien object' among the skyful of stars. He felt, he was to recall, 'uneasy and apprehensive'—as did much of America that night and in the weeks to come."

Johnson, who was planning to run for president in 1960, used the general alarm and panic to elevate his profile. "The Roman Empire controlled the world because it could build roads," he said. "Later, the British Empire was dominant because it had ships. In the air age we were powerful because we had airplanes. Now the Communists have established a foothold in outer space.... Soon they will be dropping bombs on us...like kids dropping rocks onto cars from a freeway overpass."

Fellow politicos added more doomsaying. House Speaker John McCormack said the United States faced the prospect of "national extinction." Washington senator Henry Jackson declared a "National Week of Shame and Danger." Michigan Democratic governor G. Mennen Williams penned a short ditty:

> *Oh little Sputnik flying high*
> *With made-in-Moscow beep*
> *You tell the world it's a Commie sky*
> *And Uncle Sam's asleep*

Life ran the headline "Arguing the Case for Being Panicky," and wrote, "Let us not pretend that this is anything but a defeat for America." A *New York Times* editorial said the United States was "in a race for survival." Nathan Pusey, the president of Harvard, declared that a greater percentage of the U.S. gross national product should go to education. When *Why Johnny Can't Read—and What You Can Do About It* was published in 1955, it had drawn little notice. After Sputnik, the book became a huge best-seller.

A congressional investigation was immediately opened. Physicist Edward Teller testified before LBJ's Senate Armed Services Subcommittee on Military Preparedness. He was asked what Americans would find if they got to the moon. "Russians," Teller responded. He was also asked if the Soviets had a rocket that could hit Houston. Teller said yes.

This wasn't true.

———

The White House tried underreacting. Chief of Staff Sherwin Adams said the United States had no interest in getting caught up "in an outer space basketball game." Publicly, Ike said, "One small ball in the air is something which does not raise my apprehension one iota." Privately, the president told General Andrew Goodpaster, "I can't understand why the American people have got to be so worked up over this thing. It's certainly not going to drop on their heads." A worried Walter Lippmann wrote, "The President must be in some kind of partial retirement." John Foster Dulles told Ike he should inform a shaken nation that fourteen different U-2 spy flights had provided solid evidence that the United States was not behind in the arms race. Reluctantly, Ike refused.

Once Sputnik was a smashing success, the Soviet press milked the propaganda value. A daily timetable was published showing exactly when the satellite was passing over Washington, New York, and Little Rock, where an ugly confrontation was under way as Eisenhower used the National Guard to protect black children integrating the previously all-white Central High School. At an international conference in Barcelona, Soviet space scientist Leonid Sedov tweaked the competition: "You Americans have a better standard of living than we have. But the American loves his car, his refrigerator, his house. He does not, as we Russians do, love his country."

Wernher von Braun, who had relocated to Huntsville, Alabama, was developing rockets for the Army, but the Navy had been given priority to put a satellite in orbit. After Sputnik, the ex-Nazi had a fit: "We knew they were going to do it! We have the hardware on the shelf. We can put up a satellite in 60 days!" Defense officials were soon visiting Alabama and telling von Braun to take his hardware off the shelf as soon as possible.

On November 3, 1957, American self-confidence took another huge hit when the Soviets put the first dog into space. Sputnik II—weighing 1,120 pounds, six times more than its predecessor—carried a small pooch named Laika, a stray found on the streets of Moscow. The Soviets would soon claim that the dog had died painlessly after orbiting the Earth for a week. Not until 2002 did the Russians reveal that Laika was cooked during takeoff when the heat shield failed. The Soviets would ultimately send a total of thirty-six dogs into space, all of them strays.

———

A month after the Sputnik launch, President Eisenhower was presented with a report from the Security Resources Panel of the President's Science Advisory Committee. The panel's chairman was Horace Rowan Gaither, a wealthy San Francisco lawyer, head of the Ford Foundation, and chairman of the board of RAND. Gaither's report was largely a product of the RAND brain trust, who had adopted the view that the Soviet Union was prepared to let millions of their own people die in order to win a nuclear World War III. *Pravda* called the think tank "the academy of science and death."

The report was titled *Deterrence and Survival in the Nuclear Age*. A more accurate title would have been *The Revenge of the Rather Nervous Nerds*. The big headline was that by 1959, which was less than two years away at the time of the report's release, the United States would be highly vulnerable to a sneak attack by Soviet missiles. This gave rise to the fiction that the country was on the wrong side of a "missile gap." As Eisenhower knew from the top-secret reconnaissance done by the U-2 spy flights, *there was no fucking missile gap.*

One of the reasons for the fright expressed in the report was an experience one of the RAND nerds had with General Curtis LeMay at SAC headquarters in Omaha, Nebraska. Robert Sprague— Gaither's deputy director and president of Sprague Electric—asked LeMay to stage a spontaneous alert of the command's bomb forces. After six hours, not a single SAC bomber had taken off. Sprague found this distressing. LeMay didn't.

"If I see the Russians are massing their planes for an attack," he told Sprague, "I'm going to knock the shit out of them before they take off the ground."

"But," Sprague replied, "that's not national policy."

"I don't care," LeMay responded. "It's my policy. That's what I'm going to do."

———

LeMay began ignoring the inevitable as soon as Strategic Air Command was formed in 1947, when the nerds were already telling him that bombers would soon be downgraded in a fast-approaching future of armed rockets, orbiting satellites, and supersonic jets. A decade before Sputnik, the RAND team had issued a report titled *Preliminary Design of an Experimental World-Circling Spaceship*. The proposal, wrote David Christopher Arnold, "offered a comprehensive look at what satellites could do for the military and suggested three missions: meteorology, communications and reconnaissance. The report outlined four significant technologies for research and development: long-life electronics, video recording, attitude stabilization, and spacecraft design."

In 1947, Jimmy Lipp, the head of Project RAND's Missile Division, made this prescient observation in a follow-up paper: "Since mastery of the elements is a reliable index of material progress, the nation which first makes significant achievements in space travel will be acknowledged as the world leader in both military and scientific techniques. To visualize the impact on the world, one can imagine the consternation and admiration that would be felt here if the United States were to discover suddenly that some other nation had already put up a successful satellite."

At the same time RAND thinkers were futurecasting, a forerunner of the space shuttle was being tested over the dry lake beds at Muroc Air Base in California's Mojave Desert. On October 14, 1947, twenty-four-year-old West Virginian Chuck Yeager strapped into the bullet-shaped X-1, powered by a mix of alcohol and frosty liquid oxygen, and set off four rocket chambers. Those on the ground heard a sonic boom when the jet reached Mach 1, the phenomenon

predicted many years before by physicist Theodore von Kármán
(later one of the founders of NASA's Jet Propulsion Laboratory at
Pasadena's Caltech). As he topped out at Mach 1.07, 660 miles per
hour, the sky in front of Yeager, as Tom Wolfe wrote in *The Right
Stuff*, "turned a deep purple and all at once the stars and the moon
came out—and the sun shone at the same time. [Yeager] had reached
a layer of the upper atmosphere where the air was too thin to contain
reflecting dust particles. He was simply looking out into space."

When informed about the great news that Chuck Yeager had broken the sound barrier, the senior Air Force command at Wright Field
in Ohio told the people at Muroc to keep quiet. There was to be no
announcement to the press. No one was to be informed. "Just what
was on the minds of the brass at Wright Field is hard to say," Wolfe
wrote. "Much of it, no doubt, was a simple holdover from wartime,
when every breakthrough of possible strategic significance was kept
under wraps. That was what you did—you shut up about them."

In 1953, Air Force general Bernard Schriever quietly turned an
abandoned Los Angeles schoolhouse into a missile lab with fifteen
independent-minded engineering geeks. "By the time Schriever
began to tinker with missile research," Steve Coll wrote in the *New
York Review of Books*, "[LeMay] had evolved from a pilot's pilot into
an isolated, arrogant man whose attitude toward his superiors bor-
dered on insubordination. LeMay fought Schriever over budgets,
research priorities, and the very premise that missiles should play
a significant role in America's nuclear force." Schriever eventually
established a thriving partnership with the Ramo-Wooldridge Corporation, a private California contractor on the way to becoming
aerospace giant TRW.

———

As LeMay fought progress, the Gaither Report had determined that
the Soviets were storming ahead in the production of thermonuclear
intercontinental ballistic missiles, or ICBMs. "The issue was both

real and hot," said Gaither panel member Herb York, who at the time was director of the Livermore Laboratories and tasked with calculating the Soviet missile threat. "We took the best data there were on the Soviet rocket development program, combined them with what we could learn about the availability of factory floor space [in Russia] needed for such an enterprise, and concluded that [the Soviets] would produce thousands [of ICBMs] in the next few years."

But this turned out to be as reliable as a wild guess. The Soviets had four ICBMs in 1957. A few years later, they had produced about a hundred—by which point General Bernard Schriever's team was pumping out twice as many rockets, with far superior technology. "The estimate was quite wrong," York acknowledged. "The problem was simple enough. I knew only a little about the Soviet missile development program and nothing about Soviet industry. In making this estimate, I was combing two dubious analytical procedures: worst-case analysis and mirror imaging."

Taking Soviet economic reports at face value, already problematic since the numbers were fabricated, the Gaither Report displayed charts showing the overall Soviet economy growing at twice the U.S. rate, producing twice as many machine tools as America, and reaching toward U.S. production levels in coal and steel. As Daniel Moynihan noted, this assessment would have been deemed batty by any regular visitor to the Hotel Ukraine in Moscow, where the informed traveler knew to ask for a room on a lower floor because the elevator was almost always out of service.

"Of the roughly one hundred people associated with the Gaither report," Moynihan wrote, "few were economists. None of the principals had any specialized knowledge about the Soviet system, certainly not enough to add 'investment in heavy industry' to outlays on the armed forces to produce an index of Soviet geopolitical strength defined as nuclear strike power. These passages from the report now seem absurd."

To keep America safe, the Gaither Report advocated spending an additional $44 billion on defense in the next five years. Ike rejected the conclusion, said he didn't want to turn America into a garrison state, and doubted the Soviets would launch an all-out surprise nuclear attack, knowing it would ultimately be suicidal. However, he did approach Secretary of Defense Neil McElroy about finding a way to boost the sinking public perception of the administration in the wake of the Sputnik launch.

McElroy had already proven to be a master of public relations at Proctor & Gamble, where he established himself as the father of brand management. "In the mid-1950s," Annie Jacobsen wrote in *The Pentagon's Brain*, "P&G had four major soap brands—Ivory, Joy, Tide and Oxydol. Sales were lagging until McElroy came up with the concept of promoting competition among in-house brands and targeting specific audiences to advertise to. It was McElroy's idea to run soap ads on daytime television, when many American housewives watched TV. By 1957, P&G soap sales had risen to $1 billion a year and McElroy would be credited with inventing the concept of the soap opera."

On November 20, 1957, McElroy proposed the creation of a new Pentagon agency that seemed like it was borrowed from Disney's Tomorrowland. It was called the Advanced Research Projects Agency, or ARPA. Later adding the word "Defense" and becoming DARPA, this new entity bolted into relevance as the country's central source of military innovations. One of the agency's first projects was the highly classified Vela program, which included three subprograms: Vela Hotel, Vela Uniform, and Vela Sierra. The goal, as Jacobsen wrote, was "to advance sensor technology so the United States could certify that no nuclear weapons were being detonated in secret. Vela Hotel developed a high-altitude satellite system to detect nuclear explosions from space. Vela Uniform developed ground sensors able to detect nuclear explosions underground.... Vela Sierra monitored potential nuclear explosions in space."

———

On December, 6, 1957, a 3.25-pound satellite was on top of a Navy Vanguard rocket for America's first nationally televised launch. With the Soviets ahead two satellites to zero, and success seen as critical, the Vanguard booster ascended about six inches...and exploded. "It seemed as if the gates of hell had opened up," wrote German engineer Kurt Stehling. "Brilliant stiletto flames shot out from the side of the rocket near the engine. The vehicle agonizingly hesitated for a moment, quivered again, and in front of our unbelieving, shocked eyes, began to topple. It sank like a great flaming sword into its scabbard down into the blast tube."

The *London Daily Express* ran this headline: "U.S. Calls It Kaputnik!" The launch was also called a Flopnik, a Stayputnik, a Goofnik, an Oopsnik, and a Dudnik. Said Lyndon Johnson, as he was chairing a hearing before a large crowd in the Senate Caucus Room, "How long, how long, oh, God, how long will it take for us to catch up with the Russians' two satellites?"

Just before the failed launch of Vanguard, Eisenhower had suffered a mild stroke. For a short period, his speech was affected. He admitted to a friend, "I might say 'desk' when I mean 'chair.'" After a heart attack in the fall of 1955, and emergency intestinal surgery in late spring 1956, this was the third time he'd been incapacitated within a two-year period. A few weeks later, just before Christmas, the Gaither Report—leaked by Paul Nitze—was front-page news in the *Washington Post*. Under a panic-inducing headline, "Enormous Arms Outlay Is Held Vital for Survival," the *Post* reported that "the still top-secret Gaither Report portrays a United States in the gravest danger in its history. It pictures the nation moving in a frightening course to the status of a second-class power. It shows an America exposed to an almost immediate threat by the missile-bristling Soviet Union."

By January 1958, Eisenhower's approval ratings had fallen 30 points to 52 percent. *Harper's Magazine* called for his resignation. On January 31, good news, long awaited, finally arrived. At 10:47:56 p.m. Eastern, von Braun's Jupiter-C rocket finally put a U.S. satellite into orbit. Eisenhower got the news in Georgia, while playing cards with his well-heeled buddies at his favorite golf sanctuary, Augusta National, home of the Masters. "That's wonderful," the president said. "I sure feel better now." But he also told an aide, "Let's not make too great a hullabaloo about this."

However, Wernher von Braun couldn't resist exploiting the visibility he gained through proving the reliability of German engineering. He joined the chorus raising the dire consequences of losing the space race: "If we do not match the ambitious Communist intentions to visit the Moon with an equally determined U.S. space flight program...we may in the not-too-distant future be surrounded by several planets flying the Hammer and Sickle flag."

In March 1958, an emergency meeting was held in Los Angeles with representatives from the U.S. defense establishment. The subject: getting a man into space, as soon as possible, quick and dirty. It was decided to use available rockets, such as von Braun's Redstone (70,000 pounds of thrust) and the Atlas (367,000 pounds), initially developed by General Dynamics to carry warheads or satellites. A pod was going to be stuck on top of one of these oversized Roman candles to carry a human being into orbit. This person would actually be more of a cannonball than a pilot. The job to get this done was assigned to NACA (the National Advisory Committee for Aeronautics), which was soon renamed NASA (the National Aeronautics and Space Administration). The first manned space missions were to be called Project Mercury. The initial flights would carry chimpanzees—an additional indication that the rocket program required little more than warm bodies with basic intelligence.

In *Spaceflight Revolution*, Professor James R. Hansen wrote, "In the wake of Sputnik, several interesting concepts for manned satellites had popped up. Some advocates of these alternatives disdained [the] proposed ballistic approach because...it represented such a radical departure from the airplane. This man-in-the-can approach was too undignified a way to fly.... Couldn't a pilot fly into space and back in some honest-to-goodness flying machine? Why not doctor the X-15 so a pilot could take it into orbit and back without burning up? One of the most innovative concepts for such a space plane called for a craft similar to NASA's later Space Shuttle.... Several of the ideas could have been made to work in time, but the new space agency did not have time to spare."

Yeager derided Project Mercury as "spam in a can." Engineers at NACA, the Air Force, and several aircraft companies had always assumed the X series was leading to the production of a manned spacecraft. At the time of the 1958 get-a-man-in-space-as-soon-as-possible meeting, Yeager had made rocket riding commonplace, with forty flights, and U.S. pilots were clocking speeds greater than three times the speed of sound and reaching an altitude of 125,000 feet, nearly twenty-five miles above the earth. The next generation in the series, the X-15, was designed to take a pilot fifty miles into space at speeds approaching Mach 7.

Destiny, however, determined that the soon-to-be-selected human cannonballs would become the most celebrated flyboys of the Cold War, superseding the rather more sensible and more impressive efforts taking place in the Mojave Desert. Moreover, the men of the Mercury program, even if they were glorified monkeys, would soon come to be known as "sailors among the stars"—America's very first astronauts.

CHAPTER 28

MIND GAMES

The Manchurian Candidate—published in 1959 by Richard Condon, made into a 1962 film by John Frankenheimer—imagines a perfectly terrifying Cold War conspiracy: A captured U.S. Korean War soldier named Raymond Shaw is brainwashed by the Chinese communists to become a sleeper agent ready to kill on command. After returning to the United States, Shaw is activated to assassinate a U.S. presidential candidate.

The basis for Condon's novel struck a chord. During the Korean War, it was initially believed that the Chinese had succeeded in reprogramming American POWs using mystifying conditioning techniques. In fact, what the Chinese were using were centuries-old torture methods. But gullible U.S. intelligence agencies convinced themselves that the communists were capable of controlling minds and turning American POWs into dutiful robots. In reaction, the subject of brainwashing was put on the front burner, during which time secret and largely unethical experiments were conducted with a variety of powerful drugs. What was learned from this research was that washing a brain with pharmaceuticals actually makes the subject less agreeable to *any kind of control* and more likely to report visions of demons and run naked in the streets.

The United States entered the Korean War on July 5, 1950. On July 9, a captured American soldier made a radio speech spouting North Korean propaganda. This became a routine occurrence. What the

American public didn't realize is that the soldiers were often making such statements after beatings and sleep deprivation, which together can coerce virtually any human being into saying anything in order to make the torture stop. By 1953, captured American pilots were signing false confessions saying that they had dropped germ warfare agents on Korean civilians. Eventually, five thousand of the seventy-two hundred American POWs had either petitioned the U.S. government to end the war or confessed to war crimes. Finally, at the conclusion of the Korean War, there was yet another shocking and incomprehensible development: *Twenty-one American prisoners refused to return to the United States.*

———

The term "brainwashing" was coined by Edward Hunter in his 1951 book *Brainwashing in Red China: The Calculated Destruction of Men's Minds.* Hunter had been a spy in Asia during World War II, serving in the Morale Operations section of the OSS—a.k.a., the propaganda wing. After the war, he became an outspoken anticommunist, and although he identified himself as a journalist, it appears he had remained an American spy charged with pumping out propaganda. Hunter's book on brainwashing was really an effort to brainwash Americans in order to stoke fears about the communist menace.

Hunter claimed he had been speaking with Europeans caught inside China when Mao's communist revolution took power, in 1949. His book alleged that the Chinese Red Army used a hypnotic process called *xi-nao*—the Mandarin words for "wash" (*xi*) and "brain" (*nao*). Hunter would later tell the House Un-American Activities Committee that the use of *xi-nao* could "change a mind radically so that its owner becomes a living puppet—a human robot—without the atrocity being visible from the outside." Hunter also told the committee that Mao's ultimate goal was conquering America. This was a whole lot of hokum.

As Hunter was making shit up, the torture wing of the U.S. intelligence apparatus was operating on the assumption that the Soviets and the Chinese had indeed cracked the code on mind control. "The concept began as an [Orientalist] propaganda fiction created by the CIA to mobilize domestic support for a massive military build-up," said Professor Timothy Melley. "This fiction proved so effective that the CIA's operations directorate believed it and began a furious search for a real mind control weapon."

Ex-Nazis saved by America's Operation Paperclip were ready and willing to do the necessary dirty work to make sure the United States wasn't falling behind in the race to find better interrogation techniques. Capturing disposable Soviet spies for torture was being done by Reinhard Gehlen, serving as the CIA's German-based intelligence arm. Dr. Kurt Blome, who somehow escaped punishment after being charged with war crimes at the Nuremberg trials, was unabashedly perpetuating his dubious specialties at the CIA's well-hidden German black sites. One of Blome's early post-Nazi projects was Operation Bluebird, which explored enhanced interrogation techniques, including the use of lysergic acid diethylamide—LSD.

———

LSD had been discovered during World War II by Dr. Albert Hofmann, a research chemist for Sandoz Laboratories in Basel, Switzerland. At the time, Dr. Hofmann was searching for an analeptic compound (a circulatory stimulant), and though he had not intended to make a mind-blowing agent, he was aware of the mind-altering history of lysergic acid. The substance is present in rye fungus, which may have been used by the ancient Greeks in sacred rites, and reportedly as a medicinal agent in the Middle East and China. It was also associated in medieval Europe with St. Anthony's fire, a kind of momentary plague during which entire villages went mad for several days after rye fungus was unknowingly milled into flour and baked as bread.

On April 16, 1943, Hofmann accidentally absorbed a small dose of LSD through his fingertips and went on the first known acid trip: "[I was] affected by a remarkable restlessness, combined with a slight dizziness," he testified. "At home I lay down and sank into a remarkable but not unpleasant state of intoxication...characterized by an intense stimulation of the imagination and an altered state of awareness of the world. As I lay in a dazed condition with eyes closed there surged up from me a succession of fantastic, rapidly changing imagery of a striking reality and depth, alternating with a vivid, kaleidoscopic play of colors. This condition gradually passed off after about three hours."

Three days later, on April 19, Hofmann went on the first *intentional* acid trip—a day, by the way, that is historic within the world of psychedelia. Hofmann swallowed what he thought was a very conservative dose: 250 micrograms, a millionth of an ounce. But as he bicycled home, he began experiencing symptoms even more powerful than the ones from his first use of the drug.

"I had great difficulty in speaking coherently," he recalled. "My field of vision swayed before me, and objects appeared distorted like images in curved mirrors. I had the impression of being unable to move from the spot, although my assistant told me afterwards that we had cycled at a good pace.... Occasionally I felt as if I were out of my body.... I thought I had died. My 'ego' was suspended somewhere in space and I saw my body lying dead on the sofa."

———

When Sandoz began to sell the drug, dangerous side effects were noted, including a "disturbance similar to split personality" and "pathological reactions (hysterical attacks, trances, epileptic fits)." The CIA, however, decided to adopt a fanciful spy-thriller view about the new Swiss hallucinogenic, hoping it could compel captured Soviet spies under its influence to spill the beans and even forget they had confessed.

"Many of the Russians and East Germans the agency had recruited as agents had gone sour," Tim Weiner wrote. "The need for a way to own a man's soul led to the search for mind control drugs and secret prisons in which to test them.... The goal was to find an interrogation technique so strong that an individual under its influence would find it difficult to maintain a fabrication under questioning."

One early effect of LSD was on the CIA itself. The agency became paranoid about anyone else using it. When a CIA analyst reported that the Soviets had bought fifty million doses from Sandoz, the only world supplier at the time, this led to speculation that the Kremlin might be preparing to wage a massive psy-ops attack on the United States by using America's water system to send the entire country tripping all at once. A subsequent analysis of the information revealed that the CIA employee had made a decimal point error while performing the dosage calculations. The Soviets had only purchased enough LSD for a few thousand tests, or significantly less than the number needed to send all of America briefly out of their minds. The paranoia wasn't allayed, however. After the incident, the CIA decided the United States needed its own stash of LSD and U.S.-based drug giant Eli Lilly was tasked with producing the chemical, for which there was as yet no clear medical application.

In 1951, Operation Bluebird—the search for mind control agents—was rechristened as Operation Artichoke, supposedly named after Allen Dulles's favorite vegetable. Artichoke was renamed again, to MK-ULTRA, a cryptic cryptonym combining the name of the CIA's Technical Services Division (MK) and the World War II designation for intelligence gained from breaking the German Enigma code (ULTRA). Thousands would unwittingly participate in a dangerous, unmonitored operation rivaling the scale and perversity of Nazi medicine.

"Motivation for this lawless behavior was a rampant fear of the Soviet Union," wrote David Kris and J. Douglas Wilson. "Some of the fears were outlandish but terrifying: the CIA believed, for example, that the Soviet Union was engaged in a wide-ranging program of testing LSD. It genuinely thought the Soviets might develop mind-control drugs and turn every American into an obedient, communist zombie. One CIA officer testified that he and his colleagues were 'literally terrified' at the prospect."

In the effort to control human behavior, the scope of CIA "brainwashing" experiments expanded. Virtually every substance popularized for recreational use in the sixties—LSD, Benzedrine, barbiturates, mescaline, mushrooms, marijuana, heroin, cocaine, PCP, and amyl nitrate—was used by the CIA at German black sites in the fifties. Hypnosis, electroshock, and sensory and sleep deprivation were also researched as interrogation tools.

The CIA's MK-ULTRA candy man was Dr. Sidney Gottlieb, a clubfooted former Young Socialist from Caltech with a doctorate in biochemistry. Known as the "Black Sorcerer" and "Dirty Trickster," Gottlieb doled out research dollars for mind expansion through fake foundations, such as the Society for the Investigation of Human Ecology. Nearly sixty American universities became party to the CIA's effort to tackle the outer limits of human consciousness with potent brain-altering chemicals. Although MK-ULTRA was intended for use on Soviet prisoners, far more Americans would end up as guinea pigs.

Gottlieb had a particular fascination with LSD, and reportedly went on 200 acid trips himself. Under his watch, the drug would be tested on a wide variety of people. At a federal penitentiary in Kentucky, seven prisoners were dosed with LSD for 77 consecutive days. A Kentucky mental patient was kept on the drug for 174 straight days. Drug addicts taken off the street were spooned extremely large doses. LSD was surreptitiously slipped into the beverages of unsuspecting soldiers, some of whom carried on conversations with invisible people for three or four days. Operation Midnight Climax was an MK-ULTRA project in which government-employed prostitutes lured unsuspecting customers into CIA "safe houses," where the men would be doped with LSD and have their behavior observed behind a two-way mirror.

The Pied Piper of the psychedelic era, Ken Kesey, was introduced to LSD in the 1950s when he volunteered for a CIA-backed experiment at a California Veterans Administration hospital. The experience provided Kesey with some of the raw material for his acclaimed novel *One Flew over the Cuckoo's Nest* (1962), set at a psychiatric ward. He later organized a celebrated cross-country, acid-dropping bus trip of "Merry Pranksters," which was charted in Tom Wolfe's *The Electric Kool-Aid Acid Test* (1968).

Beat poet and antiestablishment hero Allen Ginsberg, another LSD proselytizer, was also introduced to the drug as a volunteer for one of Sidney Gottlieb's university-based experiments. At a Stanford lab where two psychologists were secretly working for the CIA, Ginsburg reported that he was played recordings of Wagner and Gertrude Stein while tripping and decided LSD was "very safe."

———

Dr. Frank Olson was an Army biochemist who worked for the Special Operations Division of the Chemical Corps. He was based at Fort Detrick, Maryland—the military's top-secret lab for chemical and biological weapons—and assigned to work closely with Dr. Kurt Blome in Germany. Olson traveled on a diplomatic passport, a way of smuggling "sensitive" substances into a foreign nation free from inspection by customs.

As Olson was traveling to Germany, some of the MK-ULTRA research was moved to Haus Waldhof, a former country estate near Kronberg, in the Frankfurt area. The sequestered location was ideal for torture sessions with Soviet Bloc expendables. Guided by ex-Nazi scientists, an army interrogation unit dubbed the "Rough Boys" used electroshock along with heroin, mescaline, LSD, and Metrazol, a drug generating seizures violent enough to produce broken bones and dislocated joints. In the summer of 1953, Olson reportedly confided to a London psychiatrist that he was deeply troubled by experiments he had witnessed Dr. Blome doing in Germany. A British source speculated that Dr. Olson may have been present during the death of a captured Soviet agent.

Later that fall, just before Thanksgiving, Olson attended a work retreat in Deep Creek Lake, Maryland, an isolated lodge where CIA officials, including Dr. Gottlieb, were in attendance. Unwittingly, Olson and four others drank from a bottle of Cointreau that Gottlieb had spiked with acid. Gottlieb later claimed he told all five about what he'd done as the men began feeling the effects of the LSD. Four of the five were giggly. Olson thought they were laughing at him and didn't understand why. The LSD had induced severe paranoia and profound mental distress.

Olson's agitation persisted. The following morning, he left the retreat early. At home, he told his wife that he was being ridiculed by his colleagues for a dreadful mistake. On November 24, 1953, he told a work associate that he wanted to quit the biowarfare program and do something else with his life. Alerted, the CIA had agents escort him to New York for a psychiatric evaluation. On November 28, Dr. Frank Olson died after falling from a tenth-floor window at New York's Statler Hotel. He was forty-two.

———

The circumstances of Dr. Olson's death have remained suspicious. The family was first told that he had suffered a "fatal nervous break-down." After the 1975 Rockefeller Commission report revealed damning details about the MK-ULTRA program, the family sued the CIA for "wrongful death." They were awarded $750,000 in an out-of-court settlement, and received apologies from President Gerald Ford and then CIA director William Colby.

Sons Eric and Nils Olson later exhumed their father's body. The result of an autopsy revealed a fist-sized blow to the head. The coroner determined that the injury had occurred before their father's fall from the hotel window.

In 2012, Olson's sons filed suit in U.S. District Court in Washington, D.C., seeking unspecified damages and additional documents from the CIA. The case was dismissed, due in part to the conditions of the family's 1976 settlement with the government, but the presiding judge, James Boasberg, wrote, "While the court must limit its analysis to the four corners of the complaint, the skeptical reader may wish to know that the public record supports many of the allegations [in the family's suit], farfetched as they may sound."

In a 2017 Netflix documentary directed by Academy Award winner Errol Morris, investigative journalist and Pulitzer Prize winner

Seymour Hersh said he had been told by an anonymous source that the U.S government had a security process to identify and execute domestic dissidents who posed a risk to national security. Hersh said Dr. Olson was a victim of this initiative. Said Morris, "Examining the nature of the cover-up, and who was involved in the cover-up, is very much an ongoing investigation of mine....I believe that the assassination was ordered by the CIA, and I believe it came from the highest levels."

LSD's psychoactive potency should have made its use highly questionable by any arm of a humane society, but, in a strictly practical sense, the drug would prove to be an unreliable way to get actionable intelligence. As Sandoz had advertised, subjects given LSD often confronted a sudden battle for their sanity. They experienced extreme anxiety and severe mental confusion. Paranoid hallucinations were common, as were acute distortions of time and place, intense color perceptions, and psychic disintegration. These mental states were similar to those known to occur in schizophrenia. It was also impossible to predict how each subject would respond. One person given a dose could experience bliss, another panic. In short, the LSD experiments were both harmful and pointless. Nonetheless, the MK–ULTRA program continued until 1973, long after Frank Olson's death.

By 1955, the Army had interviewed four thousand Korean War prisoners and had more or less solved the mystery behind China's brainwashing. The answer came in a report: *POW: The Fight Continues After the Battle.* The secret proved to be very low-tech. The Chinese separated prisoners they judged the most likely to be converted and barraged them with hours of indoctrination that was sometimes accompanied by torture. "In general," wrote Louis Menand, "the Chinese used the traditional methods of psychological coercion: repetition and humiliation."

In 1961, psychiatrist Robert Jay Lifton published *Thought Reform and the Psychology of Totalism: A Study of "Brainwashing" in China.* Dr.

Lifton had conducted some of the interviews with returning Korean War POWs for the 1955 Army study. He concluded that the indoctrination of prisoners was a long-term failure. Prisoners who had come home praising communism soon reverted to American views, and by 1966, nineteen of the twenty-one American POWs who had chosen not to be repatriated were back in the United States.

Dr. Lifton also studied experiments by Nazi doctors and, assessing the interrogation methods practiced under Hitler, Stalin, and Mao, listed criteria for "thought reform." As Lorraine Boissoneault wrote in *Smithsonian*, Lifton's criteria included "'milieu control' (having absolute power over the individual's surroundings) and 'confession' (in which individuals are forced to confess to crimes repeatedly, even if they aren't true). For the American soldiers trapped in the Korean prison camps, brainwashing meant forced standing, deprivation of food and sleep, solitary confinement, and repeated exposure to Communist propaganda."

When *The Manchurian Candidate* was published, American culture was in the midst of a minor obsession with brainwashing. Frederic Wertham's *Seduction of the Innocent* (1954) warned that even comic books were capable of corrupting the minds of America's youth. Wertham claimed that the hypnotic fascination with fantastic superheroes was the cause of juvenile delinquency. In 1957, behaviorist B. F. Skinner and colleague C. B. Ferster published *Schedules of Reinforcement*, which detailed experiments in what Skinner called "operant conditioning." Free will, Skinner posited, was an illusion; instead, human beings were principally guided by *reinforcement*. He theorized that actions with positive consequences get repeated, or *positively reinforced*. Conversely, actions with negative outcomes do not. A year after *Schedules of Reinforcement*, FBI director J. Edgar Hoover repeatedly referenced communist thought control in his ghostwritten *Masters of Deceit: The Story of Communism in America and How to Fight It* (1958).

As Menand noted, *Manchurian Candidate* author Richard Condon was first trained in the art of popular persuasion, a movie publicist before becoming a novelist, and his tale about the brainwashing of Korean POW Raymond Shaw leans more toward anthropology and psychology than Cold War superpower machinations. "Even before Raymond falls into the hands of Yen Lo, he is psychologically conditioned, by his mother's behavior, to despise everyone," Menand wrote. "His mother is conditioned, by her early incest, to betray everyone. And the American people are conditioned, by political propaganda, to believe her McCarthy-like husband's baseless charges about Communists in the government. It is not, in Condon's vision, the Communist world on one side and the free world on the other. It is just the manipulators and the manipulated, the conditioners and the conditioned, the publicists and the public."

The Manchurian Candidate was a best-seller, but when the film appeared in 1962, it was a box-office disappointment. After the assassination of John F. Kennedy, in 1963, United Artists pulled it from distribution. In the meantime, the similarity between Condon's Raymond Shaw and Lee Harvey Oswald, a U.S. soldier who went to the Soviet Union and returned to assassinate a president, was inevitably noted.

Did Lee Harvey Oswald see *The Manchurian Candidate*? Maybe. In *Oswald's Trigger Films* (2000), John Loken made the case that Oswald had "motive" and "opportunity." The Kennedy assassin had a habit of going to the movies by himself, was in fact arrested trying to hide in a theater, and *The Manchurian Candidate* played for several months at a Dallas location that Oswald passed every day on the bus he took to work.

———

A case could also be made that the premise of Condon's thriller, programming the subject of an experiment to become a killer, was *successfully accomplished*—albeit inadvertently—by an American academic in Cambridge, Massachusetts.

In 1959, a search to pacify human nature in the ever more danger-ous atomic age ended up abusing virgin minds. Harvard sophomore and math major Theodore John Kaczynski was among the volunteers for an experiment designed to achieve "psychic deconstruction" by humiliation and severe stress. The author of the experiment—titled "Multiform Assessments of Personality Development Among Gifted College Men"—was the chairman of Harvard's Department of Social Relations and one of the country's most influential scientists.

Dr. Henry A. Murray, a psychologist, had pioneered the Thematic Apperception Test (TAT), a personality exam that became a routine part of industrial management and psychological assessments. At the start of World War II, the TAT brought Dr. Murray to the atten-tion of OSS leadership, which asked him to devise a screening test to determine the suitability of applicants for intelligence work and, by extension, their ability to withstand harsh interrogation. After the war, Dr. Murray was yet another academic who took research dollars from the CIA's Dr. Gottlieb in order to study the possible use for LSD and other substances.

"You could say that he was simply continuing on what he had done for the O.S.S.," said Alton Chase, a contemporary of Kaczynski's at Harvard. In 2001, Chase wrote about the Murray experiment for the *Atlantic*: "A wealthy and blue-blooded New Yorker, Murray was both a scientist and a humanist. . . . He feared for the future of civilization in an age of nuclear weapons, and advocated implementing the agenda of the World Federalist Association, which called for a single world gov-ernment. The atomic bomb, Murray wrote in a letter to [antinuclear activist Lewis] Mumford, 'is the logical & predictable result of the course we have been madly pursuing for a hundred years.'"

As a way to undo man's mad pursuit toward extinction, Mur-ray was exploring the concept of the "dyad"—a social group of two people. "Rather than follow Freud and Jung by identifying the indi-vidual as the fundamental atom in the psychological universe," Chase wrote, "Murray chose the dyad—the smallest social unit—and in this way sought to unite psychiatry, which studied the psyches of individuals, and sociology, which studied social relations."

But Murray was also hiding a deep secret, a forty-year sadomasochistic love affair with Christiana Morgan, a colleague and the coinventor of the widely hailed TAT assessment. Murray's Harvard humiliation experiments were, covertly, an extension of his own passion for sadism, with its interest in the allure of power and the indulgence of fantasies based on receiving and dispensing pain.

———

Ted Kaczynski had graduated from high school early, at age fifteen. At Harvard, he swam, wrestled, played pickup basketball, and practiced trombone. He had friends. A Harvard health-services doctor responsible for evaluating students found him to be stable, secure, and bound for success. In 1959, at age sixteen, he and twenty-one other Harvard undergraduates submitted to Murray's testing for three years.

Murray's subjects remained anonymous; Kaczynski was codenamed "Lawful." Each participant was instructed to write an essay on their philosophy of life, including details from toilet training, how often they masturbated, and the content of their erotic fantasies. "Then," said Chase, "they're told that after they've written it that they will meet with another undergraduate student and they will debate it—have a discussion about their philosophies of life. In fact— they were being duped."

The students weren't told that their opponents in the debates were law students instructed on how to demolish their arguments. These faux debates also took place in an interrogation room with a one-way mirror. The subjects were attached to electrodes and exposed to harsh, hot lights. A camera recorded the sessions. Murray himself called the counterarguments by the law students "vehement, sweeping, and personally abusive attacks." They were intended to crush egos. After being mentally and sexually debased, the volunteers relived their humiliation on film. Knowingly or unknowingly, Harvard was permitting its students to be tortured under the guise of science.

In 1967, Kaczynski would receive a PhD in math from the University of Michigan and subsequently teach at UC Berkeley. In 1971, in the grip of deepening mental illness, he retreated to a remote Montana cabin and, in 1978, sent his first mail bomb to Buckley Crist, a professor of materials engineering at Northwestern University. Over a period of eighteen years, he killed three people and maimed another twenty-three. Kaczynski became known as "the Unabomber"—the moniker bestowed by the FBI in reference to his pattern of targeting individuals attached to **un**iversities or **a**irlines.

In 1995, the Unabomber said he would "desist from terrorism" if his thirty-five-thousand-word manifesto, *Industrial Society and Its Future*, was published. The Department of Justice thought that doing so could help identify the attacker, and the document was printed in the *New York Times* and the *Washington Post*. In the essay, Kaczynski argued that the Industrial Revolution was the font of human enslavement. "The system does not and cannot exist to satisfy human needs," he wrote. "Instead, it is human behavior that has to be modified to fit the needs of the system." Kaczynski's sister-in-law recognized the similarity between the manuscript and letters sent to her husband, Kaczynski's brother, David. On April 3, 1996, a nine-man SWAT team apprehended Ted Kaczynski at his cabin in Lincoln, Montana.

In 2010, David Kaczynski told a reporter, "My brother was a victim before he victimized others—and in this he is hardly unique. Those who victimized him exercised cruelty with impunity.... What was done to my brother at Harvard should never be allowed to happen again. Our best insurance against inflicting harm on others—as was done to Ted and by Ted—is to avoid objectifying human beings, and to approach others with compassion."

CHAPTER 29

DANCE WITH DÉTENTE

In September 1959, Nikita Khrushchev became the first Soviet leader to tour the United States. On September 16, a day after his arrival, he spoke at a National Press Club luncheon in Washington, D.C. The talk was televised nationally and broadcast in the USSR by the Voice of America, the first such broadcast in ten years that the Soviets did not jam. Khrushchev's handlers agreed that the questions would not be screened in advance.

Khrushchev held his temper in check and made a largely positive impression with his blunt and folksy way of speaking. The final exchange addressed a famous comment he had made to Western diplomats in 1956, at a Polish embassy reception, where he said, "Whether you like it or not, history is on our side, we will bury you."

QUESTION: If you didn't say it, you could deny it. If you did say it, could you please explain what you meant?

KHRUSHCHEV: There is only a small section of people in this hall. My life is too short to bury every one of you.

That comment was followed by laughter. He continued:

KHRUSHCHEV: I did speak about it, but my statement has been deliberately misconstrued. It was not a question of physical burial of anyone at any time but of how the social system changes in the course of historical progress of society.... I am convinced that the winner will be communism, a social system which creates better conditions for the development of a country's productive forces, enables every individual to prove his worth and guarantees complete freedom for society, for every member of society. You may disagree with me. I disagree with you. What are we to do, then? We must coexist. Live on under capitalism, and we will build communism. The new and progressive will win; and the old and moribund will die.

In the next two weeks, Khrushchev traveled to New York, Los Angeles, San Francisco, Des Moines, Pittsburgh, and, finally, Camp David, where he met with President Eisenhower. In an assessment of the trip for the Library of Congress, Alan Gevinson wrote, "He was heckled by protesters, insulted by conservative businessmen, goaded by the mayor of Los Angeles, and belligerently challenged by labor leaders. Khrushchev responded in kind, often aggressively lashing out with colorful invective and threatening to cut the trip short."

On September 23, he visited Roswell Garst on his farm in Coon Rapids, Iowa. More than four thousand visitors showed up in the town of seventeen hundred. Garst's farm had a very efficient open-pen system for feeding the livestock, whereas in the Soviet Union, Khrushchev noted, "We provide each cow with a stall, each one is allotted with a fork and a knife... what kind of idiocy is this." Speaking later in Des Moines, he urged that the earth "be furrowed by plows, not rockets and tanks" and said he was interested in finding out how U.S. farmers—12 percent of the American population—managed "to produce enough food for everybody."

As Khrushchev flew to the West Coast and back, what he saw from multiple perspectives, from ground level and a bird's-eye view, was a country that was indeed much more affluent than his own. America was sprouting fast-food franchises, Holiday Inns, shopping malls, and drive-in movies. Office towers were being equipped with copiers, cal-culators, and high-speed computers. A forty-two-thousand-mile inter-state highway system was under construction. On bustling multilane highways, convoys of buses, trucks, and station wagons were conveying goods and people. Waterways were spotted by tankers and barges. Motorboats and sailboats navigated across hundreds of lakes. Planes, helicopters, and jets—private, commercial, and military—buzzed through the skies in abundance.

Every metropolitan area had requisite bowling alleys, golf courses, baseball fields, football stadiums, indoor arenas, performance spaces, libraries, and museums. Grocery stores bulged with enough ingredients to supply every cookbook and any meal. In the multiply-ing suburbs, there was a car in every driveway and picket fences stood guard over carefully cropped lawns. Lush farmland seemed to stretch toward infinity. Well-maintained sandy beaches outlined each coast. At night, downtowns popped with a neon glow. A youth culture twisted to the liberating beats of rock 'n' roll.

In 1959, capitalism was crushing communism.

During Khrushchev's visit, Henry Cabot Lodge Jr., U.S. ambas-sador to the United Nations, served as tour guide. At one point, Khrushchev admitted to Lodge that the Soviet standard of living had to be raised. The Soviet Union, he explained, was like "a hungry per-son who had just awakened and wanted to eat. Such a person would not wash his hands before eating. . . . Therefore, the Soviet Union was not trying now to develop the production of any sophisticated con-sumer goods; it was simply trying to satisfy the basic needs."

———

However, there was no feasible way for Khrushchev to make tangible progress toward prosperity without, at the very least, downsizing the immense national security costs of his far-flung empire. Defense may have absorbed up to a third of all spending. At the same time, the

Soviet Union seemed incapable of evolving beyond its birth as a sti-fling police state or producing goods anyone wanted. As one Western leader later put it, the USSR was little more than "Upper Volta with missiles."

As a general principle, Dwight Eisenhower had a similar goal: taming a ravenous U.S. defense industry that was eating up ever-larger portions of the federal budget. But on the subject of arms control, the two men began at different starting points.

Khrushchev, knowing his country was incapable of matching America's technological advantage, was ready to negotiate on dis-armament. He needed to slow the clock on arms development and somehow keep the United States from being emboldened to wage a first-strike nuclear attack. Eisenhower had a different worry: a matter of trust. He wasn't going to start disarming until he had a way to ver-ify that the Soviets weren't cheating. Like every American president in the Cold War, he was frustrated by how little real intelligence he had about the Soviet Union, in particular its war-making capability.

In 1955, during the Geneva Summit, the first face-to-face meet-ing in ten years between the leaders of the superpowers, Ike had pro-posed a treaty guaranteeing "Open Skies," which would require both the United States and the USSR to cough up blueprints and charts of their military installations and permit regular aerial reconnaissance as a means of verification. Khrushchev, a fundamentally insecure man at the top of an incredibly paranoid empire, immediately rejected the idea because he didn't want the world to know that his country's military was markedly inferior to America's. To his thinking, disar-mament had to precede inspection.

"Mr. President," Khrushchev said in the Geneva cocktail session that followed Eisenhower's overture, "we do not question the motive with which you put forward this proposal, but in effect who are you trying to fool? In our eyes, this is a very transparent espionage device.... You could hardly expect us to take this seriously."

In the Soviet Union, the practice of espionage, the art of deception, and the protection of secrets was as central to the culture as ballet, figure skating, and ice hockey. "If something like the Soviet regime had been envisioned both by those who had great hopes for it and by those who instinctively feared it, no one seems to have anticipated that secrecy would be its most distinctive feature," Moynihan wrote. "Everything that went on in government was closed to public view. Civil society ceased to exist."

One of Lenin's first acts was the establishment of the All-Russian Extraordinary Commission, or Cheka, a secret police organization ostensibly charged with combating counterrevolution and sabotage, but which was intended to tame the population with constant terror and senseless violence. The Cheka was renamed several times. By the start of the Cold War, it had morphed into the KGB. The organization was a gigantic twenty-headed hydra of spy agencies, with half a million employees overseeing foreign intelligence, domestic counterintelligence, technical intelligence, border security, protection of the leadership, and suppression of dissent. In size, the KGB rivaled capitalist behemoth General Motors. In Moscow alone, fifty thousand people were attached to spy work, outnumbering the combined employees of the CIA and FBI.

In his memoir *Spymaster*, ex-agent Oleg Kalugin wrote about Department Six, the KGB division tasked with tracking virtually every Earth-based object that left the Soviet orbit: "When two Soviet truck drivers delivered cargo to Europe, one or both of them would report to the KGB. When a Soviet merchant marine or scientific vessel sailed overseas, at least a quarter of the crew was KGB officers or informers.... When Aeroflot planes flew around the world, the flight crews were riddled with KGB informers. No matter what the mode of transportation, if it was Soviet and chugged, steamed, rumbled, or jetted overseas, we controlled it."

The KGB's territorial intelligence unit used various methods of entrapment to gain compromising information on foreign visitors. One of the targets was American syndicated newspaper columnist Joseph Alsop, who visited the Soviet Union in 1957. Alsop had been surprised when the Soviet authorities extended a visa. He and his younger brother Stewart, collaborators on a nationally syndicated political column, were among the most prominent anti-Soviet journalists in America. When the Alsops appeared in *Pravda*, it was to identify them as "the atom-happy" brothers who put "assassins, robbers, pirates, and rapists of all flags" to shame.

On February 17, 1957, Joe was attending a dinner at Moscow's Grand Hotel. He met a young man who identified himself as Boris Nikolaievich, described by Alsop as "an athletic, blonde, pleasant-faced, pleasant-mannered fellow." The KGB knew Alsop was gay. Boris was a plant. The columnist didn't know that the year before, a CIA officer based in Moscow had been sent home after a hidden camera recorded sexual liaisons with a KGB colonel posing as a housemaid.

The honey trap worked. The attempt to close the deal on the *kompromat* occurred the next day, when agents presented the American columnist with photos and began an interrogation, hoping to blackmail Alsop into becoming a Soviet spy. Crushed, distraught, contemplating suicide, Alsop contacted the U.S. ambassador to the Soviet Union, Chip Bohlen, a longtime friend. Bohlen put him on a plane to Paris, where Alsop was debriefed by the CIA and asked to write a sexual history.

The KGB continued efforts to expose the columnist, but Alsop had friends in high places. He was a relative of the Roosevelts and a product of Groton and Harvard. His regular houseguests included the publisher of the *Washington Post*, senior spooks of the CIA, assorted secretaries of state, and the occasional president. After finding "Joe Alsop is Queer" on the windshield of a car in front of his Georgetown address, Alsop contacted friend and head of the CIA

Richard Helms. Edwin Yoder, who authored a book on the columnist, explained that Alsop told Helms "that he planned to put an end
to the ordeal with a public declaration. Helms advised against it and
promised to fix the problem via a back channel reserved for washing
dirty laundry with Russian intelligence. The Soviets were warned
that if the defamation continued, US intelligence had plenty of retal-
iatory trash to circulate. It stopped."

Much of what the CIA knew about Russia's most important secrets
came from a plane without wheels or a gun, or what Curtis LeMay
described as "a pile of bullshit." The top-secret U-2 spy plane was
a jet glider: single-seat, single-engine, capable of flying at seventy
thousand feet, armed with nothing more than a camera, albeit one
with an extraordinary zoom lens designed by Polaroid's Edwin Land.
The U-2 provided Eisenhower with the only real intelligence he ever
received about the Soviet nuclear threat during the 1950s. As Ike's
generals and congressional hawks claimed America was behind in
bombers, and then missiles, the U-2 photographs told Eisenhower
that neither contention was even remotely true, a rather vital piece of
information he told virtually no one. "In a perverse regard for Soviet
sensibility," Max Frankel wrote, "Eisenhower withheld the evidence
that underlay his own sense of security."

The president was never comfortable with the program. He
understood that the Soviets could legitimately judge the blatant overflights as acts of war and called them "provocative pin pricking…
that might seriously give them the idea that we are seriously preparing plans to knock out their installations." In the spring of 1960,
there was an additional consideration. He didn't want a U-2 incident
to derail a May 16 summit with Khrushchev in Paris, which was to
be followed shortly thereafter by a planned visit to Moscow, a historic
first trip behind the Iron Curtain by an American president.

The Geneva meetings with Khrushchev, as Ike was keenly aware, would be his last chance to firmly establish a new era of détente, a word the president only used in private for fear of inciting reactionary Catholic conservatives such as Bill Buckley and Cardinal Francis Spellman of New York. The year before, Khrushchev had more or less done his part to lower anxiety by revealing a playful wit and genuine curiosity during his lengthy U.S. visit. The Eisenhower administration's foreign policy was also in a slightly kinder and gentler phase absent the perpetually dim view of summitry held by John Foster Dulles, who had died in 1959.

"I have one tremendous asset in a summit meeting," Eisenhower told intelligence advisors. "That is my reputation for honesty. If one of these aircraft were lost when we were engaged in apparently sincere deliberations, it could be put on display in Moscow and ruin my effectiveness." The remark was tragically prophetic.

On May 1, 1960, in central Russia, a U-2 piloted by Gary Powers was blown out of the sky by an S-75 surface-to-air missile. On May 3, NASA said it had lost a weather plane over Turkey. Then the White House said a weather plane had mistakenly strayed into the Soviet Union. Then Khrushchev, disillusioned by Eisenhower's dishonesty and silence, humiliated the president by revealing that the Soviets had remnants of the plane and "we also have the pilot, who is quite alive and kicking!"

On May 9, arriving at the Oval Office, Ike told his assistant, "I would like to resign." As Tim Weiner wrote in *Legacy of Ashes*, "For the first time in the history of the United States, millions of citizens understood that their President could deceive them in the name of national security. The doctrine of plausible deniability was dead."

At the Paris summit days later, Khrushchev demanded an apology, saying, "The Soviet Union is not Cuba, not Guatemala, not Panama, not Iceland." Ike countered by offering to stop the U-2 flights and asked Khrushchev to reconsider the "Open Skies" concept. But the U.S. president would not stoop to an apology. The Soviet leader responded by bolting the Paris talks. The impending

Moscow tête-à-tête was toast. "The summit with Khrushchev was wrecked," Weiner wrote, "and the brief thaw in the Cold War iced over. The CIA spy plane destroyed the idea of détente for almost a decade. Eisenhower had approved the final mission in the hope of putting to lie the missile gasp. But the cover-up of the crash made him out to be a liar."

"What the U-2 affair did reveal," wrote Aleksandr Fursenko and Timothy Naftali in *Khrushchev's Cold War*, "was the enormous role of reputation in the superpower confrontation. Both leaders allowed matters of personal prestige to dictate their most important decisions in May 1960.... In a war fought more on a psychological plane than a conventional battlefield, where a superpower's most potent defense involved deterring an enemy attack before it ever happened, the credibility of each leader carried enormous significance."

———

Although not in time to save détente, a better way to snoop on the Soviets arrived soon after. On August 18, 1960, the kind of satellite that RAND had urged Curtis LeMay to develop way back in 1946 became America's new and untouchable eyes in the sky. It was the work of General Bernard Schriever's team at the wonky West Coast missile works. KH-1 9009—publicly identified as a weather satellite named Discoverer 14—was the first successful low-resolution photosurveillance spacecraft ever launched, and beat the Soviets to the punch by two years.

There would be 144 more launches related to the Corona program (named for the favorite cigar of one of the staffers). During the Cold War, the real reason for these missions was kept secret and the details were not declassified until 1995. From NASA: "The primary goal of the program was to develop a film-return photographic surveillance satellite to assess how rapidly the Soviet Union was producing long-range bombers and ballistic missiles and where they were being deployed, and to take photos over the Sino–Soviet bloc to replace the U-2 spy planes."

The data from this new asset wasn't being shared with 1960 Democratic presidential candidate John Kennedy, who wantonly exploited the fresh fears produced by Sputnik. Kennedy began quoting a frightening Air Force estimate that the Soviets would have five hundred ICBMs by the end of the year. "For the first time since the war of 1812," Kennedy claimed, "foreign enemy forces potentially have become a direct and unmistakable threat to the continental United States, to our homes and to our people." After taking office, and being provided with the top-secret photos from Operation Corona, Kennedy learned that the Soviets had but a handful of intercontinental ballistic missiles.

CHAPTER 30

SEND IN THE CLOWNS

On September 9, 1960, Nikita Khrushchev sailed to New York on the steamer *Baltika* for meetings of the UN General Assembly. Before he departed, U.S. officials had instructed him that he would not be able to leave the New York City area without permission, an indication of the growing breach in relations between Moscow and Washington.

When the ship arrived ten days later, it was pouring rain. In New York harbor, longshoremen on a chartered sightseeing boat waved such placards as ROSES ARE RED, VIOLETS ARE BLUE, STALIN DROPPED DEAD, HOW ABOUT YOU? No U.S delegation was present to greet the Soviets as the *Baltika* docked at shabby Pier 73 on the East River. One of the Soviet sailors immediately defected.

The travel restrictions didn't ban Khrushchev from going uptown for his first face-to-face meeting with Fidel Castro, who was staying at the black-owned Hotel Theresa in Harlem. The encounter produced borderline chaos. In one of the photos, the two men are on the sidewalk outside the hotel, side by side. They look relaxed and chummy while being encircled by a small army of stone-faced New York City cops who are fitfully holding back a throng packed together like Times Square on New Year's Eve. The bearded Castro is wearing fatigues, a look he'd model for the next several decades, seeking to immortalize his revolutionary moment. A head shorter and far rounder, Khrushchev is the Costello to Castro's Abbott.

Khrushchev had recently indicated that the USSR would come to Cuba's aid in the event of a U.S.-sponsored invasion—a plot already in motion at CIA training camps in South Florida and Guatemala. "It should be borne in mind," Khrushchev said at a public event in the summer of 1960, "that the United States is now not at such an unattainable distance from the Soviet Union as formerly.... We have rockets we can land precisely in a preset square target 13,000 kilometers away. This, if you want, is a warning to those who would like to solve international problems by force and not by reason."

From the U.S. point of view, Castro's transition to the dark side was all but complete. He had nationalized American businesses, invited the Soviets to open an embassy in Havana, sent his brother Raúl on an official trip to Moscow, and begun receiving Soviet-made weapons. Internally, Castro had launched a crackdown on political dissent, and encouraged neighbors to begin spying on one another, instituting the kind of block surveillance system used by the East Germans. While in New York, he'd further exploit the Harlem locale to decry the U.S. record on civil rights and, in another incendiary move, entertained Nation of Islam minister Malcolm X, who, in contrast to Martin Luther King's profession of nonviolence, had begun to wage a far more militant campaign for black equality.

In his memoir about his career at the *New York Times*, Max Frankel wrote about first meeting Fidel Castro during the 1960 UN sessions. At the coffee shop of the Hotel Theresa, Frankel informed Castro he was heading to Havana for his new assignment with the *Times* and began an interview. He asked only one question. Castro spent the next hour in a "recitation of soothing platitudes" and concluded by telling Frankel that he would find much to teach the people about *La Revolución*. It was during this same New York visit that the new Cuban leader set a new UN record with a nearly five-hour speech.

Castro would ultimately be upstaged by his new friend in the Kremlin. Just before the conclusion of his nearly monthlong stay,

Khrushchev uncorked a soon-to-be-legendary tantrum. Being caged had been detrimental to the mental health of the frenetic Soviet leader, who at one point appeared on the second-floor balcony of the Soviet mission on Park Avenue and sang a verse of "The Internationale" to a gathering of journalists below. On October 12, 1960, while Khrushchev was attending a UN session in the General Assembly Hall, Filipino delegate Lorenzo Sumulong said that "the peoples of Eastern Europe and elsewhere...have been deprived of the free exercise of their civil and political rights and swallowed up, so to speak, by the Soviet Union." This instantly infuriated Khrushchev, who had spent the previous three weeks claiming that the USSR was leading the way on decolonization and self-determination.

The red-faced Soviet leader began pounding his fists on the table area in front of him and then took off his right shoe and began banging that instead. A noticeable buzz started in the hall. Next to Khrushchev, Foreign Minister Andrei Gromyko felt obliged to take off one of his shoes, although he gently tapped it on the desktop. Khrushchev's performance soon included a long denunciation of Sumulong, whom he branded "a jerk, a stooge, a lackey, and a toady of American imperialism." Disorder continued until Ireland's Frederick Boland, the Assembly president, abruptly declared the meeting adjourned and slammed his gavel down so hard that it broke, sending the head flying.

———

Frankel's assignment in Cuba would be relatively brief. By the end of 1960, Castro had ordered the U.S. ambassador to shrink his staff to a few clerks, assuming, fairly, that many of the people he was booting were CIA agents helping to plan an invasion. Eisenhower retaliated by breaking off diplomatic relations. Frankel, like all Americans, was suddenly required to apply for a visa. He applied, and was predictably denied.

After having seen *La Revolución* up close, Frankel was less than impressed: "Fidel...so despised Cuba's oligarchy of wealth that he drove out its talent and settled for an equality of privation. He so resented Cuba's exploitation by North Americans that he delivered the country for a pittance to their Soviet adversaries. A brilliant orator and a genius in mob psychology, Castro turned out to be the most durable autocrat in a time of autocrats because he was blessed with a foolish enemy."

During the 1960 Christmas holiday, when President-elect Kennedy and key members of his transition team were staying at his father's estate, in Palm Beach, Florida, Frankel and two other reporters were summoned to the compound by Pierre Salinger, JFK's press secretary in waiting. Salinger wanted to hear their thoughts on what the United States should do about Castro, which in turn would be relayed to a "grateful" Kennedy.

In short, the reporters urged engagement instead of isolation. The Kennedy administration, the reporters said, should "educate the Cuban people in the joys of democracy," a small lift since the residents "already worshiped baseball and Hollywood, drank Coke, and smoked Camels." When Salinger asked if the United States had a duty to keep Castro from stirring up revolution all over Latin America, the reporters told him to "just accept the fact" that revolutions were "not exported but homemade." Frankel and his colleagues explained to Salinger that "Cuba wasn't communized by the Soviet Army, like Poland or Hungary. It was ripe for revolution because [the United States] indulged its dictators.... Until Fidel appeared," they noted, "[the United States] never gave a damn for Latin American democracy."

Looking back, Frankel determined that "where Cuba was concerned, Kennedy's head was no match for his gut. Nothing we could have said in Palm Beach would have offset the agitations of his family, his friends, and his virile ego....John Kennedy visited Cuba two or three times *in the year before* Castro came to power. He went not to study conditions there but to go whoring around Havana with Sen.

George Smathers of Florida.... Smathers was the ambassador of the American mobsters and sugar barons dispossessed by Castro."

As Frankel suspected, Kennedy began his presidency by laying the predicate for removing Castro, claiming he was "no mere petty tyrant" but rather a dictator who "had transformed the island of Cuba into a hostile and militant Communist satellite—a base from which to carry Communist infiltration and subversion throughout the Americas." Diplomacy, from day one, was apparently not an option.

For Khrushchev, Castro was a timely gift. With the ever more defiant Mao Zedong muttering that the Kremlin had become a timid steward of the international socialist gospel, Castro was loud proof of Soviet sway. Cuba's revolution was also testimony to the inevitability of the Marxist dialectic, and a stinging rebuke to America's hubristic attempt to contain communism. In the next two years, as heated rhetoric, cheap demonization, and cynical political calculations supplanted fact, reason, and prudence, Kennedy and Khrushchev proceeded inexorably on a collision course over Cuba that would produce the most dangerous event of the entire Cold War, a very real "missile crisis" that nearly started World War III.

———

On April 19, 1961, after sixty hours of fighting, a brigade of CIA-trained Cuban refugees was routed by Castro's forces at the Bay of Pigs. Of the 1,500 men involved in the amphibious assault, 114 were killed and 1,189 captured. It was the definition of a debacle.

For starters, the covert operation, months in the planning, may have been the worst-kept secret of the entire Cold War. For example, *New York Times* reporter Tad Szulc heard all about the pending invasion without even asking. The information was volunteered by Cuban and American friends when Szulc was passing through Miami. Szulc's story about the covert operation ran in the *Times* twelve days before the Bay of Pigs landing, on April 7, 1961, although watered down; Kennedy had succeeded in convincing the publisher to delete references to the CIA and the time of the attack. Even if Castro had missed that day's *Times*, his new friends at the KGB had given him a heads-up, courtesy of Communist Party members in Guatemala, the other training site of the Cuban exiles.

Following the humiliating failure, the Kennedy administration intensified anti-Castro efforts with threatening military maneuvers and new plots to assassinate the Cuban leader. Attorney General Robert Kennedy told the CIA that it was a top priority to eliminate Castro with swift, silent sabotage. "Let's get the hell on with it," RFK told new CIA director John McCone. The plan was given the code name Operation Mongoose. One of the men in charge was Dr. Sidney Gottlieb, the very same man who was running the LSD MK-ULTRA mind control explorations.

The schemes targeting Castro included (1) spraying his television studio with LSD (of course); (2) saturating his shoes with thallium to make his beard fall out (the element was typically used as a rat poison and insect killer); (3) lacing one of Fidel's cigars with a disorienting chemical; (4) putting poison in a fountain pen; (5) secreting a fungus in his wetsuit (Castro liked to dive); (6) planting a bomb inside a conch shell in the area where Castro was known to dive; and (7) hiring a mob hit man. Fabián Escalante, in charge of protecting Castro as chief of Cuba's counterintelligence, would later estimate that from 1959 to 2000, the total number of assassination attempts on Castro by the CIA was 638.

As the CIA was pushing forward on Operation Mongoose, the Pentagon had formulated Operation Northwoods, a plan that envisioned U.S.-backed false flag terrorist operations to provide a pretext to take out the Cuban leader by military force. "Using phony evidence," James Bamford wrote in *Body of Secrets*, "all of it would be blamed on Castro, thus giving [General Lyman Lemnitzer, chairman of the Joint Chiefs] and his cabal the excuse, as well as the public and international backing, they needed to launch their war."

Seeking to avoid comparisons to the USSR's behavior in Hungary, the Joint Chiefs had ruled out a full-scale U.S. invasion of

Cuba. Instead, as Bamford detailed, Operation Northwoods "called for innocent people to be shot on American streets; for boats carrying refugees fleeing Cuba to be sunk on the high seas; for a wave of violent terrorism to be launched in Washington, D.C., Miami, and elsewhere. People would be framed for bombings they did not commit; planes would be hijacked."

Some of the Operation Northwoods proposals called for killing U.S. troops, such as bombing the American naval base at Guantánamo Bay, on the Cuban coast. The Joint Chiefs also saw the potential of blowing up a U.S. Navy ship in Cuban waters in the hope that history would repeat itself. In 1898, the explosion of the battleship USS *Maine* in Havana harbor was blamed—immediately and falsely—on the Spanish, inciting the Spanish-American War.

Until his support of the exceedingly fucked-up Operation Northwoods, General Lyman Lemnitzer had had a storied career as a daring soldier with the capabilities of a diplomat. During World War II, when he became a protégé of Eisenhower's, he took part in a secret submarine mission to North Africa that succeeded in convincing French forces to defy the Nazi-controlled Vichy regime. Later in the war, Lemnitzer was a key party in negotiating the surrender of Italian and German forces in Italy. But by September 1960, when Eisenhower, his idol, elevated him to chairman of the Joint Chiefs, Lemnitzer was among a growing wave of virulently anticommunist officers way right of the political center.

In the wake of Sputnik, a 1958 National Security memorandum recommended uniting all branches of the government with the citizenry in the cause of national unity. This resulted in a network of cooperative ventures between military and business. Public seminars were held on a "strategy for survival" and "fourth dimensional warfare," meaning that the United States had to defeat the Soviets on land, sea, air, and the so-called fourth dimension of psychological warfare. Inadvertently, this seeded a movement that opposed any compromise with communism. Giles Scott-Smith, a Cold War historian, wrote, "What was meant to be an effort to unite civilian-military interests in a moment of concern for national security and resolve instead became a stimulus for right-wing critics to push a militant vision of national identity at the grassroots level."

The emerging antidétente caucus wanted the demonization of communism intensified, supported a virtual blank check for the military, and opposed anything that reeked of collectivism, such as New Deal–style interventions by the federal government or any empowerment of the United Nations. "The uncompromising right-wing anticommunism was aimed not so much at the Soviet Union as the root of all evil, since that was a given," Scott-Smith wrote. "The real threat came from communist infiltrators and their hood-winked or 'soft allies' on the liberal left. Liberalism was equal to self-destruction due to lack of political will and a rejection of fundamental American values."

Emerging ultra-right institutions included the fanatical John Birch Society (established in 1958 by Massachusetts candy maker Robert Welch); the Foreign Policy Research Institute at the University of Pennsylvania (an ultra-conservative think tank founded in 1955, with nuclear war rationalizer Henry Kissinger as a member); the Richardson Foundation (a right-wing corporate philanthropy funded by the Vicks Chemical Company); the Christian Crusade (started by fundamentalists who were dedicated anticommunists); and the Minutemen (a shadowy militia group formed by Robert DePugh, who thought of himself as a twentieth-century Paul Revere).

General Edwin Walker, who commanded a force of ten thousand servicemen in West Germany, drew congressional notice for openly espousing ultra-right propaganda. He was a member of the John Birch Society, publicly questioned the loyalty of Harry Truman and Eleanor Roosevelt, and had initiated a "Pro-Blue" campaign in which he extolled the values of Americanism and advised his troops on how they should vote, violating the Hatch Act. After being formally admonished by the Joint Chiefs, Walker became the only U.S. general in the twentieth century to resign his commission.

In 1961, an investigation by Senator J. William Fulbright, chair of the Senate Foreign Relations Committee, provided evidence of military-sponsored programs that linked liberalism with socialism and attacked foreign aid, cultural exchanges, and disarmament negotiations. Fulbright wrote, "We must overcome the 'cold war' mentality that has persuaded millions of sensible and intelligent citizens that the prosecution of the Cold War is our only true essential national responsibility."

General Lemnitzer considered Kennedy a poor substitute for Ike, dismissing the president's military service in the South Pacific by calling him "a patrol-boat skipper." His negative opinion of the new commander in chief was amplified when the forty-three-year-old Kennedy expressed great reluctance to use nuclear weapons. Bamford wrote, "Outwardly, Lemnitzer remained stiff and correct. But deep inside he was raging at the new and youthful Kennedy White House. He felt out of place and out of time in a culture that seemed suddenly to have turned its back on military tradition. Almost immediately he became, in the clinical sense, paranoid; he began secretly expressing his worries to other senior officers."

As Lemnitzer and the nation's top generals were contriving to tilt Kennedy's foreign policy with frightening false flag proposals, journalists Charles Bailey II and Fletcher Knebel published *Seven Days in May*, a novel about a military-political cabal that plots to take over the U.S. government when the president begins negotiating a disarmament treaty with the Soviet Union. Knebel's urge to write the book followed an interview with Curtis LeMay, during which LeMay made off-the-record remarks critical of Kennedy, calling him cowardly for his handling of the Bay of Pigs.

In the film, Burt Lancaster plays General James Mattoon Scott, chairman of the Joint Chiefs and an ideological zealot leading a brewing military coup. He's no loonier than General LeMay, or Edwin

Walker, or Lyman Lemnitzer. "We're asked to believe that a piece of paper will take the place of missile sites and Polaris submarines," the fictional General Scott says contemptuously to a congressional committee, "and that an enemy who hasn't honored one solemn treaty in the history of its existence will now, for our convenience, do precisely that."

Back in the real world, as the plotting of Operation Northwoods continued without Kennedy's knowledge, Lemnitzer and the Joint Chiefs saw an opportunity to blame the death of an astronaut on the new Soviet foothold in Cuba. Such a ploy had the possibility of exploiting a raw national mood. Americans were still being reminded that the Soviets were winning the space race, which was the same thing as saying the United States was losing the Cold War.

On April 12, 1961, the country had experienced Sputnik déjà vu when Yuri Gagarin became the first man in space, and the first to orbit the planet. On August 6, 1961, Gherman Titov became the first man to make multiple orbits, a total of seventeen. (He was also the first person to sleep in orbit, photograph the Earth, and vomit in space.) Meanwhile, America's two manned missions had been suborbital—they went up and came down, only reaching the fringe of space. John Glenn—Mercury astronaut number three—had been scheduled to make another suborbital flight, on a Redstone booster, just like predecessors Alan Shepard and Gus Grissom. But Titov's flight compelled a change in plans. In the interest of national pride, Glenn's mission was upgraded. He was instead going to be put into orbit.

This required a bigger rocket, the nine-story-tall Atlas, which still had a habit of blowing up. On September 9, 1959, the first Atlas to fly as part of the Mercury program, carrying an unmanned capsule, exploded fifty-eight seconds after launch due to structural failure. Glenn was an eyewitness to that disaster, and as he prepared for his December 1961 launch date atop another Atlas, he was keenly aware that the rocket still only had a 50 percent success rate; there had been propellant feed failures, propulsion failures, electrical failures, hydraulic systems failures, and launch systems failures.

This information was well known to the plotters of Operation Northwoods. If the Atlas booster failed, the Joint Chiefs were going to blame it on "radio interference" from the Russian trawlers typically anchored off Cape Canaveral during U.S. spaceflights. If the Soviets could be credibly accused of murdering Glenn, a combat hero turned sexy astronaut, an outcry for revenge had the prospect of not only wiping out the communists in Cuba, but also starting World War III.

Ultimately, there was no opportunity for scapegoating. After the launch was delayed ten times over the course of two months, an Atlas rocket, topped by John Glenn in his Friendship 7 capsule, bolted into the Florida skies on the morning of February 20, 1962. In offices, schools, and homes, millions were glued to the TV coverage. Five hours later, when Glenn's capsule plopped down in the Atlantic Ocean near Bermuda, the country cheered for days. It was truly a moment of national catharsis.

Glenn, the clean-cut, apple-pie, good-natured midwesterner, debriefed JFK at the White House, spoke to a joint session of Congress, and was treated to a ticker tape parade up Broadway. Wrote Tom Wolfe, "And what was it that had moved them all so deeply?... They knew it had to do with the presence, the aura, the radiation of the right stuff, the same vital force of manhood that had made millions vibrate and resonate thirty-five years before to Lindbergh—except that in this case it was heightened by Cold War patriotism, the greatest surge of patriotism seen since the end of World War II."

General Lyman L. Lemnitzer formally discussed Operation Northwoods with Secretary of Defense Robert McNamara on March 13, 1962. On March 16, President Kennedy told the general that there was no chance the United States would take immediate military action against Cuba. A few months later, General Lemnitzer was reassigned to Europe, as Supreme Allied Commander of NATO.

CHAPTER 31

GRAND SETTLEMENT

Nikita Khrushchev and his East German associates had intentionally chosen to build the Berlin Wall on a weekend, when many fewer East Berliners would be going to work at their jobs in West Berlin. So it was that on a Sunday, August 13, 1961, hundreds of East German police lined up along the twenty-seven-mile sectoral boundary, including the Brandenburg Gate, and began unrolling barbed wire. Concrete barriers went up two days later. Ultimately, the wall sliced through 192 streets, thirty-two railway lines, eight S-Bahn city train lines, four subway lines, and three autobahns. On August 22, 1961, a hundred-meter no-man's-land was created on both sides of the wall.

West Berlin—a hundred miles inside East Germany—had been set aside by France, Britain, and the United States after the Grand Alliance with the Soviets defeated Hitler. It almost immediately became the political ground zero in the Cold War. An oasis of freedom, it acted like a magnet. By 1961, more than three million East Germans—a fifth of the population—had fled to the city, often using it as a way station for relocating across Western Europe.

The need for a solution became acute when, in the spring of 1961, the westward flow of refugees doubled after the East German parliament voted down a proposal to lift wages and shorten the workweek. The ugly, hastily built barrier was a brutish stopgap measure, not a long-term solution, and gave the West another propaganda gift of inestimable value. Kennedy speechwriter Teddy Sorensen summarized the view from the White House: The wall was "illegal, immoral, and inhumane, but not a cause for war." The humane way to deal with East Germany's problem—and the self-evident answer to the crisis—would have been to permit Germany's reunification. Instead, East Germany limped along, and its most notable product became young female athletes disfigured by doping. An already diseased state submitted to perversion.

The fix Khrushchev preferred he dared not attempt. He wanted to flush the Western military presence out of Berlin altogether. But during a June 1961 summit in Geneva, President Kennedy made clear such a move would mean war—"West Berlin is Western Europe," he told the Soviet leader. Khrushchev knew he was still outgunned and, overall, his communist empire was a sputtering mess.

Meeting the requirements of food and shelter remained a challenge. Taller buildings would have more expeditiously answered the USSR's desperate housing shortage, but there weren't sufficient raw materials to supply elevators for apartments above five stories. Soviet agriculture couldn't produce an adequate supply of meat and dairy. At peasant markets, eggs were selling for three dollars a dozen—this in a country habituated to paying only pennies for basic food items. The Kremlin was forced to sell twenty-three tons of gold to buy European butter.

A poster circulated in the Siberian city of Chita: "You're a blabbermouth, Khrushchev: Where's the abundance you promised?" When retail prices were raised on meat, poultry, butter, and milk, civil disturbances took place across the Soviet Union. After Red Army troops and secret police units were sent to pacify Novocherkassk, a demonstration of ten thousand ended with twenty-six dead and eight wounded. Wrote William Taubman, "The authorities were so determined to conceal the true toll that they repaved the street, which scrub brushes and fire hoses had proved unable to cleanse of blood, and buried the victims secretly in five separate cemeteries in widely dispersed parts of the Rostov Province."

As civil discontent mounted, so did crime. Khrushchev demanded a greater use of the death penalty. The KGB enlarged its police units. A one-third increase in the defense budget was authorized. Khrushchev's hope of improving the Soviet standard of living through détente and demilitarization had all but faded away.

Meanwhile, the Soviet rocket program, which the Soviet leader envisioned as a shortcut to strategic parity with the United States, was still struggling to recover from a disaster at the Baikonur Cosmodrome on October 24, 1960. During the prelaunch sequence of the new R-16 intercontinental ballistic missile, a fuel supply system, improperly repaired, caused a fire. Ten tons of fuel ignited. More than a hundred people died, many burned alive, including Mitrofan Nedelin, the head of the Strategic Rocket Forces and chief marshal of artillery. He could only be identified by the Hero of the Soviet Union award on his uniform. The Soviet media reported he had died in a plane crash.

In early 1962, Khrushchev received more depressing news about his missile program. He learned that the R-16 had been made obsolete by the second generation of U.S. missiles, the Minuteman. The corrosive liquid propellant used for the R-16 had to be drained if the rocket wasn't immediately used. As a result, the missile always required refueling, which took hours. By contrast, the U.S. Minuteman, powered by solid fuels, remained in a ready position for years; it required only minutes to launch. "Before we managed to move the R-16 and lift it into place, nothing would be left of us," a chief rocket official told Khrushchev.

The arms deficiency propelled Khrushchev to find a partial solution through geography. Although the Soviets were struggling to build a reliable intercontinental ballistic missile, they did have effective medium-range ballistic missiles (MRBMs) and intermediate-range ballistic missiles (IRBMs). These weapons provided little leverage if they remained inside the borders of the Soviet Union, but—assuming Fidel Castro's cooperation—the Soviets could spot a bunch of them in Cuba, ninety miles off the U.S. coast, close enough to imperil every city in the continental United States. "Why not throw a hedgehog at Uncle Sam's pants?" Khrushchev quipped.

"As we now know," Max Frankel wrote, "the Cuban missile ploy was cooked up in the spring of 1962 by Khrushchev, and his defense minister, Rodion Malinovksy. They faced a growing 'missile gap' in America's favor and realized that catching up in the production of ICBMs would take years and cost a czar's fortune. Quickly building nuclear bases in Cuba would let them deploy their abundant stocks of short range (1,000- to 2,000-mile) missiles and instantly multiply the number of American targets in their nuclear sights."

Khrushchev began imagining a grand settlement. "By November 6, [1962,] all the missiles would be in Cuba and operational," wrote Fursenko and Naftali, "and his Foreign Ministry would have prepared boilerplate for formal agreements on the establishment of a UN presence in West Berlin and the withdrawal of Western troops. In addition, he would have a draft of a test ban treaty that he could offer to Kennedy as a sweetener once the President had swallowed the retreat from Berlin." Providing Castro with a nuclear boost would also deter American interference. "So long as the secret [missile] deployment to Cuba could hold," Fursenko and Naftali added, "Khrushchev believed that John Kennedy would have no choice but to accept Soviet terms for ending the Cold War in 1962."

This thinking was the product of a desperate man ruling a dysfunctional state. Desperation doesn't often clarify the mind, and Khrushchev's best-laid plans would go terribly awry.

In July 1962, the Soviets began positioning a chunk of the Red Army in Cuba. The deployment would eventually include antiaircraft guns and missiles, a battalion of T-55 tanks, a wing of MIG-21 fighters, forty-two Il-28 light bombers, 162 nuclear weapons, and 41,902 troops. This large and rapid military surge was going to be hard to miss and, predictably, the goal of total secrecy was never met.

Many of the arriving Soviet soldiers were dressed as civilians and described as machine operators, irrigation specialists, and agricultural advisors; the Cuban population was not fooled. Sergey Biryuzov, head of the Soviet Rocket Forces, told Khrushchev that the missiles would be concealed and camouflaged by palm trees; this was fanciful thinking. Within weeks, the CIA had learned about the buildup from sources on the ground and U-2 photos.

After the Soviets shot down the U-2 piloted by Gary Powers, Khrushchev had seen the quality of the photos taken by the plane. This fact alone should have made him far more skeptical of being able to hide his hedgehogs from Uncle Sam. Operation Anadyr, as the Cuba plan was code-named, could only pave the way for his "Grand Settlement to End the Cold War" if the United States was suddenly and shockingly presented with a nuclear fait accompli.

On August 10, 1962, CIA director John A. McCone sent a memo to Kennedy about the Soviet arms traffic and reasoned that sending antiaircraft missiles into Cuba only made sense "if Moscow intended to use them to shield a base for ballistic missiles aimed at the United States." Three weeks later, on August 31, Republican Kenneth Keating went to the Senate floor and accused the Kennedy administration of hiding the fact that Khrushchev was building rocket bases in Cuba. With the Bay of Pigs catastrophe still resonant and midterm elections approaching, such a charge was political dynamite for the White House. "In his presidential bid," Benjamin Schwarz noted in the *Atlantic*, "Kennedy had red-baited the Eisenhower-Nixon administration, charging that its policies had 'helped make Communism's first Caribbean base.'" Roger Hilsman, the State Department's director of intelligence and research, put it this way: "The United States might not be in mortal danger, but...the administration most certainly was."

On September 7, a day before the first consignment of medium-range nuclear missiles arrived in Cuba, Soviet ambassador to the United States Anatoly Dobrynin assured U.S. ambassador to the United Nations Adlai Stevenson that the Soviet Union was supplying only defensive weapons to Cuba. (Such lies continued until October 25, when Stevenson produced reconnaissance photos of the missile sites at the UN.) In all, thirty-six R-12 MRBMs would be delivered. These were topped by a megaton-class warhead capable of reaching as far north as New York, or as far west as Dallas.

Unknown for the remainder of the Cold War, the Soviets also shipped more than a hundred smaller tactical nuclear weapons to Cuba. These were to be used to repel a prospective U.S. invasion. Some of the nuclear-tipped cruise missiles had a hundred-mile range and enough destructive power to destroy an invasion armada. Others were assigned to Soviet motorized brigades and were to be used exclusively for battlefield combat. A total of six nuclear bombs were also provided for the light bombers, and four Soviet submarines moving toward Cuba each carried a nuclear missile.

The thirteen-day period that came to be identified as the height of the crisis began on October 16, when Kennedy received solid visual evidence of the missiles from a U-2 flight. Oleg Penkovsky, a CIA agent inside Soviet military intelligence, had already provided an R-12 manual, which greatly helped analysts make sense of the photographs. JFK's military advisors, LeMay in particular, pushed for an attack.

"The Russian bear has always been eager to stick his paw in Latin American waters," LeMay told Kennedy at one point. "Now that we've got him in a trap, let's take his leg off right up to his testicles. On second thought, let's take off his testicles, too."

"These brass hats have one great advantage in their favor," Kennedy said to his closest advisors. "If we listen to them, and do what they want us to do, none of us will be alive later to tell them that they were wrong."

On October 17, 1962, Kennedy decided the initial U.S. response would be a blockade to interrupt all incoming shipping. Five more days would pass before JFK told Khrushchev—and the world—about his decision to blockade Cuba, which he'd technically call a "quarantine," so it didn't sound like an act of war, even though by any other name it was still an act of war. What propelled the idea of a blockade was smart politics: Look tough, but don't play nutty nuclear cowboy.

At 7:00 p.m. Eastern on October 22, Kennedy delivered, as the *New York Times* wrote, "an 18-minute radio and television address of a grimness unparalleled in recent times." The president announced the discovery of the missiles in Cuba, the start of the quarantine, and invoked the nineteenth-century Monroe Doctrine:

> It shall be the policy of this nation to regard any nuclear missile launched from Cuba against any nation in the Western Hemisphere as an attack by the Soviet Union on the United States, requiring a full retaliatory response upon the Soviet Union.

As Kennedy said those words, twenty-year-old college junior and future journalist Michael Mosettig was watching at a fraternity house affiliated with George Washington University. "In a room of about 20 normally talkative and garrulous fraternity men, the only sound was the occasional gasp," he recalled. "As that week spun on, seemingly in increasing danger, there was some talk of a few people here moving their families out of Washington.... Ever since the Soviets exploded their first atomic bomb in 1949, being a nuclear target was part of the subconscious price that we and our families paid to work and live in the nation's capital." The *New Yorker* wrote, "The great gate hung on its hinges, and would have to swing, but when? And in what direction? In the oddly silent wasteland of First Avenue, we could hear the ticking of the watch on our wrist."

On October 24, Kennedy put additional pressure on Khrushchev to remove the missiles by placing Strategic Air Command at Defense Condition (DEFCON) 2 for the first time since the system was established, in 1959. This was one step short of nuclear war. The order was issued on an open channel so that the Soviets could hear it. Sixty-six B-52s carrying hydrogen bombs were now constantly airborne, replaced with fresh crews every twenty-four hours.

What came next depends upon your source, or gullibility. According to the formidable Kennedy mythmaking machine, JFK calmly repelled the warmongers inside his administration and ultimately strong-armed the Soviet leader into packing up his missiles in return for a minor concession, a declaration that the United States would not invade Cuba. But that's definitely *not* what happened.

"In the midst of that crisis," Schwarz wrote, "the sanest and most sensible observers...saw a missile trade as a fairly simple solution." The quid pro quo being suggested by, among others, UN ambassador Adlai Stevenson was this: Khrushchev would take the missiles out of Cuba if Kennedy removed the U.S. missiles in Turkey. "In an effort to resolve the impasse," Schwarz added, "Khrushchev himself openly made this proposal on October 27. According to the version of events propagated by the Kennedy administration (and long accepted as historical fact), Washington unequivocally rebuffed Moscow's offer and instead, thanks to Kennedy's resolve, forced a unilateral Soviet withdrawal."

This was the way the deal *actually* went down: Without telling his top advisors, Kennedy instructed his brother, Attorney General Robert Kennedy, to meet secretly with Soviet ambassador Dobrynin. RFK told Dobrynin that the United States was willing to remove the missiles from Turkey within five months provided the concession *not be part of any public resolution to the conflict.* Vice President Lyndon Johnson was one of many who did not know about the trade. "In their effort to maintain the cover-up," wrote Schwarz, "a number of those who did, including [Secretary of Defense Robert] McNamara and [Secretary of State Dean] Rusk, lied to Congress....By successfully hiding the deal...Kennedy and his team reinforced the dangerous notion that firmness in the face of what the United States construes as aggression, and the graduated escalation of military threats and action in countering that aggression, makes for a successful national-security strategy."

What also remained hidden for decades were multiple harrowing episodes during those thirteen tense days in October that could have resulted in global nuclear war.

———

At least four nuclear weapons were detonated in space during the Cuban Missile Crisis, two by the United States, two by the Soviets. These were incredibly ill-timed tests of the Christofilos effect, named after Nicholas Christofilos, a Greek elevator repairman turned inventor who theorized that an antimissile shield of high-energy electrons—a kind of invisible Astrodome—could be created by exploding a large number of nuclear weapons in space.

The United States conducted a test related to this theory on October 20, code-named Checkmate. A rocket was launched from Johnston Atoll, 860 miles southwest of Hawaii, in the United States Minor Outlying Islands. The rocket carried a low-yield nuclear warhead that was detonated at an altitude of 91 miles. Observers on Johnston Island reported seeing a man-made version of the aurora borealis— a circular green-and-blue region "surrounded by a blood-red ring" along with "blue-green streamers and numerous pink striations."

On October 22, likely in response to the U.S. test, the Soviets exploded a warhead of their own in space. Four days later, on October 26, the United States conducted a second high-altitude nuclear test, code-named Bluegill Triple Prime. By this point, the U.S. military had been placed on DEFCON 2 alert. Commenting on the timing of the tests, CIA Soviet missile expert Raymond Garthoff said, "The danger of the situation simply getting out of control from developments or accidents or incidents that neither side—leaders on either side—were even aware of, much less in control of, could have led to war."

On October 28, 1962, in Kazakhstan, the Soviets detonated a nuclear weapon at an altitude of ninety-three miles. Russian scientists reported that the detonation caused an electromagnetic pulse that covered all of Kazakhstan, including "electrical cables buried underground."

Meanwhile, Curtis LeMay was conspiring with his successor at SAC, Thomas Powers, to raise the heat. "They began taking small steps to provoke nuclear war on their own," the *New Yorker*'s Joshua Rothman noted. "At the height of the crisis, SAC decided to go ahead with an ICBM test launch which, by all rights, should have been cancelled." This was a deliberate provocation, and there were more. "SAC airborne-alert bombers deliberately flew past their customary turnaround points toward the Soviet Union," Richard Rhodes wrote. "The bombers did eventually turn back, but the provocation was clear."

On the morning of Saturday, October 27, U-2 pilot Rudolf Anderson was approaching Cuba during what he expected to be a routine reconnaissance mission. At the same time, one of the newly constructed Soviet antiaircraft missile batteries on Cuba started the first test of its early warning and guidance system.

"[The] numbers appeared on the screen: azimuth, altitude, distance, speed," Khrushchev's son Sergei later wrote.

There could be no doubt. They'd detected a spy plane. The operators called the head of Soviet air defenses in Cuba, Col. Georgy Voronkov. He in turn tried to contact the commander of all Soviet forces in Cuba, Gen. Issa Pliyev, but no one knew where he was. Voronkov called again: "The target is leaving. We have two minutes left." The generals had no orders from Moscow to shoot down single American planes. They were authorized to use missiles only in case of an assault on the island, a massive bomber attack. But there was no categorical prohibition either. Now only seconds were left.

"Fire," one of Pliyev's deputies, Maj. Gen. Leonid Gabruz, breathed softly into the telephone.

Two SAM-2 anti-aircraft missiles broke from their launchers and tore into the clear blue sky. A small white puff of smoke appeared. The operator reported: "The target has been destroyed."

U.S. officials assumed Khrushchev had ordered the attack and were deeply shaken. "Had another American plane been hit," George Perkovich wrote in *Politico*, "the United States probably would have responded first by bombing missile installations. Depending on how Castro and his forces reacted to that, and whether the Soviets would have begun removing the detected missiles, Kennedy and the military planned that the United States would begin an invasion." The United States had expected that such an invasion would produce a quick victory; at the time, intelligence reports indicated only eight thousand to ten thousand Soviet troops were in Cuba. In fact, there were four times that many, a total not revealed until 2008.

On the same day the U-2 was shot down, USS *Beale*, an American destroyer, located a diesel-powered Soviet Foxtrot submarine in Cuban waters. The *Beale* began dropping practice depth charges, the size of a hand grenade, to force the sub to surface. The charges were actually nonlethal practice rounds, and the U.S. Navy had informed the Soviets about using this tactic. But the captain of submarine B-59, Valentin Savitsky, didn't have that information, nor did he know about Kennedy's blockade. He'd lost communication with Moscow.

The atmosphere on board the Soviet vessel was already tense and unsustainable. The battery was failing, and the air conditioning and onboard freezer had conked out. This had the effect of spoiling much of the food supply and raising the temperature inside the ship to a sweltering one hundred degrees. The crew, dripping sweat, were working in their underwear and fainting from rising levels of carbon dioxide. Due to lack of water, everyone was infected with rashes.

As the assault of depth charges continued, the Soviet seamen assumed they were under attack. "They exploded right next to the hull," said intelligence officer Vadim Orlov. "It felt like you were sitting in a metal barrel, which somebody is constantly blasting with a sledgehammer."

The U.S. Navy was also missing a critical piece of information about the B-59: The Soviet sub was carrying a 15-kiloton T-5 nuclear torpedo, approximating the explosive power of the bomb dropped on Hiroshima. Savitsky ordered the nuclear torpedo prepared for battle readiness. Then he roared, "We're going to blast them now! We will die, but we will sink them all—we will not become the shame of the fleet."

The sub's target was USS *Randolf*, a giant aircraft carrier leading the Navy task force. However, firing without a direct order from Moscow required the consent of all three senior officers on board. Political officer Ivan Maslennikov agreed that the torpedo should be launched. But the other officer, Second Captain Vasili Arkhipov, dissented. His word carried weight. The year before, he had exposed himself to deadly radiation in order to save a submarine with an overheating reactor.

Arkhipov argued that they did not know for sure that the ship was under attack. Why not surface and then await orders from Moscow? The torpedo wasn't fired. The B-59 surfaced near the American warships and set off north, returning to the Soviet Union without incident.

Thomas Blanton, the director of the National Security Archive at George Washington University, said, "The lesson from this is that a guy called Vasili Arkhipov saved the world."

———

"We know now," said Harvard political scientist Graham Allison, "that in addition to nuclear-armed ballistic missiles, the Soviet Union had deployed 100 tactical nuclear weapons to Cuba.... The U.S. air strike and invasion that were scheduled for the third week of the confrontation would likely have triggered a nuclear response against American ships and troops, and perhaps even Miami. The resulting war might have led to the deaths of over 100 million Americans and over 100 million Russians."

As more has been learned about the scope of what took place during the crisis, the actions of Khrushchev and Kennedy have received much harsher reviews. "[Khrushchev] managed to transform the years between 1958 and 1962 into the most dangerous period of the Cold War without achieving a grand settlement," wrote Fursenko and Naftali. "The threat of nuclear war was useful only if your enemy truly believed you were suicidal. Instead, with the United States aware of its strategic advantage, these standoffs turned into games of chicken that Khrushchev always called off first. It was Khrushchev's propensity to risk war to make peace that bedeviled U.S. presidents." In the meantime, Kennedy was consumed by imagery and oblivious to the downside of a Cuba policy that had completely forsaken diplomacy and essentially had only one action item: assassinating Fidel Castro.

In the immediate aftermath of the Cuban crisis, a Soviet envoy told his American counterpart, "We will honor this agreement, but I want to tell you something. You'll never do this to us again." Soviet lieutenant general Nikolai Detinov explained what came next: "Because of the strategic [imbalance] between the United States and the Soviet Union, the Soviet Union had to accept everything that the United States dictated to it and this had a painful effect on our country and our government.... All our economic resources were mobilized [afterward] to solve this problem." By 1978, the two nations would achieve numerical nuclear parity, with the Soviets slightly ahead, commanding an inventory of 25,393 total warheads to 24,243 for the United States. The Soviet stockpile would peak at 40,000 warheads during the 1980s.

CHAPTER 32

CHAOS THEORY

If you are alive in the 1960s, the assaults on the collective psyche seem to accelerate. The specter of violence dominates. Killing arrives in a greater variety and becomes even more mystifying. There's blood on the floor and in the streets. Society seems at the verge of collapse. What's next appears less and less predictable...

... **You are MIT meteorology professor Edward Lorenz**, using a computer program to make long-term weather forecasts. Your model is based on twelve variables, representing things like temperature and wind speed. You decide to repeat a simulation with the aim of letting it run longer. Not wanting to wait for the computer to recalculate the whole sequence from the beginning, you skip to the middle by simply typing in the results you already had.

When the simulation is completed, however, the entire weather pattern has diverged. This doesn't make any sense until you realize that when doing the data entry you rounded off one variable from 0.506127 to 0.506. This tiny alteration has drastically transformed the whole pattern over two months of simulated weather. A small discrepancy—in decimal points, one part in a thousand—completely changed the ultimate result. Or, a small change had a very large consequence.

You publish your results in the *Journal of the Atmospheric Sciences*. The title of the paper is "Deterministic Nonperiodic Flow." "Only one thing can happen next," you write.

Isaac Newton's tidy clockwork universe and the dream of perfect knowledge has been blown apart. You give a talk that puts the concept in layman's terms: "Predictability: Does the Flap of a Butterfly's Wings in Brazil Set Off a Tornado in Texas?" You have discovered that the more a system has the capacity to vary, the less likely it is to produce a repeating sequence. This sensitivity makes weather, and much of the activity in the natural world, very difficult to forecast far in advance. In a sense, history does turn on a dime. Your insight becomes known as chaos theory.

   ...**It is January 14, 1963**. You are George Corley Wallace and you have just taken the oath of office as governor of Alabama, the only state that has not integrated its educational system. The ceremony is taking place from the portico of the Alabama State Capitol in Montgomery, the same place where, a century earlier, Jefferson Davis split the nation over slavery. You raise the connection to that blood-soaked Civil War:

> It is very appropriate...that from this Cradle of the Confederacy, this very Heart of the Great Anglo-Saxon Southland, that today we sound the drum for freedom as have our generations of forebears before us done.... In the name of the greatest people that have ever trod this earth, I draw the line in the dust and toss the gauntlet before the feet of tyranny...and I say...segregation today...segregation tomorrow...segregation forever.

   ...**It is May 20, 1963**. You are Medgar Evers, the Mississippi field director for the NAACP, a rising figure in the civil rights movement, and about to integrate Jackson television station WLBT with a prime-time political address. You're going to integrate a station that has never shown coverage of the civil rights movement or more than a few seconds of a human being with a black face. You note your service in the U.S. Army fighting Fascism and Nazism. You provide galling statistics about the city's lack of equality. Forty percent of Jackson's 150,000 residents are black, but there are no black police officers, no black firefighters, and no black municipal clerks. You conclude by saying:

> The Negro has been here in America since 1619, a total of 344 years. He is not going anywhere else; this country is his home. He wants to do his part to help make his city, state, and nation a better place for everyone.... Let me appeal to the consciences of many silent, responsible citizens of the white community who know that a victory for democracy in Jackson will be a victory for democracy everywhere.

...It is June 10, 1963, just after midnight in Jackson, Mississippi. If you are forty-two-year-old Byron De La Beckwith, you are waiting to kill Medgar Evers with a high-powered .30-06 Enfield rifle, which you typically use to hunt deer. You are hiding behind a clump of honeysuckle vines in a vacant lot across the street from the Evers home.

Your friends call you DEE-lay. You are a wife-beating fertilizer salesman who has been battling schizophrenia since being wounded when your Marine unit stormed the beaches at Tarawa. You have been obsessed by race since coming back home. You have written to the Mississippi governor promising to "tear the mask from the face of the NAACP" and "forever rid the land of the DISEASE OF INTEGRATION."

You get ready to fire as Evers pulls into the driveway of his one-story home. He is coming back from an NAACP meeting at the New Jerusalem Baptist Church. He takes T-shirts out of his car that read "Jim Crow Must Go." You shoot. Your bullet strikes Evers in the back, pierces his heart, exits out the front, and continues, putting a hole in a picture window before ending up in the kitchen. Evers staggers to the front door, where he collapses, still holding his car keys.

T-shirts are scattered on the driveway. You flee in your white Plymouth Valiant. Evers, age thirty-seven, is survived by a wife and three young children.

...If you are Stan Lee of Marvel Comics, you know that if there is one thing your readers hate, it is the military. So you decide to create a character who represents the military to the hundredth degree—someone who is a rich weapons manufacturer, like Howard Hughes. You think it will be fun to create a character that none of your Marvel devotees will like and shove him down their throats.

His name is Tony Stark. You imagine this rich weapons manufacturer impressing a U.S. general with one of his new inventions, a miracle transistor capable of increasing the power of magnets. Tony will say to the general, "Now do you believe the transistors I've invented are capable of solving your problem in Vietnam?"

You create a story where Tony is captured by communist forces in Southeast Asia under the leadership of Wong-Chu, the "Red Guerrilla Tyrant." Tony Stark will soon figure out how to turn himself into a weapon. He will become Iron Man.

...It is June 11, 1963. If you are Associated Press photographer Malcolm Browne, you are watching sixty-seven-year-old Buddhist monk Thich Quang Duc set himself ablaze while sitting at a Saigon intersection. He is protesting the persecution of Buddhism by the U.S.-backed South Vietnamese regime. As the flames quickly consume his body, the monk does not move, nor make a sound.

...It is June 14, 1963. You are Thomas Hughes, assistant secretary of state for intelligence and research, and you have just completed a memo titled "Soviet Media Coverage of Current U.S. Racial Crisis." Your memo instructs on the ways the Soviets are exploiting the hateful treatment of black Americans to highlight the hypocrisy of America's founding creed of "equality for all." You write, "Recurrent themes of the Soviet treatment have been: that racism is inevitable in the capitalist system and can only be eradicated along with capitalism itself; that the Federal Government is actually supporting the racists by its general inertia and because of its unwillingness to antagonize Southern Democrats; and that U.S. racism is clearly indicative of policies toward colored people throughout the world."

...**It is August 28, 1963**. The March on Washington has drawn 250,000 people to the capital in a push for meaningful civil rights legislation. Speakers and performers begin a program on the steps of the Lincoln Memorial. You are twenty-two-year-old Bob Dylan, and you've been asked to perform a song you've just written about the killing of Medgar Evers. You have taken a deep and dangerous route with your lyrics, suggesting that the alleged murderer, Byron De La Beckwith, is just one more poor angry white man fed hate by manipulative politicians, a pawn in their game:

You got more than the blacks, don't complain
You're better than them, you been born with white skin, they
    explain . . .

...**It is Thursday, September 5, 1963**. Your name is Robert Chambliss, and you are one of Birmingham, Alabama's "Cahaba River Bridge Boys," an especially violent faction of the Ku Klux Klan. You are in possession of hundreds of sticks of dynamite and you are going to use a portion of them in a matter of days to send a message to the city's Negro population. You have been incited to action by the ardent segregationist in the statehouse, Governor George Wallace, who has just publicly said that what the country needs is a few first-class funerals. You tell your niece that the Cahaba Boys have enough stuff to flatten half of Birmingham. "You wait until after Sunday," you tell her. "They'll beg us to let them segregate."

...**On the morning of Sunday, September 15, 1963**, you are one of the first responders to a bombing at the Sixteenth Street Baptist Church in Birmingham. The explosion has ripped a gaping hole in the back wall. Windows in adjacent buildings are shattered. Cars parked on the street have been destroyed. Four girls, members of the choir, are dead. They are fourteen-year-old Addie Mae Collins, eleven-year-old Denise McNair, fourteen-year-old Carole Robertson, and fourteen-year-old Cynthia Wesley. One of the girls has been decapitated, another killed by a flying piece of mortar that became embedded in her skull.

...**During the fall of 1963**, you are reading John le Carré's number one best-seller *The Spy Who Came in from the Cold*. "What the hell do you think spies are?" says weary fictional British agent Alec Leamus. "Moral philosophers measuring everything they do against the word of God or Karl Marx? They're not. They're just a bunch of seedy, squalid bastards like me. Little men, drunkards, queers, henpecked husbands, civil servants playing cowboys and Indians to brighten their rotten little lives."

...**It is 1 p.m. at Parkland Memorial Hospital in Dallas on November 22, 1963**. President John Kennedy has just been pronounced dead of a gunshot wound to the brain. You are acting White House press secretary Malcolm Kilduff and it is your job to tell the world. But first you head to a hospital room where Lyndon Johnson and his wife, Lady Bird, have been waiting. As a courtesy, you ask Johnson—calling him "Mr. President"—if you can announce Kennedy's death to the press. To your surprise, Johnson asks that you wait until after he leaves. "I think I had better get out of here before you announce it," LBJ says. "We don't know whether this is a worldwide conspiracy, whether they are after me as well as they were after President Kennedy, or whether they are after Speaker McCormack, or Senator Hayden. We just don't know."

...**On November 24, 1963**, around lunchtime, you are one of millions of people watching NBC's ongoing coverage of the Kennedy assassination. A perp walk is in progress. In the basement of the Dallas city jail, presumed assassin Lee Harvey Oswald, flanked by detectives, is being transferred to another facility. Out of the lower right corner of the screen, you see a man rush toward Oswald. You hear a pop. Oswald gasps and begins to fall, grabbing his side. Off camera, you hear NBC newsman Tom Pettit say excitedly, "He's been shot! Lee Oswald has been shot! There is absolute panic— pandemonium has broken out!"

A swarm of bodies envelops a man later identified as Jack Ruby. It's a tangle of arms and legs, pushing and scuffling. A stretcher appears. A clear view is blocked by the blur of activity. There's an ambulance backing into the basement. The doors open, the motionless Oswald is lifted into it. Pettit indignantly asks an officer, "How would it have been possible for him to slip in?" The officer replies, "Sir, I can't answer that question." Pettit finds Captain Will Fritz: "Do you have the man who fired the shot?" Fritz says, "We have a man, yes."

...It is December 4, 1963. You are Nation of Islam minister Malcolm X. After making a speech in Manhattan in which you have warned white America that she is at her hour of judgment and must pay for her sins against twenty-two million Negroes, you are asked a question about the Kennedy assassination by a member of the press. You indicate that JFK's murder was a righteous act that satisfied a kind of cosmic moral balance. You say Kennedy had twiddled his thumbs at the killing of South Vietnamese president Ngo Dinh Diem and his brother Ngo Dinh Nhu. You say about the dead president:

> He never foresaw that the chickens would come home to roost so soon....Being an old farm boy myself, chickens coming home to roost never did make me sad; they've always made me glad.

...You are Martin Luther King. After receiving the Nobel Peace Prize, you return home to find a very disturbing package. It is dated September 10, 1964. The contents are FBI blackmail. There is tape of you in a hotel room engaged in extramarital sex, and a let- ter that encourages you to commit suicide. The letter says, in part, "King, there is only one thing left for you to do. You know what it is. . . . You are done. There is but one way out for you. You better take it before your filthy, abnormal, fraudulent self is bared to the nation."

You are Barry Goldwater, the 1964 Republican candidate for president. A new quarterly magazine, *Fact*, has just devoted its entire September–October issue—all sixty-five pages—to a discussion about your mental health. The cover indicates you are out of your mind:

1,189 Psychiatrists Say Goldwater Is Psychologically Unfit to Be President!

There are two main articles under the shared heading of "The Unconscious of a Conservative: A Special Issue on the Mind of Barry Goldwater." The articles report that you have a severely paranoid personality and are psychologically unfit for the high office to which you aspire. The thesis is supported by (1) alleged troubling incidents from your public and private life and (2) the results of a poll sent by the magazine to 12,356 psychiatrists.

The *Fact* magazine survey of psychiatrists asked one question: "Do you believe Barry Goldwater is psychologically fit to serve as President of the United States?" Of the 2,417 who responded, 1,189 say you are *unfit*. Two-thirds of the psychiatrists were willing to have their names and responses printed. They call you megalomaniacal, paranoid, schizophrenic, grossly psychotic, unstable, immature, cowardly, amoral, immoral, and a dangerous lunatic.

. . . It is February 21, 1965. You are New York radio reporter Gene Simpson, about to hear Malcolm X speak at the Audubon Ballroom, at 166th and Broadway in Washington Heights. "*As salaam alaikum,*" Malcom begins, offering the traditional Arabic greeting, meaning "Peace be unto you." The crowd responds, "*Alaikum salaam.*" You hear a disturbance, about eight rows back. You turn. Malcolm says, "Be cool now, don't get excited." Shots ring out all over the place. It looks like a firing squad. Three men are shooting, rushing the stage, one with a sawed-off shotgun, the other two with handguns. You duck for cover. You hear a muffled sound and you see Malcolm take a bullet with his hands still raised. He falls back stiffly over the chairs behind him, his head hitting the floor with a thud. Everyone is shouting. Malcolm's supporters are trying to subdue one of the shooters. Another man is firing like he is in some western, running backward toward the door and firing at the same time. You see Malcolm lying on the stage, alive but feebly so. People have ripped apart his bloodied shirt and are trying to give him mouth-to-mouth resuscitation, first a woman, then a man. His wife, Betty, is on her knees next to him, sobbing. She says, "They killed him!"

. . .It is August 6, 1965. You are one of nearly thirty million people watching a broadcast of the *CBS Evening News*. Correspondent Morley Safer is reporting from South Vietnam, in the village of Cam Ne. A U.S. Marine casually raises a Zippo lighter to the roof of a thatched hut. Desperate villagers cry and plead with the soldier as the house goes up in flames. We see another U.S. Marine using a flamethrower to almost instantly ignite the roof of another hut. Over shots of more smoking huts, and grieving families, and blindfolded prisoners, Safer says:

> The day's operation burned down 150 houses, wounded three women, killed one baby, wounded one Marine, and netted these four prisoners—four old men who could not answer questions put to them in English, four old men who had no idea what an ID card was.

. . .It is August 11, 1965. You are a shaken white Angeleno watching KTLA. Black men are tossing Molotov cocktails at cops in an area twenty minutes from your house. The station's novel "telecopter" isn't doing the usual traffic report—it's providing live coverage of the Watts riot: commercial buildings in flames, looters sacking department stores, police subduing and arresting scores of residents. The flashpoint is fuzzy. According to one story, it began with the arrest of Marquette Frye, a twenty-one-year-old black motorist suspected of drunk driving. After his mother appeared in the middle of Avalon Avenue and began hollering at Marquette for driving drunk, a crowd assembled and a rumor spread that mother and son were being brutalized by the cops. As Marquette was being led away, one of his friends said to him, "Don't worry; we're going to burn this mother down." More than six hundred buildings have been damaged or destroyed. More than a thousand people have been injured. Thirty-four killed. The National Guard has cordoned off a vast region of South Los Angeles. You are wondering if it's time to get out of the city. What if the violence spreads?

. . . You are twenty-five-year-old ex-Marine sharpshooter Charles Whitman. It is August 1, 1966. On a scorching day, high noon, you establish a sniper position atop the twenty-eight-story bell tower at the University of Texas, in Austin. You are an architectural student at the school. For the past year, you've been battling severe headaches. Seen five doctors, including a psychiatrist who prescribed Valium. What you don't know is that you have a brain tumor. Which may have something to do with why you murdered your mother and your wife before heading to the campus.

You have seven guns and seven hundred rounds of ammunition. The stash includes a sawed-off shotgun, a Remington 700 6-millimeter bolt-action hunting rifle, a .35-caliber pump rifle, a .30-caliber carbine (M1), a 9-millimeter Luger pistol, a Galesi-Brescia .25-caliber pistol, and a Smith & Wesson Model 19 .357 Magnum revolver. You also have a machete, and three knives, and enough supplies for mounting a long attack—food, coffee, vitamins, Dexedrine, Excedrin, earplugs, jugs of water, matches, lighter fluid, rope, binoculars, a transistor radio, toilet paper, a razor, and a bottle of deodorant. You are wearing khaki overalls. You open fire. Over the next ninety minutes, you will shoot forty-nine people, kill seventeen.

...In 1967, America's ghettoes are war zones. There are seventy-five separate urban riots, resulting in 88 deaths, 1,397 injuries, 16,389 arrests, and economic damage estimated at $664.5 million. In Detroit, 43 are killed; in Newark, 26. Stokely Carmichael, head of the Student Non-Violent Coordinating Committee, speaks openly of blacks arming for purposes of self-defense. Eldridge Cleaver, information minister of the Black Panthers, announces he will run for president under the banner of the Peace and Freedom Party. H. Rap Brown of the SNCC predicts that inner-city violence is only a "dress rehearsal for the revolution."

...You are an increasingly paranoid Lyndon Johnson. You see a communist plot behind the riots. You summon CIA director Richard Helms. You tell him you're not going to let the communists take over the government. You say you want to carefully look at who leaves the country, where they go, why they're going. Even though Hoover's FBI, under COINTELPRO, is already gathering information on American radicals using illegal break-ins, illegal wiretaps, and the illegal opening of mail, you order Helms to begin an illegal domestic surveillance program. It will be called Operation Chaos.

...It is November 16, 1967. You are CIA director Richard Helms. You tell the president that you have found no evidence that a foreign government is sponsoring leftists or members of the Black Power movement. In response, LBJ tells you to intensify the search. The Chaos program will continue for another six years.

...It is August 8, 1968. You are Richard Nixon, making your acceptance speech at the Republican convention in Miami, and you are going to split the country in two. You say:

As we look at America, we see cities enveloped in smoke and flames. We hear sirens in the night.

This is a reminder of more terrifying rioting and looting by blacks across the country, like what happened after the April assassination of

Martin Luther King, when anarchy was unloosed in a hundred cities, and twenty thousand were arrested, and fifty thousand National Guard troops were needed to put a lid on the madness.

You say:

We see Americans hating each other; fighting each other; killing each other at home.

Some of the millions listening to you think not only of King's assassination but of Bobby Kennedy's, two months later, the senator dying in a pool of his own blood in a Los Angeles hotel kitchen.

You say:

Millions of Americans cry out in anguish. Did we come all this way for this? Did American boys die in Normandy, and Korea, and in Valley Forge for this?

Who are these millions of anguished Americans? They are the Silent Majority and you will promise them law and order. They are millions of white working-class men and women who are deadly afraid of a black revolt and you know how to speak to them in artfully coded ways.

You say:

When the nation with the greatest tradition of the rule of law is plagued by unprecedented lawlessness...then it's time for new leadership for the United States of America.

On the campaign trail, you will oppose forced busing because white working-class parents don't want black children invading their schools. You will support states' rights and swear to put only strict constructionists on the Supreme Court because whites in the South want to prevent the federal government from taking apart Jim

Crow. You will keep using the words *law and order* because looters and arsonists are criminals and criminals need to be prosecuted and what does that have to do with the color of anyone's skin? Let the Democrats own civil rights and voting rights and poverty programs. Let the Democrats spout liberal pieties while the country is going to shit. Let the Democrats be the party of all those ghetto hoodlums and welfare cheats who need to be rounded up and put in jail for a very long time.

...You are Howard Hughes and you can't take it anymore. Tremors are shaking your penthouse suite at the Desert Inn. Every week, at a military site less than two hours north of the Strip, the United States has been blowing up hydrogen bombs underground. You write a memo to your fixer, Bob Maheu:

> Has anybody ever tried to compute the price paid for the privilege of laying waste, mutilating and contaminating for all the days to come millions of acres of good, fertile, vegetated Nevada earth through the damage wrought by these explosions?

You want the tests stopped and you tell Maheu to bribe Richard Nixon and Hubert Humphrey, the presidential candidates of the two major parties. Each man, without hesitation, accepts an all-cash contribution from you of $100,000.

...It is October 3, 1968. You are George Wallace and about to announce your running mate for a surging, states'-rights, segregationist, law-and-order, tell-it-like-it-is third-party presidential campaign. You would have preferred to remain a kind of lone gunman—tweaking liberal America at incendiary rallies—but many states require a matching vice presidential candidate on the ballot. Having to choose someone, you have selected retired Air Force general Curtis LeMay.

You hope LeMay will appeal to soldiers and veterans disgusted by the long-haired, left-leaning, pot-smoking, sandal-wearing, antiwar hippies. On the flip side, and potential downside, you also know that LeMay has traveled in the popular imagination from the status of World War II hero to the caricatured mad bomber of Strategic Air Command, most notably satirized in Stanley Kubrick's *Dr. Strangelove*. As the press conference begins, you quickly find out that the guy you picked is more like the caricature than the war hero.

Le May is asked, "What do you feel your experience can bring to the solution of the nation's domestic problems...and secondly, as a potential president, what would be your policy in the employment of nuclear weapons?"

LeMay responds:

> We seem to have a phobia about nuclear weapons. I think to most military men that a nuclear weapon is just another weapon in our arsenal. I think there are many occasions when it would be most efficient to use nuclear weapons. However, the public opinion in this country and throughout the world throws up their hands in horror when you mention nuclear weapons, just because of the propaganda that's been fed to them.

The self-destruction continues. LeMay soon adds, "I don't believe the world would end if we exploded a nuclear weapon."

Only minutes earlier, before LeMay had almost instantly proved that he was the mad bomber everyone thought he was, it seemed the sky was the limit for the Wallace for President campaign. You had been siphoning blue-collar workers from Humphrey, stealing southern whites from Nixon, polling at 20 percent, leading in seven states, featured on the covers of *Time*, *Life*, and *Newsweek*, with pundits seriously entertaining the notion that you might prevent Humphrey or Nixon from reaching the necessary 270 electoral votes.

After LeMay's catastrophic normalization of thermonuclear war, you try to rescue your immediate political future by physically nudging your new running mate aside and playing translator:

General LeMay hasn't advocated the use of nuclear weapons, not at all. He discussed nuclear weapons with you. He's against the use of nuclear weapons and I am too.

But that dog don't hunt for Jack Nelson, the seasoned political reporter for the *Los Angeles Times*, who raises the logical tie between LeMay's willingness to use nukes and the stalemated war in Vietnam. Nelson asks, "If you found it necessary to end the war, you would use them, wouldn't you?"

LeMay is almost barking as he responds:

If I found it necessary, I would use anything that we could dream up, anything we could dream up . . . including nuclear weapons, if it was necessary.

Goodbye to you. Goodbye to the surging third-party Wallace presidential campaign.

LeMay starts speaking at length about a film showing a revival of one of the most radiated spots on the planet: Bikini Atoll, the coral islands used for twenty-three nuclear tests. The film, LeMay says, indicates that the crabs are "still a little bit hot," but "the fish are all back in the lagoons; the coconut trees are growing coconuts; the guava bushes have fruit on them; the birds are back." LeMay also claims the rats are doing the best of all the creatures—"bigger, fatter, and healthier than they were before."

It is October 24, 1968. You are Stephen Roberts, a reporter for the *New York Times* interviewing some of the people attending a Wallace–LeMay rally at Madison Square Garden.

Richard Brady is a policeman from Poughkeepsie and his face grows darker with rage as he speaks: "I was in the Navy for six and a half years. You sing 'God Bless America' and say the Pledge of Allegiance and you really believe it—and some people think you're a kook. That's why I'm here tonight."

Joseph Delaney tells you he runs a catering firm in Garfield, New Jersey: "Wallace will get rid of all the Communists in government. This country is going to pot, it's being run down, little by little. And people are sick and tired of what's going on. Those college demonstrators and everything—everybody is against the country, even the people who live here."

Walter Grabowy is a sanitation worker from Rockland County, with a tattoo on one of his thick arms reading *USS Spencer.* He speaks in a growl: "I want a change. All those giveaway programs. They'd rather give them money than put them to work."

Jeff Dady, who lives in Queens and works for one of the airlines at JFK, says, "It's about time people woke up in this country, they've been taken advantage of long enough. Look at your paycheck every week. That money they take out isn't going to the man who breaks his back—it goes to the man who stays at home in bed."

. . . It is October 31, 1968, six days before the election. You are Nixon campaign manager John Mitchell watching Lyndon Johnson unleash an October surprise that, with the polls so close, could secure the presidency for Hubert Humphrey. In a nationally televised address, the president makes two major announcements: a total halt to the three-year U.S. bombing campaign in Vietnam, and a deal with the North Vietnamese to restart peace talks in Paris. Johnson encourages South Vietnam to join the talks.

As soon as LBJ's speech ends, you search for Anna Chennault and end up finding her at a party. For months, Chennault has been the Nixon campaign's conduit to the South Vietnamese government. She is the attractive, outgoing widow of Claire Lee Chennault, leader of the Flying Tigers in China during World War II. She is a prominent Republican fund-raiser, hostess, and supporter of Taiwan, and views communism as the worst thing that ever happened to Asia. You tell Chennault to stop the South Vietnamese from going to Paris.

. . . It is November 4, 1968, the day before Election Day. You are Lyndon Johnson and the *Christian Science Monitor* is calling for a comment about a story that says Republican aides have tried to scuttle your efforts to restart peace talks between North and South Vietnam. You read and agonize over an unpublished draft of the story by Saigon reporter Beverly Deepe:

> Purported political encouragement from the Richard Nixon camp was a significant factor in the last-minute decision of President Nguyen Van Thieu's refusal to send a delegation to the Paris peace talks—at least until the American Presidential election is over.

You know the story is true. A week earlier, you had even called Everett Dirksen, the top Republican in the Senate, to warn Nixon to stop interfering or you would put the story on the front pages and shock America.

"This is treason," you told Dirksen. "They're contacting a foreign power in the middle of a war."

You know it's true because you've had the CIA, NSA, and FBI spying on Nixon and all his top staffers. You ask for a conference call with your three wise men, National Security Advisor Walt Rostow, Secretary of Defense Clark Clifford, and Secretary of State Dean Rusk. These pillars of the establishment are unanimous that you should say nothing, because such scandalous information might reflect very badly on the U.S. government.

One of your press officials calls the *Monitor* about the blockbuster story and says the president is not going to "get into this kind of thing in any way, shape or form."

Beverly Deepe's story is diluted and trimmed and put on page two under a single-column headline.

...It is 12:03 Eastern on November 6 when the results from Illinois are reported and Richard Nixon is declared president. What you the American voter do not know is that the next president of the United States has conspired to prolong the

Vietnam War and another twenty thousand young Americans will die before it is over.

...Killer zombies emerge, shambling suddenly undead humans who are besieging seven people trapped in a western Pennsylvania farmhouse. There is speculation that this unnatural and horrifying occurrence may have something to do with a radiation-covered NASA satellite returning from Venus. These ghouls have an insatiable appetite for human flesh. They dine on shredded skin, intestines, and severed limbs. A resurrected daughter eats her mom. The police and military are useless. All of the central characters die. It's the *Night of the Living Dead*.

...You are wannabe musician and violent sociopath Charles Manson, and you are listening to the Beatles' latest album over and over again. Distributed in an all-white sleeve, with the only text being the band's name embossed in Helvetica typeface, fans are calling the spare look the "White Album." You have told your followers—"the Family"—that the music is a coded prophecy of a coming civil war over civil rights in which racist and nonracist whites will exterminate each other and black militants will use this vacuum of leadership to seize control.

You tell your "family" they are going to avoid the conflict by hiding in an underground city and will later emerge to rule the remaining black population, which will have proved to be incapable of governing.

"Helter Skelter" is your term for this course of events. The name comes from a heavy metal track on side three of *The White Album*:

Will you, won't you want me to make you
I'm coming down fast but don't let me break you

You are absolutely certain that the Beatles have tapped into your spirit, into your truth. Everything is gonna come down and the black man is gonna rise. The Beatles are talking about what you have been expounding for years. Every single song on *The White Album* is about you and your followers.

"Blackbird" and "Piggies" are calls to a violent revolution of black men and women against the U.S. government.

You believe "Revolution 9" is a reference to the Book of Revelation, the ninth chapter, which foretells of a hellish bottomless pit opening up in the world, and a plague of locusts with long hair coming to torture the unfaithful until an angel blows a trumpet to God.

"I Will" is a direct message to you. It's telling you it's time to make your own album and declare yourself the new messiah:

Oh, you know I will
I will

But there's been a recent setback with the plan. Terry Melcher—Doris Day's son, the guy who produced the Byrds—has backed out of helping you. He promised he'd get your songs recorded. But after he saw you beat the shit of out of someone he's going back on his word. Not cool.

...It's August 8, 1969. You tell your fiercest followers at the Spahn Ranch that the time for Helter Skelter has come. You send Tex Watson, Susan Atkins, Patricia Krenwinkel, and Linda Kasabian to Terry Melcher's former address at 10050 Cielo Drive in Benedict Canyon. You know the house is being leased by someone else, the guy who directed *Rosemary's Baby*, Roman Polanski, but if some really scary things go down at his old place, Terry will get the message.

...When everyone gets back to the ranch, you ask what happened. You're told five people were shot and stabbed, and just before leaving Melcher's place, Tex told Susan Atkins to go back in and write something that would shock the world. So Susan went to the woman who was pregnant. She was making gurgling sounds, like the blood was flowing into the body out of the heart. Susan took a towel and touched the woman's chest and then with her blood wrote *Pig* on one of the doors.

Everyone played a role, as you had demanded. But you're not happy with Patricia. When you asked her to talk about it, she said, "Charlie, they were so young."

...It is August 9, 1969. You are displeased by the sloppiness of the Benedict Canyon murders. The killing is all over the news. Victims were stabbed 102 times. The names are Sharon Tate, the pregnant one; Wojciech Frykowski, some Hollywood writer; Abigail Folger, called the coffee heiress; Jay Sebring, Tate's hairstylist; and Steven Parent, a guy who knew the gardener or something.

You go back into Los Angeles in search of more victims. Joining you in a beat-up four-door Ford, which is missing the backseat, are all the participants in the Tate murders, plus two others: Leslie Van Houten and Steve Grogan.

In Los Feliz, on the outskirts of Hollywood, you break into a house next door to one where you had attended several parties. You have no idea who lives there. You find out they're Leno LaBianca and his wife, Rosemary. You tie them up by yourself, leave the house, and send Watson, Krenwinkel, and Van Houten to kill them. Then you drive off with Atkins, Grogan, and Kasabian, expecting the three left in Los Feliz to hitchhike back to the Spahn Ranch.

Using blood from the victims, your followers scrawl *Rise* and *Death to Pigs* on the living room walls, and put the words *Healter Skelter* on the refrigerator—spelling it wrong.

...In court, you place some of the blame for the killings on the Beatles. You say, "Is it a conspiracy that the music is telling the youth to rise up against the establishment because the establishment is rapidly destroying things?" You say that people are too deaf, dumb, and blind to even listen to the music. You say it is not your music. It says "Rise." It says "Kill." Why blame it on you? You didn't write the music. "Helter skelter" is confusion, you say, confusion coming down around you fast.

...It is July 4, 1969. You are nineteen-year-old Michael Mageau, sitting with twenty-two-year-old Darlene Ferrin in a Corvair at Blue Rock Springs Park in Vallejo, California. A car parks behind you. A man holding a light emerges from the car and walks to the passenger-side window and without warning opens fire with a 9-millimeter pistol. At 12:38 p.m., Darlene is pronounced dead on arrival at the local hospital. In spite of being shot in the face, neck, and chest, you survive and describe the assailant as a white male with light brown curly hair, twenty-six to thirty years old, 195 to 200 pounds, five foot eight.

A few weeks later, three Bay Area newspapers receive handwritten letters and printed symbols. "Dear Editor—This is the murderer of the 2 teenagers last Christmas at Lake Herman & the girl on the 4th of July.... To prove I killed them I shall state some facts which only I & the police know..."

A crossed circle is drawn at the bottom of the page. The next week, another letter arrives: "Dear Editor—This is the Zodiac speaking."

...Detective "Dirty Harry" Callahan is lunching at a nondescript San Francisco eatery when he hears the sound of an alarm from a nearby bank. He briefly grimaces and exits the hot dog joint. While still jawing on his food, Dirty Harry stands in the middle of the street *High Noon* cowboy style, shooting the robbers—all black—as they try to make their getaway. He walks over to a bloodied culprit whose shotgun is just out of reach. Pointing his gun at the robber's head, he says smugly:

> I know what you're thinking. "Did he fire six shots or only five?" Well, to tell you the truth...I kinda lost track myself. But being this is a .44 Magnum, the most powerful handgun in the world and would blow your head clean off, you've gotta ask yourself one question: "Do I feel lucky?" Well, do ya, punk?

A Red Army POW. The Soviets suffered more combat deaths at the Battle of Stalingrad alone (approximately 500,000) than did U.S. forces in all of World War II. *(Military Museum of Finland)*

Lieutenant William Robertson with Lieutenant Alexander Sylvashko of the Red Army in late April 1945, as U.S. and USSR forces converged in Torgau, Germany, on the Elbe River. A poll soon after showed that 60 percent of Americans expressed confidence about cooperation between the USSR and Western Allies. *(U.S. Department of Defense)*

In July 1945, Harry Truman and Joseph Stalin met for the first and last time, in the Berlin suburb of Potsdam. There wouldn't be another summit between the leaders of the two countries for another ten years. *(National Archives & Records Administration)*

Ex-Nazi scientists with U.S. Operation Paperclip coordinator. In the forefront is pioneering rocket engineer Herman Oberth with, from left to right, rocket scientist Dr. Ernst Stuhlinger, U.S. Army Major General H.N. Toftoy, rocket scientist Dr. Werner von Braun (on table), and engineer and aircraft designer Dr. Robert Lusser. *(U.S. Army/ NASA)*

A Soviet observer of the 1946 U.S. atomic tests at Bikini Atoll reported that the U.S. was not interested in nuclear disarmament and recommended that the USSR suspend negotiations about international control of atomic power. *(U.S. Department of Defense)*

After the conclusion of the Cold War, State Department policy guru George Kennan would say: "My thoughts about containment were of course distorted by the people who understood it and pursued it exclusively as a military concept." *(Harris & Ewing photo via Library of Congress)*

J. Edgar Hoover viewed civil rights, gay rights, women's liberation, and the antiwar movement as communist plots. Said a close colleague: "He hated liberalism, he hated blacks, he hated Jews—he had this great long list of hates." *(Harris & Ewing photo via Library of Congress)*

Explaining why Harry Truman chose James Forrestal as the first-ever secretary of defense, Clark Clifford said: "If Forrestal had remained secretary of the navy, he would have made life unbearable for the secretary of defense. If, on the other hand, he was the secretary [of defense], he would have to try to make the system work." *(National Archives & Records Administration)*

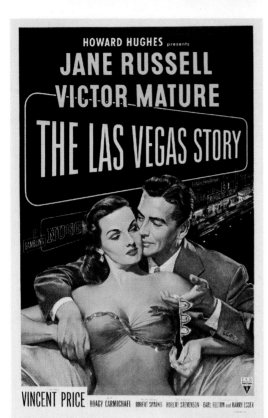

When RKO boss Howard Hughes stripped Communist Party member Paul Jarrico from the credits of *The Las Vegas Story*, Hearst columnist Hedda Hopper applauded: "I have said for many years, let's stand up and fight instead of coddling them, let's clean them out...One rotten apple in the barrel can affect the other apples." *(RKO Radio Pictures)*

In 1954, Japanese fishermen poisoned by the radioactive fallout of the Castle Bravo H-bomb test spurred producer Tomoyuki Tanaka to envision a film about a nuclear explosion stirring a monster from the ocean floor. *(Toho Company Ltd)*

Strategic Air Command's B-47 Stratojet was the world's first intercontinental nuclear bomber. U.S. military technology remained a step ahead of the Soviet Union throughout the Cold War. *(USAF)*

In 1958, U.S. and Canadian air defenses against the Soviet threat were combined as the North American Air Defense Command, or NORAD. During the Cold War, command-and-control systems regularly faced false alarms that could have caused all-out thermonuclear war. *(USAF)*

As of 1962, just 1.4 percent of Americans had a bomb shelter. A signature *Twilight Zone* episode envisioned the madness following a national emergency when a member of that 1.4 percent locks out everyone else in his neighborhood. *(Federal Emergency Management Agency)*

NOTICE

OFFICE OF CIVILIAN DEFENSE
WASHINGTON, D.C.

INSTRUCTION TO PATRONS ON PREMISES
IN CASE OF NUCLEAR BOMB ATTACK:

UPON THE FIRST WARNING:

1. STAY CLEAR OF ALL WINDOWS.

2. KEEP HANDS FREE OF GLASSES, BOTTLES, CIGARETTES, ETC.

3. STAND AWAY FROM BAR, TABLES, ORCHESTRA, EQUIPMENT AND FURNITURE.

4. LOOSEN NECKTIE, UNBUTTON COAT AND ANY OTHER RESTRICTIVE CLOTHING.

5. REMOVE GLASSES, EMPTY POCKETS OF ALL SHARP OBJECTS SUCH AS PENS, PENCILS, ETC.

6. IMMEDIATELY UPON SEEING THE BRILLIANT FLASH OF NUCLEAR EXPLOSION, BEND OVER AND PLACE YOUR HEAD FIRMLY BETWEEN YOUR LEGS.

7. THEN KISS YOUR ASS GOODBYE.

A bit of gallows humor expressed in a satirical Civil Defense notice. President Eisenhower came to believe that in the event of a nuclear attack, "You might as well go out and shoot everyone you see and then shoot yourself." *(Yanker Poster Collection, Library of Congress)*

President Eisenhower and Secretary of State John Foster Dulles greeting South Vietnam's President Ngo Dinh Diem at Washington National Airport on May 8, 1957. *(U.S. Department of Defense)*

Gold-coated telephone presented to Cuban dictator Fulgencio Batista in 1957 by International Telegraph and Telephone (ITT), after Batista approved the company's steep rate hike. *(Museo de la Revolución [Havana], Wikimedia Commons)*

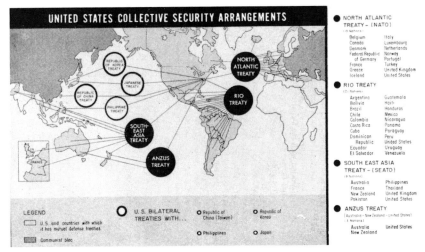

During the Cold War, the United States established military alliances with 50 nations and had as many as 1.5 million soldiers posted in 117 countries. *(U.S. Department of Defense)*

In December 1957, after the Soviets had twice beaten America into space (with a satellite named Sputnik and a dog named Laika), a Navy Vanguard rocket blew up on the launch pad, compounding hysteria about Russia's perceived technological supremacy. *(U.S. Navy)*

Before the desperation created by Sputnik, the first U.S. astronauts were supposed to pilot a version of the X-15, a rocket plane that reached Mach 7 and flew fifty miles above the Earth's surface. However, a "space shuttle" concept was shelved for a down-and-dirty man-in the-can approach. *(NASA)*

In 1958, when a B-47 accidentally dropped a Mark 6 nuclear bomb on a children's playhouse in Mars Bluff, South Carolina, only the bomb's conventional explosives ignited. But the Soviet press claimed all of South Carolina had been contaminated by radioactive fallout. *(Creative Commons)*

Fidel Castro and Nikita Khrushchev on a Soviet poster that reads (in English translation): "Long live the eternal, indestructible friendship and cooperation between the Soviet and Cuban people." *(Creative Commons)*

Soviet cosmonaut Gherman Titov (right) with astronaut John Glenn and President Kennedy at the White House on May 3, 1962. Titov was the first person to sleep in orbit and vomit in space. *(NASA)*

Soviet medium-range ballistic missile launch site, from a U-2 aerial reconnaissance photo. By October 1962, Soviet forces in Cuba included a battalion of T-55 tanks, a wing of MIG-21 fighters, forty-two Il-28 light bombers, 162 nuclear weapons, and 41,902 troops. *(National Archives)*

To protest persecution of Buddhism by the U.S.-backed South Vietnamese regime, Thich Quang Duc set himself ablaze at a Saigon intersection in 1963. *(Malcolm Browne for the Associated Press)*

Lee Harvey Oswald in his backyard in Dallas, March 1963. Oswald defected to the Soviet Union in 1959 and spent two and a half years in Minsk before returning to the United States. *(Marina Oswald, from Warren Commission Report)*

Martin Luther King Jr. and Malcolm X were shot and killed by assassins—Malcolm in 1965, King in 1968—and were each thirty-nine at the time of their deaths. *(U.S. News & World Report Collection, Library of Congress)*

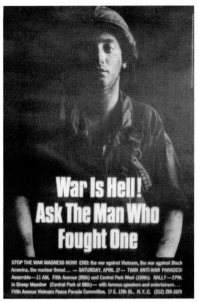

The CIA's most extensive domestic spying campaign was the illegal Operation CHAOS (1967–74). The program gathered and evaluated information about foreign links to the civil rights and antiwar movements and also tracked the activity of Americans traveling abroad. *(Fifth Avenue Vietnam Peace Parade Committee)*

Editorial cartoon by Yoel Buchwald depicts Warsaw Pact forces crushing Czechoslovakia's 1968 Prague Spring. During the Cold War, the "Iron Curtain" military alliance attacked only its own member nations. *(Yoel Buchwald's Collection, The Israeli Cartoon Museum)*

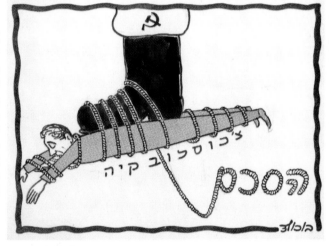

General Curtis LeMay's public life concluded ignominiously when, as George Wallace's 1968 running mate, he spoke positively about using nuclear weapons in Vietnam. *(USAF)*

President Nixon during a 1970 TV address discussing battles in Cambodia. The 2.7 million tons of bombs dropped on Cambodia exceeded the amount of all Allied bombing during World War II, including Hiroshima and Nagasaki. *(Richard Nixon Presidential Library, National Archives & Records Administration)*

On April 29, 1974, President Nixon told the nation he was releasing edited transcripts of taped White House conversations. Expletives were deleted, but Nixon's criminal culpability in the Watergate coverup was not. *(National Archives & Records Administration)*

President Gerald Ford and General Secretary Leonid Brezhnev at a 1974 arms control summit in Vladivostok. A year later, Brezhnev blundered in Helsinki by agreeing to human rights provisions. *(National Archives & Records Administration)*

A butcher at a Russian market in 1975. The USSR earned several derisive nicknames: "Upper Volta with rockets," "Nigeria with snow," and "China's gas station." *(Thomas Taylor Hammond, University of Virginia Center for Russian, East European, and Eurasian Studies)*

The Reverend Jim Jones, founder of the Peoples Temple, at a San Francisco "anti-eviction" rally. In the hours preceding the 1978 mass suicide in Jonestown, Jones ordered the transfer of $7 million to the Soviet government for the benefit of "oppressed people" around the world. *(Nancy Wong, Creative Commons)*

President Carter with advisor Pat Caddell, author of the 1979 "Apocalypse Now" memo, which claimed the United States was experiencing "a crisis of confidence marked by a dwindling faith in the future." *(Jimmy Carter Library, National Archives & Records Administration)*

The Ohio-class Trident submarine was capable of stealthily approaching the Soviet coast and launching a shower of nuclear missiles that could strike within minutes. In response, the Soviets installed a Dead Hand system—or doomsday device—in order to maintain a second-strike capability. *(U.S. Navy)*

At their first summit, in 1985, Mikhail Gorbachev told President Reagan that the Soviets would team with the United States in the event of an alien invasion. *(Ronald Reagan Presidential Library, National Archives & Records Administration)*

The Cessna 172 used by Mathias Rust to fly from Finland to Moscow's Red Square in 1987. *(German Museum of Technology, Creative Commons)*

The ugly, hastily built Berlin Wall, erected in 1961, was a brutish stopgap measure to stem East Germany's brain drain. It gave the West an ongoing propaganda gift of inestimable value. *(FOTO: FORTEPAN/Urbán Tamás, Creative Commons)*

Wounded mujahideen are led from a U.S. military medical evacuation flight in 1989. The CIA's massive covert operation to kick the Soviets out of Afghanistan incubated global jihad. *(Staff Sergeant F. Lee Corkran, U.S. Department of Defense)*

CHAPTER 33

NIXON BY THE NUMBERS

Richard Nixon won the 1968 presidential election by one of the narrowest margins in U.S. history. He received 43.4 percent of the popular vote (31,770,000), with Hubert Humphrey winning 42.7 percent, losing to Nixon by 500,000 votes, or less than 1 percent. Nixon's treason—conspiring with Anna Chennault to sabotage the Paris peace negotiations on Vietnam—was not revealed for decades.

"It is my personal view that disclosure of the Nixon-sanctioned actions by Mrs. Chennault would have been so explosive and damaging to the Nixon 1968 campaign that Hubert Humphrey would have been elected president, " said Tom Johnson, who worked in the Johnson White House and later became publisher of the *Los Angeles Times* and chief executive of CNN.

"The tactic 'worked,'" wrote Christopher Hitchens, "in that the South Vietnamese junta withdrew from the talks on the eve of the election, thereby destroying the 'peace plank' on which the Democrats had contested it. In another way, it did not 'work,' because four years later the Nixon Administration concluded the war on the same terms that had been offered in Paris....The impact of those four years on Indochinese society, and on American democracy, is beyond computation."

Timothy Naftali, who served as director of the Nixon library from 2007 to 2011, said, "This covert action by the Nixon campaign laid the ground for the skullduggery of his presidency."

The skullduggery that followed started with Nixon demanding

that the FBI, CIA, NSA, and Defense Intelligence Agency (DIA) conduct a coordinated and sweeping domestic intelligence operation to spy on Vietnam War dissidents. The plan was put to paper by White House aide Thomas Charles Huston and ratified by Nixon in July 1970. The forty-three-page report called for burglary, illegal surveillance, mail opening, and the creation of camps in western states where antiwar protestors could be detained.

Concentration camps for hippies didn't happen. But many other proposals in the Huston Plan did. The Plumbers, a rogue White House counterintelligence unit, was created when Nixon had a fit about the 1971 leak of the Pentagon Papers. The NSA continued to monitor all overseas communications sent or received by Americans. The FBI created files on more than one million citizens, and carried out more than half a million investigations of so-called subversives (without a single conviction).

"The executive branch," Loch Johnson wrote, "had concluded, wrongly, that the youthful dissenters were agents of Moscow. As a result, the United States would have to move outside the framework of the Constitution and the law; the legal system had become too confining in the struggle against the Soviet Union.... The enemy was sinister and lawless, so the United States would have to become that way, too."

During the 1975 hearings by the Church Committee—officially called the Special Select Committee to Investigate Intelligence Activities—then Minnesota senator Walter Mondale would be flabbergasted by the "enormous unrestricted paranoid fear about the American people...no meeting was too small, no group too insignificant."

Huston later told congressional investigators, "The risk was that you would get people susceptible to political considerations as opposed to national security considerations, to move from the kid with a bomb to a kid with a picket sign, and from the kid with the picket sign to the kid with the bumper sticker of the opposing candidate. And you just keep going down the line."

———

Amount of money raised by Richard Nixon for his 1968 presidential campaign: **$30 million**.

Prior campaigns that raised more: **0**.

Amount of illegal contribution to 1968 Nixon campaign from Greece's governing junta: **$549,000**.

Number of government officials and journalists illegally wiretapped by Henry Kissinger: **17**.

Number of U.S. citizens National Security Agency illegally wiretapped from 1967 to 1973: **1,600**.

Days spent by Richard Nixon at Key Biscayne compound in Florida during his presidency: **198**.

Number of waterfront bungalows at the Florida compound: **5**.

Holes on private golf course at Nixon's San Clemente estate in California: **7**.

Number of hobbies Nixon was said to have by one of his aides: **0**.

Percentage of poll respondents who blamed demonstrators for May 4, 1970, killing of four Kent State students: **58**.

Percentage who blamed National Guard: **11**.

Date two hundred construction workers attacked a thousand antiwar demonstrators on Wall Street: **May 8, 1970**.

Date Nixon met at White House with union leaders who instigated the Wall Street riot: **May 26, 1970**.

Number of retired New York City cops secretly hired by Nixon to investigate Democratic rivals: **2**.

Number of political opponents Nixon ordered the IRS to audit: **490**.

Number the IRS audited: **0**.

Nixon's total adjusted gross income in 1970: **$262,942**.

Total federal income tax Nixon paid in 1970: **$792**.

Nixon's total adjusted gross income in 1971: **$262,384**.

Total income tax Nixon paid in 1971: **$878**.

Amount Nixon owed in back taxes and interest following a subsequent government investigation: **$476,451**.

Total number of Americans Nixon estimated would be killed in a nuclear war: **70 million**.

Number of hidden microphones installed in Oval Office by Nixon's Secret Service: **7**.

Of Oval Office microphones, number hidden in the fireplace: **2**.

Number of hidden microphones in the Cabinet Room: **2**.

Number of hidden microphones at Nixon "hideaway" in Old Executive Office Building: **4**.

Number of hidden microphones at Camp David: **3**.

Number of Nixon's White House telephones that were tapped: **3**.

Number of people aware of the bugging system: **4**.

Total hours of conversation recorded: **3,700**.

Total U.S. troops in Vietnam in 1969: **539,000**.

In 1971: **239,000**.

Date on which Nixon calls India's prime minister Indira Gandhi "a bitch": **November 5, 1971**.

Pledged amount offered to Nixon reelection campaign by donor seeking British ambassadorship: **$3 million**.

Maximum B-52 sorties on one day during 1972 Operation Linebacker bombing of North Vietnam: **110**.

Approximate number of killed or wounded by Operation Linebacker: **100,000**.

Amount spent on U.S. arms by the shah after Nixon's 1972 visit to Iran: **$25 billion**.

Total number of break-ins of Democratic Party headquarters at Watergate complex by Nixon operatives: **4**.

Date on which five Nixon campaign associates were arrested for burglarizing Watergate DNC headquarters: **June 17, 1972**.

Date on which Nixon told the CIA to block FBI's investigation of Watergate break-in: **June 23, 1972**.

Date on which *Washington Post* reported Nixon campaign funds were sent to bank account of a Watergate burglar: **August 1, 1972**.

States carried by Nixon in the 1972 presidential election: **49**.

Price of *Washington Post* stock in 1972, one share: **$38**.

Price after Nixon administration challenged licenses of two *Post*-owned TV stations in Florida: **$17**.

Amount of cash in White House safe managed by Nixon secretary Rose Mary Woods: **$400,000**.

Amount of "hush money" Nixon said could be rounded up to pay Watergate burglars: **$1 million**.

Total, in minutes, of gap on one of the Nixon tapes subpoenaed during Watergate scandal: **18.5**.

Portion of gap, in minutes, that is white noise: **5**.

Nixon approval rating at start of second term, January 1973: **67 percent**.

Nixon approval rating at time of his resignation, August 1974: **24 percent**.

Total number of FBI agents involved in Watergate investigation: **330**.

Total number of government officials found guilty of crimes connected to Watergate: **48**.

Number of House seats gained by the Democrats in the 1974 midterm elections: **49**.

Amount paid to Nixon for memoirs: **$2 million**.

Amount Nixon was paid to appear with David Frost for a series of interviews: **$600,000**.

Total Oscar nominations for Watergate saga *All the President's Men*: **8**.

Amount of screen time, in minutes, for Supporting Actress nominee Jane Alexander: **8**.

Percentage of Americans, in 1994, who said Nixon would be remembered as a great President: **27**.

Percentage who said he would be remembered as a dishonest leader: **44**.

CHAPTER 34

WATERGATE DICTIONARY

After Howard Hughes sent $100,000 to both Richard Nixon and Hubert Humphrey in order to stop nuclear testing, the Atomic Energy Commission created a new underground facility more than two hundred miles north of Las Vegas. However, the multimegaton hydrogen bombs, even when detonated farther away and thirty-two hundred feet below ground, still rattled the penthouse suite at the Desert Inn. In 1970, Hughes left Las Vegas for good. He was reportedly carried out of the hotel on a stretcher, driven to Nellis Air Force Base, and flown by private jet to the Bahamas.

When Richard Nixon gladly pocketed the bribe from Hughes in 1968, this was at least the second time that his family had been assisted by the baldly transactional tycoon. In 1956, while Hughes was waging a campaign to persuade the IRS to grant tax-exempt status to his fraudulent charity, the Howard Hughes Medical Institute, he had suspiciously "loaned" Nixon's brother Donald $205,000. The payment surfaced during the 1960 election campaign; Nixon believed the disclosure was one of the reasons he lost to Kennedy.

As Nixon sought reelection, in 1972, he had reason to fear that the Democrats would reveal the history of his corrupt arrangements with Hughes, including the 1968 bribe, a portion of which had been used to add a putting green and pool table to his Key Biscayne home. In 1972, Nixon nemesis Larry O'Brien was the head of the Democratic

National Committee. Previously, O'Brien had been the campaign manager for JFK, LBJ, and RFK, and in 1968 had been hired by Hughes ($25,000 up front, then $15,000 monthly) to act as a Washington lobbyist.

On June 17, 1972, the most significant date in Nixon's infamy, O'Brien's office at the Watergate complex was burglarized.

In 2005, CBS's *60 Minutes* connected the dots in a story that included an interview with Terry Lenzner, the chief investigator for the Senate Watergate Committee.

"Well, Nixon assumed [O'Brien] knew about [the payment from Hughes]," Lenzner said. "So he could be thinking, 'Gosh, I bet if O'Brien was tied into the Hughes Organization maybe he knows about things we did for Hughes, on the casinos, on the airlines.' I don't know if it was the sole motive for the [Watergate] break-in, but I'm absolutely certain it was a significant part of the president's thinking that this has to be done. This has to be taken care of."

Lenzner wrote a whole section on Hughes for the Senate Watergate report, but it wasn't included in the published document. "I don't remember any explanation [why]," he told journalist Lesley Stahl.

PLUMBERS

Definition: *Covert White House Special Investigation Unit, so called because its founding mission was to plug the leaks of classified information, such as the Pentagon Papers.*

Plumber in Chief: The unit branched out into illegal activities on behalf of the Committee to Re-elect the President (CREEP). On January 27, 1972, a meeting related to the campaign was held at the Justice Department, in the office of Attorney General John Mitchell, who was doing double duty as head of the reelection campaign. The meeting was run by G. Gordon Liddy (full name George

Gordon Battle Liddy), a then forty-year-old ex–FBI employee who had become, officially, a White House counsel and, unofficially, "Plumber in Chief." Liddy had a distinctive bushy mustache and the bearing and intensity of a drill sergeant. He had a reputation for being reckless, hotheaded, loud, flamboyant, and politically ambitious. In 1968, he had nearly won a congressional race in western New York State. In *All the President's Men*, Hal Holbrook's Deep Throat (who turned out to be FBI associate director Mark Felt) says of Liddy, "Once, at a gathering, he put his hand over a candle. And he kept it there. He kept it right in the flame until his flesh seared. A woman who was watching asked, 'What's the trick?' And he replied, 'The trick is not minding.'" The other attendees at the January 27 meeting were Jeb Stuart Magruder, CREEP deputy, and White House counsel John Dean. In total, three of the four attendees were lawyers, including, in Mitchell, the country's top law enforcement official.

Account of the meeting: In *One Man Against the World: The Tragedy of Richard Nixon*, Tim Weiner writes, "The Office of the Attorney General of the United States is an enormous room exuding the grandeur of the rule of law," and in this most decorous setting Liddy "had prepared an elaborate plan code-named *Gemstone*... which he now formally presented...along with seven separate flow charts propped up on easels. *Gemstone* was a conspiracy to violate federal laws including kidnapping, burglary, and warrantless wiretapping, all in the name of the reelection of the president of the United States." The charts were titled *Nacht und Nebel* (Night and Fog), a term used by Nazi stormtroopers for making people disappear. The components of the plan were Diamond (kidnapping anti-Nixon demonstrators at the Republican National Convention, drugging them, and dumping them in Mexico); Opal (mounting black bag jobs for planting bugs inside key Democratic campaign sites); Emerald (electronic eavesdropping); Quartz (intercepting microwave telephone traffic); Topaz (photographing documents at the Democratic headquarters in Washington, D.C., and at the Democratic convention in Miami Beach); Ruby (placing spies inside Democratic organizations); Turquoise (sabotaging the air conditioning at the Democratic convention); Sapphire (hiring prostitutes during the convention for a houseboat docked in Miami Beach); Crystal (recording and photographing Democratic politicians on the Sapphire houseboat for use as blackmail); and Coal (overtly racist description of a plan to finance the long-shot campaign of Shirley Chisholm, the first black woman to run for president, in order to divert black Democrats from the likely nominee). After the presentation, Attorney General John Mitchell had two reactions: He asked Liddy to scale back Gemstone, which Liddy had estimated would cost a million dollars ($6 million today), and he wanted to make sure Liddy would burn the charts.

THIRD-RATE BURGLARY

Definition: *An attempt at criminal activity so lacking in sense or intelligence as to be laughable—but, in fact, devastating by its very existence. . . . The expression is since used with heavy irony to imply that any attempt to minimize a transgression (usually a political one) is asking for trouble and to remind the world that what seems like a low-grade burglary can bring down a President. (*Merriam-Webster's Dictionary of Allusions*)*

Example: On June 20, 1972, asked about the five men who had been arrested three days earlier for an early-morning break-in of the Democratic National Committee headquarters at the Watergate complex, White House press secretary Ron Ziegler said, "I'm not going to comment on a third-rate burglary attempt." Ziegler had become Nixon's press secretary at age twenty-nine, the youngest ever in the role. Reporters would come to call him Zig Zag and his obfuscations Zieglaratta.

SMOKING GUN

Definition: *Incontrovertible evidence of guilt.*

Example: In a conversation recorded on June 23, 1972, Nixon is heard telling chief of staff H. R. Haldeman that the CIA should be directed to ask the FBI to stop the Watergate investigation as a matter of "national security." This was the "smoking gun" evidence clearly indicating Nixon's guilt in the Watergate cover-up. The tape was released to the public on August 5, 1974. After its release, ten Republicans on the House Judiciary Committee who had voted against impeachment in committee announced that they would now vote for impeachment once the matter reached the House floor. Nixon announced his resignation on the evening of Thursday, August 8, 1974, effective as of noon the next day.

DEEP THROAT

Definition: *Pseudonym of secret informant used by* Washington Post *reporters Bob Woodward and Carl Bernstein in their reporting of the Watergate scandal. Named after title of 1972 pornographic film of the same name.*

Example: In one of the signature scenes of *All the President's Men*, Bob Woodward (played by Robert Redford) heads into a parking garage. According to William Goldman's script, *It's an eerie place, and his heels make noise and if you wonder is he edgy, yes he's edgy.* We cut to a cigarette being lit, but in the pitch-black of the garage, we only see the orange glow of the match. Said Oscar-winning cinematographer Gordon Willis about the shot, "I like going from light to dark, dark to light, big to small, small to big, and good and evil." Deep Throat (played by Hal Holbrook) tells Woodward, "Look, forget the myths the media's created about the White House—the truth is, these are not very bright guys, and things got out of hand." Woodward tells Deep Throat some of what he and Bernstein have learned. He says, "Howard Hunt's been found—there was talk that his lawyer had twenty-five thousand in cash in a paper bag." Deep Throat responds, "Follow the money. Always follow the money."

STONEWALL

Definition: *To be uncooperative, obstructive, or evasive, especially if one is guilty of directing a massive cover-up.*

Example: On the Watergate tapes, Nixon confirms he wants to frustrate investigators. Nixon says, "I don't give a shit what happens. I want you all to stonewall it, let them plead the Fifth Amendment, cover up, or anything else."

NON-DENIAL DENIAL

Definition: *A carefully worded official statement which ostensibly rejects allegations of wrongdoing but does not quite say they are false. A statement of equivocation.* (Merriam-Webster)

Example: On October 16, 1972, commenting on the simmering Watergate scandal just weeks before the presidential election, Ziegler said, "I will not dignify with comment stories based on hearsay, character assassination, innuendo or guilt by association." *Post* executive editor Ben Bradlee responded to the charge with a statement saying that everything the paper had reported on Watergate was factual and "unchallenged by contrary evidence." In *All the President's Men*, the reaction to Ziegler is played this way: Bradlee (Jason Robards): "All non-denial denials—we're dirty guys and they doubt we were ever virgins but they don't say the story is inaccurate." Bernstein (Dustin Hoffman): "What's a real denial?" Bradlee: "If they ever start calling us goddamn liars, it's time to start circling the wagons."

TWIST SLOWLY IN THE WIND

Definition: *The abandonment of a political subordinate to suffer prolonged and politically fatal public agonies alone.* (Merriam-Webster)

Example: During confirmation hearings, acting FBI director L. Patrick Gray admitted that he had used his home fireplace to burn two files of incriminating Watergate-related documents given to him by the White House. On March 7, 1973, commenting on Gray's disastrous testimony, Nixon aide John Ehrlichman said, "Let him hang there. Hell, I think we ought to let him hang there. Let him twist slowly, slowly in the wind." On March 22, 1973, Nixon said, in reference to Gray, "The problem with him is he is a little bit stupid." On April 23, 1973, Gray resigned.

OPERATIVE STATEMENT

Definition: *The creation of a rhetorical shuffle to avoid clear responsibility for a past misstatement, error, falsehood, or lie.*

Example: From the *New York Times*: "On April 17, 1973, Nixon stunned reporters by saying that he had conducted an investigation that raised the prospect of involvement by White House officials. Mr. Ziegler told a puzzled press corps that this was now the 'operative statement,' repeating the word operative six times. Finally, R. W. Apple Jr. of *The New York Times* asked, 'Would it be fair for us to infer, since what the president said today is now considered the operative statement, to quote you, that the other statement is no longer operative, that it is now inoperative?' Eventually Mr. Ziegler consented to Apple's logic and replied: 'The president refers to the fact that there is new material; therefore, this is the operative statement. The others are inoperative.'"

WITCH HUNT

Definition: *As used by Richard Nixon, and later Donald Trump, the term is used to claim that an investigation into your own misdeeds is a corrupt conspiracy to falsely accuse you.*

Example: The term was used in a July 21, 1973, *Washington Post* story by Woodward and Bernstein that was headlined "Nixon, Aides Believe Hearing Is a Witch-Hunt." The article quoted several anonymous White House sources. The leaking by anonymous staffers was rather hypocritical since the same White House was regularly maligning the *Washington Post* and other members of the media for using leakers who remained anonymous. The story reported that President Nixon and his top aides believed that the Senate Watergate hearings were unfair and constituted a "political witch-hunt." The anonymous sources said that the president had expressed bitterness and deep hostility toward the two-month-old proceedings. "The President sees the hearings as an attempt to get Richard Nixon and do it just damn unfairly," one source said. Another source said, "The Ervin committee is out to destroy the President."

EXPLETIVE DELETED

Definition: *A profanity, or several profanities, censored in a text.*

Context: On April 29, 1974, Richard Nixon went on national television to speak for the third time about Watergate. This time he had gifts he would be sharing: a pile of snazzy dark blue loose-leaf notebooks that he said contained transcripts of the tapes. "The president has nothing to hide," he said. This "will tell it all." Not quite. As it turned out, Nixon had doctored the transcripts and cleaned up his language by replacing profanities with such words as "expletive" and "unintelligible."

Example: A May 18, 1973, meeting with H. R. Haldeman in the Old Executive Office Building was included on one of the released transcripts. Nixon is recalling how Attorney General Richard G. Kleindienst had advised him that Haldeman and Ehrlichman needed to resign immediately. This is what was released to the public, as Nixon speaks to Haldeman: "A bunch of [expletive] stuff.... What I mean to say is this. We're talking in the confidence of this room. I don't give a [expletive] what comes out on you or John or even on poor, damn, dumb John Mitchell. There is going to be a total pardon."

Reaction: The June 6, 1974, issue of *Rolling Stone* commented, "With blue pencil in hand, Richard Nixon has brought to the point of charm the curious inversion of priorities and moral values which has always characterized him. In his personally edited transcripts of many of the White House conversations, he has, by some grotesque system of default, left in material which demonstrates clear guilt in criminal as well as other impeachable offenses, while carefully pruning out language which might make him seem vulgar or—is it possible?—even more culpable. The transcripts show that he is guilty of obstructing justice, ordering the payment of 'hush money,' counseling perjury, tampering with grand jury proceedings and proposing offers of clemency in return for perjured testimony." In the same article, *Rolling Stone* offered to finance an all-expenses-paid weekend at the Watergate Hotel in Washington, D.C., "for the individual who supplies the most fitting expletives and deletions." The magazine provided a few suggestions of its own, as a guide, such as prospective "fill-in the deleted word" from a conversation in which John Dean talks about when he first heard about the Watergate burglary:

> "DEAN: The next point in time that I became aware of anything was on June 17th when I got the word that there had been this break-in at the DNC and somebody from our committee had been caught in the DNC. And I said, 'Oh [EXPLETIVE DELETED].'
> a) darn!
> b) Tannenbaum
> c) shoot!
> d) dash it all!
> e) shit, those Cuban cocksuckers have really fucked us up this time.
> f) horse hockey!
> g) where am I? What's the date?
> h) ..."

DEAD MOUSE ON THE KITCHEN FLOOR

Definition: *An item that needs to be disposed of as quickly as possible so a sense of normalcy can be resumed.*

Example: From 1970 to 1974, syndicated *Washington Post* columnist Nicholas von Hoffman went to the CBS Studios on M Street in

Washington, D.C., to tape a weekly *60 Minutes* "Point-Counterpoint" segment. Von Hoffman spoke for the left, James Kilpatrick for the right. "By early summer of 1974," Kilpatrick later wrote, "it was evident that Nixon's presidency was in deep trouble. Impeachment hearings began in the House in May. The Supreme Court was about to order the president to reveal more than 60 incriminating tapes. Rumors of a Nixon resignation were so intense that Nick and I were instructed to tape on Sunday afternoon July 28." By waiting to tape the segment until the day of air for *60 Minutes*, CBS was giving von Hoffman and Kirkpatrick the ability to react to any late-breaking developments. The only immediate development that took place, however, was that von Hoffman got himself fired. On July 28, 1974, he told viewers of *60 Minutes* that Nixon was "a dead mouse on the kitchen floor that nobody wants to throw away. The question," he continued, "is who is going to pick it up by the tail and drop it in the trash? At this point it makes no difference whether he resigns, thereby depositing himself in a sanitary container, or whether Congress scoops him up in the dustpan of impeachment. But as an urgent national health measure, we've got to get that decomposing political corpse out of the White House."

Kilpatrick explained what happened after the segment aired: "Regrettably, on that Sunday afternoon, Don Hewitt [executive producer of *60 Minutes*] and others at CBS who usually monitored our eloquence were out of town or unavailable. Our tapes went on the air unedited and unrestrained. Switchboards exploded. Fire alarms rang! The CBS brass ordered Nick to apologize, which he did a week later. Not enough."

———

By 1974, Nixon was a broken, empty, bewildered figure, lost in the grip of paranoia. The seeds of his ultimate destruction were already evident when he first ran for public office, in 1946, and blithely exploited anticommunist hysteria because it presented the clearest route to victory. He was, from the beginning, someone corrupted by blind ambition and fraying from a raging insecurity. Behind a studied mask, he was irretrievably cold and lonely and fated to never be loved.

After disgracing the office of the presidency and being forced to resign, Nixon would confront too late his fatal flaw. "Always remember," he said in a farewell to White House staff, "others may hate you, but those who hate you don't win unless you hate them, and then you destroy yourself."

CHAPTER 35

MAD AS HELL

As the seventies rolled on, we the people weren't sure who we could trust. We suspected precious secrets were being hoarded by nefarious forces. Shadowy conspiracies appeared to multiply. Paranoia was in fashion.

As the universe of people out to get us widened in the public imagination, fabled Nazis and actual Russians were joined by alleged threats from a proliferating roster of secretive societies, criminal enterprises, deadly cults, hypnotic charlatans, international terrorists, lurking creatures, curious extraterrestrials, and men in black. Many of these entities were beyond belief, which didn't stop people from insisting they were real. Further, a significant portion of Americans were confident that a secret power elite with a globalist agenda was conspiring to rule the planet through a world government. In the night skies, unmarked helicopters joined flying saucers.

In early 1975, when then little-known Jimmy Carter was campaigning in Iowa, he uttered the words that defined the essence of his appeal to voters in a disillusioned age: "I will not lie to you." As Bob Woodward wrote, "It was the backbone of the rationale for his candidacy. He was not Nixon. He was not a lawyer. He had never held office in Washington—the seat of a government few any longer trusted. He was an outsider, and he would tell the truth—always."

"Those were the days," said Don DeLillo, novelist of the nightmare behind the Great American Dream, "when the enemy was some presence seeping out of the government, and the most paranoid sort of fear was indistinguishable from common sense."

It was the decade when America the Beautiful became America in Need of Repair. Citizens of the seventies learned of criminal behavior by a lawless executive branch through persistent congressional investigations, absorbed a humiliating defeat in a foreign war fought with doublespeak, and confronted severe recession, high inflation, factory closings, gas lines, and one of the worst crime waves in U.S. history. A ravenous cocaine high became the deadly crack epidemic. AIDS was judged a biblical plague.

As my classmate Fred Balzac wrote in our college yearbook, students of the seventies "came of age at a time when the loss of innocence meant the gain of not knowledge but cynicism, when trust gave way to distrust, when idealism was replaced with pessimism." As the class of 1980 "came to collect our inheritance," Fred added, we discovered "all that's left is the debt of a world gone materially and morally bankrupt."

———

At the very start of the seventies, we the people were put on notice that some of our corporations were inherently rotten. For the first time, all cigarette packages were required to include a warning from the surgeon general that the product could kill anyone who used it. After Ralph Nader published *Unsafe at Any Speed* (1965), documenting how U.S. automakers were sacrificing safety for profit, General Motors hired a private detective agency to investigate him, had his phone tapped, and paid prostitutes to catch him in a compromising situation. When the Cuyahoga River in Cleveland caught fire and made the cover of *Time*, this "open sewer through the center of the city," the result of effluvia wantonly released by heavy industry, spurred the creation of the Environmental Protection Agency and the Clean Water Act.

The decade's most effective public service announcement shamed us all and made littering a sin. It showed a Native American in costume shedding a very noticeable tear after trash is thrown from the window of a car. "People start pollution," narrator William Conrad intoned. "People can stop it." Later, the *New Orleans Times-Picayune* revealed that the actor in the commercial, who called himself Iron Eyes Cody, was a second-generation Italian American born in Louisiana.

On the first Earth Day, in 1971, Walt Kelly's popular comic strip, titled after a pithy opossum named Pogo, chided America for its crappy stewardship of the planet. As Pogo and his friend Porkypine stare at a swamp choked with garbage, Kelly's opinionated critter observes, "We have met the enemy and he is us." That same year, the newly established, in-your-face Greenpeace provoked global outrage about the largest-ever U.S. underground nuclear test, a five-megaton bomb that was to be detonated on Alaska's Amchitka Island. Critics feared that the blast could trigger an earthquake and cause a tsunami in the tectonically unstable region. A Greenpeace ship that sailed to the testing site was turned back by a U.S. Coast Guard vessel, but the daring protest raised awareness about the blast's destructive force—which ended up registering a 7.0 on the Richter scale—and the Amchitka site was never used again for testing.

Charles Reich wrote one of the first manifestos of the seventies, a hosanna to the sixties counterculture called *The Greening of America*. It would sell two million copies. "The logic of the new generation's rebellion," he wrote, "must be understood in light of the rise of the corporate state under which we live & the way in which the state dominates, exploits, & ultimately destroys both nature & man. Americans have lost control of the machinery of their society & only new values & a new culture can restore control." Reich was speaking in particular to the 750,000 Americans who had traded private homes and apartments for nonhierarchical consciousness-raising communal living.

Teenager William Powell, angry that the U.S. government wanted to send him to fight and die in Vietnam, wrote another manifesto that sold two million copies: *The Anarchist Cookbook*. The do–it–yourself manual instructed readers on guerrilla training, electronic surveillance, modifying guns, and blowing things up. "As almost everyone knows," Powell wrote, "silencers are illegal in virtually all the countries of the world, but then a true revolutionary believes that the government in power is illegal, so following that logic, I see no reason that he should feel restricted by laws made by an illegal body."

Some scars from the sixties failed to heal. As Kennedy's Camelot proved to be more sordid than initially advertised, fewer of us were prepared to believe JFK was killed by a lone wolf, as concluded by the 888-page Warren Commission Report. No Cold War–era conspiracy was as tenacious. A growing list of theorized new culprits included Fidel Castro (who, as we found out, was repeatedly targeted for assassination by the Kennedy White House); the CIA (hated by JFK after the Bay of Pigs); and the Mafia (not only did Bobby Kennedy expose organized crime figures, but the wildly libidinous Jack was apparently sharing a lover with a mob boss).

Abraham Zapruder's eight-millimeter home-movie camera had captured the moment of the fatal shot (frame 313 of 486), but it wasn't seen in full by any members of the public until the late sixties, when New Orleans DA Jim Garrison had it subpoenaed from *Life*, which had bought it from Zapruder for $150,000. In 1971, as part of his ongoing investigation into JFK's assassination, Garrison was ready to add a new name to the growing list of alleged conspirators: Air Force general and deputy CIA director Charles Cabell, whose brother Earle was the Dallas mayor in 1963. "What happened at Dealey Plaza in Dallas on November 22, 1963, was a coup d'état," Garrison claimed. "I believe that it was instigated and planned long in advance by fanatical anti-Communists in the United States intelligence community...and that its purpose was to stop Kennedy from seeking détente with the Soviet Union and Cuba and ending the Cold War."

If one uses the logic of Occam's razor—the simplest solution being the most likely to be true—the Soviets probably deserved more scrutiny for orchestrating the deed: (a) They were Cold War Enemy number one and (b) Lee Harvey Oswald was one of only seventeen Americans ever to defect to the USSR. "If any assassin might plausibly have been a Communist puppet," Louis Menand wrote, "it was Oswald, a man who had lived in the Soviet Union for three years, who had a Russian wife, and who once handed out leaflets for an outfit called the *Fair Play for Cuba Committee.* These facts were widely known within hours of Oswald's arrest, and yet the theory that he was an agent who was directed, wittingly or not, by Communist handlers has never been an important part of the folklore of the Kennedy assassination."

As the conspiracy theories flowered madly through the seventies, the tally of alternative assassins began heading toward one hundred. "There's the shattering randomness of the event," DeLillo explained in a 1993 interview, "the missing motive...the uncertainty we feel about the basic facts that surround the case—number of gunmen, number of shots, and so on. Our grip on reality has felt a little threatened. Every revelation about the event seems to produce new levels of secrecy, unexpected links....But mainly we have the individual in the small room, the nobody who walks out of the shadows and changes everything."

———

Hollywood captured the dark and unsettled mind-set of gathering gloom and indulged our growing appetite for supernatural terror. *Serpico,* Sidney Lumet's 1973 neo-noir, told the true story of Frank Serpico, who went undercover to expose rampant corruption in the New York City police force and nearly died in a shooting that may have been set up by his fellow detectives. *The Exorcist,* William Friedkin's thriller about the demonic possession of a twelve-year-old, compelled some moviegoers to seek exorcisms for family members they believed to be consumed by satanic evil. In *Network* (1976), a corporate cosmology is preached by the head of a conglomerate that owns the TV station:

> There is no America. There is no democracy. There is only IBM, and ITT, and AT&T, and DuPont, Dow, Union Carbide, and Exxon. Those are the nations of the world today. What do you think the Russians talk about in their councils of state, Karl Marx? They get out their linear programming charts, statistical decision theories, minimax solutions, and compute the price-cost probabilities of their transactions and investments, just like we do. We no longer live in a world of nations and ideologies. . . . The world is a college of corporations, inexorably determined by the immutable bylaws of business.

Carrie (1976) was the first of more than a hundred film and TV productions based on the typically chilling, genre-fluid work of Stephen King. As directed by Brian De Palma, King's morality tale about violence and anger builds to a blood-splattered prom holocaust, when the main character, a bullied teen girl, unleashes devastating telekinetic powers. In *Capricorn One* (1977), three astronauts (one played by O. J. Simpson) fake a Mars mission from a TV studio at an abandoned Air Force base. As pessimism deepened even further by decade's end, *Mad Max* (1979), directed by Australian George Miller, skipped ahead to what seemed to be our inevitable future: a lawless post-Armageddon wasteland.

A rising tide of Protestant evangelicals were convinced our time was running out. *The Late Great Planet Earth*, written by Christian Zionist Hal Lindsey, was the best-selling nonfiction book of the entire decade, at ten million copies, and told us that the ultimate cosmic conspiracy, the era of the Antichrist, was under way. Lindsey foresaw increasing famine, earthquakes, and a Soviet invasion of Israel—the Battle of Gog and Magog, as prophesied by the Book of Ezekiel. But while awaiting our inevitable trip into the valley of death, the author was somehow enjoying the ride.

In 1977, *Publisher's Weekly* wrote, "Hal Lindsey...is an Advent-and-Apocalypse evangelist who sports a Porsche racing jacket and tools around Los Angeles in a Mercedes 450 SL. And even though his best-selling books warn that the end is near, Lindsey maintains a suite of offices in a posh Santa Monica high-rise for the personal management firm that sinks his royalties into long-term real estate investments." Meanwhile, as Erin A. Smith reported in *Humanities*, "scholars and intellectuals condemned *The Late Great Planet Earth* for being theologically wrong, historically inaccurate, and aesthetically bad."

As spirituality won increasing credibility, polls showed that only a third of Americans had confidence in science. Alternative explanations of nature began to prosper. In the early seventies, Princeton University established an Engineering Anomalies Research Lab to investigate paranormal phenomena. *The Secret Life of Plants*, published in 1973, told us that the Food and Drug Administration, in league with agribusiness, had conspired to suppress evidence that plants were sentient. In 1974, the National Wildlife Foundation funded a study to track down Bigfoot, the giant hairy beast reportedly living in the forests of the Pacific Northwest. The International Association for Near-Death Studies was formed after several nearly dead people said they'd glimpsed the afterlife. In *Against Method: Outline on Anarchistic Theory of Knowledge* (1975), Paul Feyerabend argued that "voodoo has a firm though still not sufficiently understood material basis and a study of its manifestations can be used to enrich, and perhaps even revise, our knowledge of physiology."

The mushrooming of magical thinking even affected the military. In response to intelligence reports that the Soviets were spending millions of dollars on "psychotronic" research, the U.S. Defense Department tested psychics, explored a psychic spy unit, and researched the potential of precognition—the ability to see future events. According to Jon Ronson's *The Men Who Stare at Goats* (2004), the U.S. Army's Project Stargate established a unit of commandos who believed they could adopt the cloak of invisibility, pass through walls, and kill goats by staring at them.

The idea that the waters of the Bermuda Triangle regularly gobbled up planes and ships was popularized in the mid-seventies by Charles Berlitz, from the family of the famed language schools. Mr. Berlitz had previously worked at a travel agency where customers were alleged to have told him tales of this deadly mystery and insisted he book flights avoiding the area. *The Bermuda Triangle: An Incredible Saga of Unexplained Disappearances*, published in 1974, suggested that the haunted seas might be connected to survivors of the lost city of Atlantis. It was soon noted that neither Lloyd's of London nor the U.S. Coast Guard classified the Bermuda Triangle as especially dangerous.

As Berlitz's book was becoming a raging best-seller, eventually selling twenty million copies in thirty languages, a reference librarian at Arizona State University, Larry Kusche, was getting tired of demystifying the incredible saga for all-too-credulous students and published *The Bermuda Triangle Mystery—Solved*. "The Legend of the Bermuda Triangle is a manufactured mystery," he wrote. "It began because of careless research and was elaborated upon and perpetuated by writers who either purposely or unknowingly made use of misconceptions, faulty reasoning and sensationalism. It was repeated so many times that it began to take on the aura of truth."

Chariots of the Gods, written by convicted Swiss embezzler Erich von Däniken, posited that extraterrestrial visitors provided the blueprints for the Egyptian pyramids, Stonehenge, and the massive statues on Easter Island. The documentary made from the book was nominated for an Oscar, but the academic community called von Däniken's ideas pseudohistory, pseudoarcheology, and pseudoscience.

In the *New York Times Book Review*, Richard R. Lingeman analyzed the outrageous success of the books by Berlitz and von Däniken:

"As those who ordered their secret decoders already know, there are strange, unexplained things going on in the Triangle, a.k.a. the Hoodoo Sea, Twilight Zone, Vile Vortex. Since they are unexplained, the pseudo-sci boys are happy to run up a theory.... Perhaps psychologists would say that there is a mild anxiety neurosis at work here causing an ambivalent projection on the unknown of fears that take the form of extraterrestrial menaces at work, coupled with a secret childlike wish that there really are benevolent higher intelligences capable of running things better than the present people in charge."

L. Ron Hubbard managed to turn science fiction into pseudoscience and pseudoscience into the Church of Scientology, which stipulates that each of us are the children of godlike aliens who were destroyed long ago by nuclear weapons used by an evil dictator of a Galactic Confederacy. By the late seventies, Hubbard was in hiding, communicating only through ten trusted Messengers. He had been named as an unindicted co-conspirator for a bevy of crimes associated with Operation Snow White, a plot by high-level church officials to infiltrate, wiretap, and steal documents from federal attorneys and the IRS in order to purge unfavorable information about Scientology activities. At the time, it was the largest incident of domestic espionage in the history of the United States.

Before *Close Encounters of the Third Kind* was released, in 1977, Steven Spielberg told the *Washington Post* that he felt the government "was sitting on an incredible compilation of information" about visitors from outer space and said "in many ways, this movie is a cosmic Watergate." The film's opening scene takes place in a howling Mexican sandstorm and presents the mysterious reappearance of Flight 19, five Navy torpedo bombers reportedly lost while flying over the Bermuda Triangle in 1945.

Spielberg's title was true to the ufology classification system established by J. Allen Hynek's 1972 book *The UFO Experience: A Scientific Inquiry*. In subsequent years, Hynek's scale of extraterrestrial intersections would be extended to Close Encounters of the Fourth Kind (abduction by a UFO or its occupants); Fifth Kind (direct communication between aliens and humans); Sixth Kind (death of a human or animal associated with a UFO sighting); and Seventh Kind (sex leading to the creation of an alien/human hybrid).

———

The NRA became fully radicalized in 1977, when hard-liners grabbed power at the organization's annual meeting and advanced the argument that the Second Amendment guaranteed every individual's right to carry a gun. "Fights over rights are effective at getting out the vote," Jill Lepore wrote in the *New Yorker.* "Describing gun-safety legislation as an attack on a constitutional right gave conservatives power at the polls that, at the time, the movement lacked. Opposing gun control was also consistent with a larger anti-regulation, libertarian and anti-government conservative agenda."

As America's murder rate was reaching an all-time peak, having doubled between 1962 and 1979, the every-good-guy-should-have-a-gun theory gained traction and became entrenched. America's percolating lunatic fringe also decided that the founders truly wanted citizens packing heat in case violence was required to vanquish a tyrannical federal regime.

Anarchists and white supremacists appeared to reach alignment. The *New Yorker*'s Mike Kelly called it "fusion paranoia," a philosophical solidarity, Kelly deduced, from the tenet that "international bankers and the Wall Street money men and the bought-up pols of Washington are conspiring to destroy America and usher its citizens into the New World Order." Anticipating the imminent activation of fused bogeymen and other conjectured calamities, survivalists began flocking to the sparsely populated tristate region of northwestern Montana, the Idaho panhandle, and eastern Washington. Huddled in weaponized communes stocked with canned goods and freeze-dried protein, they prepared themselves to prosper off the grid should the agents of the globalists ever attack or a brutish *Mad Max* brand of dystopia finally arrive.

Cult leader Jim Jones, narcissistic and charismatic, fused fervid faith with leftist politics, attaching evangelical Christianity and New Age spirituality to social equality and Marxist collectivism. He also forced his followers to prove their loyalty by signing blank power-of-attorney forms containing false confessions that they had molested their children or conspired to overthrow the U.S. government.

In 1977, Jones suddenly moved his Peoples Temple from California to the small South American country of Guyana. The uprooting followed the publication of a story charging that Jones conducted fake healings, beat church members, and demanded that they turn over all their money and possessions. In establishing the new jungle location, an inhospitable tract of land called Jonestown, he told members they were building a utopia free of meddling by government agencies, such as the CIA, and would be safe from an imminent nuclear holocaust.

After a family in the United States won a custody order for a child living in Jonestown, Jones became a disintegrating paranoid speed freak shadowed by bodyguards, and the commune was converted into an armed camp patrolled by members carrying guns and machetes. At one point, Black Panthers Huey Newton and Angela Davis spoke to Jonestown inhabitants by radio to voice their solidarity. Jones had long spouted progressive racial views and a majority of the residents were black. Davis provided cover for Jones's mania by saying the Peoples Temple was at the vanguard of revolution and encouraged resistance against the church's unseen conspirators.

In 1978, after Jones ordered the killing of visiting congressman Leo Ryan, he commanded all the residents, many of them children, to drink a cyanide-laced fruit punch. Nine hundred and twelve died slowly and painfully. It was the largest mass suicide in American history. Jones left a will stating that his assets should go to the Communist Party of the USSR.

"The Peoples Temple was—as many communes, cults, churches and social movements are—an alternative to the established social order, a nation unto itself," Tim Raven wrote in his history of the cult. "The Temple I knew was not populated by masochists and half-wits, so it followed that the members who gave years of labor, life savings, homes, children and, in some cases, their own lives had been getting something in return."

CHAPTER 36

A MINUET WITH MALAISE

By the end of the seventies, we were learning how many "friend-lies" in Vietnam had been poisoned by the indiscriminate use of chemical weaponry. Thousands of U.S. troops were sprayed with the toxic herbicide Agent Orange. The use of the chemical—meant to deny enemy troops jungle cover—had begun under President Kennedy, and even though Presidents Johnson and Nixon had been publicly warned by hundreds of scientists about the lethality of the aerial spraying of defoliants, the program—called Operation Ranch Hand—was active until 1971. Ironically, one of the Nazi chemists recruited through Operation Paperclip, Dr. Fritz Hoffmann, warned against using the substance. He was ignored, too.

By 1978, soldiers attached to Ranch Hand were seen dying on national television. Paul Reutershan, a former helicopter crew chief in Vietnam responsible for transporting supplies to the 20th Engineering Brigade, appeared on *The Today Show* and told viewers, "I died in Vietnam, but I didn't even know it." Reutershan had flown daily through clouds of herbicides discharged by C-123 cargo planes. He told of watching mangrove forests turn brown and die, said the Army told him that Agent Orange was "relatively nontoxic to humans and animals," and revealed that he was dying of a spreading cancer, which indeed would kill him only months after his TV interview.

In 1979, a decade of disillusionment and despair, of black comedies and biting satire, concluded, appropriately, with a year validating

Murphy's law—anything and everything that could go wrong did go wrong, day after day, month after month. Our paranoia was enflamed by regular examples of entropy, order surrendering to disorder, often a product of sheer incompetence, and it began this way: The shah, that ruthless bedrock of Middle East stability, was forced out by an Islamic revolution. The CIA had failed to figure out that Iran was at long last fed up with the shah's ceaseless corruption and brutality. Nor did its analysts grasp that religious zeal could still be translated into political action.

As fighting raged in the streets of Tehran, National Security Advisor Zbigniew Brzezinski told U.S. ambassador William Sullivan he expected the American military attaché to round up the Iranian army and "overthrow" the new regime. But much had changed since the CIA had last saved the shah, in 1953. Sullivan had to explain to Brzezinski that the American military attaché in question, Lieutenant General Philip C. Gast, was hiding in the basement of the Iranian army headquarters, pinned down by gunfire.

A hostile Islamic Republic—with something called an ayatollah—took charge, and under this new and exceedingly anti-American regime, Iran's oil exports were interrupted, oil prices rose as demand exceeded supply, and very long and very irritating lines began forming at every gas station in America. Previously, the shah had been pumping enough oil to address more than 10 percent of the needs of the Western world.

The prospect that another form of energy was less than reliable entered the public square on March 16, 1979, when *The China Syndrome* was released. Jane Fonda and Michael Douglas play TV reporters who secretly film a major nuclear accident. The phrase "China Syndrome" is a reference to the fascinating but implausible notion that during a nuclear meltdown, the reactor components will melt through their containment, into the earth, and all the way to China. The more likely scenario, as a character in the film explained, was that a meltdown could "render an area the size of Pennsylvania permanently uninhabitable."

This menacing message very quickly turned into an all-too-real I-told-you-so. On March 28, just twelve days later, the possibility that "an area the size of Pennsylvania" could become permanently uninhabitable by a nuclear accident became a very real thing when a partial meltdown occurred at Pennsylvania's Three Mile Island Nuclear Generating Station, on the Susquehanna River near Harrisburg. Compounding the accident, blundering plant workers inadvertently released radioactive gases that created a potentially explosive hydrogen bubble above the core. An evacuation zone with a twenty-mile radius was established, and 140,000 people temporarily left the area. It was the worst accident in U.S. commercial power plant history.

On April 23, 1979, White House pollster Pat Caddell produced what came to be called the "Apocalypse Now" memo—named for Francis Ford Coppola's beautifully photographed but wholly depressing Vietnam War film. "America is a nation deep in crisis," Caddell wrote. "Unlike civil war or depression, this crisis, nearly invisible, is unique from those that previously have engaged Americans in their history. Psychological more than material, it is a crisis of confidence marked by a dwindling faith in the future.... There are no armies of the night, no street demonstrations, no powerful lobbies.... This crisis threatens the political and social fabric of the nation.... One out of every three Americans see their own lives going straight downhill.... This is a psychological crisis of the first order."

———

On Friday, May 25, at the start of the Memorial Day weekend, the rampage of Murphy's law continued. A DC-10 taking off from Chicago's O'Hare Airport lost its left engine. The jet stalled, rolled, and plunged. Loaded with fuel, it exploded on impact. All 271 on board were killed instantly. The heat from the blaze was so intense, firefighters couldn't approach the crash site for close to an hour. It was the worst air disaster in American history. An American Airlines maintenance crew was found to be at fault. After removing the engine for repairs, they had failed to follow procedures while refastening it to the wing.

Meanwhile, the other superpower was preparing to wage war against God through his holy messenger in the Vatican. Poland's fifty-eight-year-old Karol Wojtyła was the youngest pope in 132 years, the first Slavic pope ever, and the first non-Italian pope in 456 years. KGB head Yuri Andropov had concluded that Pope John Paul II was the product of an Anglo-German conspiracy orchestrated by Polish American Zbigniew Brzezinski to undermine Soviet control of largely Catholic Poland, with the larger aim to foment the collapse of the entire Soviet Union.

When the pope announced his first pilgrimage to Warsaw, in June 1979, Andropov issued a secret memorandum to Soviet schoolteachers: "The Pope is our enemy.... Due to his uncommon skills and great sense of humor he is dangerous, because he charms everyone.... [He] puts on a highlander's hat, shakes all hands, kisses children, etc.... It is modeled on American presidential campaigns.... Because of the activities of the Church in Poland our activities designed to atheize the youth not only cannot diminish but must intensely develop."

Back in America, the annoying gas shortages of the spring of 1979 became a Great Gas Panic by the summer. Snaking gas lines caused traffic jams. Stations started closing on Sundays. Some states limited sales to $3 per customer. The country was encouraged to be more fuel-efficient by not exceeding 55 miles per hour, which was perhaps the final insult. A lead foot on the pedal had become a national birthright. In Hollywood, a Cadillac driver crashed a gas line and brandished a pistol while filling up his tank. In Queens, a woman offered sex for gas. A Shell Oil truck was hijacked, the driver bound and blindfolded.

Political journalist Theodore White later observed, "The gasoline shortage of 1979 would have been at all times manageable by a severe, disciplinary government. The overall shortfall of approximately 3 percent from the previous year's summer gasoline consumption had struck the country unevenly. The pinpoints of acute shortage, in growing states like California, provoked anxiety and panic; and the panic provoked the gorging of gas in jerry cans by frightened motorists."

On July 4, the *New York Post* found nothing to celebrate: "As a nation, we appear to have become steadily more dependent on forces seemingly beyond our control, losing confidence in our ability to master events, uncertain of our direction.... The United States is now a victim of a loss of nerve and will, wracked by indecision and groping for a glimpse of inspirational and innovative leadership."

A week later, on July 11, Skylab was falling, but no one knew where. In 1973, under the Nixon administration, NASA had put the space station into orbit without having any way of bringing it down safely. When it was discovered that Skylab's orbit was decaying faster than anticipated, the best NASA engineers could do to fix the problem was fuzzy math, telling the world they'd endeavor to land the seventy-seven-ton house-sized loose cannon over a large body of water by firing the station's booster rockets at just the right time. This plan gave no one comfort.

A Soviet satellite had just fallen out of the sky and spilled radioactive debris over a four-hundred-mile stretch of northern Canada. Channeling the unsettled mood, an editorial cartoon in the *Philadelphia Inquirer* asked readers, "Pick the best example of good ol' American know-how: Three Mile Island, DC-10, Skylab, Pinto, mass transit." On *Saturday Night Live*, John Belushi appeared on "Weekend Update" in his recurring Science Editor role to provide insight on Skylab's landing spot. Shortly, he began destroying his two props, attacking an inflated globe with a handheld model of the spacecraft, becoming increasingly enraged to the point of incoherence and collapse.

BELUSHI: Hey [continuing to puncture globe with plastic model], here's John Belushi in his apartment in New York, here he's not worried about Skylab, no. That's silly....Do I have any reason to be worried or be afraid? The government takes 50 percent of my money that I earn every year. They should be spending it on mass transit, solar energy, clean up the environment!...But no, no, they have to spend millions on a few chunks of steel so it could come screaming back at us!

In advance of the calculated crash, people in Devon, England, took shelter in an old smuggler's cave; a St. Louis gathering of the just-formed Skylab Watchers and Gourmet Diners Society wore hard hats for protection; and in Charlotte, North Carolina, a local hotel designated itself an official Skylab crash zone, while also advertising a poolside disco party.

No one in Devon, St. Louis, or Charlotte would be struck. The largest chunks of the space station ended up in the Indian Ocean, as theorized, but a notable amount of debris was scattered across Australia. Seventeen-year-old Stan Thornton of Esperance—a town of thirteen thousand on Australia's western coastline, near Perth—collected several of the fragments that struck his home, hopped on a flight to the United States, and claimed a $10,000 prize offered by the *San Francisco Examiner* as the first person to deliver a piece of Skylab debris to the paper's office within seventy-two hours of the crash.

———

On July 15, 1979, following ten days of seclusion at Camp David, Jimmy Carter addressed the nation to calm fears about gas shortages. He acknowledged that the gap between the government and its citizens had "never been so wide," and conceded that the nation had "an intolerable dependence on OPEC oil," but also admonished Americans for their "worship of self-indulgence and consumption." It was soon called the "malaise" speech, even though the president never actually used the word. Two days after the address, Carter asked his entire cabinet for their resignations.

By Labor Day, the former peanut farmer from Plains, Georgia, had an approval rating of 19 percent. Six weeks later, Carter made the two biggest mistakes of his entire presidency by (1) permitting the exiled and ailing shah to come to America for treatment at a New York hospital while (2) failing to evacuate the U.S. embassy in Tehran. As the shah landed in the United States, anti-American street demonstrations erupted in Iran. On November 1, the ayatollah said, "The United States, which has given refuge to that corrupt germ, will be confronted in a different manner by us." On November 4, a mob seized the U.S. embassy and sixty-five Americans were held hostage for another 444 days.

On November 9, 1979, at 3 a.m. Eastern Time, the computers at all the top command centers—the North American Aerospace Defense Command's Cheyenne Mountain site, the Pentagon's National Military Command Center, and the Alternate National Military Command Center in Maryland—showed that the Soviets had launched a massive nuclear strike against the United States. Ten fighters were immediately launched. The National Emergency Airborne Command Post—the "doomsday plane" meant to get the president to safety—mistakenly took off from Andrews Air Force base without President Jimmy Carter. Fortunately, moments before Zbigniew Brzezinski was going to call the president and advise him to launch a nuclear counterattack against the Soviet Union, the Pentagon learned that none of the early warning posts outside the United States had noticed anything different. A software program simulating a Soviet missile attack had somehow found its way into the regular warning display.

After the incident, Marshall Shulman, a senior State Department advisor, told Carter and other senior staffers that the false alerts were not a rare occurrence and that there was a "complacency about handling them" he found disturbing. The Kremlin was also heard from. On November 14, 1979, after reading about the fuckup in the *New York Times* and the *Washington Post*, Soviet Communist Party general secretary Leonid Brezhnev wrote secretly to Carter bitching that the erroneous alert was "fraught with a tremendous danger." Brezhnev added, "I think you will agree with me that there should be no errors in such matters."

In forming a response to Brezhnev, Carter let the hard-liners within his administration prevail, and he told the Soviet leader that his complaint about the United States nearly killing tens of millions of Soviets was "inaccurate and unacceptable." Shulman called Carter's language "snotty" and "gratuitously insulting."

Two months later, the Soviets invaded Afghanistan. The country was being ruled by a Soviet puppet named Hafizullah Amin, a brutal and unpopular psychopath. Brezhnev decided to stage an invasion followed by a coup d'état to replace Amin before the Afghans, like the Iranians, took matters into their own hands.

In response, and mindful of reelection, President Carter maximized his bully pulpit. He decried the Soviet aggression as the act of a powerful atheistic government subjugating an independent Islamic people in order to take their oil; issued a trade embargo preventing U.S. businesses from selling the USSR desperately needed grain and information technology; restricted Soviet fishing in U.S. waters; tabled SALT II arms talks; called on the United Nations to provide military equipment, food, and other assistance to Afghanistan's possibly imperiled neighbors; announced the restart of the draft; requested a 5 percent increase in defense spending; and, for good measure, said the United States was boycotting the 1980 Summer Olympics in Moscow.

Quickly, the Carter administration discovered that U.S. athletes would not be compliant. A group of fifty potential Olympians issued a statement denouncing the use of sports as a political lever. "We must use actions which will achieve results," the statement read, "not symbolic gestures which only vent emotions." On March 30, 1980, the Moscow Olympic boycott was opposed at a meeting of all thirty-two sports federations. A headline in the next day's *Washington Post* read: CARTER GETS WORD: TRY AND STOP US.

Vice President Walter Mondale was sent to speak before the 341 voting members of the U.S. Olympic Committee. Mondale suggested it had been wrong to send an American team to Hitler's Berlin Olympics in 1936, and presented the Carter boycott as a second chance to oppose world evil.

"The athletes here, and the athletes you represent, may have been born a full generation after the Berlin Olympics," Mondale said. "But as their advisers and trustees, you bear the responsibility of linking that history to their duty. For the story of Hitler's rise is more than an unspeakable tragedy, more than a study in tyranny. It is also a chronicle of the free world's failure—of opportunities seized, aggression not opposed, appeasement not condemned."

For the first time, the USOC voted to reject an invitation to participate in the Olympic Games. So the TV sets in America in the summer of 1980 would not see butterfly world record holder Craig Beardsley attempt to slay the Soviets in the pool; or Jesse Vassallo (who was dedicating his races to his late father) sweeping the 200- and 400-meter individual medley; or Renaldo Nehemiah looking to lower his world record in the hurdles. They wouldn't see gymnast Kurt Thomas, who at the 1978 Worlds in Strasbourg, France, had become the first U.S. world champion in forty-six years. No chance of seeing the young Villanova-trained Don Paige try to outkick Britain's Sebastian Coe and Steve Ovett in the 800 meters. Or discover the potential of a nineteen-year-old quarter-miler named Gwen Gardner. No Stanley Floyd blazing in the 100. No Carol Blazejowski lighting up the scoreboard in basketball. Or Isiah Thomas feeding a no-look pass to an open teammate.

"What made the feelings of bitterness and emptiness worse was that the boycott didn't work," wrote John Powers in the *Boston Globe*. "Multiple American allies—notably Great Britain, France, Italy, Spain, Ireland, Switzerland, Mexico, Australia—went to Moscow anyway.... And the Soviets remained in Afghanistan for another decade."

On September 18, 1980, near the conclusion of Jimmy Carter's first—and, as it turned out, only—term in office, one of the most frightening "broken arrow" episodes of the Cold War era took place just outside Damascus, Arkansas. During a routine maintenance procedure at Launch Complex 347-7, a worker dropped an eight-pound wrench that ricocheted inside the silo and put a hole in the fuel tank of a Titan II intercontinental ballistic missile. At the time, the Titan II was the largest thermonuclear missile in the U.S. arsenal, topped by a nine-megaton warhead—three times the explosive force of all the bombs dropped during World War II.

As the missile leaked a cloud of aerozine 50 fuel, there was the possibility that it could blow up at any second and detonate the warhead. As the Air Force scrambled a containment team to the site, the Arkansas Democratic Convention was taking place in the state capital, Little Rock, just fifty miles south of Damascus. The attendees at the convention included then Arkansas governor Bill Clinton, his wife, Hillary, and Walter Mondale.

The commotion of emergency vehicles and military personnel at the Damascus silo drew the attention of the local press and live TV coverage from a new name in national round-the-clock news, CNN, which had launched on June 1, 1980. Meanwhile, Mondale received a requested briefing about the incident from three officers with Strategic Air Command. He asked if the missile was carrying a nuclear warhead. The officers told the vice president that SAC headquarters had instructed them neither to confirm nor deny the presence of a nuclear weapon. Pissed, Mondale called Harold Brown, the secretary of defense. He wouldn't tell him, either.

"Goddamn it, Harold," Mondale replied angrily, "I'm the vice president of the United States!"

Brown relented and confirmed that the Titan II was in fact carrying a nuclear device.

At 3 a.m. the following morning, the missile exploded. The 740-ton silo door was flung into the air, as was the second stage of the rocket and the nine-megaton warhead, which landed a hundred feet away from the entry gate of the launch complex. The warhead did not detonate, nor did it leak radiation. One member of the Air Force investigation team was killed. Twenty-one others in the vicinity of the blast were injured.

"This is the one and only time that a warhead of this design was involved in a serious accident," said *Command and Control* author Eric Schlosser. "Obviously it didn't detonate because we would know if it had. But you wouldn't want to try this accident five times."

In CNN's twentieth anniversary show, anchor Bernie Shaw said the Damascus incident was a turning point for the network: "The Air Force was saying no problem, even though one person was killed, 'Don't worry, folks, there was no nuclear warhead on the missile.' Well, I made a call to a totally unimpeachable source at the Pentagon, and while a U.S. Air Force officer was standing out there at ground zero telling the American people and the world, 'There is no nuclear warhead atop this missile,' my source at the Pentagon said, 'Not only was there a warhead, but guess what? They are looking for it.' And we had pictures of skirmish lines out there, and they found the warhead a couple days later."

"Again and again," Schlosser wrote, "safety problems were hidden not only from the public but also from the officers and the enlisted personnel who handled nuclear weapons every day." Just as bad, Schlosser indicated, "the strict, compartmentalized secrecy hid safety problems from the scientists and engineers responsible for weapons safety." Using the Freedom of Information Act, Schlosser was able to obtain a document that listed the *Accidents and Incidents Involving Nuclear Weapons* from the summer of 1957 until the spring of 1967. It was 245 pages long.

CHAPTER 37

TIT-FOR-TAT

Two members of a criminal gang are arrested. They are believed to have participated in the same crime, a burglary. Their names are Bill and Jim. They are placed in separate interrogation rooms, without any way to communicate with each other. Each will be offered a plea deal.

The prosecutor has enough evidence to convict Bill and Jim of a parole violation, but not enough evidence to convict them of burglary, which carries a greater penalty. The prosecutor offers Bill and Jim the same three-part bargain:

1. If Bill and Jim both betray each other—that is, if Bill testifies that Jim committed burglary and Jim does the same to Bill— they will each get five years in prison.
2. However, if Bill testifies that Jim committed burglary, and Jim remains silent about Bill's role, Bill will be set free and Jim will serve ten years in prison. The same is true if Jim betrays Bill and Bill remains silent.
3. Finally, if Jim and Bill both remain silent, they will only serve one year in prison on the lesser charge of a parole violation.

They are told that the deal is on the table for a finite amount of time.

The above scenario is known as the prisoner's dilemma. It is a standard example from game theory, a field of study that became very popular during the Cold War, and this particular "game," the prisoner's dilemma, was first formulated by the people at RAND, the Air Force think tank that, among other things, thought about how to defeat the Soviets in a thermonuclear war. The reason why this game came from the people thinking about thermonuclear war is because it was, in theory, a way to understand how and why rational individuals might choose to cooperate, or not. A world with two adversaries who possessed devastating armaments capable of destroying one another in a matter of minutes made the concept of cooperation very relevant.

In the prisoner's dilemma, if both parties remain silent, scenario number three, there is a guaranteed but lesser punishment. If only one party decides to cooperate, betrayal potentially offers the greatest reward: no jail, scenario number two. But if both parties choose betrayal, scenario number one, it leads to a worse result than if both parties had chosen cooperation. Put another way: If Bill and Jim rat each other out, it leads to a greater punishment than if they had each shut up—or cooperated.

Ultimately, the theoretical Bill and Jim of the prisoner's dilemma, "defined" as rational and self-interested actors, *should betray* each other, because betrayal offers the greatest possible guaranteed reward: no jail time. Cooperation is less attractive because it requires a leap of faith: a level of trust. How can you be sure the other guy won't sell you out?

Merrill Flood and Melvin Dresher were the RAND analysts who created the prisoner's dilemma, and as Annie Jacobsen wrote, they "learned something unexpected from the results. The outcome of the Prisoner's Dilemma seemed to depend on the human nature of the individual players involved—whether the player was guided by trust or distrust."

Dresher and Flood also discovered that behavior during the game revealed the inherent philosophical and political dispositions of the players. The majority of those who were politically conservative, Jacobsen added, "chose to testify against their criminal partner. They did not trust that partner to follow the concept of self-preservation, gamble against his own best interests, and refuse to talk. Five years in prison was better than ten." By contrast, liberals generally refused to testify against their partner, willing to put themselves at risk to get the best possible outcome for both parties: a single year in jail.

———

In March 1980, computational modeling was paired with game theory and conflict resolution. University of Michigan political scientist Robert Axelrod held an "iterated" prisoner's dilemma tournament for celebrated game theorists. Attendees submitted strategies premised by the essence of the paradigm: choosing to betray or cooperate.

Economists, sociologists, biologists, political scientists, computer scientists, mathematicians, physicists, and hobbyists were partnered against one another, as if in a round-robin sports tournament. Instead of the games being framed by minutes or quarters, the players faced off against one another—strategy versus strategy—over the course of two hundred moves executed by a computer, through a software code. The strategy that had the lowest total amount of "prison time" would be the winner.

One of the players was sixty-eight-year-old Anatol Rapoport, whose life had been tossed and turned by the tides of twentieth-century history, from the rise of Hitler, to World War II, and into the Cold War. He was born in Ukraine, immigrated to the United States with his family in 1922, and became a naturalized citizen in 1928, when he turned seventeen. Rapoport ventured to Vienna to study music, a pursuit that abruptly concluded when the rise of Nazism prevented Jews like himself from enjoying any kind of normal existence. Returning to the United States, he shifted to mathematics and received a PhD from the University of Chicago. He joined the Communist Party, was a member for three years, and quit before enlisting in the U.S. Army Air Corps in 1941.

His experience in the war inspired him to turn peacemaking into a science. In 1955, Rapoport became professor of mathematical biology and senior research mathematician at the University of Michigan, where he founded the Mental Health Research Institute—applying "scientific methods to the study of human behavior." He'd also play an active role in the school's antiwar activity.

In 1960, the Students for a Democratic Society (SDS) was founded on the Michigan campus, and Michigan student Tom Hayden authored the founding political manifesto of the New Left, the Port Huron Statement, which argued for participatory democracy, nonviolent civil disobedience, and nuclear disarmament. As the Michigan campus became embroiled in demonstrations against the Vietnam War, Rapoport was a leading organizer of the first teach-ins. At one of those events, he said, "By undertaking the war against Vietnam, the United States has undertaken a war against humanity.... This war we shall not win."

His political activity, prior association with the Communist Party, and "suspicious" origins—born and raised in Ukraine, a Soviet republic—made him a target of J. Edgar Hoover's COINTELPRO program. FBI agents were directed to "neutralize" Rapoport. "The Bureau," wrote Loch Johnson, "mailed anonymous letters to senior administrators at the university, as well as to prominent citizens in Ann Arbor and throughout the state, claiming without a shred of evidence that Rapoport was, if not a Communist, then at least an apologist for communism and a troublemaker. The letters were typically signed 'a concerned citizen' or a 'concerned taxpayer.' ... The FBI had placed informants in Rapoport's classrooms to report on his 'subversive' activities.... These pressures, whose underlying source Rapoport never comprehended, eventually led him to resign from the University of Michigan and take up a faculty post at the University of Toronto. The FBI had won."

In 1980, however, Professor Rapoport was the winner, victorious in the first-ever "iterated" prisoner's dilemma tournament. He used a simple strategy called *Tit-for-Tat*, which had only four lines of code. The strategy starts with cooperation on the first move, and then mirrors whatever the opponent does for the following moves. If matched against a strategy of betrayal, or "defecting from cooperation," it always betrays, or defects—tit for every tat. Conversely, if matched against a cooperative strategy, it always cooperates.

Tit-for-Tat proved to be applicable to conflict resolution in the business world: It's (1) inherently *nice* (the first move of Tit-for-Tat is always cooperation); (2) it's *clear* (those who betray receive immediate retaliation); and (3) it's *forgiving* (no matter what the prior move, Tit-for-Tat responds to a cooperative move with immediate cooperation).

For someone in a long-term work relationship inside an established institution, Tit-for-Tat indicated that informed cooperation can be a better strategy than a default setting of cutthroat competition. As Metta Spencer wrote in *Peace Magazine*, the program "punished the other player for selfish behaviour and rewarded her for cooperative behaviour—but the punishment lasted only as long as the selfish behaviour lasted. This proved to be an exceptionally effective sanction, quickly showing the other side the advantages of cooperating. It also set moral philosophers to proposing this as a workable principle to use in real life interactions."

When Professor Rapoport won the Axelrod competition with Tit-for-Tat, he had recently founded the Peace and Conflict Studies program at the University of Toronto, for which he was, at the time, the only teacher—and unpaid. "I'm for killing the institution of war," he'd say. Rapoport taught his students using an interdisciplinary approach to the study of peace, integrating math, politics, psychology, philosophy, science, and sociology. His ultimate goal was to legitimize peace studies as a worthy academic pursuit.

A few years later, he would have two unwitting students in Ronald Reagan and Mikhail Gorbachev. They would use Tit-for-Tat to conclude the Cold War.

CHAPTER 38

ARMING FOR BEAR

On December 11, 1980, CIA Director Stansfield Turner gave President-elect Ronald Reagan a detailed intelligence briefing. During the campaign, Reagan had charged that the Carter administration had allowed America to become vulnerable to a Soviet attack. He had claimed that the Soviets not only had nuclear superiority but, further, had engaged in a massive civil defense project to shelter their population in order "to win" a nuclear war.

Turner gave Reagan a reality check. He told the president-elect that the Soviet Union's economy was starting to crater: The population was aging, economic inefficiency was persistent, growth had been halved. Next, he told Reagan that the Soviets did not have nuclear superiority; in the event of a first strike by the Soviets, the United States would still have enough nuclear weapons to destroy every Soviet city with a population over one hundred thousand. Finally, Reagan was told that less than 10 percent of the Soviet population could be sheltered in an attack. Turner suggested that Reagan envision the difficulty of getting eight million people out of Moscow during the Russian winter.

Reagan, however, was not ready to listen. Instead, he was paying attention to such people as General Alexander Haig, his incoming secretary of state, who insisted that the Soviet Union "possessed greater military power than the United States." Again, this was just not true. Nor was Haig's contention that America's defense had "gone into a truly alarming military decline even before the withdrawal from Vietnam accelerated the weakening trend."

Upon taking office, Reagan announced he wanted to spend $1.6 trillion on the U.S. military in the next five years. This represented a 10 percent increase in the defense budget and was the largest peacetime arms buildup in U.S. history. "Defense is not a budget item," he told the Pentagon. "Spend what you need." Reagan restarted the building of the B-1 supersonic bomber; approved the development of the B-2 stealth bomber; accelerated deployment of both the MX mobile missile system and the next generation of Trident submarines; and set a target of increasing the Navy from 450 to 600 ships. He also tossed the CIA more money for covert operations.

"In the morning of an Administration," Haig said, "the air is fresh and still relatively quiet, and friends and adversaries are alert and watchful. It is the best time to send signals."

———

Near the conclusion of *Dr. Strangelove*, Soviet ambassador de Sadesky reveals that the Soviets have built a doomsday device:

> We could not keep up with the expense involved in the arms race, the space race, and the peace race. And at the same time our people grumbled for more nylons and washing machines. Our doomsday scheme cost us just a small fraction of what we'd been spending on defense in a single year. But the deciding factor was when we learned that your country was working along similar lines, and we were afraid of a doomsday gap.

Following this admission, Dr. Strangelove castigates the Soviet ambassador:

> The whole point of the doomsday machine is lost...if you keep it a secret! Why didn't you tell the world, eh!

As it turned out, the Soviets *did* build a doomsday machine—and the United States *didn't* know about it. The system ensured that even if the Soviet political and military leadership was decapitated, a computer would take over as a cybernetic command and control system—a kind of Skynet, the neural net–based group mind imagined in *The Terminator* (1984).

The project was a not unreasonable response to a perception that Ronald Reagan and the United States were attempting to gain a decisive nuclear superiority. As America's arsenal was rapidly being updated and increased, it was being accompanied by disturbing rhetoric. For example, during a Senate confirmation hearing in 1981, the incoming head of the Arms Control and Disarmament Agency, Eugene Rostow, argued that Japan had flourished after the nuclear attack and said that even if a nuclear war killed one hundred million Americans, "that is not the whole of the population."

For the Kremlin, perhaps the greatest threat was the introduction of the gigantic and fearsome U.S. Trident nuclear submarine, which was as long as two football fields, as wide as a city bus, and perhaps the most destructive weapon system ever created. By 1982, four had been launched, with more on the way. Since each submarine carried 24 nuclear missiles, and since each of those 24 missiles was topped by a multiple independently targetable reentry vehicle (MIRV) with eight warheads, the four boats alone were capable of attacking the Soviet Union with 768 nuclear explosives—a number sufficient to flatten every Soviet target of consequence. As advertised by the builder, the Electric Boat Division of General Dynamics, the Trident was also faster and quieter than existing submarines, making it very difficult to detect.

By the logic of nuclear deterrence, the Trident ensured that the United States would have an adequate counterstrike capability. "While a first strike might wipe out a country's land–based missiles and nuclear bombers," Sebastien Roblin wrote in *The National Interest*, "it's *very* difficult to track a ballistic-missile submarine patrolling quietly in the depths of the ocean—and there's little hope of taking them *all* out in a first strike. Thus, ballistic-missile submarines promise the unstoppable hand of nuclear retribution—and should deter any sane adversary from attempting a first strike or resorting to nuclear weapons at all."

But in turn, the mandate of the security dilemma required the Soviets to immediately counteract yet another technological breakthrough by the United States. The Trident was capable of stealthily approaching the Soviet coast and launching a shower of incredibly accurate and speedy missiles that could reach their targets in as little as three minutes. Since this would permit virtually no warning time to duck and cover, much less decide on how to respond, the Soviets created a Dead Hand system—a doomsday device—in order to maintain a second-strike capability. In the event that the entire Soviet leadership perished, this computerized system was capable of bypassing the established command authority and transferring it to a junior officer.

As to why the Soviets didn't tell anyone about the Dead Hand, author Nicholas Thompson explained, "One, they're extremely secretive. They didn't tell their own arms negotiators. Number two is if you tell the United States about it, there's a better chance that we could disable, or trick it, or destroy it. But then the third reason is that it wasn't built as a classic deterrent. It was built to deter the Soviet Union. It was built to prevent this issue of launch on false warning.... If you have this doomsday machine, it means you don't feel like you need to respond immediately.... You can wait and see whether the radars are correct and whether it really is a nuclear strike or whether it's a flock of geese. My sense is that overall, it made us safer."

———

Oleg Gordievsky became a KGB agent in 1963 and was posted to the Soviet embassy in Denmark. In 1968, he became deeply disturbed by the USSR's invasion of Czechoslovakia. He'd later write that the suppression of the Prague Spring made clear to him that a "Communist one-party state leads inexorably to intolerance, inhumanity, and the destruction of liberties." In 1974, Gordievsky agreed to betray his country and become a double agent. In 1982, his value to the West increased significantly when the KGB moved him to the Soviet embassy in London, where he took over as head of station, in charge of all Soviet intelligence operations in the United Kingdom. As Kim Philby had once exposed all of British intelligence to the Kremlin, so Gordievsky did more or less the same in reverse, conveying to MI6, Her Majesty's Secret Service, the extent of Kremlin espionage in the British Isles.

By 1985, the Soviets had begun to suspect his disloyalty, summoned him to Moscow, and began interrogating him. While his superiors were deciding if he indeed was a mole, Gordievsky was placed in a KGB sanitarium and kept under surveillance. One day, he went on a jog and managed to disappear. In 1990, he published a book about his spying with Cambridge historian Christopher Andrew. One of the most chilling revelations in the book is Gordievsky's full account of the very precarious and truly paranoid state of the aging Soviet Politburo in the early 1980s.

The reason reformer Mikhail Gorbachev had the opportunity to fill a power vacuum in 1985, at the age of fifty-four, is because his rivals were so feeble and dropped dead so swiftly. Leonid Brezhnev, suffering from what was likely Alzheimer's and hardening of the arteries, was already a figurehead, barely able to speak coherently, when he died in 1982 at age seventy-five. Brezhnev's successor, KGB head Yuri Andropov, lasted one year and eighty-nine days as general secretary, spending most of it attached to dialysis machines treating his failing kidneys, a condition that killed him in 1983, at age sixty-nine. Andropov was followed by Konstantin Chernenko, who served an even shorter term than Andropov. He had emphysema, contracted pneumonia, and died of heart failure in 1985, at age seventy-three.

This gerontocracy was a goofy bunch who were obsessed with

miracle cures dispensed by a mysterious Assyrian faith healer who came to be known as the "Soviet Rasputin." Brezhnev, Andropov, and Chernenko were all being treated by Kremlin "health advisor" Juna Davitashvili, who did not have a medical degree, but claimed to have the power to cure cancer and prolong life. Her personal brand of pharmacology included a special time-released rejuvenating pill said to contain an "autonomous stimulator" giving off impulses identical to those naturally transmitted by the brain of a young, robust person. This Fountain of Youth in a pill supposedly regenerated body tissue and vital organs. "The stark truth," said historian Peter Bogdanov, "is that a system ostensibly based on immutable scientific theories of economics and sociologies was being run by credulous ignoramuses willing to believe any old wives' tales to prolong their lives."

In May 1981, the credulous ignoramuses addressed a major closed-session conference of senior KGB officers in Moscow. Brezhnev denounced Ronald Reagan's policies. Andropov, head of the KGB at the time, declared that the new U.S. administration was actively preparing for nuclear war. Wrote Gordievsky, "The Politburo had accordingly decided that the overriding priority of Soviet foreign intelligence operations must thenceforth be to collect military-strategic intelligence on the nuclear threat from the United States and NATO. To the astonishment of most of his audience, Andropov then announced that the KGB [civilian intelligence] and the GRU [military intelligence] were for the first time to cooperate in a worldwide intelligence operation code-named RYaN: a newly devised acronym for *Raketno Yadernoye Napadenie*—Nuclear Missile Attack."

In London, Gordievsky and his fellow agents were put on round-the-clock Apocalypse watch, told to monitor the number of lights on at night in government offices and military installations, the movements of key personnel, and the meetings of committees. They were also ordered to "carry out a regular census of the number of cars... both in and out of normal working hours at all government buildings and military installations involved in preparations for nuclear

warfare, and to report immediately any deviations from the norm."
Cattle were counted, in the belief that large quantities of meat would
be frozen in advance of a nuclear attack. Moscow also told its London spies that "an important sign of British preparations for nuclear
war would probably be increased purchases of blood and a rise in the
price paid for it," and the agents were "ordered to report any change
in blood prices immediately." The KGB leadership in Moscow was
unaware that blood donors in Britain were unpaid volunteers.

The Kremlin had also long suspected that the West was run by
a secret cabal who, given their privileged status, would naturally
have been tipped off to a coming war. Gordievsky explained that the
"bizarre, conspiratorial image of the clerical and capitalist elements
in the establishment, which, it believed, dominated British society,
also led to exploring the possibility of obtaining advance warning of
a holocaust from church leaders and bankers."

Operation RYaN would be the largest and most comprehensive peacetime intelligence-gathering operation in Soviet history.
It was also relentlessly dopey. Had Brezhnev been capable of having a coherent and frank discussion with Ronald Reagan, as Gorbachev would ultimately be able to do, he would have learned that
the American president thought the reverse was true: that the Soviets
were the ones seeking to develop a first-strike capability in order to
erase the United States.

In fairness, it should also be noted that the first-term Reagan,
blithely playing the role of gunslinger, might not have tolerated such
a discussion. Brezhnev, then Andropov, and then Chernenko all
wrote Reagan, offering arms control proposals and other measures
to build better relations between the two countries, but, as historian
Jason Saltoun-Ebin wrote, "Reagan just was not interested. Between
1981 and 1985 . . . he was interested in achieving his 'strength through
peace' agenda. Plus, his hard-line anti-communism kept him from
trusting these hard-line communists."

The Cold War had become a block of ice. Carter and Brezhnev

had met in Vienna in June 1979; it would turn out to be the last face-to-face sitdown between the leaders of the superpowers for another six years. In the absence of communication, both sides erred wildly on the side of paranoia. Gordievsky described a kooky Catch-22 world at the Kremlin. "[Operation] RYaN created a vicious circulation of intelligence collection and assessment," he wrote. "Residencies were required to report alarming information even if they themselves were skeptical of it. The Center was duly alarmed by what they reported and demanded more."

Top U.S. Soviet analyst Bob Gates later acknowledged, "We did not then grasp the growing desperation of the men in the Kremlin... how pedestrian, isolated, and self-absorbed they were; how paranoid, fearful they were."

CHAPTER 39

PEAK PARANOIA

On February 25, 1983, the KGB instructed its spies in the United States to begin planning "active measures" to thwart Ronald Reagan's reelection. According to Gordievsky, the Kremlin had decided that "any other Presidential candidate, whether Republican or Democrat, would be preferable to Reagan." The KGB instructed residencies to acquire contacts in the staffs of all possible presidential candidates and in both party headquarters. "The main purpose of these contacts," wrote Gordievsky, "was to gather as much information as possible to discredit Reagan during the campaign and to open up new channels for dissemination." In addition, Soviet spies stationed across the globe were ordered to popularize the slogan "Reagan means war!"

Gordievsky indicated the "active measures" fell into several topical categories. It was suggested to attack Reagan for his:

1. militarist adventurism . . .
2. personal responsibility for accelerating the arms race . . .
3. support for repressive regimes around the world . . .
4. administration's attempts to crush national liberation movements . . .
5. responsibility for tension with his NATO allies . . .
6. alleged discrimination against ethnic minorities . . .
7. administration's corruption . . .
8. subservience to the military-industrial complex.

Two weeks later, Reagan provided the KGB with another reason to sink his reelection. During a speech to the National Association of Evangelicals in Orlando, he first used the phrase "evil empire" to describe the USSR—wording exquisitely suited for the Moral Majority in front of him, or a movie hero president, but less so for improving relations during the Cold War:

> I urge you to beware of declaring yourselves above it all and label both sides equally at fault, to ignore the facts of history and the aggressive impulses of an evil empire, to simply call the arms race a giant misunderstanding and thereby remove yourself from the struggle between right and wrong and good and evil.

The speechwriter who authored the words admitted he had channeled George Lucas's Nazi-tinged *Star Wars* series, in which Darth Vader's head is buried inside a stylistic conflation of a feudal samurai *kabuto* with a German army "coal scuttle" *Stahlhelm* and the foot soldiers of the evil Empire are known as "stormtroopers," the name of the Führer's brownshirted bullyboy vigilantes.

"I heartily welcome the reaction that it was likened to *Star Wars*," said Tony Dolan. "Some even called it the Darth Vader speech. But why was the movie *Star Wars* so popular? Because it was a fantasy which did what Bruno Bettelheim says fantasy performs: it is a healthy expression of reality. Kids know there is evil in the world, and no matter how many nice words we use to buffer ourselves from that insight, the reality is that there is evil, and that it has to be fought against."

But a Fantasyland version of an all-evil Soviet empire was not a healthy expression of reality. In fact, the country was impossible to stereotype in any coherent way. The USSR had a population of 270 million, split into a hundred distinct national ethnicities, spread across the entire expanse of the world's largest continent. Commenting on

Dolan's "evil empire" speech, a predecessor, Carter speechwriter Hendrik Hertzberg, judged the notion harmful. "If the Russians are infinitely evil and we are infinitely good," Hertzberg said, "then the logical first step is a nuclear first strike. Words like that frighten the American public and antagonize the Soviets. What good is that?"

Wrote Roger Morris, "The postwar Soviet leadership were creatures of their preconceptions and preoccupations, and of their odious politics, as much as any ruling class in history. Yet to relegate them to caricature, to ignore the touchstones of their lives, was ultimate folly. What American specialists saw were not fearful, compromised 'human beings like ourselves,' but monstrous, implacable, mythically evil enemies in ill-fitting suits, to be opposed at all costs, with the end—the 'defeat' of Russia one way or another—justifying the means."

On March 23, 1983, Reagan used a nationally televised address to announce the development of the Strategic Defense Initiative— soon to be scornfully branded as the "Star Wars program" by Senator Ted Kennedy in yet another name check of Lucas's sci-fi blockbuster. This proposed defense system would incinerate inbound missiles by using lasers, particle beams, and other "directed energy" weapons that would be deployed on orbiting space platforms. Reagan explained that such a weapon had a virtue unlike any other by being strictly for protection, not warmaking:

> What if free people could live secure in the knowledge that their security did not rest upon the threat of instant U.S. retaliation to deter a Soviet attack.... Wouldn't it be better to save lives than avenge them?

One of the chief authors of the "space shield" concept was H-bomb inventor Dr. Edward Teller. "Dr. Teller," Reagan biographer Edmund Morris wrote, "represented all that the President admired in a scientist, being distinguished, individualistic, sonorously spoken, and short on academic circumspection. For half an hour, Teller deployed X-ray lasers all over the Oval Office, reducing hundreds of incoming Soviet missiles to radioactive chaff, while Reagan, gazing up ecstatically, saw a crystal shield covering the Last Best Hope of Man."

Former defense secretary James Schlesinger ridiculed the "Star Wars" defensive shield as an "astrodome" defense. Richard DeLauer, the Pentagon's chief scientist, called it "nonsense."

But what was being missed at the time, and what would prove critical in building a rapport with Gorbachev, was that Reagan saw SDI *as a way to get rid of all nuclear weapons*. If there was a way to literally zap missiles out of the sky, then missiles would become obsolete. Further, Reagan was prepared to share the technology, once developed, with everyone—including the Soviets. Gorbachev, like many, would judge Reagan's credulous attachment to space lasers a bit ridiculous, but he found common ground with the president over the notion of trying to achieve a nuclear-free world.

Predictably, Reagan had virtually no support for "nuclear abolition" within the military-industrial complex. General John Vessey, chairman of the Joint Chiefs of Staff, said, "We're not going to wish away nuclear power, fusion or fission, whether for weapons or for heat." Secretary of State George Shultz, who had replaced Haig and would ultimately back Reagan's abolitionist impulses, was at first an opponent of SDI because it freaked out America's NATO allies, who viewed the space shield as a way for the United States to withdraw from its obligation to defend Europe from Soviet attack. When Shultz was telling his chief arms strategist, Richard Burt, that the president had an idea of a world without nuclear weapons, Burt shot back, "He can't have a world without nuclear weapons! Doesn't he understand the realities?"

As *New Yorker* writer John Newhouse reported, the Kremlin's paranoid clan of elders who preceded Gorbachev were not so dismissive: "Only in Moscow was SDI seen then as deadly serious. Only the Soviets could have persuaded themselves of America's ineffable gift for squaring the circle technologically.... The Soviets may have felt as if they were condemned to an endless and exhausting game of catch-up with a power that held higher cards."

———

On September 1, 1983, near the Sea of Japan, two air-to-air missiles fired by a Soviet Su-15 interceptor shot down a Korean Air Lines 747 en route to Seoul from Anchorage, Alaska. The commercial airliner had inadvertently strayed into Russian airspace. All 269 passengers were killed, including Georgia congressman Larry McDonald.

The Soviet fighter pilot did not know what kind of jet he was attacking, which violated Soviet Air Force rules of engagement requiring visual identification of the intruder before shooting it down. In the immediate aftermath, however, some in the Soviet chain of command suspected that the plane was not a 747, but a U.S. RC-135 intelligence-gathering aircraft. This was a genuinely held assessment, not simply Soviet propaganda, and it had the effect of intensifying the crisis.

In the *New York Times*, Max Fisher delineated how the Soviets and the Americans misread each other: "In an atmosphere of distrust, technical and bureaucratic snafus drove each to suspect the other of deception.... Moscow received contradictory reports as to whether its pilots had shot down an airliner or a spy plane, and Soviet leaders were biased toward trusting their own. So when they declared a legal interception of an American military incursion, American leaders, who knew this to be false, assumed the Soviet leaders were lying.... Washington made a mirror mistake, suggesting such misreadings were not possible."

On September 2, 1983, Reagan went on national television to denounce the Soviets for what he called the "Korean airline massacre." He went on to describe the incident as an "act of barbarism, born of a society which wantonly disregards individual rights and the value of human life." The rhetoric was overwrought, especially since the CIA, in that morning's presidential briefing document, had concluded that the incident was likely an error. Reagan had apparently missed this important piece of information.

Wrote Fisher, "Soviet leaders had not considered this. They assumed Reagan was lying about their intentions. Some concluded he had somehow lured the Soviet Union into downing the aircraft as cover for a massive pre-emptive attack, which they feared would come at any minute. Each read the other's blundering and dissembling as intentional, deepening suspicions among hardliners that the other side was laying the groundwork for war."

Looking back on the incident for his memoir, Reagan wrote, "The KAL incident demonstrated how close the world had come to the nuclear precipice and how much we needed nuclear arms control."

———

Less than a month later, on September 26, 1983, a siren wailed just after midnight in a Moscow bunker housing an early warning satellite monitoring station. The alert indicated a missile had been fired by the United States and was heading for the Soviet Union. Lieutenant Colonel Stanislav Petrov leapt off his chair and froze. He later explained, "All I had to do was to reach for the phone, to raise the direct line to our top commanders, but I couldn't move. I felt like I was sitting on a hot frying pan."

Petrov knew that if he made the call to senior military officials, he could be starting all-out thermonuclear war. Instead, he gambled on a hunch. The satellite system was new and had been prone to error. He was only looking at *one missile*. He decided that this was a system malfunction of some kind. Minutes passed. The attack didn't expand, and ground radar didn't corroborate the existence of a U.S. ICBM.

More sirens followed, indicating four more missiles were on the way. The size of the attack still seemed too small. Petrov was sure that the United States wouldn't start World War III this way. It wasn't logical. He said to himself, "Idiots who would start such war with only five missiles don't exist."

It turned out that the Soviet satellites had picked up sunlight reflecting off high-altitude clouds and read them as missiles. Bruce Blair, an expert on Cold War nuclear strategies, provided this perspective: "I think that this is the closest our country has come to accidental nuclear war.... The situation had deteriorated to the point where the Soviet Union as a system—not just the Kremlin, not just Soviet leader Yuri Andropov, not just the KGB—but as a system, was geared to expect an attack and to retaliate very quickly to it. It was on hair-trigger alert. It was very nervous and prone to mistakes and accidents."

Because World War III did not erupt during the Cold War, it became common wisdom that nuclear deterrence—and, more specifically, the idea of mutually assured destruction—had proven to be a successful innovation in human relations. Since starting a nuclear conflict was self-defeating, the logic of doom had worked to cool the animal spirits of even the most cold-blooded rulers. However, there will likely never be a full accounting of how many times members of the U.S. and Soviet armed forces—plus those from other nuclear states—either narrowly prevented or nearly caused Armageddon. Was the world on the razor's edge of extinction a hundred times? A thousand times? More? A valid and less than comforting argument can also be made that the reason we didn't blow ourselves up during the Cold War was a combination of sheer luck and an unknown number of sensible people who ably shepherded weapons of irrevocable damnation. In reality, our military doctrine was an interplay of MAD and Russian roulette.

On May 6, 1992, before a receptive audience of ten thousand in Fulton, Missouri, where Winston Churchill formally kicked off the Cold War in 1946, the last leader of the USSR unofficially declared its end. He didn't think anyone should gloat. "We should under no circumstance," said Mikhail Gorbachev, "make the intellectual and, consequently, the political error of interpreting victory in the Cold War narrowly as a victory for oneself, one's own way of life, one's own values and merits. . . . It was a shattering of the vicious circle into which we had driven ourselves. This was altogether a victory for common sense, reason, a victory for democracy, a victory for common human values."

———

Andropov disappeared from public view around the time of the KAL incident. But, Gordievsky noted, "from his sickbed he issued on September 28 [1983], a denunciation of American policy couched in apocalyptic language unprecedented since the depths of the Cold War. The United States, he said, was a 'country where outrageous militarized psychosis is being imposed.' . . . Andropov spent the last five months of his life after the shootdown as a morbidly suspicious invalid, brooding over the possible approach of a nuclear Armageddon."

On November 7, the North Atlantic Treaty Organization began its annual Able Archer military exercise, scheduled to last for five days. It involved forces throughout Western Europe, and was coordinated from Belgium, at Supreme Headquarters Allied Powers Europe (SHAPE). The purpose was to simulate an escalation of conflict with the Warsaw Pact, culminating in a simulated DEFCON 1 all-out nuclear exchange.

The 1983 exercise introduced a new, unique format of coded communication, radio silences, and, for the first time, the participation of heads of government. This increase in realism—in concert with the anticipated arrival of new intermediate-range nuclear missiles in West Germany—further unnerved an already frazzled Soviet political and military leadership, who suspected Able Archer 83 was a ruse to obscure preparations for a nuclear first strike. In response, the Soviets readied their nuclear forces and placed air units in East Germany and Poland on alert.

"Paranoia in the Center reached its peak during the NATO command-post exercise Able Archer 83," Gordievsky wrote. "Soviet contingency plans for a surprise attack against the West envisaged using training exercises as cover for a real offensive. The Center was haunted by the fear that Western plans for a surprise attack on the Soviet Union might be the mirror image of its own.... Among the members of the Politburo who followed the crisis generated by Soviet paranoia and American rhetoric was its rising star Mikhail Gorbachev. He cannot have failed to draw the conclusion that East-West détente was an urgent priority."

Two weeks after the conclusion of the Able Archer exercises, the Reagan administration began the planned delivery of 572 intermediate-range nuclear missiles to Western Europe. The British received the ground-launched Tomahawk cruise missile, a pilotless, subsonic weapon that had a range of 1,500 miles, sufficient to reach all likely targets in Eastern Europe. The West Germans were supplied with the Pershing II, a two-stage, mobile, supersonic ballistic missile with a range of about 1,130 miles, making it capable of attacking Russian targets. The Reagan administration argued that the deployment was designed to counter the existing 360 Soviet SS-20 missiles, two-thirds of which could hit NATO allies in Europe. In response to the start of the deployment, the Soviet delegation walked out of the Geneva negotiations on intermediate nuclear forces.

"Neither the Pershing II nor the cruise missiles are essential to the defense of West Germany or other European NATO countries," said the Center for Defense Information, which was founded in 1971 by a group of retired U.S. military officers. "Their introduction is purely political and unneeded militarily."

———

As all this was happening, Reagan watched the film *War Games*. This Cold War sci-fi thriller followed a hacker, played by Matthew Broderick, who unwittingly accesses a U.S. military supercomputer and prompts the machine to nearly launch an all-out nuclear attack on the Soviet Union.

A few days later, in the Oval Office, Reagan was discussing nuclear forces with his advisors, members of Congress, and the Joint Chiefs of Staff. At one point, he put down his index cards and asked if anyone else had seen *War Games*. No one had, so he described the plot in detail.

"Don't tell the ending," one of the lawmakers cautioned.

After finishing his synopsis, Reagan turned to General Vessey, chairman of the Joint Chiefs, and asked, "Could something like this really happen?"

General Vessey said he would look into it.

One week later, the general returned to the White House with his answer.

"Mr. President," he said, "the problem is much worse than you think."

On Sunday October 30, 1983, *Parade* magazine's ten million readers were presented with a chilling warning written by the country's best-known scientist. On a cover picturing a gray, desolate Earth dotted with snow, there was this text:

> Would nuclear war be the end of the world? In a major "exchange," more than a billion people would be instantly killed. But the long-term consequences could be much worse.

The author was Carl Sagan. As Matthew R. Francis wrote in *Smithsonian*, "He was a charismatic spokesperson for science, particularly the exploration of the solar system by robotic probes. He hosted and co-wrote the PBS television series *Cosmos*, which became the most-watched science program in history and made him a household name."

Inside the magazine, Sagan's article introduced the general public to a new term: *nuclear winter*. Sagan made the argument that science had failed to fully grasp the toxifying effects to the planet of a nuclear war. According to the article, after all the bombs were detonated, the atmosphere would be choked by prolonged dust and smoke. Due to blocked sunlight, a precipitous drop in Earth's temperatures would occur, leading to widespread crop failure and global famine.

———

In November, Reagan received an advance screening of ABC's television movie *The Day After*, which depicted a nuclear attack on Lawrence, Kansas, and showed the anticipated large-scale suffering from radioactive fallout. Reagan wrote in his diary that the movie "was very effective & left me greatly depressed." He expected it would embolden the nuclear freeze movement.

On November 18, 1983, the Friday before the Sunday ABC broadcast, the *Washington Post* reported that the White House was "launching an all-out effort to reemphasize President Reagan's commitment to arms control...starting with an ABC interview of Secretary of State George P. Shultz immediately after the film. Other Administration members were expected to write newspaper articles and 'make speeches' emphasizing Reagan's efforts to control nuclear weapons."

White House communications director David Gergen was quoted saying that the film was one of "unrelenting despair...very powerful, very emotional. It will leave many people feeling a sense of hopelessness....The film poses an important question: what will happen in a nuclear war, which all agree would be horrible. But the film does not address an even more important question: how do you prevent such a catastrophe?"

The Day After would be seen by one hundred million Americans, making it the most-watched TV film of all time.

"Throughout much of the period," Alex Wellerstein wrote in *Harper's*, "Americans felt that the risk of nuclear war was, as political psychologists would say, salient....Nuclear war could happen at any moment and many felt that it would happen potentially in their lifetime. In 1983, some 24 percent of Americans identified, without being prompted, nuclear war as the most important problem facing the country—more important than the economy, unemployment, crime or morality." In addition, 50 percent of Americans polled thought they would die in a nuclear war.

——

On January 12, 1984, the almost eighty-year-old children's book author Theodore Seuss Geisel, better known as Dr. Seuss, published—as his forty-fourth book—an antinuclear Cold War parable about the arms race in which the warring parties are battling over the best way to butter bread. The Yooks eat their bread with the butter side up. The Zooks eat their bread with the butter side down. In *The Butter Battle Book*, an arms race leads to mutually assured destruction. It starts when a Zook uses a slingshot against the Yooks' best weapon, a Snick-Berry Switch ("a many pronged whip").

1. In response, the Yooks develop a Triple-Sling Jigger (a machine with three slingshots).
2. The Zooks go the Yooks one better by building a Jigger-Rock Snatchem (a machine with three nets to fling the rocks fired by the Triple-Sling Jigger back to the other side).
3. The Yooks create a Kick-A-Poo Kid (loaded with "powerful Poo-A-Doo powder...and dried-fried clam chowder").
4. The Zooks counter with the Eight-Nozzled Elephant-Toted Boom Blitz (a machine that shoots "high-explosive sour cherry stone pits").
5. Next, the Yooks devise an Utterly Splutter (a large blue vehicle to sprinkle blue goo over the Zooks).
6. Copying their adversaries, the Zooks make their own Utterly Splutter.

7. Finally, each side possesses the Bitsy Big-Boy Boomeroo, but neither side has any defense against it.

The Butter Battle Book ends with Grandpa—the top Yook general—holding the pink hand-sized Bitsy Big-Boy Boomeroo and his grandson saying:

"Grandpa! Be careful! Oh, gee! Who's going to drop it? Will you... Or will he?"

"Be patient," Grandpa says, "We'll see. We will see..."

CHAPTER 40

NINE REASONS

Although the Cold War was in theory not an actual war but a political battle, investing in "guns" generally took precedence over investing in "butter." The cost of the U.S. intelligence community was five times that of the U.S. State Department, and the overall U.S. military budget was equal to the total spent by the countries with the six next largest defense budgets: the Soviet Union, China, Japan, France, Germany, and the United Kingdom. The weapons spending spree during the 1980s was so costly, the United States switched from being the world's greatest creditor to one of the leading debtors.

However, as the United States and the USSR built enormous nuclear stockpiles, nuclear war became unwinnable. At the same time, both nations remained lost in the security dilemma. They acted on the assumption of inevitable betrayal by the opponent, didn't believe in the possibility of cooperation, and continued to divert giant chunks of national wealth to enlarging and improving their nuclear capabilities. Yet more was only more. No additional strategic advantage was gained. In fact, larger stockpiles made each side feel even less secure. But if both sides could agree to disarm at the same time, the ultimate in cooperation, a war that might end life on the planet could be avoided and immense savings would result. *Cooperation had the best outcome.*

Expecting betrayal while maintaining self-interest prevailed between the United States and the Soviet Union until 1985, which was when change agent Mikhail Gorbachev took over at the Kremlin and the second-term version of Ronald Reagan made a 180-degree turn, determining that he wanted history to judge him most of all as a peacemaker.

Gorbachev took over as general secretary of the Soviet Union on March 11, 1985. Eight months later, he and Reagan held their first face-to-face summit in Geneva, on November 19 and 20, 1985. They would meet three more times in the next three years, in Reykjavik, Iceland (1986); Washington, D.C. (1987); and Moscow (1988).

Ending the state of paranoia required overcoming a paralysis of ignorance. Reagan and Gorbachev had the courage to trust each other against an onslaught of naysayers. This trust wasn't achieved instantly, but through a commitment to keep communicating, in spite of various and ongoing disagreements. The two men were frequent correspondents. Reagan enjoyed writing letters and was artful in the practice. In his autobiography, he spoke of the importance of writing privately—and regularly—to Gorbachev: "I realize those first letters marked the cautious beginning on both sides of what was to become the foundation of not only a better relationship between our countries, but a friendship between two men." This rapport was essential to winding down the Cold War.

Nine Reasons Why the Cold War Cooled Off

1: MIKHAIL GORBACHEV WAS A DECENT AND MORAL MAN: In his biography of Gorbachev, William Taubman wrote, "Gorbachev's decency showed in his family life. His wife, Raisa, was a woman of intellect and good taste.... Unlike too many politicians, Gorbachev loved and cherished his wife, and rare for a Soviet boss, he was a committed and involved father to his daughter, and grandfather to his two granddaughters." Russian scholar Dmitry Furman said, "Gorbachev is the only politician in Russian history who, having full power in his hands, voluntarily opted to limit it and even risk losing it, in the name of principled moral values."

2: NEW WORLD ORDER: One of Gorbachev's detractors called him "a genetic error of the system." He was more than that. He was a once-in-a-millennium kind of figure. Taubman suggested that Russia's autocratic history should have completely discouraged Gorbachev: "What possessed him to think he could overcome Russian political, economic, and social patterns dating back centuries in a few short years: Czarist authoritarianism morphing into Soviet totalitarianism, long stretches of near slavish obedience to authority punctuated by occasional bursts of bloody rebellion, minimal experience with civic activity, including compromise and consensus, no tradition of democratic self-organization, no real rule of law?" Gorbachev was the first Soviet leader from the generation that came of age after World War II and, as such, not consumed by the deep-seated fear of a unified Germany returning to power. He was also worldly enough to know that his discouraged workforce had no answer to the disruptive innovations bursting from America's Silicon Valley. Further, he adopted a liberal big-picture view that the fate of all nations had become inextricably tied together. "Global interdependence is such," said Gorbachev, "that all peoples are similar to climbers roped together on a mountainside. They either can climb together to the summit or fall together into the abyss." Finally, regarding defense spending, he also surmised, accurately, "Any striving for military superiority means chasing one's own tail."

3: FIRST LADY ALSO SEES THE BIG PICTURE: As the *New Yorker*'s John Newhouse wrote, "Mrs. Reagan wanted her husband remembered for having lowered the risk of nuclear war. Only in 1984 had she begun to show an interest in her husband's place in history. [Reagan] himself had been unconcerned with posterity's judgement or the demands of historiography. But Mrs. Reagan, once aroused, was determined."

4: MAGGIE GOT IT RIGHT: In December 1984, when Gorbachev met in London with British prime minister Margaret Thatcher, he was a rising star in the Politburo, but not yet in charge.

After the meeting, Thatcher told the BBC, "I am cautiously optimistic. I like Mr. Gorbachev. We can do business together." Thatcher also said she and Gorbachev had agreed that "we should both do everything we can to see that war never starts again, and therefore we go into the disarmament talks determined to make them succeed." In the very same week she met with Gorbachev, Thatcher traveled to Camp David to debrief Reagan on her positive assessment of the USSR's new face. As Bill Keller wrote in the *New York Times*, Thatcher "was the first important Western leader to suggest that Gorbachev sincerely wanted to fix his miserable country, and that to do it would entail halting the exorbitant arms race with the West.... Thatcher's endorsement won Gorbachev important credibility in Washington and other western capitals."

5: GORBACHEV COULD HANDLE THE TRUTH: The Soviet Union's economy had become overly dependent on the extraction and export of oil and gas and, as a result, hostage to the highly unpredictable and uncontrollable conditions of the oil and gas markets. In 1985, the Saudi Arabians announced plans to increase oil production. Within months, the world price of oil plummeted to $30 per barrel. Without hard-currency oil revenue, the Soviets would be unable to (1) pay for imports of grain; (2) service foreign debt; and (3) keep up in the arms race. Gorbachev told a colleague, "The United States has an interest in keeping the negotiations machine running idle, while the arms race overburdens our economy. That is why we need a breakthrough, we need the process to start moving." That Gorbachev was prepared to acknowledge the failings of the Soviet economy gave Reagan hope that he was dealing with a Soviet leader who was capable of admitting fault and speaking with candor. Reagan later wrote to a friend, "[Gorbachev] is practical and knows his economy is a basket case. I think our job is to show him he and they will be better off if we make some practical agreements, without attempting to convert him to our way of thinking."

6: REAGAN IGNORED THE PEANUT GALLERY: Many of the president's fellow Republicans, inside and outside the administration, judged his support of radical arms control foolish and insisted Gorbachev was a phony. As planning began for the 1985 Geneva summit, Secretary of Defense Caspar Weinberger, CIA director Bill Casey, and Deputy Chief of Staff Edwin Meese were, said one American diplomat, "mau-mauing the enterprise." Congressman and future Speaker Newt Gingrich declared that Reagan's Geneva meeting with Gorbachev was "the most dangerous summit for the West since Adolf Hitler met with Neville Chamberlain in 1938 in Munich." Former secretary of state Henry Kissinger, with typical pessimistic pedantry, offered ill-informed logic, proposing that because Gorbachev's mentor in the Politburo was Yuri Andropov, who had run the often murderous KGB, Gorbachev therefore had to have demonstrated an appetite for cruelty and violence in order to have been endorsed by Andropov. What Kissinger didn't know is that Andropov supported Gorbachev because he was one of the few senior Communist Party officials who had resisted a career of bribery and corruption. When Kissinger's former boss, Richard Nixon, wouldn't stop slamming Reagan's collegial treatment of Gorbachev, the ex-president was invited to the White House and politely asked to cut the shit. Nixon refused. Instead, he told Reagan that a deal with the Soviets would not help him politically. Nixon based this judgment on polls that had shown military action helps a president far more than diplomacy does. He said to Reagan, "Many people felt my popularity had gone up because of my trip to China. In fact, it had improved only slightly. What really sent it up was the bombing and mining of Haiphong Harbor."

7: UNRAVELING THE SECURITY DILEMMA: Even though no U.S. president ever contemplated a preemptive nuclear war on the Soviet Union and no Soviet leader ever thought of doing the same against the United States, leadership in the White House and the Kremlin habitually suspected that their rival superpower was constantly plotting a devastating surprise attack. When Gorbachev and Reagan met in Geneva, and Reagan spoke of getting rid of all nuclear weapons and Gorbachev made clear that he thought that was a fine idea, the two men concluded by agreeing on a joint statement that did not announce any far-reaching accords, but was nonetheless a big deal because it contained this language: "A nuclear war," Gorbachev and Reagan told the world, "cannot be won and must never be fought." Gorbachev aide Anatoly Chernyaev explained at the time why such a concession from Reagan mattered so much: "[Gorbachev] is dedicated to ending the arms race...He is [now] taking the risk because, as he understands it, it is no risk at all, because nobody would attack us even if we disarmed completely. And in order to get the country on solid ground, we have to relieve it of the burden of the arms race, which is a drain on more than just the economy." In a classic "security dilemma" scenario, no nation ever takes the first step to disarm for fear that its opponent will continue to add weaponry and ultimately gain oppressive superiority. But, as Gorbachev and Reagan understood like few of their predecessors, having thirty thousand active nuclear warheads didn't make you any safer than having three thousand. Massive shared cuts were a logical first step.

8: NECESSARY WINGMAN: Given that a large portion of American conservatives were critical of Reagan's diplomatic efforts with Gorbachev, it was important for Reagan to have at least one credible, high-level conservative supporter. After the Geneva summit, he found one in Secretary of State George Shultz, an elder statesman whose wide-ranging list of credentials included chapters as a U.S. Marine, MIT-educated economist, the dean of the University of Chicago School of Business, and executive vice president of Bechtel. Shultz was also one of only two men in U.S. history to have held four different cabinet positions (Labor, Office of Management and Budget, Treasury, and State). Shultz shared Reagan's favorable opinion of Gorbachev, saying, "In Gorbachev we have an entirely different kind of leader in the Soviet Union than we have experienced before." The *New Yorker*'s Newhouse wrote, "The [Geneva] summit boosted George Shultz's stock to an all-time high, and [Defense Secretary Caspar] Weinberger's appeared to have been a heavy loser. He hadn't gone to Geneva, but instead had tried to sabotage the meeting by leaking a letter that he had sent to the White House—a letter that urged Reagan to avoid any of the steps that might lead to negotiation."

9: FELLOW ABOLITIONISTS: On January 15, 1986, two months after the Geneva summit, Gorbachev made a speech in which he publicly unveiled a sweeping proposal to eliminate all of the world's nuclear weapons by the year 2000. He did this *without telling the White House in advance.* The details appeared through TASS, the Soviet news service. Soviet ambassador Anatoly Dobrynin later admitted, "It would not be honest to deny that Gorbachev's proclamation carried elements of propaganda." Virtually the entire Reagan administration wanted it rejected outright. Said an American diplomat, "Gorbachev soured the atmosphere with the January 15th speech and then a procession of initiatives, mostly aimed at the gallery. Reagan was the only exception. His comment was, 'Why did it take so long?'"

CHAPTER 41

TEEN PILOT

On May 28, 1987, Mathias Rust, an eighteen-year-old German pilot, took off in a single-engine Cessna Skyhawk 172 from Malmi Airport in Helsinki, Finland. It was 12:21 p.m. The four-seat airplane, which Rust had signed out from his Hamburg flying club, was equipped with four auxiliary fuel tanks. His luggage included a motorcycle crash helmet.

He had filed a flight plan for Stockholm, Sweden. About thirty minutes into the flight, near the Finnish town of Nummela, Rust made a dramatic course alteration, from west to east, and began heading across the Gulf of Finland, passing through restricted Finnish airspace. Controllers attempted to alert him, but could not make contact, and Rust's plane disappeared from the radar screen.

At about 1:15 p.m., a Finnish helicopter pilot radioed that he saw an oil slick and debris in the waters where Rust's plane had last been detected. A search-and-rescue operation was activated. Rust was still airborne, however. Later, Finland would investigate why several planes, including Rust's, had vanished from radar in the same spot over the Gulf of Finland.

Rust turned to a heading of 117 degrees, flying in a southeasterly direction. Over the Soviet Republic of Estonia, he climbed to twenty-five hundred feet, a standard altitude for a cross-country flight. As the plane glided on a straight and level path, he put on the motorcycle helmet.

All foreign aircraft flying into the Soviet Union were required to get prior approval. Rust had not done so. The Soviets noticed the intruder. Three missile units were put on alert and two Soviet fighter-interceptors were scrambled to investigate Rust's plane. One of the pilots, looking through a hole in the clouds, reported seeing what he suspected was a Yak-12, a single-engine Soviet sports airplane, which looks similar to a Cessna. No further action was taken by the local Soviet command.

About two hours into his flight, as Rust reached a new sector of the Soviet air defense system, he saw a black shadow blaze across the sky. Seconds later, a MiG-23 materialized out of the nearby clouds.

"It was coming at me very fast, and dead-on," Rust said later. "And it went whoosh!—right over me.... I remember how my heart felt, beating very fast. This is exactly the moment when you start to ask yourself: is this when they shoot you down?"

The MiG-23 was ten times the size of the Cessna, but it was designed to fly at twice the speed of sound, about 1,500 miles per hour. It was definitely *not* meant to track a single-engine recreational plane with a cruising speed of 140 mph. "The swing-wing fighter had to be put into full landing configuration," Tom LeCompte wrote in *Air & Space* magazine, "gear and flaps extended, wings swung outward—in order to slow it enough to fly alongside the Cessna. Its nose rode high as it hovered at the edge of a stall."

The Soviet fighter pilot tried to reach Rust on the radio, but since he was using a high-frequency military channel, Rust couldn't hear him. After the pilots exchanged glances, the MiG rocketed away. The command at the local Soviet sector did not inform senior leadership in Moscow about the Cessna.

Rust's joyride was taking place only four years after a Soviet fighter had mistakenly shot down a Korean passenger jet. That humiliating error had spooked the entire Soviet Air Force into behaving with an abundance of caution. Wrote LeCompte, "Strict orders were given that no hostile action should be taken against civilian aircraft unless orders originated at the very highest levels of the Soviet military."

As it happened, the day Rust had chosen for this unannounced flight was the same day that Soviet defense minister Sergei Sokolov and other top commanders were in East Berlin with Mikhail Gorbachev at a secret Warsaw Pact meeting, where Gorbachev was promising the Iron Curtain countries that the USSR would never invade them again.

At 3 p.m. local time, Rust entered a Soviet Air Force training zone, where about a dozen military aircraft were flying. They had performance characteristics and a radar signature similar to the Cessna's. The Soviet trainees were practicing takeoffs and landings.

These pilots were supposed to reset their transponder codes at a designated time. Rust's plane didn't do this. But thinking Rust was a student who simply forgot, a commander at the local Soviet radar station ordered an operator to switch the Cessna from a designation of "hostile" to "friendly." The commander said, "Otherwise we might shoot some of our own."

At 4 p.m., about three hours into the flight and two hundred miles west of Moscow, the Cessna became visible on a new set of radar screens. Two more Soviet fighters were scrambled. Commanders aborted the mission because of the danger presented by low-lying clouds. No visual contact was made.

Near the town of Torzhok, on the Tvertsa River, Rust's airplane crossed into the area of another air defense technician, but he assumed the signal was from one of two helicopters that had been performing search-and-rescue missions nearby.

Rust headed into Moscow's so-called Ring of Steel, where anti-aircraft missiles were set at distances of forty-five nautical miles, then twenty-five, then ten. They were built to knock down U.S. bombers, not a puttering low-altitude Cessna. Wrote LeCompte, "Soviet investigators would later tell Rust, radar controllers realized something was terribly wrong, but it was too late for them to act."

At 6 p.m., local time, about five hours and almost six hundred miles into his flight, Rust reached Moscow, where all overflights by civilian and military aircraft were prohibited. He removed his helmet and looked for a place to land. He'd later explain, "At first, I thought maybe I should land inside the Kremlin wall, but then I realized that although there was plenty of space, I wasn't sure what the KGB would do with me. If I landed inside the wall, only a few people would see me, and they could just take me away and deny the whole thing. But if I landed in the square, plenty of people would see me, and the KGB couldn't just arrest me and lie about it."

Rust saw a wide bridge crossing the Moscow River into Red Square. But landing on it was going to be tricky. There were overhead wires at both ends and in the middle. Normally, the entire bridge would have been wrapped in wires, but that morning a public works crew had removed the majority of them for maintenance. Rust thought he could fly over the first set of wires and quickly land, so he could taxi under the other wires.

On this early Thursday evening in Moscow, the Cessna Skyhawk 172 made a steep dive and flared for a landing as soon it passed over the first set of wires. A Volga automobile was right in front of Rust on the bridge. "I moved to the left to pass him," said Rust, "and as I did I looked and saw this old man with a look on his face like he could not believe what he was seeing. I just hoped he wouldn't panic and lose control of the car and hit me."

He parked the plane next to St. Basil's Cathedral in Red Square. He looked up at the Spasskaya Clock Tower and saw that the time was 6:43 p.m. As he got out of the plane, he expected to be immediately smothered by troops and KGB agents. Instead, a very curious crowd formed.

Rust didn't speak Russian, but he did speak English and, finding an English-speaking Russian among the onlookers, he told everyone why he had made the flight. He told them he had come from the West and wanted to speak with Gorbachev. Rust later said, "I wanted to deliver this peace message that would convince everybody in the West that [Gorbachev] had a new approach."

After the 1986 U.S.-USSR summit in Reykjavik had failed to produce a comprehensive arms reduction deal, Rust had envisioned his flight being an "imaginary bridge" between the two men. Rust explained, "How would Reagan continue to say it was the 'Empire of Evil' if me, in a small aircraft, can go straight there and be unharmed?"

A woman gave Rust a piece of bread as a sign of friendship. After an hour, there was a commotion at the fringe of the crowd. KGB agents were interviewing people and confiscating cameras and notebooks. Two truckloads of soldiers arrived and began to disperse the crowd. They started to put up barriers around the airplane. A black sedan pulled up, three men introduced themselves to Rust, and, after a few questions, they asked him to get in the car.

———

Pravda suggested that Rust was part of a plot, a patsy who was supposed to be shot down and thereby create an international incident to remind the world again of KAL Flight 007. Gorbachev exploited the embarrassing episode to dismiss hundreds of senior military officials, many of whom had been opposing his radical reform efforts. Those fired included Defense Minister Sokolov, and the commander in chief of the Soviet Air Defense Forces, former World War II fighter ace Alexander Koldunov. "It was the biggest turnover in the Soviet military command since Stalin's bloody purges of the 1930s," wrote LeCompte.

Rust was sentenced to four years in prison, but given special privileges, allowed to work in a garden and receive visits from his parents every two months. The USSR released him after fourteen months, in what the Kremlin described as a "goodwill gesture."

CHAPTER 42

BASKET THREE

On August 1, 1975, President Gerald Ford signed the Helsinki Accords at the conclusion of the first Conference on Security and Co-operation in Europe, held in Helsinki. In addition to the United States, Canada, and the Soviet Union, the signees included the rest of Europe, except Albania. The primary purpose of the accords was to reduce tension between the Soviet and Western blocs. Not having the power of clairvoyance, or the technology of time travel, Ford had to eat a lot of shit before a consensus emerged that the accords were a rather momentous diplomatic achievement immensely favorable to the West.

In 1975, as soon as the ink was dry, Ford was pummeled. None of his critics were focusing on "Basket three" of the Helsinki agreement: human rights. Instead, "Basket one" was highlighted. This codified the post–World War II status quo in Europe: All borders were understood to be inviolable, and not to be altered by force. Basket one was the favorite basket of the Soviets because it fully legitimized the Warsaw Pact arrangement. It was also used by certain elements on the American right, such as then presidential aspirant Ronald Reagan, to imply that the United States had surrendered the idea of using military force to free the captive peoples of Eastern Europe.

On July 25, 1975, Reagan dumped on the Helsinki pact before it was even finalized: "I am against it, and I think all Americans should be against it." (A few months later, he announced his plans to run against Ford in 1976.) Senator Henry Jackson—the strident hawk of the Democratic Party—savaged the agreement, saying that Eastern Europe had been given away in exchange for human rights promises that were "so imprecise and so hedged as to raise considerable doubt about whether they can and will be seriously implemented." The Polish-American Congress noted that "the Soviet Union rarely, if ever, honored treaties." A *New York Times* editorial remarked, "Nothing signed in Helsinki will in any way save courageous free thinkers in the Soviet empire from the prospect of incarceration in forced labor camps, or in insane asylums, or from being subjected to involuntary exile." Alexander Solzhenitsyn described the deal as "the funeral of Eastern Europe."

Ford remembered that his mail "showed 122 letters condemning the accords; only eleven letters approved of what I had done." His approval rating, as polled by Gallup, was 52 percent before Helsinki, and slid to 45 percent shortly after the signing.

Of course, since the very start of the Cold War, it had been American policy to *contain* the Soviet empire, not invade it. This meant, at least to the author of the policy, George Kennan, that the United States had decided to accept Stalin's conquest of Eastern Europe as a fait accompli once the Soviet dictator had left tanks, troops, and secret police units in place after the war. The CIA once had big plans of stirring popular revolts behind the Iron Curtain, but were overmatched by the suffocating suppression maintained by communist puppet regimes that effectively made prisoners of their entire populations. Eventually, American presidents feared that any attempt to liberate Eastern Europe through U.S. military action had the prospect of starting a nuclear World War III.

In short, Basket one looked backward and enshrined something that was obvious: The United States was not prepared to risk another global war to free the Warsaw Pact satellites. On the other hand, Basket three—in which Moscow formally capitulated to the centrality of human rights—contained the means to alter the present and the future. As it turned out, the Helsinki Accords were truly a Trojan horse.

The Soviet Union was fundamentally incapable of providing basic freedoms, but, with the Helsinki agreement, had committed to doing so—in front of the entire world. It made the issue of human rights far more black and white. Either people were allowed to speak their minds, or they weren't. After Helsinki, the Soviets paid a price for allowing only undercover spies out of the country. Change was letting dissident Andrei Sakharov do and say whatever he pleased, when he pleased. At the same time, muzzling or harassing him suddenly echoed as a clear violation of the liberalizing imperative of Basket three, which was now the business of all the signees. This kind of change was incredibly simple to understand and impossible for the Kremlin to permit. Something would have to give.

In *The National Interest*, under an article titled "Did the West Undo the East?," Stephen Sestanovich wrote, "By assuming the obligations contained in 'basket three' of the Act . . . the result was a steady sharpening of the international focus on human-rights practices, not only in the Soviet Union but in its Eastern European dependencies as well. Just how important Eastern Europe's growing anti-communist activism was became clear more than a decade later, when Gorbachev's reforms metastasized into the revolutions of 1989. . . . The creation of an international human rights test of political respectability had a fundamental impact: the Soviet empire became increasingly illegitimate."

On May 27, 1988, President Ronald Reagan spoke at Helsinki's Finlandia Hall, where the accords were signed. The moment was invested with a palpable gravitas. The largely Finnish audience all stood when Reagan entered the hall and listened without interruption. Reagan told them the thirteen-year-old Helsinki process had succeeded:

> For all the bleak winds that have swept the plains of justice
> since that signing day in 1975, the accords have taken root

in the conscience of humanity and grown in moral and diplomatic authority.... The front line in the competition of ideas that has played in Europe and America for more than seventy years has shifted east. Once it was the democracies that doubted their own view of freedom and doubted whether Utopian systems might not be better. Today, the doubt is on the other side.

Reagan said the accord's "new standards of conduct in human rights" would be carried forward to his next stop, a Moscow summit with Gorbachev. He received a standing ovation when he finished.

From 1946 to 1988, more or less the expanse of the Cold War, there were eight American presidents. Only three—Nixon, Ford, and Reagan—ever traveled to the Soviet Union. When Reagan did, in 1988, he and Gorbachev took a walk in Red Square. They stopped to talk with Muscovites. Gorbachev picked up a small boy in his arms and said, "Shake hands with Grandfather Reagan."

As the two leaders were walking back toward the Kremlin, a reporter asked Reagan, "Do you still think you're in an evil empire, Mr. President?" Without hesitation, Reagan said, "No. I was talking about another time and another era."

CHAPTER 43

STIRRED-UP MUSLIMS

On February 15, 1989, the last Soviet soldiers left Afghanistan. The USSR had lost fifteen thousand troops during the almost ten-year occupation. One million Afghans had died. Three million were maimed. Five million fled to refugee camps in neighboring countries. State Department official Peter Thomsen predicted Afghanistan could become unique as "a training ground and munitions dump for foreign terrorists and the world's largest poppy field." Warlords flush with ammunition turned on one another.

Afghanistan was the site of the final proxy battle of the Cold War. In 1977, the Carter administration had begun a covert CIA program to destabilize the Soviet Union by encouraging ethnic violence and radical Islam in Afghanistan, Soviet Georgia, Azerbaijan, and Chechnya. When the Soviets sent one hundred thousand troops into Afghanistan on December 27, 1979, the U.S. commitment to the anti-Soviet mujahideen surged.

"Our ultimate goal is the withdrawal of Soviet troops from Afghanistan," National Security Director Zbigniew Brzezinski said at the time. "Even if this is not attainable, we should make Soviet involvement as costly as possible...give the Soviets their Vietnam." In the next decade, arms and explosives were supplied to more than three hundred thousand fighters, and the battle against the Soviets became the biggest and most expensive operation in the CIA's history.

The middleman was the diabolical general running Pakistan, Muhammad Zia-ul-Haq, who funneled arms to the guerrillas under an extraordinary set of conditions: (1) The United States would deliver weapons to Pakistan's corrupt and rapacious Inter-Services Intelligence, or ISI, which would in turn pass them along to the Afghans, and (2) no Americans were to enter Afghanistan or have contact with guerrilla commanders.

Zia was yet another morally challenged leader the United States chose to tolerate during the Cold War. In 1977, the four-star general had seized power in a military coup, overthrowing elected prime minister Zulfikar Ali Bhutto. In a subsequent trial, Zia framed Bhutto and had him executed by hanging. General Zia also made martial law permanent; obtained an atomic bomb; established a hateful Islamic culture; introduced public floggings; and tortured thousands of dissidents and journalists. As a committed theocrat, Zia channeled the bulk of the CIA military aid to a subset of Afghan fighters who were Islamic extremists.

In 1984, as Afghanistan was indeed becoming a Soviet quagmire like Vietnam, Ronald Reagan attached the Saudi royal family to the funding of mujahideen insurgents. The Saudis were already tied to General Zia as the generous benefactors of new religious schools catering to two vulnerable populations: poorer Pakistanis and Afghan refugees. To ensure that these schools taught only the Saudi strain of Islam—puritanical Wahhabism—the kingdom also shipped hundreds of religious teachers to Pakistan.

The Saudis agreed to match America's military spending on a dollar-for-dollar basis. The U.S. aid to the Afghan rebels, which was $30 million a year when Reagan took office, would rise to $470 million in 1986, and be bumped to $630 million in 1987. Adding the Saudi matching dollars, the covert operation against the Soviets reached into the billions. At well-financed CIA-sponsored camps inside Pakistan, the mujahideen used sniper rifles and time-delayed bomb detonators while being trained in sabotage, ambush, and assault.

As the Pakistanis skimmed off a large portion of the U.S. money and arms, the country's largest city, Karachi, became a black market for the sale of military-grade weaponry. The Afghan rebels also pocketed a percentage of what finally came their way. Concerned that the CIA's billion-dollar covert operation was not actually arming enough of the insurgents fighting the Soviets, CIA agent John McMahon convened a meeting of the seven leaders of the Afghan rebel groups.

"We didn't try to tell the Afghan rebels how to fight the war," McMahon said. "But when we saw some of the Soviet successes against the mujahideen, I had become convinced that all the arms we had provided were not ending up in Afghan shooters' hands. . . . I told them I was concerned that they were siphoning off the arms and either caching them for a later day or, I said, 'God forbid you're selling them.' And they laughed. And they said, 'You're absolutely right! We're caching some arms. Because some day the United States will not be here, and we'll be left on our own to carry on our struggle.'"

In this period, the son of a Saudi construction magnate, Osama bin Laden, based himself in Pakistan, where he recruited foreign fighters and played the lead role in the birth of al-Qaeda, a militant multinational Sunni Islamist organization. Assessing the long-term effect of the religious radicalization, one secular Afghan warned an American colleague, saying, "For God's sake, you're financing your own assassins!"

In 1986, the fight between the Soviets and Afghan rebels became *Charlie Wilson's War*, a story made notorious by a 2007 Mike Nichols film, and so named because of Congressman Charlie Wilson's role in securing money for five hundred Stinger portable antiaircraft rockets for the Afghan forces. "All these things happened," Congressman Wilson said of the covert measures turned into legend, "and they were glorious, and they changed the world. Then we fucked up the endgame."

A particular Islamic extremist group best exploited the departure of the Soviets to seize power. They had recruited Afghan refugees from the thousands of Saudi-financed religious schools in Pakistan and organized them into military units. Because each of these recruits had been a *talib*, or religious student, they called their movement the Taliban. Many of its militants had learned the art of modern warfare at camps paid for by the CIA.

In 1998, the French newsmagazine *Le Nouvel Observateur* interviewed Zbigniew Brzezinski about the covert Afghan operation:

QUESTION: When the Soviets justified their intervention by asserting that they intended to fight against a secret involvement of the United States in Afghanistan, people didn't believe them. However, there was a basis of truth. You don't regret anything today?

BRZEZINSKI: Regret what? That secret operation was an excellent idea. It had the effect of drawing the Russians into the Afghan trap and you want me to regret it?...Indeed, for almost 10 years, Moscow had to carry on a war unsupportable by the government, a conflict that brought about the demoralization and finally the breakup of the Soviet empire.

QUESTION: And neither do you regret having...given arms and advice to future terrorists?

BRZEZINSKI: What is most important to the history of the world? The Taliban or the collapse of the Soviet empire? Some stirred-up Muslims or the liberation of Central Europe and the end of the Cold War?

CHAPTER 44

SOUND OF SILENCE

It is December 5, 1989, and you are a thirty-seven-year-old lieutenant colonel in the KGB who is shaking with fear and furious with disgust. East Germany is collapsing into madness and now you know they are coming for you—you and all the Russian overlords in Dresden. If that wasn't enough, there is this, too: Moscow is choosing silence. How easy for them.

After you, Vladimir Vladimirovich Putin, had successfully dispersed a swarm mobbing the KGB mansion by threatening to shoot them all, you then made a logical phone call to a Red Army tank unit and, incredibly, found out you were all alone. No help would be forthcoming. The Red Army officer told you, "We cannot do anything without orders from Moscow, and Moscow is silent." *Moscow is silent.* The words are being seared into your memory as you now prepare to pack and leave—to flee.

You will have to say *auf wiedersehen* to your slice of paradise, where your two daughters were born and raised in a world of splendid German order and comfort. Your wife, Lyudmila, will be crushed, too. She won't welcome a return to dreary, backward Leningrad. She admires how in Dresden all the people take pride in their neighborhoods. How everyone washes their windows at least once a week. You'll pack a case of Radeberger, the local beer, and you'll have to savor every bottle. There'll be no more weekly beer deliveries from your friends at the Ministry of State Security—the once impregnable

Stasi. They're getting ready to run, too. Lyudmila has told you about Stasi wives crying all day, every day. You've heard that some of the top Stasi officers have committed suicide.

You are amazed at how quickly it all went to shit.

When East Germany turned forty in October, you watched the Sozialistische Einheitspartei Deutschlands celebrating the anniversary in Berlin—one hundred thousand praising the Communist Party in a torchlight procession. But hooligans inspired by Western media were also in the streets, shouting Western claptrap like *We are the People.*

In Dresden, you witnessed a riot when ten thousand demonstrators rushed trains headed to West Germany. The police were being assaulted with paving stones. Then the West German chancellor came to Dresden and talked about restoring the *Vaterland* and everyone roared. It was the kind of Nazi rhetoric you thought your father's generation had buried forever in the Great Patriotic War.

All of a sudden, on November 9, people were dancing on the wall. An idiotic bureaucrat named Schabowski had a press conference on GDR TV and misinterpreted a new Politburo order. It made everyone think they could cross to West Berlin anytime they wanted. Everyone turned out to be half a million East Berliners and all at once. Confronted with these mobs, the border guards said fuck it. A month later, the party on the Kurfürstendamm is still going, like a long, continuous shout.

After all that, you and everyone else in the Dresden KGB mansion were ordered to start burning documents. You were burning so many documents that the furnace became clogged. The Stasi people were doing the same thing across the street. The constant black smoke from torched paper acted like a signal to journalists and activists. They had finally figured out where the spies lived and where all the secrets were kept and they were ready to break down the doors.

Which brings us to the events of the night of December 5, 1989, when a guard at the gate of the KGB compound comes rushing inside, and you go back out and confront the rabble, telling them, "Don't try to force your way into this property. My comrades are armed, and they are authorized to use their weapons in an emergency."

After you go inside, you then learn that the Red Army tanks will not be rolling like they did when Hungary erupted in 1956 or like Czechoslovakia in 1968. The great reformer Gorbachev has decided upon an ignominious and spineless retreat. The West has won without a fight.

You are deeply proud of your family's sacrifice for Mother Russia. Your grandmother was killed by the Nazis in 1941. Your father was badly wounded in 1942 while serving in the Red Army. Your brother Viktor died of diphtheria during the nine-hundred-day siege of Leningrad, when Hitler's forces aspired to kill every last city resident. You had wanted to join the KGB since you were a teenager. You watched movies of Soviet espionage heroes, where you learned that one man's effort could achieve what whole armies could not. Now, after sixteen years in your dream job, after discovering your dream socialist paradise, you wonder if you'll have to drive a taxi.

When you and your wife confront this new reality, Lyudmila will say, sadly and poignantly, "I have the horrible feeling that East Germany, our new home, will soon no longer exist." Shortly, towing a twenty-year-old German washing machine, you and Lyudmila will return to a country that has changed in ways you won't want to accept. Leningrad is to become St. Petersburg. The city named for the author of the Bolshevik Revolution will revert to honoring a czar. After Moscow's dominion over Eastern Europe vanishes, the fifteen republics of the Soviet Union will assume their independence. The guidepost of the world communist movement will be condemned to the dustbin of history. You, Vladimir Putin, will never forget the fright and humiliation of a December night in 1989. Nor will you ever again forget how a popular will, once united, brought a glorious empire to its knees.

ACKNOWLEDGMENTS

I remember the moment like it was yesterday.

It was a fast-fading spring afternoon. I was in Astoria, Queens, nearing a station of the elevated N line of New York's comprehensive subway system. I had just concluded a creative spitballing session with the internationally famous set designer George Tsypin—working at his studio on a sales pitch to Turkmenistan president Gurabanguly Berdimuhamedow for the opening ceremony of the 2017 Ashgabat Asian Indoor and Martial Arts Games (I'm not kidding). With the distinctive high-decibel squealing of subway trains attacking my ears, I checked my horribly uncool BlackBerry and saw a message from my book agent, Bob Mecoy, of Creative Book Services. This is what it said: "If you'd rather do something more fun than staring at your navel, I know an editor who's looking for a history of American paranoia from 1947 to last week. . . . Does that interest you?"

For a couple of reasons, this email was amazingly prescient. First, I would indeed soon be staring at my navel, because George and I didn't get the job in Ashgabat, which was just as well. Like Donald Trump, the leader of Turkmenistan's desert republic has a thing for autocracy, nepotism, and expensive self-edification. The fifth annual Asian and Indoor Martial Arts Games (featuring competition ranging from bowling to jiujitsu) would turn out to be a $7.3 billion justification for Mr. Berdimuhamedow's iron rule and an avenue for more unfettered corruption. Meanwhile, to pay for it, the country's citizens lost subsidies for water, gas, and electricity, followed by shortages of flour, cooking oil, and sugar.

Second, the date of Bob's email—March 1, 2016—also speaks to its timeliness. The editor expressing interest in the subject was Sean Desmond at Twelve, and I want to make crystal clear that, in retrospect, Mr. Desmond (who is also publisher at Twelve) was clearly clairvoyant. A return to the Cold War was about to become additionally resonant, though on March 1, 2016, the writing wasn't yet on the wall for most of us.

The dark anxiety of Cold War 2.0 had yet to descend. Hillary Clinton was the presumptive next president and Donald Trump was unapologetically using his short-staffed campaign to get the most amount of attention for the least amount of his own money. Only months later, and subsequent to Trump's shocking victory, did our national security establishment seriously wonder if the forty-fifth president of the United States was a wholly owned subsidiary of the Kremlin, and, in particular, beholden to the ex-communist spy who judges the collapse of the USSR as the greatest tragedy of the twentieth century.

However, what Sean did not foresee was the undisciplined tonnage I delivered as my first draft of this book, or Cold War Paranoia in three volumes. The timeline of draft number one began in medieval Russia, detoured into the Crimean War (1853–56), and noted the efforts of American socialist Eugene V. Debs to keep the United States out of World War I. Superbly, concisely, and unemotionally, Sean steadily helped me carve away my indulgent wanderings and refocus on the roots and effects of a malignant paranoia that strangled the party atmosphere of late summer 1945, when Alfred Eisenstaedt's V-J photo of the kissing sailor in Times Square encapsulated a short-lived surrender to unmitigated and infectious joy.

As I am immensely grateful for Sean's repeated leaps of faith and tireless diligence, I am also truly appreciative of the free editorial therapy sessions provided during my self-made odyssey by Mr. Mecoy, who at one point boosted my spirits by confiding that he was married to a writer who also produced very, very comprehensive first drafts. I'd also like to extend my special thanks to Sean Desmond's devoted colleagues at Twelve: editorial assistant Rachel Kambury; associate publisher and director of marketing Brian McLendon; director of publicity Paul Samuelson; assistant publicist Rachel Molland; designer Jarrod Taylor; production editor Bob Castillo; and copy editor Roland Ottewell.

Two of the smartest and most well-read people I've ever known, Charlie Ditkoff and Joe Gesue, generously agreed to read the final manuscript.

Very importantly, my darling daughter, Marisa, did not flee when I asked her once again to play a role of great importance, significant pressure, and invisible compensation: unpaid personal assistant, researcher, and editor. As I was finishing the project, Marisa was moving out of the house to Brooklyn, which is not a good thing for me, or my son, Luke, who will now have to add unpaid personal assistant to his long-standing job of being my unpaid information technology specialist.

I am also undeserving of the steadfast support of my dear wife, Maryellen, who has always acted as captain of the ship while I was allowed to confine myself to the happier task of cruise director. Not one word of this enterprise would have even been possible without her.

BIBLIOGRAPHY, NOTES, AND CONTEXT

In a recent *New Yorker*, Pulitzer Prize winner Robert Caro wrote about the paper trail he's been following for his multivolume biography of Lyndon Johnson. The piece opens with Caro speaking about an early and vital lesson in journalism. The year is 1959 and *Newsday*'s crusty managing editor at the time, Alan Hathway, has summoned Caro to his office. Following an "attaboy" for dogged work, Hathway supplies Caro with what will be the essential commandment of his life as an investigative journalist and historian. "Just remember," the editor tells him. "Turn every page. Never assume anything. Turn every goddam page."

Caro goes on to paint the scene of his first research visit to the Johnson Library and Museum in Austin. It's now 1976 and he's confronted by an almost unimaginable blizzard of documents.

"In front of me," he writes, "was a broad, tall marble staircase. At its top was a glass wall four stories high. Behind the glass, on each of the four stories, were rows of tall, red boxes—a hundred and seventy-five rows across, each row six boxes high.... There were about forty thousand boxes, the archivist told me; each had a capacity of eight hundred pages.... There were thirty-two million pages in all. I had a bad feeling: during all the years since Alan Hathway had given me that first piece of advice—'Turn every page. Never assume anything. Turn every goddam page'—I had never forgotten it; it was engraved in my mind. There would be no turning every page here."

When I began working in journalism, some twenty years later, turning the page still meant literally turning the page. At the *New York Times*, we visited "the morgue"—not to see dead bodies, but to obtain small packets with articles individually cut out of past editions and other major publications. When I became a TV producer, investigation was still hands-on. The search for audiotape, videotape, and film often required hunting in dusty basements, garages, and attics. When I was tasked by NBC with creating a research binder for the opening ceremony of the 1988 Seoul Olympics, my first step was buying a global almanac from the U.S. government diced up into handy index cards, which I received via snail mail.

Old habits run deep and I went old-school as I began research on this topic. I roamed the Strand Book Store in Manhattan ("legendary home of 18 miles of new, used and rare books") and left with four bags containing fifty or so purchases. I was also ready to make the hike to the Truman Library and Museum in Independence, Missouri (for insight on the first U.S. president of the Cold War), and take a train to the National Security Archive at George Washington University in Washington, D.C. ("founded in 1985 by journalists and scholars to check rising government secrecy…leading non-profit user of the U.S. Freedom of Information Act").

As soon became clear, however, both the Truman Library and the National Security Archive are institutions that can now be visited remotely, at all hours, at their web address in cyberspace. Moreover, almost every brick-and-mortar establishment relevant to my education on this topic maintains a 24/7 virtual reality in our brave new digital century, where every day we are multiplying Everything We've Ever Learned by Everything We've Ever Learned, creating (as per computer scientists) more new data every twenty-four hours than all of the information amassed by the ten thousand years of civilization that came before us. In short, I didn't have to go anywhere to find almost everything.

With a click, you can access the contents of Harry Truman's diary and declassified CIA memos. You don't need a projector to watch the totemic 1951 U.S. Federal Civil Defense film *Duck and Cover*, starring Bert the Turtle. It's instantly available on YouTube. You don't need an employee ID to gain access to the *New York Times* morgue; the paper's online archive contains articles going back to 1851. As of this writing, there are 5,802,421 submissions in English on Wikipedia. The ever-multiplying feast of cyber research includes the nonprofit JSTOR, which "provides access to more than 12 million academic journal articles, books, and primary sources in 75 disciplines." The Hathi Trust Digital Library—an international community of universities "committed to long-term curation"—provides access to nearly 17 million volumes, or 5,922,762,300 pages. Cold War historians are tweeting, blogging, and podcasting. While sitting on my ass in the comfort of my home office—wearing sweats, picking my nose, noshing on pretzels—I can stream every notable Cold War film, hear Curtis LeMay tell John Kennedy he's a coward, and listen to Richard Nixon obstructing justice.

Given this instantaneous and enlarged frame of reference, I believe I've been able to more deeply grasp the mentalities and foibles that fostered and maintained the Cold War. However, I also feel obligated to profess a giant measure of humility. As more and more previously inaccessible documents and media are uploaded to computing clouds across the world, my version of events—at least a portion—will in some future be revealed as incomplete and perhaps wholly naïve. I'm put in mind of Donald Rumsfeld's response when, as secretary of defense in 2002, he was asked about the lack of evidence linking Iraq with supplying weapons of mass destruction to terrorists. Said Rumsfeld:

"Reports that say that something hasn't happened are always interesting to me, because as we know, there are known knowns; there are things we know we know. We also know there are known unknowns; that is to say we know there are some things we do not know. But there are also unknown unknowns—the ones we don't know we don't know. And if one looks throughout the history of our country and other free countries, it is the latter category that tend to be the difficult ones."

———

These "analog" texts below also provided important big-picture perspective and assistance:

Chang, Jung, and Jon Halliday. *Mao: The Unknown Story.* Alfred A. Knopf, 2005.
The Concise Columbia Encyclopedia. 3rd ed. Columbia University Press, 1994.
Evans, Harold. *The American Century.* Alfred A. Knopf, 1998.
Finder, Henry, ed. *The 50s: The Story of a Decade; The New Yorker.* Modern Library, 2016.
———. *The 60s: The Story of a Decade; The New Yorker.* Random House, 2016.
Finder, Henry, ed., with Giles Harvey. *The 40s: The Story of a Decade; The New Yorker.* Modern Library, 2014.
Gaddis, John Lewis. *The Cold War: A New History.* Penguin, 2005.
Garraty, John, ed. *The Columbia History of the World.* Harper & Row, 1972.
Glover, Jonathan. *Humanity: A Moral History of the Twentieth Century.* Yale University Press, 2001.
Halberstam, David. *The Fifties.* Villard, 1993.
Johnson, Paul. *Modern Times: The World from the Twenties to the Eighties.* Harper & Row, 1983.

McMahon, Robert J. *The Cold War: A Very Short Introduction*. Oxford University Press, 2003.

Moore, Kathryn. *The American President: A Complete History*. Barnes & Noble, 2007.

Webber, Elizabeth, and Mike Feinsilber. *Merriam-Webster's Dictionary of Allusions*. Merriam-Webster, 1999.

Woodward, Bob. *Shadow: Five Presidents and the Legacy of Watergate*. Touchstone, 1999.

Zinn, Howard. *A People's History of the United States*. Harper Perennial, 1995.

These were some of my principal sources for a broad view of Soviet history:

Alexievich, Svetlana. *Secondhand Time: The Last of the Soviets*. Random House, 2016.

Amalrik, Andrei. *Will the Soviet Union Survive Until 1984?* Harper & Row, 1970.

Applebaum, Anne. *Iron Curtain: The Crushing of Eastern Europe, 1944–1956*. Anchor, 2013.

———. *Red Famine: Stalin's War on Ukraine*. Doubleday, 2017.

Remnick, David. *Lenin's Tomb: The Last Days of the Soviet Empire*. Vintage, 1994.

Solzhenitsyn, Aleksandr. *The Gulag Archipelago: An Experiment in Literary Investigation*. Harper Perennial, 2002.

The Cold War coincides with the birth of the nuclear era. These books acted as tutorials on the development of the atom and hydrogen bombs and their effects:

Fussell, Paul. *Thank God for the Atom Bomb, and Other Essays*. Ballantine, 1988.

Hersey, John. *Hiroshima*. Vintage, 1989.

Holloway, David. *Stalin and the Bomb*. Yale University Press, 1996.

Isaacson, Walter. *Einstein: His Life and Universe*. Simon & Schuster, 2007.

Kelly, Cynthia C., ed. *The Manhattan Project: The Birth of the Atomic Bomb in the Words of Its Creators, Eyewitnesses, and Historians*. Black Dog & Leventhal/ Atomic Heritage Foundation, 2007.

Lanouette, William. *Genius in the Shadows: A Biography of Leo Szilard, the Man Behind the Bomb*. University of Chicago Press, 1994.

Lifton, Robert Jay, and Greg Mitchell. *Hiroshima in America: Fifty Years of Denial*. G. P. Putnam's Sons, 1995.

Rhodes, Richard. *Dark Sun: The Making of the Hydrogen Bomb*. Simon & Schuster, 1995.

———. *The Making of the Atomic Bomb*. Simon & Schuster, 1986.

Soviet Russia had a suffocating security bureaucracy from its birth, in 1917. The organization was first known as the Cheka; it became the KGB in 1954. The KGB officially ceased operations in 1991. The United States had a foreign intelligence organization during World War II, the Office of Strategic

Services (OSS), which was disbanded after the war. The Central Intelligence Agency (CIA) was established in 1947, and the National Security Agency (NSA) in 1952. The Federal Bureau of Investigation (FBI) began in 1908 as an unnamed investigative arm of the Justice Department. Britain's intelligence bureaucracy was established in 1909. MI5 is the British equivalent of the FBI; MI6 is the equivalent of the CIA. During the Cold War, the Soviet Union, the United States, and the British also maintained separate military-run intelligence organizations. Russian military intelligence is still known by its Soviet-era name: the GRU. These books were immensely helpful in sorting out the alphabet soup of Cold War spydom:

Andrew, Christopher. *The Sword and The Shield: The Mitrokhin Archive and the Secret History of the KGB*. Basic Books, 1999.

Andrew, Christopher, and Oleg Gordievsky. *KGB: The Inside Story*. HarperCollins, 1990.

Bamford, James. *Body of Secrets: Anatomy of the Ultra-Secret National Security Agency*. Anchor, 2001.

Garthoff, Raymond L. *A Journey Through the Cold War: A Memoir of Containment and Coexistence*. Brookings Institution Press, 2001.

Haslam, Jonathan. *Near and Distant Neighbors: A New History of Soviet Intelligence*. Farrar, Straus & Giroux, 2015.

Hoffman, David E. *The Billion Dollar Spy: A True Story of Cold War Espionage and Betrayal*. Anchor, 2015.

Hunter, Edward. *Brain-Washing in Red China*. Vanguard, 1953.

Kalugin, Oleg. *Spymaster: My Thirty-Two Years in Intelligence and Espionage Against the West*. Basic Books, 2009.

Kessler, Ronald. *Inside the CIA: Revealing the Secrets of the World's Most Powerful Spy Agency*. Pocket Books, 1992.

Kinzer, Stephen. *The Brothers: John Foster Dulles, Allen Dulles, and Their Secret World War*. St. Martin's Griffin, 2013.

———. *Overthrow: America's Century of Regime Change from Hawaii to Iraq*. Times Books/Henry Holt, 2006.

Kris, David S., and J. Douglas Wilson. *National Security Investigations and Prosecutions*. 2nd ed. Thomson/West, 2012.

le Carré, John. *The Pigeon Tunnel: Stories from My Life*. Viking, 2016.

———. *The Spy Who Came in from the Cold*. Penguin, 2013. (First published 1963.)

Lifton, Robert Jay. *Thought Reform and the Psychology of Totalism: A Study of "Brainwashing" in China*. University of North Carolina Press, 1989.

Marton, Kati. *True Believer: Stalin's Last American Spy*. Simon & Schuster, 2016.

Miller, Scott. *Agent 100: An American Spymaster and the German Resistance in WWII*. Simon & Schuster, 2013.

Moynihan, Daniel Patrick. *Secrecy: The American Experience.* Yale University Press, 1998.

Powers, Thomas. *The Man Who Kept the Secrets: Richard Helms and the CIA.* Alfred A. Knopf, 1979.

Roberts, Sam. *The Brother: The Untold Story of the Rosenberg Case.* Random House, 2003.

Talbot, David. *The Devil's Chessboard: Allen Dulles, the CIA, and the Rise of America's Secret Government.* Harper Perennial, 2015.

Trento, Joseph J. *The Secret History of the CIA.* MJF Books, 2001.

Wall, W. H. *From Healing to Hell.* Author House, 2018.

Weiner, Tim. *Legacy of Ashes: The History of the CIA.* Doubleday, 2007.

Woodward, Bob. *Veil: The Secret Wars of the CIA, 1981–1987.* Simon & Schuster, 1987.

The hazards of an out-of-control U.S. "military-industrial complex" were first famously noted by President Dwight Eisenhower in his farewell address to the nation on January 17, 1961. These books deconstruct and assess the contours of the exploding U.S. defense establishment:

Brzezinski, Matthew. *Red Moon Rising: Sputnik and the Hidden Rivalries That Ignited the Space Race.* Macmillan, 2007.

Graff, Garrett. *Raven Rock: The Story of the U.S. Government's Secret Plan to Save Itself—While the Rest of Us Die.* Simon & Schuster, 2017.

Jacobsen, Annie. *Area 51: An Uncensored History of America's Top Secret Military Base.* Little, Brown, 2011.

———. *Operation Paperclip: The Secret Intelligence Program That Brought Nazi Scientists to America.* Little, Brown, 2014.

———. *The Pentagon's Brain: An Uncensored History of DARPA, America's Top Secret Military Research Agency.* Little, Brown, 2015.

Kenney, L. Douglas. *15 Minutes: General Curtis LeMay and the Countdown to Nuclear Annihilation.* St. Martin's Griffin, 2011.

Knebel, Fletcher, and Charles Bailey II. *Seven Days in May.* Bantam, 1962.

Marks, John D. *The Search for the "Manchurian Candidate": The CIA and Mind Control; The Secret History of the Behavioral Sciences.* W. W. Norton, 1991.

Mills, Charles Wright. *The Causes of World War Three.* Literary Licensing, 2011.

Schlosser, Eric. *Command and Control: Nuclear Weapons, the Damascus Accident, and the Illusion of Safety.* Penguin, 2013.

Simpson, Christopher. *Blowback: The First Full Account of America's Recruitment of Nazis and Its Disastrous Effect on the Cold War.* Collier, 1989.

The principal Soviet political figures during the Cold War were Joseph Stalin (1926–53); Nikita Khrushchev (1953–64); Leonid Brezhnev (1964–82); and Mikhail Gorbachev (1985–91). I consulted these biographies and assessments:

Amis, Martin. *Koba the Dread: Laughter and the Twenty Million.* Vintage International, 2002.

Conquest, Robert. *Stalin: Breaker of Nations.* Penguin, 1991.

Fursenko, Alexander, and Timothy Naftali. *Khrushchev's Cold War: The Inside Story of an American Adversary.* W. W. Norton, 2006.

Medvedev, Roy, and Zhores Medvedev. *The Unknown Stalin: His Life, Death, and Legacy.* Overlook Press, 2004.

Montefiore, Simon Sebag. *Stalin: The Court of the Red Tsar.* Vintage, 2005.

Service, Robert. *Stalin: A Biography.* Pan Macmillan, 2004.

Taubman, William. *Gorbachev: His Life and Times.* W. W. Norton, 2017.

———. *Khrushchev: The Man and His Era.* W. W. Norton, 2003.

The Cold War–era U.S. presidents were Harry Truman (1945–53); Dwight Eisenhower (1953–61); John F. Kennedy (1961–63); Lyndon Johnson (1963–69); Richard Nixon (1969–74); Gerald Ford (1974–77); Jimmy Carter (1977–81); Ronald Reagan (1981–89); and George H. W. Bush (1989–93). I consulted these biographies and assessments:

Ambrose, Stephen. *Nixon: The Education of a Politician.* Simon & Schuster, 1987.

Bernstein, Carl, and Bob Woodward. *All the President's Men.* Warner Paperback, 1975.

Brands, H. W. *Reagan: The Life.* Anchor, 2016.

Caro, Robert. *Master of the Senate: The Years of Lyndon Johnson.* Alfred A. Knopf, 2002.

Ferrell, Robert E. *Harry S. Truman, A Life.* University of Missouri Press, 1994.

Mann, James. *The Rebellion of Ronald Reagan: A History of the End of the Cold War.* Viking, 2009.

McCullough, David. *Truman.* Simon & Schuster, 1992.

Minutaglio, Bill, and Steven L. Davis. *Dallas 1963.* Twelve, 2013.

Morris, Edmund. *Dutch: A Memoir of Ronald Reagan.* Random House, 1999.

Newton, Jim. *Eisenhower: The White House Years.* Doubleday, 2001.

Summers, Anthony. *The Arrogance of Power: The Secret World of Richard Nixon.* Viking, 2000.

Thomas, Evan. *Ike's Bluff: President Eisenhower's Secret Battle to Save the World.* Little, Brown, 2012.

Unger, Irwin, and Debi Unger. *LBJ: A Life.* John Wiley & Sons, 1999.

Weiner, Tim. *One Man Against the World: The Tragedy of Richard Nixon.* Henry Holt, 2015.

I consulted these biographies and histories involving other principal U.S. figures during the Cold War: J. Edgar Hoover (head of the FBI from 1924 to 1971); Senator Joe McCarthy; Roy Cohn (McCarthy's Senate staff attorney); British spy and traitor Kim Philby; iconic author George Orwell; and iconic tycoon Howard Hughes:

Bartlett, Donald L., and James B. Steele. *Howard Hughes: His Life and Madness.* W. W. Norton, 1979.

Buckley, William F., and L. Brent Bozell. *McCarthy and His Enemies.* Regnery, 1995.

Cook, Fred J. *The Nightmare Decade: The Life and Times of Senator Joe McCarthy.* Random House, 1971.

Gentry, Curt. *J. Edgar Hoover: The Man and the Secrets.* W. W. Norton, 1991.

Hoover, J. Edgar. *Masters of Deceit: The Story of Communism in America and How to Fight It.* Henry Holt, 1958.

Jewell, Richard B. *The RKO Story.* Arlington House, 1985.

Kessler, Ronald. *The Bureau: The Secret History of the FBI.* St. Martin's, 2002.

Macintyre, Ben. *A Spy Among Friends: Kim Philby and the Great Betrayal.* Broadway Books, 2014.

Orwell, George. *Animal Farm.* New American Library, 1974.

———. *Collected Essays, Journalism and Letters of George Orwell.* 4 vols. Edited by Sonia Orwell and Ian Angus. Harcourt Brace Jovanovich, 1968.

———. *Nineteen Eighty-Four.* Penguin, 2008.

Ricks, Thomas E. *Churchill and Orwell: The Fight for Freedom.* Penguin Press, 2017.

von Hoffman, Nicholas. *Citizen Cohn: The Life and Times of Roy Cohn.* Doubleday, 1988.

Weiner, Tim. *Enemies: A History of the FBI.* Random House, 2013.

These books discuss and dissect the architects of Cold War U.S. policy:

Acacia, John. *Clark Clifford: The Wise Man of Washington.* University Press of Kentucky, 2009.

Hitchens, Christopher. *The Trial of Henry Kissinger.* Twelve, 2002.

Issacson, Walter, and Evan Thomas. *The Wise Men: Six Friends and the World They Made.* Simon & Schuster, 1986.

Kennan, George. *At a Century's Ending: Reflections, 1982–1995.* W. W. Norton, 1996.

Robertson, David. *Sly and Able: A Political Biography of James F. Byrnes.* W. W. Norton, 1994.

Smith, Hedrick. *The Power Game: How Washington Works.* Ballantine Books, 1988.

Thomas, Evan. *The Very Best Men: Four Who Dared; The Early Years of the CIA.* Simon & Schuster, 1996.

Thompson, Nicholas. *The Hawk and the Dove: Paul Nitze, George Kennan, and the History of the Cold War.* Picador/Henry Holt, 2009.

Notable Cold War journalism took place in print, on the radio, and on TV:

Alsop, Joseph W., with Adam Platt. *"I've Seen The Best of It": Memoirs.* W. W. Norton, 1992.

Cloud, Stanley, and Lynne Olson. *The Murrow Boys: Pioneers on the Front Lines of Broadcast Journalism.* Houghton Mifflin, 1996.

Frankel, Max. *The Times of My Life, and My Life with The Times.* Random House, 1999.

Gabler, Neal. *Winchell: Gossip, Power and the Culture of Celebrity.* Alfred A. Knopf, 1994.

Keever, Beverly Deepe. *Death Zones and Darling Spies: Seven Years of Vietnam War Reporting.* University of Nebraska Press, 2013.

Moyers, Bill. *Moyers on America: A Journalist and His Times.* New Press, 2004.

These books address the kaleidoscope of the Cold War zeitgeist and culture:

Álvarez de Toledo, Lucía. *The Story of Che Guevara.* Quercus Publishing, 2016.

Andersen, Kurt. *Fantasyland: How America Went Haywire.* Random House, 2017.

Arnold, Jeremy. *52 Must-See Movies, and Why They Matter.* Running Press, 2016.

Bartholomew, Robert E., and George S. Howard. *UFOs and Alien Contact: Two Centuries of Mystery.* Prometheus Books, 1998.

Berlitz, Charles. *The Bermuda Triangle.* Doubleday, 1974.

Blanchard, Paul. *Communism, Democracy and Catholic Power.* Nabu Press, 2011.

Bryan, C. D. B. *Close Encounters of the Fourth Kind.* Penguin, 1995.

Burdick, Eugene, and William Lederer. *The Ugly American.* W. W. Norton, 1999. (Originally published in 1958.)

Carter, David. *Stonewall: The Riots That Sparked the Gay Revolution.* St. Martin's Griffin, 2010.

Chase, Alton. *Harvard and the Unabomber: The Education of an American Terrorist.* W. W. Norton, 2003.

Cohen, Michael A. *American Maelstrom: The 1968 Election and the Politics of Division.* Oxford University Press, 2016.

Condon, Richard. *The Manchurian Candidate.* Pocket Star, 2004. (Originally published in 1959.)

DeLillo, Don. *Underworld.* Scribner, 1997.

Feldman, Jay. *Manufacturing Hysteria: A History of Scapegoating, Surveillance, and Secrecy in Modern America.* Anchor, 2011.

Ferster, C. B., and B. F. Skinner. *Schedules of Reinforcement.* Appleton-Century-Crofts, 1957.

Feyerabend, Paul. *Against Method: Outline of an Anarchist Theory of Knowledge.* New Left Books, 1975.

Greene, Graham. *The Quiet American.* Penguin, 2002. (Originally published in 1955.)

Hansen, James R. *Spaceflight Revolution: NASA Langley Research Center from Sputnik to Apollo*. Forgotten Books, 2018.

Hitchens, Christopher. *Arguably: Essays*. Twelve, 2011.

Hughes, Robert. *Culture of Complaint: The Fraying of America*. Oxford University Press, 1993.

Hynek, J. Allen. *The UFO Experience: A Scientific Inquiry*. Ballantine, 1972.

Johnson, Paul. *Intellectuals*. Harper & Row, 1988.

Lindsey, Hal. *The Late Great Planet Earth*. Zondervan, 1970.

Loken, John. *Oswald's Trigger Films: The Manchurian Candidate, We Were Strangers, Suddenly?* Falcon Books, 2000.

Miller, Arthur. *Collected Essays*. Penguin, 2016.

Munn, Michael. *John Wayne: The Man Behind the Myth*. Berkley, 2005.

Perlstein, Rick. *Nixonland: The Rise of a President and the Fracturing of America*. Scribner, 2009.

Reich, Charles A. *The Greening of America*. Crown, 1995.

Ronson, Jon. *The Men Who Stare at Goats*. Simon & Schuster, 2004.

Sagan, Carl, and Ann Druyan. *The Demon-Haunted World: Science as a Candle in the Dark*. Ballantine, 1997.

Saunders, Frances Stonor. *The Cultural Cold War: The CIA and the World of Arts and Letters*. New Press, 1999.

Seuss, Dr. *The Butter Battle Book*. Random House, 1984.

Thomson, David. *The New Biographical Dictionary of Film*. Alfred A. Knopf, 2003.

Tompkins, Peter, and Christopher Bird. *The Secret Life of Plants: A Fascinating Account of the Physical, Emotional, and Spiritual Relations Between Plants and Man*. Harper Perennial, 1973.

von Däniken, Erich. *Chariots of the Gods*. G. P. Putnam's Sons, 1968.

Wertham, Frederick, MD. *Seduction of the Innocent: The Influence of Comic Books on Today's Youth*. Clarke, Irwin, 1953.

Wolfe, Tom. *The Right Stuff*. Picador, 1979.

Other sources—interviews, memos, letters, government reports, unclassified documents, diary entries, newspapers, magazines, academic studies, websites, blogs, videos, radio and TV broadcasts, films, and more—are noted below, by chapter:

Introduction

Yuri Bezmenov: Interview with Edward Griffin, 1984.

Russian hacking: William Burns, "How We Fool Ourselves on Russia," *New York Times*, January 8, 2017; Michael Smith, "The Trump Campaign and the Russians' 'Active Measures,'" *Washington Examiner*, September 4, 2014; Mark Kramer, "The Deep Roots of the Russian Election-Hacking

Campaign," *Cognoscenti* (WBUR), January 10, 2017; Julia Ioffe, "What Putin Really Wants," *Atlantic*, January/February 2018; Anton Troianovski, "A Former Russian Troll Speaks," *Washington Post*, February 17, 2018.

Nuclear launch codes: If a president decides to launch nuclear weapons, he turns to a military aide who is always within easy reach. The aide carries the so-called nuclear football, the nickname derived from the code word for the first set of nuclear war plans, DROPKICK. From Garrett M. Graff, "The Madman and the Bomb," *Politico*, August 13, 2017: "There is no one who has to confirm a launch order, no one has to certify that the man giving the order is of sound mind, no congressional leader or Cabinet secretary who has to countersign the order."

Joseph Stalin: Anne Applebaum, "How Stalin Hid Ukraine's Famine from the World," *Atlantic*, October 13, 2017.

Effects of World War II on the USSR: From Sheila Fitzpatrick, "War and Society in Soviet Context: Soviet Labor Before, During, and After World War II," *International Labor and Working Class History*, no. 35 (Spring 1989): "The total number of working adults in 1946 was only 71 percent of what it had been in 1940 and the number of male working adults was less than half of what it had been at the beginning of the war."

Communists in the United States: Wendy Wall, "Anti-Communism in the 1950s," Gilder-Lehrman Institute of American History.

Reader's Digest: Joanne Sharp, "Rise and Fall of Reader's Digest," CNN, February 20, 2013.

Advanced Aerospace Threat Identification Program: Helene Cooper, Ralph Blumenthal, and Leslie Kean, "Glowing Auras and 'Black Money': The Pentagon's Mysterious U.F.O. Program," *New York Times*, December 16, 2017.

Roger Morris: Roger Morris, "Tomgram: Roger Morris, the CIA and the Gates Legacy," *TomDispatch*, June 25, 2007.

Primal scream therapy: Publicly introduced in 1970 by California psychotherapist Arthur Janov.

1. Scorch, Boil, and Bake

Curtis LeMay: "World Battlefronts: Battle of Japan: V.L.R. Man," *Time*, August 13, 1945; Richard Rhodes, "The General and World War

III," *New Yorker,* June 19, 1995; Joshua Rothman, "Waiting for World War III," *New Yorker,* October 16, 2012.

B-29: Daniel Wyatt, "World War II: 40th Bomb Group," *Aviation History,* September 1994.

Strategic bombing: Richard Overy, *The Bombers and the Bombed: Allied Air War over Europe, 1940–1945* (Viking, 2014).

Robert Pape: Alastair Gee, "Aerial Bombing: Turns Out It Almost Never Works," Ideas.Ted.com, November 17, 2014.

Sexiest branch: From Louis Menand, "Fat Man," *New Yorker,* June 27, 2005: "In 1945, when the United States dropped atomic bombs nicknamed Little Boy and Fat Man on Japan, the Air Force was still a branch of the Army. The bombs changed that. An independent department of the Air Force was created in 1947; the nation's nuclear arsenal was put under its command; and the Air Force replaced the Army as the prima donna of national defense."

Bombing Japan: Richard Tanter, "Voice and Silence in the First Nuclear War: Wilfred Burchett and Hiroshima," *Asia-Pacific Journal,* August 3, 2005.

Air Force on film: Sam Edwards, "12 O'Clock High and the Image of American Air Power, 1946–1967," in *American Militarism on the Small Screen,* ed. Anna Froula and Stacy Takacs (Routledge, 2016).

Strategic Air Command: Col. Phillip S. Meilinger, "How LeMay Transformed Strategic Air Command," *Air and Space Power Journal,* March–April 2014.

Above and Beyond: Screenplay by Melvin Frank and Norman Panama; released by MGM (1952).

Bombing during the Korean War: Blaine Harden, "Rocket Man Should Know His History," *New York Times,* September 24, 2017.

Warrior truism: Novelist Viet Thanh Nguyen: "All wars are fought twice, the first time on the battlefield, the second time in memory."

Dr. Strangelove, or: How I Learned to Stop Worrying and Love the Bomb: Screenplay by Stanley Kubrick, Terry Southern, and Peter George; released by Columbia (1963). Principal photography started at Shepperton Studios, England, in January 1963. From Louis Menand, "Fat Man," *New Yorker,* June 27, 2005: "Stanley Kubrick began reading intensively on nuclear strategy after he finished directing *Lolita,* in 1962. His original plan was to make a realistic thriller. One of his working titles was taken from an article by [Albert] Wohlstetter [the head of Air Force think tank RAND] in *Foreign Affairs*, in 1959: *The Delicate Balance of Terror*....But Kubrick could not invent a plausible story in which a nuclear war is started by accident, so he ended up making a comedy adapted from a novel by a former R.A.F. officer called *Red Alert*." Additional source material: Grant Stillman, "Two of the MAD-dest Scientists: Where Strangelove Meets Dr. No; or, Unexpected Roots for Kubrick's Cold War Classic," *Film History* 20, no. 4, Politics and Film (2008).

2. Operation Paperclip

Wernher von Braun: Brian Crim, "Wernher von Braun's 'Rocket Team' and America's Military-Industrial Complex," A Library of Social Science Essay; Daniel Lang, "A Romantic Urge," *New Yorker*, April 21, 1951.

Operation Paperclip: Annie Jacobsen, "What Cold War CIA Interrogators Learned from the Nazis," *Daily Beast*, February 11, 2014.

Hill Project: Derek R. Mallett, "Western Allied Intelligence and the German Military Document Section, 1945–6," *Journal of Contemporary History* 46, no. 2 (April 2011).

3. Face-to-Face

Elbe: *Swansong 1945: A Collective Diary of the Last Days of the Third Reich*, ed. Walter Kempowski (W. W. Norton, 2015); Mary Williams Walsh, "Battling to Save a Bridge to Peace: The Elbe River Span Where U.S. and Soviet Soldiers Joyously Met in World War II Is Slated for Demolition," *Los Angeles Times*, April 26, 1994.

Russia's image in America: After the August 1945 Gallup poll indicated that 54 percent of Americans had a positive view of the Soviet Union, that figure dropped to just 25 percent in a January 1946 poll. In March 1946, following Winston Churchill's "Iron Curtain" speech and the first revelations of Soviet spying in America, 71 percent of the U.S. public named the Soviet Union as "a nation seeking world domination."

Jimmy Byrnes: "The Nations: The Year of the Bullbat," *Time*, January 6, 1947; Kenneth Davis, "Mr. Assistance," *New York Times*, December 18, 1994; Jason Spencer, "A House in Converse Heights Played a Role in the Use of the Atomic Bomb," GoUpstate.com, August 9, 2005.

Leo Szilard: "Memorandum of Szilard Correspondence," NuclearFiles .org; "Leo Szilard Interview: President Truman Did Not Understand," *U.S.*

News & World Report, August 15, 1960; Leo Szilard, *Reminiscences*, ed. Gertrud Weiss Szilard and Kathleen R. Winsor (1968); Nicholas and Robert Halasz, "Leo Szilard: The Reluctant Father of the Atomic Bomb," *New Hungarian Quarterly*, November 30, 1974; interview with William Lanouette by Cindy Kelly, Atomic Heritage Foundation, April 11, 2014; Alex Wellerstein, "Remembering the Chicago Pile: The World's First Nuclear Reactor," *New Yorker*, December 2, 2017.

Albert Einstein: Dennis Overbye, "New Details Emerge from the Einstein Files; How the F.B.I. Tracked His Phone Calls and His Trash," *New York Times*, May 7, 2002.

Soviet atomic spies: Marian Smith Holmes, "Spies Who Spilled Atomic Bomb Secrets," Smithsonian.com, April 19, 2009.

Decision to drop the atomic bomb: Gar Alperovitz, "Did America Have to Drop the Bomb? Not to End the War, but Truman Wanted to Intimidate Russia," *Washington Post*, August 4, 1985; Evan Thomas, "Why We Did It," *Newsweek*, August 23, 1995; Margaret Mary Barrett, "Atomic Bomb: Why Did President Harry S. Truman Order the Bombings of Hiroshima and Nagasaki?," *History in Dispute*, 2000; Margo Dowling, "Viewpoint: President Truman Used the Atomic Bombs in Order to Bring a Quick End to the War," *History in Dispute*, 2000; William Barr, ed., "The Atomic Bomb and the End of World War II: A Collection of Primary Sources," *National Security Archive Electronic Briefing Book No. 162*, August 5, 2005); Douglas J. MacEachin, *The Final Months of the War with Japan: Signals Intelligence: U.S. Invasion Planning, and the A-Bomb Decision*, Central Intelligence Agency, March 19, 2007; Josette H. Williams, *The Information War in the Pacific, 1945*, Central Intelligence Agency, April 14, 2007.

U.S. reaction to the atomic bomb: "Atomic Yellow Pages," Conelrad .com.

Soviet entry into the Pacific theater: Tsuyoshi Hasegawa, "The Soviet Factor in Ending the Pacific War," University of California–Santa Barbara, National Council for Eurasian and East European Research, October 28, 2003.

Norman Cousins: Norman Cousins, "Modern Man Is Obsolete," *Saturday Review*, August 10, 1945.

Edward R. Murrow comments: August 12, 1945, radio broadcast.

Who started the Cold War: From a 2016 *New York Times* letter to the editor by Eric Alterman: "No one would argue that the Soviets 'held' to the spirit of the Yalta Accords with their brutal behavior in Poland and elsewhere in Eastern Europe. But even allowing for some misunderstanding and ambiguity on the American side regarding Poland, it was the United States that undertook the first indisputable repudiation of the agreement's letter. Roosevelt and Stalin had agreed there that only countries that had declared war on Nazi Germany by March 1 would be admitted to the General Assembly. But once the UN talks got underway in San Francisco, the United States went back on its word and voted to seat Argentina, which had failed to meet that rather generous deadline—a decision promoted by Nelson Rockefeller, the assistant secretary of state for Western Hemisphere affairs."

4. Cold War Bibles

George Orwell profiles and assessments: Murray N. Rothbard, "George Orwell and the Cold War: A Reconsideration," in *Reflections on America, 1984: An Orwell Symposium*, ed. Robert Mulvihill (University of Georgia Press, 1986); Jacob Weisberg, "Orwell, Listing: The Author of 1984 Was Right to Name Names," *Slate*, August 16, 1998; Louis Menand, "Honest, Decent, Wrong," *New Yorker*, January 27, 2003; Thomas E. Ricks, "What Orwell Saw—and What He Missed—About Today's World," *Politico*, May 23, 2017.

Communist Manifesto: From Peter Gordon, "Call Him Karl," *New York Times Book Review*, October 23, 2016: "Just a year before his death and gravely ill, Marx wrote with [Friedrich] Engels a short preface to the Russian edition of the Manifesto. It entertained the prospect that the common ownership system in the Russian village might serve as 'the starting point for a communist development.' Three and a half decades later, the Bolsheviks seized power in Russia, and by the late 1920s, the government commenced its brutal collectivization of agriculture. Like all intellectual legacies, Marx's work remains open to new interpretation. But it seems clear that the man himself would never have accepted the inhumanity undertaken in his name."

Joseph Stalin: From Robert S. Robins and Jerrod M. Post, "The Paranoid Political Actor," *Biography* 10, no. 1 (Winter 1987): "As we have noted, sooner or later the paranoid will indeed be surrounded by enemies. . . . Consider Joseph Stalin, who while highly suspicious for most of his life was probably not clinically ill. His exaggerated alertness to conspiracy—appropriate in the plot-laden Kremlin—was highly adaptive and time and time again permitted him to eliminate potential rivals before they eliminated him. At the same time, however, it created an atmosphere of fear and produced a widening circle of rivals and enemies. As Stalin's fear magnified, so too did the extent of his actions to eliminate threats to his power; witness the extent of the purges, variously estimated to be upwards of twelve million victims."

H. P. Smollett/Smolka: Peter Foges, "My Spy: The Story of H. P. Smolka, Soviet Spy, and Inspiration for *The Third Man*," *Lapham's Quarterly*, January 14, 2016.

Superstates: In a 1947 essay for *The Partisan Review*, "Toward European Unity," Orwell wrote, "The fear inspired by the atomic bomb and other weapons yet to come will be so great that everyone will refrain from using them. . . . It would mean the division of the world among two or three vast super states, unable to conquer one another and unable to be overthrown by any internal rebellion. In all probability, their structure would be hierarchic, with a semi-divine caste at the top and outright slavery at the bottom, and the crushing out of liberty exceeding anything the world has yet seen. Within each state the necessary psychological atmosphere would be kept up by complete severance from the outside world, and by a continuous phony war against rival states. Civilization of this type might remain static for thousands of years."

5. Concepts of Containment

Bolshoi speech: Transcript of "Speech Delivered by Joseph Stalin at a Meeting of Voters of the Stalin Electoral District, Moscow," February 9, 1946, Wilson Center, Digital Archive. The multiple titles given to Stalin were tracked in one of the definitive texts about the final days of the USSR, the Pulitzer Prize–winning *Lenin's Tomb*, by David Remnick. His book is based in part on his superb reporting as the Moscow correspondent for the *Washington Post*.

Kennan profile: Louis Menand, "Getting Real: George F. Kennan's Cold War," *New Yorker*, November 14, 2011.

Kennan's containment: Transcript of telegram, "The Change in the Soviet Union (Kennan) to the Secretary of State," received in Washington, D.C., February 22, 1946, at 3:52 p.m. (known informally as the "long telegram"); X, "The Sources of Soviet Conduct," *Foreign Affairs*, July 1947; Walter Lippmann, "The Cold War," Courtesy of the Office of Recording Secretary—President & Fellows of Harvard College; Nicholas Thompson, "A War Best Served Cold," *New York Times*, July 31, 2007.

Winston Churchill's "Iron Curtain" speech: Transcript of "Sinews of Peace" at Westminster College, Fulton, Missouri, March 5, 1946.

Princess Ileana: Transcript from Senate Judiciary Committee, *The Scope of Soviet Activity in the United States*, hearings before the Subcommittee to Investigate the Administration of the Internal Security Act and Other Internal Security Laws, May 1956.

6. Small and Devastating

Bernard Baruch's UN speech: Transcript of text of speech presented to the United Nations Atomic Energy Commission, June 4, 1946, NuclearFiles.org.

"Billy's Blacklist": Wilkerson's "A Vote for Stalin" appeared in the July 28, 1946, issue of the *Hollywood Reporter*. From Kat Eschner, "The Columnist Who Shaped Hollywood's Most Destructive Witch Hunt," Smithsonian.com, July 28, 2017: "Despite personal misgivings and career ones, Wilkerson went forward with identifying people as communists in his column....By 1950, a pamphlet naming more than 150 movie workers helped to formalize the blacklist—but there was never just one list, which was part of what made this period in Hollywood history so frightening and dangerous for performers and workers. People of color, Jewish actors and those who were not born in the United States were under particular threat."

7. Communism and Republicanism

"The American Century": Essay by Henry Luce in the February 17, 1941, issue of *Life*. His call to wean America from—in his view—a pinkish New Deal philosophy also included this language: "We start into this war with huge Government debt, a vast bureaucracy and a whole generation of young people trained to look to the Government as the source of all life.

The Party in power is the one which for long years has been most sympathetic to all manner of socialist doctrines and collectivist trends....The President of the United States has continually reached for more and more power, and he owes his continuation in office today largely to the coming of the war. Thus, the fear that the United States will be driven to a national socialism, as a result of cataclysmic circumstances and contrary to the free will of the American people, is an entirely justifiable fear."

8. Dachau Model

The Nuremberg trials: R. F. Tannenbaum, "The Devil's Chemists," *Commentary*, January 1, 1953.

U.S. interest in Nazi science: Alfred McCoy, "Science in Dachau's Shadow," *Journal of the History of Behavioral Sciences* 43 (Fall 2007).

9. United States of Surveillance

Dean Acheson's "rotten apples" comment: Made to senators visiting the Oval Office on February 27, 1947.

10. Unidentified Objects

Science fiction: The genre, as defined by author Brian Aldiss: "The world is in some sort of state, and something awful happens. It may not be evil, it may be good or neutral, just an accident. Whatever they do in the novel, at the end the world is changed forever."

NICAP: Dan Barry, "Dad Believed in U.F.O.s. Turns Out He Wasn't Alone," *New York Times*, December 30, 2017.

Day the Earth Stood Still: J. Hoberman, "The Cold War Sci-Fi Parable That Fell to Earth," *New York Times*, October 31, 2008.

11. Hollywood on Trial

Ayn Rand: Josh Jones, "Ayn Rand Helped the FBI Identify *It's a Wonderful Life* as Communist Propaganda," Open Culture, December 25, 2014. In her 1957 novel *Atlas Shrugged*, Rand wrote: "The man at the top of the intellectual pyramid contributes the most to all those below him, but gets nothing except his material payment, receiving no intellectual bonus from others to add to the value of his time. The man at the bottom who, left to himself, would starve in his hopeless ineptitude, contributes nothing to those above him, but receives the bonus of all their brains."

HUAC: Rand, Walt Disney, and Ronald Reagan testified during hearings before the Committee on Un-American Activities, House of Representatives, October 20–30, 1947.

Disney labor issues: Ken Tucker, "'Walt Disney': The Genius, the Empire Builder, the Vindictive Jerk," Yahoo Entertainment, September 14, 2015.

12. Cultural Content

I Married a Communist: Daniel Leab, "How Red Was My Valley: Hollywood, the Cold War Film, and I Married a Communist," *Journal of Contemporary History* 19, no. 1 (January 1984).

I Was a Communist for the FBI: From Tony Perucci, "The Red Mask of Sanity: Paul Robeson, HUAC, and the Sound of Cold War Performance," *TDR: The Drama Review* 53, no. 4 (Winter 2009): "The Communist was always seen to be acting, while the anti-Communist American was transparently truthful. The American citizen, constituted in noble sincerity, refused mimesis and instead inhabited an authentic citizenship. So strong was the belief in the anti-Communist dishonesty, that the fictionalized film adaption of professional informer Matt Cvertic's memoir, *I Was a Communist for the FBI*, was nominated for Best Documentary Oscar."

The Third Man: Screenplay by Graham Greene; released by British Lion Films and Selznick Releasing Organization (1949); Julia Driver, "Justice, Mercy, and Friendship in The Third Man," *Ethics at the Cinema*, August 20, 2010; Lawrence Osborne, "Agents of Betrayal," *Lapham's Quarterly*; Madeline Ashby, "Noir Films Perfected: The Third Man," Tor.com, August 17, 2011.

13. Insane Era

Hughes profile: Purnell W. Chopin (president of the Howard Hughes Medical Institute), "Three-Headed Bit to a Major Philanthropy: The Surprising Legacy of Howard Hughes," *Proceedings of the American Philosophical Society* 142, no. 3 (September 1998).

Paul Jarrico: In 1958, still blacklisted, Jarrico renounced his membership in the Communist Party: "I thought the Soviet Union was a vanguard country fighting for a better future for the entire world, including the United States. That was an illusion, I discovered....Even the slowest of us realized that the accusations against Stalin and Stalinism were true...and that we had been defending indefensible things....But the illusion didn't make me disloyal; it made me a fool. And that's what I wound up feeling like. Not that I'd been deceived, but that I'd deceived myself."

Hughes in Las Vegas: Mary Manning, "Howard Hughes: A Revolutionary Recluse, *Las Vegas Sun*, May 15, 2008; Ken Cooper, " 'Zero Pays the House': The Las Vegas Novel and Atomic Roulette," *Contemporary Literature* 33, no. 3 (Autumn 1992).

14. Impossible Missions

CIA radio and Soviet attacks on U.S. race relations: In 1954, when the Supreme Court overturned school segregation in *Brown v. Board of Education*, "the opinion gave the State Department the counter to Soviet propaganda it had been looking for," wrote Mary L. Dudziak in "Desegregation as a Cold War Imperative," *Stanford Law Review* 41, no. 1 (November 1988), "and the State Department wasted no time in making use of it. Within an hour after the decision was handed down, the *Voice of America* broadcast the news to Eastern Europe." On May 18, 1954, the *New York Times* quoted a VOA official saying that behind the Iron Curtain "the people would know nothing about the decision except what would be told them by the Communist press and radio, which you may be sure would be twisted and perverted. They have been told that the Negro in the United States is still practically a slave and a declassed person." In contrast, Robert Patterson, the founder of the white Citizens' Council, judged Brown as a symptom of a "communistic disease" and that "people are resigning themselves to seeing their children crammed into schools and churches with children of other races and being taught the Communist theme of all races and mongrelization." Georgia's segregationist governor Herman Talmadge wrote, "In some instances, we have shaped our national policy by trying to please the Communists....Who cares what the Reds say? Who cares what *Pravda* prints?"

Willis Conover: "The Voice of Jazz Behind the Iron Curtain," broadcast of NPR's *Weekend Edition Saturday* with Scott Simon, July 25, 2015. From his May 19, 1996, obituary in the *New York Times*, "Willis Conover Is Dead at 75; Aimed Jazz at the Soviet Bloc," by Robert McG. Thomas Jr.:

"There were immediate grumblings in Congress about wasting taxpayers' money by broadcasting frivolous music, but Mr. Conover, a scholar who discussed music and interviewed musicians but never mentioned politics, won the day. In 1993 the House of Representatives honored him with a resolution praising the man who had been called one of the country's greatest foreign policy tools. An independent-minded man, Mr. Conover had his share of run-ins with Voice of America officials but never backed down. As an independent contractor, he had full control over his programming choices, and besides, he had listened to too much jazz to do things any way but his own."

The power of jazz in the Cold War: From Billy Perrigo, "How the U.S. Used Jazz as a Cold War Secret Weapon," *Time*, December 22, 2017: "The music of jazz, which was structured around improvisation within a set of commonly agreed-upon boundaries, was a perfect metaphor for America in the eyes of the State Department. Here was music of democracy and freedom.... By sending bands comprised of black and white musicians to play together around the world, the State Department could engineer an image of racial harmony to offset the bad press about racism at home."

Radio Free Europe: Kenneth Osgood, "The C.I.A.'s Fake News," *New York Times* (op-ed), October 14, 2017.

Ukrainian covert operations: Kevin C. Ruffner, "Cold War Allies: The Origins of CIA's Relationship with Ukrainian Nationalists," CIA report, 1998.

15. Charming Betrayal

Psychology of the Magnificent Five/access to "Inner Ring": From David Brooks, "The Art of Thinking Well," *New York Times*, October 10, 2017: "In every setting—a school, a company, or a society—there is an official hierarchy. But there may also be a separate prestige hierarchy, where the cool kids are. They are the Inner Ring.... There are always going to be people who desperately want to get into the Inner Ring and will cut all sorts of intellectual corners to be accepted. As [C. S.] Lewis put it: 'The passion for the Inner Ring is most skillful in making a man who is not yet a bad man do very bad things.'"

John le Carré: Interview by Sarah Lyall, *New York Times Book Review*, August 21, 2017.

Harvey's Oyster House: Pamela Kessler, "Cloak-and-Swagger," *Washington Post*, March 3, 1989.

"Wilderness of mirrors": From Arthur Redding, "A Wilderness of Mirrors: Writing and Reading the Cold War," *Contemporary Literature* 51, no. 4 (Winter 2010): "[James] Angleton himself likened the duplicitous world of intelligence to the paradoxical play of signs in modern poetry.... If the 'intentional fallacy' suggests a radical break between intent and utterance, then it is just a short, contrarian step to disbelieving everyone's account of themselves: the more reliable an agent's credentials, the more likely he was, in Angleton's mind, to be a Soviet agent." Author Terrence Hawkes noted that Angleton described his work as "the practical criticism of ambiguity."

Yuri Nosenko: John Hart, "Monster Plot: Counterintelligence in the Case of Yuriy Ivanovich Nosenko," CIA, December 1976; James Risen, "What Cold War Intrigue Can Tell Us About the Trump-Russia Inquiry," *New York Times*, March 30, 2017.

Angleton's madness: Jefferson Morley, "Wilderness of Mirrors: Documents Reveal the Complex Legacy of James Angleton, CIA Counterintelligence Chief and Godfather of Mass Surveillance," *The Intercept*, January 1, 2018.

Kim Philby in the USSR: Ron Rosenbaum, "Kim Philby and the Age of Paranoia," *New York Times*, July 10, 1994.

16. Tragic Climax

Motive for Forrestal's suicide: Alexander Wooley, "The Fall of James Forrestal," *Washington Post*, May 23, 1999.

World petroleum market: David S. Painter, "Oil and the American Century," *Journal of American History* 99, no. 1 (June 2012).

17. Approaching Midnight

Kennan's opposition to the hydrogen bomb: "Memorandum by the Counselor (Kennan)," Department of State Atomic Energy Files, Top Secret [Washington, D.C.], January 20, 1950.

Kennette Benedict: Interviewed in Chicago on November 17, 2016, by Cindy Kelly as part of the Atomic Heritage Foundation's Voices of the Manhattan Project.

NSC-68: From Louis Menand, "Fat Man," *New Yorker,* June 27, 2005: "The early Cold Warriors... were at least as worried about American attitudes as they were about Soviet intentions. Obsessed with preparedness, they sometimes did not scruple about overstating the threat for which preparation was necessary. They practiced psychological warfare on their own people." From Samuel Moyn and David Priestland, "A Problem Worse Than Tyranny," *New York Times,* August 13, 2017: "Focusing on exaggerated threats to freedom and stigmatizing the communist enemy undermined... progressive goals. [NSC-68] argued that the Cold War justified the reduction of non-military expenditure by the 'deferment of certain desirable programs,' including welfare. And while the New Deal was not dismantled, efforts to extend it were denounced as pink tyranny. Casualties included attempts to create a national health care program. The consequences for American politics have been huge." From Tony Perucci, "The Red Mask of Sanity: Paul Robeson, HUAC, and the Sound of Cold War Performance," *TDR: The Drama Review* 53, no. 4 (Winter 2009): "NSC-68 can be seen as an example of... 'crisis talk,' which is often used to create an illusion of scarcity of resources as well as of permanent political stasis.... As a result, political dissent must be restricted, 'extravagant' social services must be cut or canceled, and labor must cooperate with the liberal corporate establishment to maintain labor stability."

Norman Cousins: Norman Cousins, "Literacy of Survival," *Saturday Review,* September 14, 1946.

Henry Stimson: Henry L. Stimson, "The Decision to Use the Atomic Bomb," *Harper's Magazine,* February 1947.

U.S. opinion on dropping atomic bombs: A 1945 Gallup poll conducted immediately after the bombing found that 85 percent of Americans approved the attacks on Hiroshima and Nagasaki. By 1991, approval had fallen to 63 percent, according to a survey by the *Detroit Free Press.*

CIA report on the Korean War: P. K. Rose, "Two Strategic Intelligence Mistakes in Korea, 1950," CIA, May 8, 2007.

Truman says U.S. fighting for survival in Korea: Transcript of presidential news conference, November 30, 1950.

U.S. national security infrastructure: Loch Johnson, "Congressional Supervision of America's Secret Agencies: The Experience and Legacy of the Church Committee," *Public Administration Review* 64, no. 1 (January/February 2004).

"two scorpions in a bottle": Robert Oppenheimer, "Atomic Weapons and American Policy," *Foreign Affairs*, July 1953.

John Sommerville: Mike Granberry, "Octogenarian Coined 'Omnicide' During Lifelong Push for Peace," *Los Angeles Times*, November 30, 1986.

U.S. obsession with the USSR: "Never in the history of the world was one people as completely dominated, intellectually and morally, by another as the people of the United States by the people of Russia in the four years from 1946 through 1949," Archibald MacLeish wrote in *The Conquest of America* (1949). "American foreign policy was a mirror image of Russian foreign policy: whatever the Russians did, we did in reverse. American domestic politics were conducted under a kind of upside-down Russian veto: no man could be elected to public office unless he was on record as detesting the Russians, and no proposal could be enacted, from a peace plan at one end to a military budget at the other, unless it could be demonstrated that the Russians wouldn't like it. American political controversy was controversy sung to the Russian tune; left-wing movements attacked right-wing movements not on American issues but on Russian issues, and right-wing movements replied with the same arguments turned round about.... All this took place not in a time of national weakness or decay but precisely at the moment when the United States, having engineered a tremendous triumph and fought its way to a brilliant victory in the greatest of all wars, had reached the highest point of world power ever achieved by a single state."

18. Absent Evidence

Judith Coplon profile: Posted in www.spartacus-educational.com by John Simkin, August 2014.

VENONA intercepts and surplus of secrets: From Jack Shafer, "America's Secret Fetish," *Columbia Journalism Review*: "Official secrets have been reproducing faster than a basket of mongooses thanks to the miracle of 'derivative classification,' and this rapid propagation has compounded the maintenance costs. Whenever information stamped as classified is folded into a new document—either verbatim or in paraphrased form—that new derivative document is born classified. Derivative classification—and the fact that nobody ever got fired for overusing the classified stamp—means that 92.1 million "classification decisions" were made in FY 2011, according to a government report, a 20 percent increase over FY 2010. Once created, your typical secret is a stubborn thing. The secret-makers' reluctance to declassify their trove is legendary: In 1997, 204 million pages were declassified, but since 9/11 only an average of 33.5 million pages have been declassified annually."

Ex-RAND and Pentagon analyst Daniel Ellsberg on first having access to the highest level of security clearance: "After you've started reading all this daily intelligence input and become used to using what amounts to whole libraries of hidden information, which is more closely held than mere top secret data, you will forget there ever was a time when you didn't have it, and you'll be aware only of the fact that you have it now and most others don't . . . and that all the other people are fools." Kevin Drum, "Daniel Ellsberg on the Limits of Knowledge," *Mother Jones*, February 27, 2010.

Alger Hiss case: Allen Weinstein, "The Alger Hiss Case Revisited," *American Scholar* 41, no. 1 (Winter 1971–72); John Ehrman, "The Alger Hiss Case: A Half-Century of Controversy," CIA, August 3, 2011.

19. Crime of the Century

Roy Cohn: Alvin Krebs, "Aide to McCarthy and Fiery Lawyer Dies at 59," *New York Times*, August 2, 1986; Jerry James, "The Stories Behind the Story of Tony Kushner's 'Angels in America,'" TheRogueTheatre .org; Frank Rich, "The Original Donald Trump," *New York* magazine, April 29, 2018.

Donald Trump: Jonathan Mahler and Matt Flegenheimer, "What Donald Trump Learned from Joseph McCarthy's Right-Hand Man," *New York Times*, June 20, 2016; Marie Brenner, "How Donald Trump and Roy Cohn's Ruthless Symbiosis Changed America," *Vanity Fair*, June 28, 2017.

Eisenhower's reaction to the Rosenberg case: From Tony Perucci, "The Red Mask of Sanity: Paul Robeson, HUAC, and the Sound of Cold War Performance," *TDR: The Drama Review* 53, no. 4 (Winter 2009): "For Eisenhower, policy decisions were to be made for their theatrical efficacy. Statecraft for him was indeed a form of stagecraft. In anticipation of the execution of Julius and Ethel Rosenberg, he explained to his Cabinet that preventing the execution would only be justified when 'statecraft dictated in the interests of the American public opinion or of the reputation of the United States government in the eyes of the world.' As enactments of the statecraft of stagecraft, domestic political acts were theatrical expressions of the United States Government in the eyes of the world."

Other sources: Peter Daniels and Bill Van Auken, "Fifty Years Since the Execution of the Rosenbergs," World Socialist Web Site, June 15, 2013.

20. Third-Rate Speaker

The onset of McCarthyism: From the *1950 CQ Almanac*: "[Joe] McCarthy took the Senate floor Feb. 20, [1950,] and in a six-hour speech described, but did not name, 81 persons whom he said were disloyal employees of the State Department....McCarthy refused to name names despite repeated efforts by Senate Majority Leader Scott Lucas (D Ill.) to pry them out....As the Senate continued into the night, Brien McMahon (D Conn.), recalled from a black-tie party, entered the chamber in formal attire to challenge briskly McCarthy's information sources. McCarthy again refused to divulge them on the floor....The Senate did not quit for the night until 11:43 p.m....The following day, Feb. 21, Lucas convened a Senate Democratic caucus which approved his plan of introducing S Res 231 calling for an investigation of McCarthy's charges....Loyalty files of the FBI would be involved, and Lucas and McMahon declared that confidential data and methods of the FBI could be impaired if the records were revealed during the course of the probe....The investigating subcommittee was named by the Foreign Relations Committee Feb. 25 [soon to be referenced as the Tydings Committee]. On it were: Millard E. Tydings (D Md.), chairman, Brien McMahon (D Conn.), Theodore F. Green (D R.I.), Henry Cabot Lodge, Jr. (R Mass.), and Bourke B. Hickenlooper (R Iowa). The Subcommittee was given the following instructions by the full Committee: 'Make a full and complete study and investigation of all government employees now in the Department of State and former employees of the Department of State now in other agencies of the government against whom charges are made, in order to determine whether or not said employees are, or have been, disloyal to the United States and to use the power of subpoena whenever necessary.'...McCarthy was the principal witness during the initial hearings which began on March 8, [1950,] under the authorizing provisions of S Res 231. During the course of his appearances before the Tydings Subcommittee, McCarthy charged 10 individuals by name with varying degrees of Communist activity: Prof. Frederick L. Schuman, Williams College; Prof. Owen J. Lattimore, Johns Hopkins University; Prof. Harlow Shapley, Harvard; Dorothy Kenyon, New York attorney; Gustavo Duran, former State Dept. employee, and then a UN official; Haldore Hanson, State Dept. officer; Philip C. Jessup, Ambassador at large; Mrs. Esther Brunauer, State Dept. Officer; John Service, Foreign Service officer; and Stephen Brunauer, Navy scientist."

McCarthy's dishonesty: A newsman of the period was quoted as saying, "My own impression was that Joe was a demagogue. But what could I do? I had to report—and quote—McCarthy. How do you say in the middle of your story, 'This is a lie?' The press is supposedly neutral."

The church's holy war: On March 30, 1930, the *New York Times* reported that Pope Pius XI conducted a "solemn rite" to a Vatican congregation of fifty thousand praying for Russians and denouncing atheism. The pope reportedly concluded by chanting a psalm "for the repose of the souls killed in the Russian persecutions."

Mary Ann Van Hoof: Susan Hogan, " 'Pray and Pray Hard': When 100,000 Waited to See the Virgin Mary on a Wisconsin Farm," *Washington Post*, August 26, 2018.

Greater Christian anticommunism: From Molly Werthen, "A Match Made in Heaven," *Atlantic*, May 2017: "By the 1950s, Billy Graham was rallying huge crowds with his dark predictions about the communist menace, an ideology 'masterminded by Satan.' ... In blending their movement's libertarian inclinations with anti-communist hysteria and anxieties about cultural change ... evangelical leaders helped catalyze the most powerful ideology in modern American politics: Christian free-market mania. ... In the United States, conservative white Protestants ensured that the welfare state remained anemic." From Sam Tannenhaus, "The Right Idea," *New Yorker*, October 24, 2016: "The Conservative Rally for World Liberation, held in March 1962, drew a crowd of eighteen thousand, with pickets and protestors gathered outside. Organized by a new rightist group, the Young Americas for Freedom, the event was greeted as evidence that the 'silent generation' might be shaking off its apathy and finding a political voice.... The star of the event was L. Brent Bozell.... Bozell gave a speech... equating the 'heresy of Gnosticism' in Kennedy's liberalism with Khrushchev's Communism, and then summoned conservatives to reject both in order to 'build a Christian civilization.' Its divine mission was to harry Communists across the globe—in Africa, in Cuba, in Europe."

21. Notoriously Disgraceful Conduct

Sources: Richard Hofstadter, "The Paranoid Style in American Politics," essay adapted from the Herbert Spencer Lecture delivered at Oxford University in November 1963.

Supposed link between homosexuality and communism: In a 1955 report, RAND analyst Nathan Leites claimed that the "Bolshevik belief" in an imminent attack by the West was a "classical paranoid defense against latent homosexuality," and Soviet aggression was "an effort to ward off fear-laden and guilty wishes to embrace men and be embraced by them."

Judith Atkins: Judith Atkins, "'These People Are Frightened to Death': Congressional Investigations and the Lavender Scare," *Prologue* magazine 48, no. 2 (Summer 2016).

Roy Cohn profile: Ken Auletta, "Don't Mess with Roy Cohn," *Esquire*, December 1978.

Cohn and Schine: Richard H. Rovere, "The Adventures of Cohn and Schine," *The Reporter*, July 21, 1953.

Eric Sevareid's criticism of Edward R. Murrow: From Nicholas Lemann, "The Murrow Doctrine," *New Yorker*, January 23, 2006: "By the time the first *See It Now* program on McCarthy aired, on March 9, 1954, McCarthy was past the height of his powers.... At that point, the most powerful press baron in the country was Henry Luce, and his magazines had been intermittently critical of McCarthy for years. Of the major news organizations, only Hearst was ardently pro-McCarthy.... Murrow picked an opportune moment to strike; if he'd waited even two more months, it would have been difficult to present him now as the man who discredited McCarthy."

22. Cross of Iron

Dwight Eisenhower profile: Rick Atkinson "Ike's Dark Days," *U.S. News & World Report*, October 28, 2002.

Military-industrial complex: Robert Biggs, "The Cold War Economy: Opportunity Costs, Ideology, and the Politics of Crisis," *Explorations in Economic History*, July 1, 1994; William D. Hartung, "Eisenhower's Warning: The Military-Industrial Complex Forty Years Later," *World Policy Journal* 18, no. 1 (Spring 2001); Stephen Schwartz, "The Cost of U.S. Nuclear Weapons," Nuclear Threat Initiative (NTI), October 1, 2008; John Swift, "The Soviet-American Arms Race," *History Review*, issue 63 (March 2009).

First SIOP: Andrew Rice, "403 Minutes with Daniel Ellsberg: Staring into the Abyss with the Famous Pentagon Papers Leaker," *New York* magazine, November 27–December 10, 2017; Thomas Powers, "The Nuclear Worrier," *New York Review of Books*, January 18, 2018; interview by Dan Amira, "Daniel Ellsberg Thinks We're in Denial About Nuclear War," *New York Times Magazine*, February 11, 2018.

Castle Bravo test: Daniel Lang, "Fallout," *New Yorker*, July 16, 1955.

Godzilla: John Rocco Roberto, "Study of the Effects of the Atomic Bomb on Japanese Culture," HistoryVortex.org, 2000; Steve Ryfle, "Godzilla's Footprint," *Virginia Quarterly Review*, Winter 2005; Brian Merchant, "A Brief History of Godzilla, Our Walking Nuclear Nightmare," *Motherboard Blog*, August 23, 2013.

23. Civil Defense

Fallout shelters: Garrett M. Graff, "The Doomsday Diet: Meet the All-Purpose Survival Cracker, the US Government's Cold War–Era Nutrition Solution for Life After a Nuclear Blast," *Eater*, December 12, 2017. From Alison McQueen, "How to Be a Prophet of Doom," *New York Times*, May 13, 2018: "In a series of works published in the early 1960s, Herman Kahn, a RAND strategist, was arguing that the United States could survive an all-out nuclear war and even resume something like a normal life.... Within a few days of a nuclear attack, a *Time* article predicted that people might begin to emerge: 'With trousers tucked into sock tops and sleeves tied around wrists, with hats, mufflers, gloves, and boots, the shelter dweller could venture forth to start ensuring his today and building for tomorrow.'" From Louis Menand, "Fat Man" *New Yorker*, June 27, 2005: "[Kahn] was the champion salesman of the fallout shelter, and was especially excited by the potential of mineshafts as evacuation centers...."

But—and this is the strange logic of deterrence—the essential purpose of investing billions in civil defense was not to save lives but to enhance the credibility of America's nuclear threat.... [Kahn] contemplated the possibility of several mass evacuations every decade in order to bolster American credibility."

U.S. government doomsday plans: Transcript of interview with author Garrett Graff, NPR's *Fresh Air* with Terry Gross, June 21, 2017.

U.S. bases overseas: From Jimmy Carter, *Faith: A Journey for All* (Simon & Schuster, 2018): As of 2017, "there were 240,000 American troops stationed in at least 172 foreign nations, plus more than 37,000 others in places militarily classified as secret." At the same time, U.S. "infrastructure investment gap," Carter noted, "is the largest of the 50 richest nations."

Bomber gap: "Weapons of Mass Destruction/The Bomber Gap," GlobalSecurity.org.

Vulnerability of nuclear command-and-control system: Eric Schlosser, "World War Three, by Mistake," *New Yorker*, December 23, 2016.

The peace sign: Zoe Levornik, "What the Campaign to Stop Killer Robots Can Learn from the Antinuclear Weapons Movement," *Bulletin of the Atomic Scientists*, August 29, 2018.

24. Serving Money

John Foster Dulles: John M. Mulder, "The Moral World of John Foster Dulles: A Presbyterian Layman and International Affairs," *Journal of Presbyterian History* 19, no. 2 (Summer 1971); Peter Dale Scott, "The Dulles Brothers, Harry Dexter White, Alger Hiss, and the Fate of the Private Prewar International Banking System," *Asia-Pacific Journal*, April 20, 2014; William Jefferson Hedrick II, "John Foster Dulles and the Gospel of Corporate Internationalism" (BA honors thesis, Florida Atlantic University, April 28, 2015).

Edward Lansdale: Marc D. Bernstein, "Ed Lansdale's Black Warfare in 1950s Vietnam," *Vietnam Point of View*, February 16, 2010. From Louis Menand, "Made in Vietnam," *New Yorker*, February 26, 2018: "[Lansdale] was a fabricator of fronts, the man behind the curtain. He manipulated events—through payoffs, propaganda, and sometimes more nefarious means—to insure that indigenous politicians friendly to the United States would be 'freely' elected. Internal opposition to these leaders could then be characterized as 'an insurgency.'...(The Soviets, of course, operated in exactly the same way, through fronts and election fixing. The Cold War was a looking-glass war.)" Menand continued, "The Vietnam he imagined was a Western fantasy....He was a liberal internationalist. He believed if you scratched a Vietnamese or a Filipino, you found a James Madison under the skin." Lansdale did not speak either of the principal languages in South Vietnam: French and Vietnamese.

Ho Chi Minh: More from the same Menand essay: "[Ho] was a Communist but he was a Communist because he was a nationalist. Twice he had appealed to American Presidents to support his independence movement—to Woodrow Wilson after the First World War, and Truman at the end of the Second—and twice he had been ignored. Only the Communists, he had concluded, were truly committed to the principle of self-determination in Asia. The Geneva Accords called for a national election to be held in Vietnam in 1956....Many people in the American government thought Ho would have won."

Nepotism: Diem's brother Ngo Dinh Nhu reportedly funded the family's political party with piracy, extortion, opium trading, and currency exchange manipulation. Menand: "Thousands of Vietnamese suspected of disloyalty were arrested, tortured and executed by beheading or disembowelment."

Marilyn Young: Her obituary: Sam Roberts, "Historian Who Challenged Foreign Policy," *New York Times*, March 9, 2017.

Doolittle report: From Wikipedia: "*The Report on the Covert Activities of the Central Intelligence Agency* is a 69-page formerly classified comprehensive study on the personnel, security, adequacy, and efficacy of the Central Intelligence Agency written by Lieutenant General James H. Doolittle. United States President Dwight Eisenhower requested the report in July 1954."

H. Stuart Hughes: H. Stuart Hughes, "A Politics of Peace: Reflections on C. Wright Mills's 'The Causes of World War III,' " *Commentary*, February 1959.

25. Dry the Grass

Failure in Vietnam: Thomas L. Ahern Jr., "CIA and the House of Ngo: Covert Actions in South Vietnam (1954–63)," CIA History Staff,

Center for the Study of Intelligence, June 2000. CIA agent Donald P. Gregg in a 2017 *New York Times* letter to the editor wrote, "We should have seen it as the end of the colonial era in Southeast Asia, which it really was. But instead, we saw it in Cold War terms, and we saw it as the defeat for the free world that was related to the rise of China. And that was a total misreading of a pivotal event, which cost us very dearly." During Senate hearings in 1966, George Kennan opposed the U.S. policy of regime change: "Our country should not be asked, and should not ask of itself, to shoulder the main burden of determining the political realities in any other country." In 2008, Henry Kissinger told *Newsweek*, "Hanoi's leaders had fought a decade against France and battled the United States for a similar length of time, not to achieve a political compromise, but to prevail." From Louis Menand, "Made in Vietnam," *New Yorker*, February 26, 2018: "Political terms are short, and so politics is short term. The main consideration that seems to have presented itself to . . . Presidents, from Harry Truman to Richard Nixon, who insisted on staying the course was domestic politics—the fear of being blamed by voters for losing Southeast Asia to Communism. If Southeast Asia was going to be lost to Communism, they preferred that it be on another President's head." From Vietnam veteran Karl Marlantes, "The War That Killed Trust," *New York Times*, January 8, 2017: "Vietnam changed us as a country. In many ways, for the worse: It made us cynical and distrustful of our institutions, especially of government. For many people, it eroded the notion, once nearly universal, that part of being an American was serving your country."

Castro's revolution: The October 19, 1959, issue of *Time* reported that Fidel Castro had even nationalized the country's bat guano caves.

The Godfather: Part II: Screenplay by Francis Ford Coppola and Mario Puzo; released by Paramount Pictures (1974).

Cambodia: Fred Branfman, "Henry Kissinger: Enlightened Statesman or Odious Schlumpf?," *Salon*, November 15, 2002; Ben Kiernan, "The American Bombardment of Kampuchea, 1969–1973," *Vietnam Generation* 1, no. 1, article 3 (1989).

Proxy conflicts during the Cold War: Milton Leitenberg, "Deaths in Wars and Conflicts in the 20th Century," Cornell University, Peace Studies Program, Occasional Paper #29, August 2003. Wars "won" by Soviet-backed forces included: China (6 million combatants and civilians killed); Vietnam (3 million killed); Cambodia (2 million killed); Angola (1.6 million killed); and Mozambique (1 million killed). Wars "won" by U.S.-backed forces included: Afghanistan (1 million killed); Ethiopia (1 million killed); Guatemala (212,000 killed); Greece (154,000 killed); and Congo (100,000). The Algerian civil war (1 million killed) was a military victory for the West, but a political victory for the Soviets, who supported an insurgency that ultimately gained independence from France. Wars in Korea (4.5 million killed), Sudan (750,000 killed), and Lebanon (130,000 dead) ended in stalemate.

26. Burying History

Soviet living conditions: Dmitry Sudakov, "What Was It Like to Live in the Soviet Union?," Pravda.ru, March 6, 2016. One of David Remnick's most noteworthy Moscow dispatches was a *Washington Post* story on December 4, 1989, headlined "Meanwhile, Soviets View a Hit Parade of Shoddy Goods": "Thousands of Soviets...caught the metro out to northern Moscow's Exhibition of Economic Achievements and looked at a collection of economic underachievements...['The Exhibit of Poor Quality Goods'] features oblong volleyballs, cross-eyed teddy bears, rusted samovars, chipped stew pots, putrid lettuce, unraveled shuttlecocks, crushed cans of fish and, perhaps the show-stopper, a bottle of mineral water with a tiny dead mouse floating inside.... 'It was time to inject a little reality into the scene here,' said one of the park's guides, Sveta Redichova. The sheer crumminess of nearly every product sold in Soviet stores is an appalling fact of life. Towels scratch, milk sours, cars collapse. The leading cause of house fires in the Soviet Union is exploding televisions. In order to assemble the exhibit, [Maria] Nitchkina said, 'We didn't have to go to much effort. We just went into a few stores picked at random and that was that.'"

Peter Preston: Peter Preston, "The Dead Hand by David Hoffman—Review," *Guardian*, February 4, 2011.

27. Space Race

Sputnik: Marina Koren, "How Sputnik Launched an Era of Technological Fragility," *Atlantic*, October 4, 2017; Jacey Fortin "Orbit of Sputnik Surprised Many, but American Spies Saw It Coming," *New York Times*, October 7, 2017.

Soviet space dogs: "Remembering Laika, Space Dog and Soviet Hero," Alex Wellerstein, *New Yorker*, November 3, 2017.

Bernard Schriever: Steve Coll, "The Cabinet of Dr. Strangelove," *New York Review of Books*, February 25, 2010.

Kurt Stehling: Constance McLaughlin Green and Milton Lomask, *Vanguard: A History* (National Aeronautics and Space Administration, Office of Technology Utilization, 1970).

28. Mind Games

Manchurian Candidate: Screenplay by George Axelrod; released by United Artists (1962).

Brainwashing: Louis Menand, "Brainwashed: Where the 'Manchurian Candidate' Came From," *New Yorker*, September 15, 2003; Lorraine Boissoneault, "The True Story of Brainwashing and How It Shaped America," Smithsonian.com, May 22, 2017; Susan Carruthers, "Who's Afraid of Brainwashing," *New York Times*, January 21, 2018.

Korean War POWs: *POW: The Fight Continues After the Battle*, report by the Secretary of Defense's Advisory Committee on Prisoners of War, August 1955.

LSD: Albert Hofmann, "Exploring an Alternate Universe: Albert Hofmann Discovers the Effects of LSD," *Lapham's Quarterly*.

MK-ULTRA: W. Henry Wall Jr., "How the CIA's LSD Mind-Control Experiments Destroyed My Healthy, High-Functioning Father's Brilliant Mind," AlterNet, August 8, 2012 (excerpt from *Healing to Hell*, NewSouth Books); Chris Calton, "When the CIA Partied with LSD on the Taxpayers' Dime," *Mises Wire*, March 15, 2017.

Errol Morris: Matthew Gault, "Wormwood Is an LSD-Soaked True Crime Masterpiece," Motherboard, December 28, 2017.

Masters of Deceit: In the book, Hoover describes communists as "ordinary looking people, like your seatmate on the bus or a clerk in one of your neighborhood stores."

Ted Kaczynski: Alton Chase, "Harvard and the Making of the Unabomber," *Atlantic*, June 2000; Janet Maslin, "The Unabomber and the 'Culture of Despair,'" *New York Times*, March 3, 2003.

29. Dance with Détente

Soviet secrecy: From Sheila Fitzpatrick, "War and Society in Soviet Context: Soviet Labor Before, During, and After World War II," *International Labor and Working Class History*, no. 35 (Spring 1989): "It is remarkable . . . to think that the systematic falsification of all published maps of the Soviet Union, instituted around 1938 as a method of battling foreign spies and potential invading armies, was still practiced as late as 1988, when it was likely to baffle nobody but the car-driving grandchildren of Soviet war veterans."

Joe Alsop: Edwin M. Yoder Jr., "Joe Alsop Resisted Soviet Blackmail in the 1950s," *Raleigh News & Observer*, January 18, 2017.

30. Send in the Clowns

Cold War rhetoric: From Louis Menand, "Fat Man," *New Yorker*, June 27, 2005: "If the United States assigned the Soviets the role of mechanized Enemy Other, the Soviets did their best to play it. . . . It served both sides in the Cold War to take each other's rhetoric at face value. We have yet to learn how not to do this."

Ultra-right fanatics: From the *San Francisco Chronicle*, July 31, 1964: "The John Birch Society is attempting to suppress a television series about the United Nations by means of a mass letter-writing campaign to the sponsor. . . . The Xerox Corporation, however, intends to go on with the programs. . . . Birch official John Rousselot said, 'We hate to have a corporation of this country promote the U.N. when we know it is an instrument of the Soviet Communist conspiracy.'" *None Dare Call It Treason* was a 1964 privately published best-seller by John Stormer claiming communist infiltration at all levels of government, from school boards to the White House. As Jim Dwyer reported in the *New York Times*, January 11, 2017, "a full-fledged excavation of the book's footnotes, *None Dare Call It Reason*, was published in a monograph form in 1965 by Julian Foster, a political science professor at California State University, Fullerton, and five colleagues. It catalogued twisted quotes and distorted paraphrasing everywhere."

William Fulbright: Giles Scott-Smith, "Bill and Ed's Big Adventure: Cold Warriors, William Fulbright and Right-Wing Propaganda in the U.S. Military, 1961–62," *Histoire@Politique*, no. 35 (May–August 2018).

John Glenn: John Noble Wilford, "John Glenn, American Hero of the Space Age, Dies at 95," *New York Times*, December 8, 2016.

31. Grand Settlement

Berlin Wall: An estimated 5,000 East Germans escaped over the Berlin Wall, and 138 were killed in the attempt.

Cuban Missile Crisis: Graham Allison, "The Cuban Missile Crisis at 50: Lessons for U.S. Foreign Policy Today," *Foreign Affairs*, July/August 2012; Michael Mosettig, "Cuban Missile Crisis: Memories of a Young Reporter," *PBS NewsHour*, October 22, 2012; Benjamin Schwarz, "The Real Cuban Missile Crisis," *Atlantic*, January/February 2013; Ross Douthat, "The Missiles of August," *New York Times*, August 12, 2017; George Perkovich, "The Other Terrifying Lesson of the Cuban Missile Crisis," *Politico*, January 4, 2018; "Nuclear Close Calls: The Cuban Missile Crisis," Atomic Heritage Foundation, June 15, 2018.

Downing of U-2: Sergei Khrushchev, "How My Father and President Kennedy Saved the World: The Cuban Missile Crisis as Seen from the Kremlin," *American Heritage*, October 2002.

Vasili Arkhipov: Avery Thomson, "The Time a Single Soviet Officer Averted a Nuclear War," PopularMechanics.com, September 27, 2016.

32. Chaos Theory

Chaos theory: Peter Dizikes, "When the Butterfly Effect Took Flight," *MIT Technology Review*, February 22, 2011.

Byron De La Beckwith: From Kelly J. Baker, "White-Collar Supremacy," *New York Times*, November 25, 2016: "The 1950s saw another surge of 'respectable' racism, this time in the form of Citizens Councils, founded in Mississippi by Robert B. Patterson in response to the Supreme Court's Brown v Board of Education decision. Rather than the vigilantism and terrorism of the 1950s and '60s Klan, the councils relied on more middle-class methods of opposing civil rights: boycotting black-owned businesses and denying mortgages to black people. The sociologist Charles M. Payne describes them as 'pursuing the agenda of the Klan with the demeanor of the Rotary Club.'"

Bob Dylan: "Only a Pawn in Their Game" was released on Dylan's *The Times They Are a-Changin'* album (1964).

Thomas Hughes: Mary Dudziak, "Desegregation as a Cold War Imperative," *Stanford Law Review* 41, no. 1 (November 1988).

Stan Lee: Tegan O'Neil, "How the Cold War Saved Marvel and Birthed a Generation of Superheroes," *A.V. Club*, March 31, 2016.

FBI letter to Martin Luther King: Beverly Gage, "What an Uncensored Letter to M.L.K. Reveals," *New York Times*, November 11, 2014.

Malcolm X's assassination: Wayne Drash, "Malcolm X Killer Freed After 44 Years," CNN, April 28, 2010; Garrett Felber, "50 Years on, Mystery Still Clouds Details of the Case," *Guardian*, February 21, 2015; DeNeen L. Brown, "Malcolm X Didn't Fear Being Killed," *Washington Post*, February 26, 2015.

Watts riots: From Kurt Andersen, "Hands Up. It's Showtime," *New York Times*, September 8, 2017: "Yet long before President Trump, the militarization of the police was being shaped by fantasy and entertainment with roots in 1960s Los Angeles....Darryl Gates was persuaded that the department needed its own special-ops corps, with military equipment and outfits, so that the cops could look and act like soldiers. He wanted to call the new units Special Weapons Attack Teams: SWAT....The first SWAT team trained on a Universal back lot."

Conservative backlash: From Rick Perlstein, "Apocalyptics," *New York Times Magazine*, April 16, 2017: "In 1965, Congress once more allowed large-scale immigration to the United States—and it is no accident that this date coincides with the increasing conservative backlash against liberalism itself, now that its spoils would be more widely distributed among nonwhites."

1968 presidential election: Louis Menand, "Been There," *New Yorker*, January 8, 2018. More from Perlstein's *New York Times Magazine* piece: "Educated whites in the prosperous metropolises of the New South sublimated the frenetic, violent anxieties that once marked race relations in their region into more palatable policy concerns about 'stable housing values' and 'quality local education,' backfooting liberals and transforming conservatives into mainstream champions of a set of positions with an enormous appeal to the white middle class."

Curtis LeMay's famous "Stone Age" quote about Vietnam: The quote comes from *Mission with LeMay: My Story* (Doubleday, 1965): "My solution to the problem would be to tell [the North Vietnamese communists] frankly that they've got to draw in their horns and stop their aggression or we're going to bomb them into the Stone Age. And we would shove them back into the Stone Age with Air power or Naval power—not with ground forces."

1968 Wallace-LeMay rally at Madison Square Garden: After the rally, fights between Wallace supporters and Wallace protestors became so violent that *New Republic* columnist Richard Strout observed, "Never again will you read about Berlin in the 1930s without remembering this wild confrontation here of two irrational forces."

Nixon subverts LBJ Vietnam peace talks: John Farrell, "Tricky Dick's Vietnam Treachery," *New York Times* (op-ed), December 31, 2016.

Night of the Living Dead: A. O. Scott and Jason Zinoman, "Provocative Old Masters of Horror," *New York Times*, July 18, 2017.

The White Album: Released on November 22, 1968, the ninth studio album by the Beatles—officially titled *The Beatles*—was recorded largely at London's Abbey Road Studios in the summer of 1968 and ultimately distributed in an all-white sleeve. It is a so-called double album of two vinyl records with tracks on both sides. Other than the name of the band embossed in Helvetica typeface, there is no other graphic or text. The first track of thirty is "Back in the USSR." Like virtually all the songs on the album, it was conceived in the first few months of 1968, while the band was chilling in Rishikesh, India, at the ashram of Transcendental Meditation guru Maharishi Mahesh Yogi. The song had an unofficial collaborator, Mike Love of the Beach Boys, who had joined the Beatles on the retreat and provided McCartney with feedback. As Love recalled, "Paul came down to the breakfast table one morning, saying, 'Hey Mike, listen to this.' And he starts strumming and singing 'Back in the USSR.' And I said, 'Well, Paul, what you ought to do is talk about the girls around Russia, Ukraine girls and then Georgia on my mind, and that kind of thing." In one nod to Love's Beach Boys, McCartney's lyrics would flip "California Girls" to "Moscow Girls," and the background harmonies would include a definitive Beach Boys "Oooeeeeooooo." The double entendre suggested by Mike Love, "Georgia on My Mind," was a tip of the hat to Ray Charles. The tone and texture was deeply influenced, like much of the Beatles' music, by the formative American rockers of the fifties: The title and the bluesy feel evokes Chuck Berry's 1959 hit "Back in the USA," and the percussive propulsion was informed by the manic style of Jerry Lee Lewis. After melding the pop genres, McCartney supplied his inimitable lighthearted, cheeky narrative. Said McCartney, "In my mind it's just about a [Russian] spy who's been in America for a long time and he's become very American but when he gets back to the USSR he's saying, 'Leave it 'til tomorrow to unpack my case, Honey, disconnect the phone,' and all that, but to Russian women." "Back in the USSR" opens with the sound of a screaming British Viscount jet flying from left to right across the speakers, an innovation of the new stereo age. When the song was released, it was criticized by conservative voices in the United States. The John Birch Society charged the Beatles with fomenting communism. Others judged it as a "tactless jest" because it was released not long after the Soviets had invaded Czechoslovakia. In the USSR, where the Beatles were seen as a welcome "belch of Western culture," the song was heard through smuggled tapes. There was even a rumor inside the country that the Beatles had secretly visited the USSR and given a private concert for the children of top communist party members, and had written the song for that occasion.

Charles Manson: Kory Grow, "Charles Manson: How Cult Leader's Twisted Beatles Obsession Inspired Family Murders," *Rolling Stone*, August 9, 2017; Margalit Fox, "Mass Killer with a Dark, Indelible Place in the American Psyche" (obituary), *New York Times*, November 21, 2017.

Dirty Harry: Screenplay by Harry Julian Fink, R. M. Fink, Jo Helms, and Terrence Malick; released by Warner Brothers (1971).

Vigilante justice: Rick Perlstein, "Apocalyptics," *New York Times Magazine*, April 16, 2017: "In 1973, the reporter Gail Sheehy joined a group of blue-collar workers watching the Watergate hearings in a bar in Astoria, Queens. 'If I was Nixon,' one of them said, 'I'd shoot every one of them.' (Who 'they' were went unspecified.) This was around the time New Yorkers were leaping to their feet and cheering during screenings of *Death Wish*, a hit move about a liberal architect, played by Charles Bronson, who shoots muggers at point-blank range."

Decade of violence: Author Heather Anne Thompson (*Blood in the Water: The Attica Prison Uprising of 1971*), interviewed by Ana Marie Cox, *New York Times Magazine*, May 14, 2017: "When you tell the nation that hippies are violent, the anti-war protestors are violent, prisoners are violent, civil rights is really about thuggery instead of genuine rights, then, all of a sudden, you look at Kent State, you look at the Chicago convention of

'68, you look at Attica and you completely miss the fact that all the violence was state violence."

33. Nixon by the Numbers

Pentagon Papers: They were leaked in 1971 by Daniel Ellsberg, and assessed U.S. involvement in Vietnam. From Greg King, in a 2018 *New Yorker* letter to the editor: "The Pentagon Papers...revealed a pattern of deception and subversion by American leaders going back as far as 1945. Those documents clearly demonstrate that the people who initiated American involvement in Vietnam were neither decent nor acting in good faith. They understood exactly what they were doing: propping up French imperialism through force...then inventing the Gulf of Tonkin incident to generate popular support for entering the conflict."

34. Watergate Dictionary

Nixon's enemies: In a *New York Times* op-ed, December 19, 2016, "Will Trump Play Spy vs. Spy?," Evan Thomas wrote, "The bureaucracy can find ways to fight back. During the Nixon Administration, the Joint Chiefs of Staff grew so distrustful of the White House that they planted a spy on the staff of the national security advisor [Henry Kissinger]. Deep Throat, the famous source behind some of the earliest Watergate revelations...turned out to be the deputy director of the FBI, Mark Felt."

Watergate overview: Joseph Okpaku and Bonnie Schulman, "Who's Who and What's What in Watergate," *Transition*, no. 45 (1974).

All the President's Men: Screenplay by William Goldman; released by Warner Bros. (1976).

Nicholas von Hoffman fired: From a 2005 syndicated column by James J. Kilpatrick, headlined "My Gifted Counterpoint on '60 Minutes' Wrote Like an Angel."

35. Mad as Hell

Don DeLillo: Adam Begley, "Don DeLillo, The Art of Fiction No. 135" (interview), *Paris Review*, issue 128 (Fall 1993).

Cigarettes: A committee established by the surgeon general released a report in 1964 linking smoking to a 70 percent increase in rates of mortality, lung cancer, bronchitis, and other diseases (*New York Times*, "On This Day in History").

Heroes and villains: On its one hundredth anniversary, the American Film Institute named its "100 Greatest Heroes and Villains." Movies from the seventies placed multiple characters in the top twenty. These are the seventies-era Heroes, with ranking: no. 7: Rocky Balboa (*Rocky*, 1976); no. 14: Han Solo (*Star Wars*, 1977); no. 15: Norma Rae Webster (*Norma Rae*, 1979); no. 17: Harry Callahan (*Dirty Harry*, 1971). Villains, with ranking: no. 3: Darth Vader (*Star Wars*, 1977); no. 5: Nurse Ratched (*One Flew over the Cuckoo's Nest*, 1975); no. 9: Regan MacNeil (*The Exorcist*, 1973); no. 11: Michael Corleone (*The Godfather: Part II*, 1974); no. 12: Alex De Large (*A Clockwork Orange*, 1971); no. 16: Noah Cross (*Chinatown*, 1974); no. 18: The Shark (*Jaws*, 1975). Overall, the no. 1 Hero was Atticus Finch (*To Kill a Mockingbird*, 1962); the no. 1 Villain was Dr. Hannibal Lecter (*The Silence of the Lambs*, 1990).

William Powell: Richard Sandomir, "Writer of 'The Anarchist Cookbook,' a Mayhem Manifesto," *New York Times*, March 30, 2017.

JFK assassination theories: Marcus Raskin, "JFK and the Culture of Violence," *American Historical Review* 97, no. 2 (April 1992).

Network: Screenplay by Paddy Chayefsky; released by MGM (1976).

Hal Lindsey: Erin A. Smith, "'The Late Great Planet Earth' Made the Apocalypse a Popular Concern," *Humanities* 38, no. 1 (Winter 2017).

Science vs. superstition: David Ropeik, "The Rise of Nuclear Fear—How We Learned to Fear the Radiation," *Scientific American*, June 15, 2012. From Carl Sagan's *Demon-Haunted World* (1995): "Science is more than a body of knowledge; it is a way of thinking. I have a foreboding of an America in my children or grandchildren's time—when the United States is a service and information economy; when nearly all the key manufacturing industries have slipped away to other countries; when awesome technological powers are in the hands of the very few, and no one representing the public inter-est can even grasp the issues; when people have lost their ability to set their own agenda or knowledgeably question those in authority; when, clutching our crystals and nervously consulting our horoscopes, our critical faculties in decline, unable to distinguish between what feels good and what's true, we slide, almost without noticing, back into superstition and darkness. The dumbing down of America is most evident in the slow decay of substantive content in the enormously influential media...lowest common denominator programming, credulous presentations on pseudoscience and superstition, but especially a kind of celebration of ignorance."

Escalating crime: The FBI's behavioral science unit introduced the term "serial killer" in the 1970s to distinguish between a mass murderer (someone who killed all at once) and a "spree killer." A number of factors contributed to a rise in serial killers: easy access to guns and hallucinogenic drugs; escape made easier by a vast interstate highway system; cheap gas; and a lack of coordination between police departments.

The NRA: Jill Lepore, "Battleground America," *New Yorker*, April 23, 2012. From Nicholas Kristof, "Let's Talk About the N.R.A.," *New York Times*, November 4, 2018: "N.R.A. advocacy is one reason the United States diverged from the path of other advanced nations—and one reason there are now more guns in America (393 million) than people (326 million).... Americans in their late teens are 82 times more likely to be murdered with guns than their peers in other advanced nations."

The Second Amendment: In 1979, one of the first campaigns by conservative direct-mail pioneer Richard Viguerie falsely warned that "federal and state legislatures" were "literally flooded with proposed laws" aimed "at total confiscation of firearms from law-abiding citizens."

Fusion paranoia: Michael Kelly, "The Road to Paranoia," *New Yorker*, June 19, 1995.

Peoples Temple: J. Oliver Conroy, "An Apocalyptic Cult, 900 Dead: Remembering the Jonestown Massacre, 40 Years On," *Guardian*, November 17, 2018.

36. A Minuet with Malaise

Agent Orange: From a 2017 *New York Times* letter to the editor by Debra J. Bardavid: "My husband was [in Vietnam] for only 40-plus days, but that was long enough for Agent Orange to leave its mark in the form of three separate cancers over the past 49 years. And during the two trips we took to Vietnam in 2013 and 2015, when we visited orphanages and homes for the elderly and infirm, we saw firsthand the diseases and deformities that are still affecting generations of Vietnamese people."

Apocalypse Now: From Vietnam veteran Michael J. Gorman, in a 2018 *New Yorker* letter to the editor about Francis Ford Coppola's *Apocalypse Now* (1979): "The war was an immoral political game played by politicians who lacked respect for human beings. As Coppola's movie showed (and came to symbolize), the mission was corrupt from the start, and it cost the lives of almost sixty thousand American soldiers (millions more were mentally and physically damaged), and more than two million Vietnamese people. It's not possible to reframe this war as something noble."

Carter White House: Theodore H. White, "The Party That Lost Its Way," *New York Times Magazine*, May 2, 1982.

Olympic boycott: John Powers, "Lost Games," *Boston Globe*, July 28, 2010.

37. Tit-for-Tat

Tom Hayden: Robert D. McFadden, "Tom Hayden, Civil Rights and Peace Activist Turned Lawmaker, Dies at 76," *New York Times*, October 25, 2016.

Prisoner's dilemma tournament: Artem Kaznatcheev, "Short History of Iterated Prisoner's Dilemma Tournaments," The EGG (Theory, Evolution and Games Group), March 2, 2015.

Peace Magazine: Metta Spencer, "Rapoport at Ninety," *Peace Magazine*, October–December 2001.

38. Arming for Bear

CIA analysis of USSR: James Risen, "Files Show CIA Warned of Soviet Decline," *Los Angeles Times*, September 26, 1995.

Trident submarine: Sebastien Roblin, "This Picture Is North Korea's Worst Nightmare: The Story of America's Ohio-Class Submarines," *The National Interest*, January 18, 2019.

Nicholas Thompson: "Dr. Strangelove's 'Doomsday Machine': It's Real," transcript of interview with Nicholas Thompson, NPR's *All Things Considered* with Guy Raz, September 26, 2009.

Magic healer: Hearst Newspapers, "Soviet Leaders Took 'Rejuvenating' Pills, Records Show," April 8, 1994.

Letters between Reagan and Gorbachev: Jason Saltoun-Ebin, "Recently Released Letters Between Reagan and Gorbachev Shed Light on the End of the Cold War," *HuffPost*, April 29, 2013.

39. Peak Paranoia

Tony Dolan: Fred I. Greenstein, *Leadership in the Modern Presidency* (Harvard University Press, 1988).

Hendrik Hertzberg: Juan Williams, "Writers of Speeches for President Claim Force Is With Him," *Washington Post*, March 29, 1983.

Star Wars/Geneva summit: John Newhouse, "Annals of Diplomacy: The Abolitionist—I," *New Yorker*, January 2, 1989; John Newhouse, "Annals of Diplomacy: The Abolitionist—II," *New Yorker*, January 9, 1989.

KAL 007: Max Fisher, "Hawaii False Alarm Hints at Thin Line Between Mishap and Nuclear War," *New York Times*, January 14, 2018.

Stanislav Petrov: Fiza Pirani, "'The Man Who Saved the World' Died and the World Didn't Notice—Who Was Stanislav Petrov?," *Atlanta Journal-Constitution*, September 18, 2017; Eresh Omar Jamal, "The Man Who Saved the World," *Daily Star* (Bangladesh), September 22, 2017.

War Games: Fred Kaplan, "'War Games' and Cybersecurity's Debt to a Hollywood Hack," *New York Times*, February 19, 2016.

Nuclear winter: Matthew R. Francis, "When Carl Sagan Warned the World About Nuclear Winter," Smithsonian.com, November 15, 2017. In a letter to the *New Yorker* on February 27, 2017, Rutgers climate change expert Alan Robock wrote, "Despite the overall decrease in Russia and the U.S.'s nuclear arsenal, the two countries still have the capability to produce a nuclear winter: a nuclear war that used less than one percent of the current global arsenal would cause a climate change unprecedented in recorded human history."

The Day After: David Hoffman and Lou Cannon, "ABC's 'The Day After,'" *Washington Post*, November 18, 1983.

Alex Wellerstein: Alex Wellerstein, "What We Lost When We Lost Bert the Turtle," *Harper's Magazine*, December 2017.

40. Nine Reasons

Ronald Reagan's transition from hawk to dove: Jacob Weisberg, "Ronald Reagan's Disarmament Dream," *Atlantic*, January 1, 2016.

Thatcher: Bill Keller, "Maggie and Gorby," *New York Times* (op-ed), April 8, 2013.

41. Teen Pilot

Principal source: Tom LeCompte, "The Notorious Flight of Mathias Rust," *Air & Space Magazine*, July 2015.

42. Basket Three

Helsinki Accords: Stephen Sestanovich, "Did the West Undo the East?," *The National Interest*, no. 31, Special Issue: The Strange Death of Soviet Communism: An Autopsy (Spring 1993).

43. Stirred-Up Muslims

Global blowback from Afghanistan: From Lawrence Wright, "The Man Behind bin Laden," *New Yorker*, September 16, 2002: "After the Soviet pullout, many of the Afghan Arabs returned home or went to other countries, carrying the torch of Islamic revolution. In the Balkans, ethnic hostility among Muslims, Croats, and Serbs prompted Bosnia-Herzegovina to vote to secede from Yugoslavia; that set off a three-year war in which a hundred and fifty thousand people died. In November of 1991, the largely Muslim region of Chechnya declared its independence from Russia—an act that soon led to war. In 1992, civil war broke out in Algeria when the government cancelled elections to prevent the Islamist party from taking power.... The conflict has taken a hundred thousand lives. In Egypt, the Islamic Group launched a campaign against tourism and Western culture in general.... And the war in Afghanistan continued, only now it was Muslims fighting Muslims for political control."

44. Sound of Silence

Vladimir Putin in the DDR: Chris Bowlby, "Vladimir Putin's Formative German Years," BBC News, March 27, 2015; Simon Kuper, "The Long Shadow of 1989," *FT Magazine*, November 3, 2016.

INDEX

Sheen, Fulton J., 188, 189
Shepard, Alan, 293
Sherry, Kenneth, 193
Shulman, Marshall, 363, 364
Shultz, George, 384, 391, 399–400
Sichel, Peter, 84
SIMA, 163, 164, 167. *See also* Coplon, Judith
Simpson, Gene, 315
Single Integrated Operational Plan (SIOP), 207–8
Sixteenth Street Baptist Church, 312–13
Skinner, B. F., 269
Skylab falling, 361–62
Smith, Merriman, 210
"smoking gun," 338
Smollett, H. P., 42–43, 44
Smollett, Peter, 45–46
Snyder, John, 85
Sobell, Martin, 173, 177, 178
Sokolov, Sergei, 403, 405
Solzhenitsyn, Alexander, 20, 39, 407
Sommerville, John, 162
Song of Russia (Mayer), 95–96, 115
Sorensen, Teddy, 295–96
Sorrell, Herb, 98, 100, 101–2
"The Sources of Soviet Conduct" (Kennan), 55
South Vietnam, 316
Soviet Communist Party, 39, 47
Soviet power, 54
Soviet Union. *See also* Cold War
    Afghanistan and, 364, 365
    CIA destabilization program, 410–13
    defense-related activities, 208
    doomsday machine, 375, 376
    Eisenhower on relationship with, 22
    Europe under it's control, 56
    as evil, 39
    first atomic bomb, 149
    as incapable of providing basic freedoms, 408
    as nuclear power, 33
    as police regime, 53

post-war conditions in, 151–52
    poverty, 50, 244
    practice of espionage, 278
    republics assume their independence, 416
    rocket program, 297
    totalitarian playbook, 57–58
    Truman and, 23
    U.S. and Britain as allies, 56
    U.S. hostility (1949), 149
space race
    beginning, media and, 250
    Gagarin and Titov and, 293
    Glenn and, 293–94
    planned start of, 249
    Shepard and Grissom and, 293
    Sputnik and, 248, 249
    Sputnik II and, 251–52
    Vanguard rocket and, 257
Spain, 42, 45
Spanish Civil War, 41
Special Operations Division, 74
Spellman, Francis, 281
Spielberg, Steven, 353
Sputnik, 19, 248, 249, 283, 290
Sputnik II, 251–52
Stalin, Joseph
    assassination fear, 242
    atomic bomb and, 29
    Big Lie, 39
    Bolshoi speech, 49–51
    British moles, 30
    cleansing in Romania, 122
    collectivization, 41
    "Declaration of World War III" and, 51
    enforcing the myth of history, 48
    Five-Year Plans, 50
    Great Terror, 41
    Hiroshima and, 32
    jobs and titles of, 49–50
    Moscow residence, 241
    opposing realities of, 39
    Poland and, 96
    at Potsdam Conference, 28–29

ABOUT THE AUTHOR

Brian T. Brown is the author of *Ring Force* (Rodale, 2012) and *TV: A Novel* (Crown, 2001). He is also a journalist, a fifteen-time Emmy winner, and the cowriter and director of *The Last Gold*, a 2016 feature-length documentary. His work has appeared on CBS, NBC, ABC, FOX, PBS, TBS, ESPN, NBCSN, HBO, and the Discovery Channel. As a writer and producer for twelve Olympic broadcasts, he has been attached to some of the most-watched shows in American TV history. Since 2017, he has served as an adjunct professor at Fordham University. Brown's professional career began in newspapers, at the *New York Times* and the *San Diego Union*.